Dallas

Dallas

Proud Heritage ~ Shining Future

FOREWORD
By The Greater Dallas Chamber

PARTNERS IN DALLAS
Corporate Profiles

Produced in Cooperation with
The City of Dallas and
The Greater Dallas Chamber

Marcoa Publishing Incorporated
Dallas, Texas

Acknowledgments

No project of this magnitude is conceived and executed without the contributions and hard work of many people. The editor would like to extend a generous word of appreciation to: the individuals, businesses and organizations who took the time to tell us and show us all they know about Dallas; the writers and photographers who were dispatched throughout the area and returned with wonderful stories and images of Dallas; and the "Partners in Dallas" who gave their time and economic support to this project. Special thanks goes to Clive Bates and Charles Parks who got the project off the ground and who rallied the business community around the cause; to Ruth Glady who kept the paper traffic flowing and the public informed; and to Mike Bolger, Rudy Rey, Brenda Bell and Kristine Sawyer who put all the pieces together in a package worthy of a city like Dallas.

Library of Congress Catalog Card Number: 89-63693

© 1990 by MARCOA Publishing, Inc.
All rights reserved.
Published 1990
Printed in the United States of America
First Edition

MARCOA Publishing, Inc.

Photo by Martin Vandiver

This book is dedicated
to that spirit and vitality
known as Dallas.

CONTENTS

Proud Heritage ~ Shining Future

PROUD HERITAGE
By Bill Sloan

Dallas is a city that some historians say never should have been. Nonetheless, a great city was built and nurtured by people who set out to make something out of nothing, turn deficits into abundance, transform vision into reality.

SPIRIT OF ENTERPRISE
By Yvonne Saliba

The story of Dallas is one of entrepreneurs, from John Neely Bryan who established a small settlement on the banks of the Trinity River to today's business pioneers who take ideas and concepts and build booming enterprises.

THE HEART OF THE CITY
By Bill Sloan

Dallas has one of the most impressive and unique skylines in the world, but there is more to downtown than tall buildings. Downtown Dallas is the financial, cultural, governmental, entertainment and psychological heart of the city as well.

STRENGTH IN DIVERSITY
By Bill Sloan

At various times in its history Dallas has leaned heavily on certain industries: cotton, oil and real estate among them. But individual industries have been assimilated to become part of a broad mix of business that gives Dallas economic strength and balance.

TECHNOLOGY LEADS THE WAY
By Candace Talmadge

High tech is an industry that adds strength to the local economy, but it also touches every part of daily life. Area high-tech companies develop and produce everything from switches and computers to communications equipment and missile guidance systems.

ROOM FOR GROWTH
By Bill Sloan

One of Dallas' major drawing points is real estate — homes, office buildings, shopping malls, strip shopping centers, industrial parks, planned developments. An abundance of quality real estate has been both a result of and a cause of explosive growth.

THE WORLD COMES TO DALLAS
By Alex Burton

Tourism and conventions is a major industry and contributor to the local economy. With a world-class airport and convention center and attractions and events to match, Dallas is one of the nation's top three convention cities, and the No. 1 tourist destination in Texas.

Partners in Dallas

Networks

Dallas' transportation and communications firms, as well as its business networks, keep people, information and power circulating throughout the region.

Quality of Life

Medical, educational and religious institutions, as well as recreation and leisure-oriented companies, all contribute to the quality of life enjoyed by Dallas' residents and visitors to the city.

Manufacturing

Producing goods for individuals and industry world-wide, Dallas' manufacturing firms also provide employment for its residents and balance to its economic base.

Business and Finance

Banking institutions, insurance, securities and diversified holding companies provide the financial foundation for a host of Dallas enterprises.

Foreword

By The Greater Dallas Chamber

"This vast metropolitan center . . . has become the most diverse and dynamic economic base in the U.S. It has become a true national center, one that is extraordinarily rich in human resources."

"The Best Cities for Business," Fortune *magazine, October 1989*

When *Fortune* magazine selected Dallas-Fort Worth as the nation's No. 1 business center, the buzz of excitement swept quickly throughout the community. And of course, the magazine was an instant sell-out.

The cause of the excitement was not so much that the area held the No. 1 ranking, as it was that others had recognized what local residents had known for a long time.

Those who have lived and worked in Dallas for any period of time know that ours is a unique and special city. We know it has an outstanding business environment, and that there is so much more that makes Dallas such a great city in which to live and work.

Aesthetically, Dallas is one of the most attractive and cleanest cities in the nation. From its handsome skyline to the numerous green parks and well-trimmed neighborhoods, Dallas is pleasing to the senses. A prevalence of "clean" industry and environmentally concerned businesses and residents help keep it that way.

Dallas is rich artistically. The downtown Arts District boasts a critically acclaimed art museum and world-class symphony hall. Performing nightly throughout the city are dance and theatre companies, as well as a delightful variety of artists and musicians.

Quality education is a priority in Dallas. Outstanding public and private facilities and a world-class faculty attest to that fact.

Likewise, the availability of quality health care is a top community priority, and Dallas long has been recognized as one of the nation's prime centers for medical care, research and education.

When it comes to shopping, dining, entertainment, sports and recreation, nobody beats Dallas for quality and quantity. Dallas has more shopping centers and restaurants per capita than any city in the country. Add to that the nightclubs and theaters, four professional sports teams and numerous other sports and recreational opportunities, and the choices can boggle the mind.

Of most importance, though, is the fact that Dallas has people who are dedicated, ambitious, energetic, concerned and genuinely friendly. Its people give Dallas its sparkle; its extra edge; its spirit and energy. From the pioneers who settled this prairie crossroads and forged it into one of the nation's great cities, the people of Dallas work individually and together to keep the fires of opportunity and prosperity burning brightly.

Dallas: Proud Heritage — Shining Future, uses words and pictures to capture the essence of Dallas and to let you feel the pulse of one of America's most dynamic cities.

Long-time Dallas residents will enjoy recalling just how the city's past built a strong foundation for a very promising future. For those who are new to the city or who never have had the opportunity to visit, each chapter of this book provides a colorful snapshot of the "Can-Do City" that knows no limits — today or tomorrow.

As Dallas celebrates its sesquicentennial in 1991, we view this publication as a tribute to the city's past and a toast to its future.

Richard D. Upton, CCE
President
Greater Dallas Chamber

Introduction

Several years ago during a trip to London, our wanderings took us to Parliament where we hoped to get a peek inside the House of Commons. Seeing a line in the middle of a great antechamber, we took our place. There, we struck up a conversation with a gentleman from the English countryside who had traveled to London to have an audience with his Member Parliament.

After this man politely informed us that we were in the wrong line for the tour, he asked where we were from. We said "Dallas," but had to say nothing more. The man's eyes lit up, he smiled, and in a few short sentences he spoke of ranches, cowboys, oil wells, John F. Kennedy and J.R. Ewing.

Few cities in the United States enjoy that kind of immediate name identification and recognition in other parts of the world. While the man's knowledge of Dallas bordered on myth and folklore, he had a strong understanding of the "essence" of Dallas nonetheless. He had never been to Dallas, but he knew Dallas.

In publishing, *Dallas: Proud Heritage–Shining Future*, it was our goal to explain in words and pictures the essence of Dallas — the myths and the truths, the unusual and the ordinary.

We wanted to show people that Dallas is more than cowboy hats, boots and horses, although that is very much a part of the city's past and present. We wanted to show that Dallas is more than just oil, money and mansions, although those elements do figure into the local lifestyle. We wanted to let people know that there was more to see in Dallas than Neiman-Marcus and Dealey Plaza, although if you come to Dallas you will want to visit those sites.

In short, we wanted to show Dallas as it really is: A vast metropolitan area inhabited by people with diverse cultural backgrounds, lifestyles, career goals and personal ambitions. The common thread weaving this great patchwork of humanity together is opportunity. There is an oft-spoken philosophy here that anything is possible if one works hard and contributes to the community.

Hard work is nothing new to Dallas residents. In the first two chapters of this book, "Proud Heritage" and "Spirit of Enterprise," we see how the early settlers of Dallas turned disadvantages into advantages and built a great city, and how their modern counterparts are building on that tradition of enterprise and innovation.

In the ensuing chapters, we see the fruits of those labors and how Dallas has as much if not more to offer its citizens in terms of opportunities and quality of life than any other city. And in "Shining Future," we see how Dallas continues to evolve and how its leaders are turning new challenges into opportunities.

Finally, in the "Partners in Dallas" section, businesses, organizations and institutions tell their own stories and explain how they contribute to and benefit from Dallas.

As in any project such as this, words and pictures may soon become dated, especially when the subject is an ever-changing city such as Dallas. But greatness is a journey and not a destination, so this book should be viewed simply as a stop along the road; a chance to take stock of all that has been accomplished, and to survey the road ahead.

As might be expected, *Dallas: Proud Heritage–Shining Future* is a somewhat boastful, proud look at the city. But then, the citizens of Dallas have much to be proud of. For that reason, we dedicate this volume to the citizens of Dallas — past, present and future.

Jeff Hampton

PART ONE

Dallas

Proud Heritage ~ Shining Future

Old City Park just south of downtown offers a striking view of Dallas past and present. Photo by Scott Metcalfe.

CHAPTER 1

Proud
Heritage

By Bill Sloan

Nobody knows what strange combination of forces led a young Tennessean named John Neely Bryan, in the autumn of 1841, to an uninhabited wilderness at the Three Forks of the Trinity River where he laid claim to 640 acres with the idea of starting a town.

Dallas celebrates July fourth as most cities do — with music and fireworks. Photo by Benjamin Stewart.

15

Dallas could be called an unsolved mystery. The birth of America's eighth largest city and its emergence as one of the great commercial centers of the Western World has been chronicled but never explained.

Even today, nobody knows exactly how it happened, or why. As nearly as anyone can tell, it was a peculiar accident of time, place and personality that caused Dallas to be born at all. And it was only through some fortuitous, inexplicable chemistry of entrepreneurship, vision and sweat — not to mention a major portion of luck — that Dallas was able to grow from a single crude log cabin to what it is today in less than 150 years.

Railroads, highways, cotton and other crops, petroleum, manufacturing, banking, communications, electronics, medicine, science, education, aviation and one of the world's great airports have all been important ingredients in the Dallas phenomenon. But no single ingredient has been more vital than the indomitable, visionary, almost evangelical spirit that has woven everything together to fashion a "Super City" where once there was only prairie.

Nobody knows what strange combination of forces led a young Tennessean named John Neely Bryan, in the autumn of 1841, to an uninhabited wilderness at the Three Forks of the Trinity River, where he laid claim to 640 acres with the idea of starting a town. From all indications, Bryan gave careful consideration to the site, but it can be rationally argued that there were scores of better, and perhaps safer potential town sites scattered across North Texas.

Although the Caddo Indians and their prehistoric predecessors had camped and hunted in the area for thousands of years, there had never been a permanent settlement on or near Bryan's site. The Indians were not particularly friendly, either. Just a year before Bryan's arrival, they had attacked a surveying party a few miles south of where Dallas now stands and killed one of the soldiers assigned to guard the surveyors. Three years earlier, nine Texas soldiers had been killed in an Indian ambush not far away on the West Fork of the Trinity.

These outbreaks led to a raid of Indian villages by General Edward H. Tarrant (for whom neighboring Tarrant County is named) and to the establishment of a small fort on the West Fork to keep the Indians in line. This outpost, known as Bird's Fort, had been completed a few months before Bryan arrived, but it did little to curb Indian depredations in the area.

However, like many who would follow him to Dallas during the ensuing decades, Bryan was a freewheeler, a dreamer and an independent thinker. He had lived for a time with the Cherokees in Arkansas and so had little fear of the red men. He also was something of an enigma in his own right — a private man who had few close friends, had little use for files or records, and who left behind no diaries or personal papers. Almost all of what is known about Bryan today is based on the secondhand, sometimes conflicting recollections of those who knew him.

As a result, even the name of the city he founded remains part of the mystery that surrounded him. Bryan's associates remembered him voicing the intention to name his town after "my friend, Dallas," but a century-and-a-half later, lingering questions remain about this "friend's" identity. For many years, it was assumed that Bryan had referred to George Mifflin Dallas, who was elected vice president of the United States as James K. Polk's running mate in 1844 and who was an outspoken advocate of Texas' annexation to the Union. But few believe that Bryan knew anything about George Mifflin Dallas or his pro-annexation stance in early 1842 when he began calling his site "Dallas." Others have speculated that the town was named for Commodore Alexander Dallas, the future vice president's brother, who once served in the Gulf of Mexico, or for some even more obscure person Bryan had known before coming to Texas.

Although Bryan definitely marched to his own drummer, he also had seemingly logical reasons for pitching his first camp where he did — at the western terminus of present-day Main Street where it enters the Triple Underpass. At that time, before the Trinity River was straightened and channeled between levees, the spot was on a bluff at the edge of the stream, which Bryan was convinced could be navigated by steamboats all the way to the Gulf of Mexico. The site also was at a natural ford on the river where the floodplain was narrow, the water usually shallow (except during spring floods) and the limestone footing solid enough to support horses and wagons. Bryan also knew that the proposed route of a new national highway, recently authorized by the Republic of Texas, passed very near his campsite. With the potential for both highway and river travel, he concluded, this was an ideal location for his town.

It was here, then, that Bryan erected a one-room log cabin which became the first permanent structure in Dallas, a reconstructed version of which stands today a few hundred yards from where Bryan originally built it. And it was here that he hired surveyor J.P. Dumas to lay out the original town of Dallas in a half-mile square and began enticing other settlers to join him in his town-building venture.

It was slow going at first. By late 1842, a visitor to Dallas described the settlement as "two small log cabins ... (with) chimneys made of sticks and mud and old mother earth serving as floors." In 1843, a treaty was signed with the Indians, which greatly reduced the threat of attack, and thousands of settlers began pouring into North Texas. But even then,

Dallas added new residents at a ponderous pace. Other settlements sprang up nearby, including Farmers Branch and Cedar Springs to the northwest and Hord's Ridge (now Oak Cliff) on the high west bank of the river directly opposite Bryan's town. Some of these communities grew temporarily larger than Dallas.

In 1845, 32 Dallas voters cast their ballots in the election that made

LEFT: The seal of Dallas is cast in bronze on a wall at City Hall Plaza. Photo by Allan Kaye.

ABOVE: Viaducts built in the 1920s span the Trinity River and connect West Dallas and Oak Cliff with downtown Dallas. Photo by Dan Hatzenbuehler.

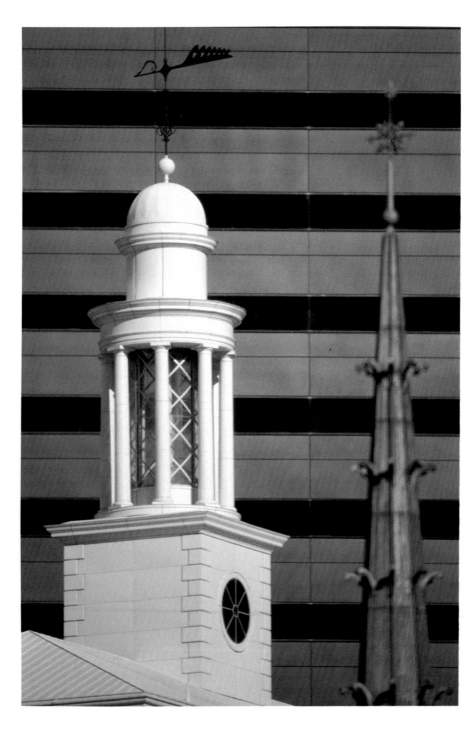

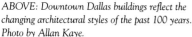

ABOVE: Downtown Dallas buildings reflect the changing architectural styles of the past 100 years. Photo by Allan Kaye.

CENTER: The Micajah Goodwin log cabin is part of the history of Grand Prairie, now the home of such industrial giants as LTV. Photo by Martin Vandiver.

RIGHT: Pegasus, or "the flying red horse," has flown above Dallas since 1934. Photo by Martin Vandiver.

Texas part of the Union. That same year, Bryan's log cabin became Dallas' first post office and Bryan its first postmaster. The first school was established in another log cabin, and the first saloon began serving drinks in a tent. Bryan, ever the entrepreneur, began operating a ferryboat on the Trinity River, and after Dallas County was organized in 1846, he offered free ferry service to all county

residents to help Dallas win the designation of county seat. In an 1850 election to decide the county seat, Dallas edged out Hord's Ridge by only 28 votes. After that, Dallas was assured of being the dominant town in Dallas County, but not of very much else.

Indeed, for more than three decades after its establishment, Dallas was destined to remain an isolated frontier village, far removed from principal trade routes and suffering from the inability either to ship its agricultural bounty to distant markets or to import the quantity of manufactured goods it needed to thrive as a commercial center. Everything that traveled to or from Dallas had to be hauled by oxcart over the terrible roads connecting it with the river port of Jefferson, Texas, 150 miles to the east.

Bryan himself grew disillusioned, both with his town, where he had given away many lots for promotional

purposes and sold many others for a negligible return, and with his failure to bring navigation to the upper Trinity. In 1853, after an abortive trip to California in search of gold, Bryan returned to Dallas, sold all his holdings for a mere $7,000 and departed. He would return years later and play a brief role in the evolution of the town he had founded.

Fortunately, the people who acquired Bryan's holdings were Alexander Cockrell, another energetic entrepreneur, and his wife, Sarah. Cockrell built the first bridge across the Trinity and opened the town's first steam-powered sawmill. He was killed in a shooting incident in 1858, and his widow became one of the wealthiest and most powerful women in Texas, owning and operating enterprises ranging from flour mills to hotels. By the time Sarah Cockrell died in 1892, she owned about one-fourth of downtown Dallas.

But even more important to the future development of Dallas, Bryan and the Cockrells established a promising climate for entrepreneurship that helped attract such risk-taking commercial pioneers as William and Walter Caruth, G.H. Schoellkopf, William L. Cabell, John M. Stemmons, Alex and Philip Sanger, William H. Gaston, Thomas L. Marsalis, George B. Dealey and others. Together, they gave the fledgling town of Dallas a core of dynamic, civic-minded, business-oriented leadership that would carry it far.

These leaders would find ways to counteract natural and manmade disasters, the lack of a navigable waterway, the remoteness and primitive nature of their town, the long distances to major markets and other formidable obstacles. And these early entrepreneurs, along with innumerable others who came after them, would create out of their own tireless enterprise, fierce determination and fertile imaginations, the mystic for-

mula that enabled Dallas to become a leading international city while other communities with greater natural advantages remained mere towns.

In 1860, on the eve of the Civil War when Dallas was still a village of less than 800 people, much of the downtown business district was wiped out in a calamitous fire that was officially blamed on abolitionist agitators and rebellious slaves. But by this time the population of the surrounding county had swelled to more than 8,000, and the town quickly rebuilt. After the Civil War began, Dallas never was in danger from Northern armies despite its designation as a Confederate quartermaster and commissary headquarters, and so it continued to grow and prosper, both during the war and the reconstruction that followed.

As the 1870s dawned, Dallas had become a quietly thriving — but still isolated — town of nearly 3,000 "thrifty, law-abiding, enterprising" inhabitants, in the words of Sarah Cockrell. The downtown area around the courthouse boasted more than 20 stores, two hotels, two flour mills and an assortment of other businesses. But anyone who ventured to Dallas from anywhere else still had to travel by horseback or stagecoach, and goods that could not be produced locally had to hauled in by wagon. In short, nearly 30 years after its founding, the little community at the Three Forks of the Trinity River gave absolutely no indication that it would one day blossom into one of the world's principal transportation centers and the largest landlocked metropolis in America.

Within the space of just three or four years, however, all this was to change dramatically as the arrival of two mainline railroads, one from the south and one from the east, suddenly transformed Dallas into one of the major crossroads of the Southwest. In the process, it triggered a population explosion and building boom that stunned even the most optimistic Dallasites. In terms of both their proportion and permanent impact, the events of the first half of the 1870s still eclipse every other economic surge in Dallas history, including the great oil boom of the 1930s and the unprecedented outburst of real estate development in the 1980s.

Dallas simply never would be the same again. During a few short months in 1872, coinciding with the arrival of the first Houston & Texas Central Railway (H&TC) train that July, the sleepy farming hamlet called Dallas vanished forever. And by the time the first Texas & Pacific Railroad (T&P) train pulled into town in late 1873, a bustling city had taken its place. Between January and September 1872, the population of Dallas more than doubled from about 3,000 to more than 7,000.

In less than two years, 1,660 new structures were erected, including more than 50 major commercial buildings and no less than 33 boarding houses to help absorb the influx of new residents. There also was a new iron bridge across the Trinity, a streetcar line connecting the "Old Town" around the new limestone courthouse with the "New Town" that had sprouted around the H&TC

station a mile to the east, a newly organized municipal fire department, an opera house and gaslights along the city's main streets.

None of this might ever have happened — present-day Dallas might be just another county seat the size of Corsicana, Waxahachie, Greenville or McKinney — had it not been for a farsighted bit of trickery carried out by John W. Lane, Dallas' representative in the Texas Legislature in the early 1870s.

As the T&P Railroad was soliciting bids from communities along its

proposed route for the privilege of having its trains pass through their boundaries, Lane quietly attached a rider to a bill concerning railroad grants that required the T&P to cross the H&TC within one mile of a place called Browder Springs. Almost no one outside Dallas knew that Browder Springs was located at what is now Old City Park, just a stone's throw from downtown Dallas. The bill passed without incident, and the only town in North Texas that got two railroads instead of just one was Dallas. That was the key to most of

ABOVE: *The cabin believed to have been built by Dallas founder John Neely Bryan sits on the Dallas County Historical Plaza downtown. Photo by Jeff Hampton.*

what has happened since. The Missouri, Kansas & Texas ("Katy") Railway arrived in 1881, and within a few years the city was served by five separate rail lines.

The advantages stemming from the gleaming rails that now stretched out in all directions fueled a flurry of economic growth that continued unabated through the 1890s and into the 20th century. Rail connections made Dallas both an excellent place for manufacturing and a chief distribution point for manufacturers in the North and East. By the turn of the century, Dallas was the leading distribution center of the Southwest.

Of even greater economic significance, however, was the railroads' role in making Dallas the undisputed "Cotton Capital of the World" by the early 1900s. Dallas was the largest inland cotton market on earth and also led the world in the manufacture of cotton gin equipment. The area's bountiful cotton crop, which had never been able to reach market by way of the Trinity River, could finally be shipped to any point on the globe. An agricultural revolution resulted as farmers who had concentrated on wheat, corn and other food crops now devoted the bulk of their land to cotton. By 1925, nearly one-third of all cotton produced in Texas was grown and ginned within 100 miles of Dallas.

In the spring of 1908, heavy rains turned the Trinity River, which Dallas leaders had long hoped to use to their advantage, into the city's mortal enemy. The river went on its worst rampage in memory, rising more than 52 feet above flood stage, leaving 4,000 persons homeless and destroying a vast section of the business district. Determined that the Trinity should never again wreak such havoc, city fathers abandoned the area of downtown west of Houston street and commissioned George E. Kessler to draft a master plan encompassing flood control, street and railroad relocation and beautification for the entire city.

Under the famed Kessler Plan of 1911, the Trinity River eventually was diverted into an artificial channel between two high levees, and many other improvements were carried out. Beginning in the late 1930s, hundreds of acres of former floodplain now protected by the levees would be developed as the sprawling Trinity Industrial District, one of the largest concentrations of business and industry in the Southwest.

The new century brought an even greater obsession with growth and bigness. The Dallas Chamber of Commerce was formed in 1909, and that organization, along with George B. Dealey's *The Dallas Morning News* and Edwin J. Kiest's *Dallas Times Herald*, launched a campaign to push the city's population past the 100,000 mark. It almost reached that level by 1910 when the federal census found more than 92,000 residents; it zoomed far beyond that by 1920 when the census counted almost 160,000 Dallasites.

Between 1901 and 1912, the first genuine skyscrapers also rose downtown, including such surviving landmarks as the eight-story Wilson Building, hailed as the finest office building south of St. Louis; the 14-story Praetorian Building, for a time the tallest structure west of the Mississippi; and the 20-story Adolphus Hotel, a renowned architectural gem and the city's first world-class hotel.

The first "horseless carriages" appeared in Dallas in 1902, and soon thousands of automobiles were wheezing and clattering along local streets and roads. The proliferation of the automobile touched off significant suburban development. Oak Cliff, which had been developed as a separate municipality by Thomas Marsalis, was annexed to the city of Dallas in 1903. Oak Lawn became a fast-growing residential area north of downtown, and the town of Highland Park was incorporated in 1913 as the exclusive brainchild of Marsalis' ex-partner, John S. Armstrong. Meanwhile, across the county such towns as Carrollton, Farmers Branch,

TOP: The Dallas County Courthouse, or "Old Red," was built in 1893 and is still occupied by various county offices.

ABOVE: An exhibit hall at Fair Park shows the symmetry and simple style of the art deco of the 1930s. Photo by Benjamin Stewart.

RIGHT: The DeGolyer Estate, once the residence of Dallas Oilman Everette DeGolyer, is now home of the Dallas Arboretum and Botanical Society. Photo by Jeff Hampton.

Garland, Irving, Lancaster, Mesquite and Richardson were enjoying gradual but steady growth.

Dallas' reputation as a banking and financial center was greatly enhanced by its designation in 1914 as headquarters for one of the banks of the newly formed Federal Reserve System. The smallest of all the cities selected, Dallas and her dogged, outspoken leadership successfully challenged such giants as Chicago, Kansas City and St. Louis for this honor, which overnight doubled the city's total banking capital and extended its financial influence throughout Texas and into Louisiana, Oklahoma, New Mexico and Arizona. Such aggressive, community-minded bankers as R.L. "Uncle Bob" Thornton, who parlayed a $20,000 investment in 1916 into the huge Mercantile National Bank, added immeasurably to that influence and reputation. Thornton's admonition to "keep the dirt flying" symbolized his city's passion for building on an ever-larger, ever-grander scale.

When the U.S. Army established Love Field as a pilot training facility during World War I, it signaled the birth of the aviation industry in Dal-

las. After the war, a group of Dallas businessmen took over the unused facility and converted it into one of the nation's busiest commercial airports by the early 1930s.

Air transportation has been an integral part of the Dallas success story ever since, and the city's role as an air hub has attracted many aviation-related companies to the area. The opening of Dallas/Fort Worth International Airport in 1973 made the Metroplex a crossroads for the world and was the decisive factor in the 1979 decision of American Airlines to relocate its headquarters from New York to D/FW. Love Field, meanwhile, remains among America's top commercial airports and is the home of Southwest Airlines, the nation's 5th largest commercial air carrier.

While the Great Depression of the 1930s was creating the hardest of "hard times" in the form of business stagnation and economic chaos in many American cities, the phenomenal East Texas oil boom was bringing another era of rapid growth and expansion to Dallas. Although there never has been a producing oil well in Dallas County, the city became an important center for the oil industry as early as the immediate post-World War I period. The 29-story headquarters building for Magnolia Petroleum, topped by its neon-lit Pegasus, has been among the most identifiable components of the famous Dallas skyline since its completion in 1921. But prior to the moment in October 1930 when the discovery well for the vast East Texas Oil Field "blew in" 100 miles east of Dallas, no one had envisioned anything like the sequence of events that was about to unfold. In a sense, it may have been the most important single moment in the history of Dallas.

While banks were failing from coast to coast, those in Dallas profited immeasurably from oil invest-

ments, and the Dallas business community as a whole achieved unprecedented wealth and prosperity. Incalculable personal fortunes were made — fortunes exemplified by H.L. Hunt, perennially recognized as the "richest man in the world," and his children, by John and Clint Murchison, Angus and Toddie Lee Wynne, Everette DeGolyer and others who helped shape the character and personality of Dallas. Oil-related companies swarmed into town by the hundreds, and by 1940 it was estimated that one in every five Dallasites derived his livelihood directly or indirectly from oil.

Even in the relatively tough times of the late 1980s, the city's oil-rich legacy remained. Hundreds of millions of television viewers around the world have received a graphic, if somewhat distorted view of that legacy through the monumental TV series "Dallas." And in a more factual

vein, Dallas remains the headquarters city for many major oil companies, including Exxon Corp.

Although Dallas had attracted large gatherings of visitors at various times, the Texas Centennial Exposition of 1936 was by far the biggest extravaganza ever staged in the city during its first 100 years. The six-month-long World's Fair came at the height of the oil boom and attracted President Franklin Roosevelt and some 10 million visitors. It also marked the real beginning of a convention and tourism industry that now comprises an important part of the total Dallas economy.

The State Fair of Texas, which celebrated its 100th anniversary in 1986, annually draws some 3 million visitors to the same Fair Park where the Centennial Exposition was held. The annual Cotton Bowl football classic and parade, staged each New Year's day since 1937, and the establish-

ment of such professional sports teams as the Dallas Cowboys in 1960, the Texas Rangers in 1972 and the Dallas Mavericks in 1982 have brought millions of additional visitors to the city.

The vast electronics and aerospace industries represented by such Dallas giants as Texas Instruments (TI) and LTV also had their beginnings in the late 1930s as America began to tool up for World War II. TI grew out of a small firm called Geophysical Services Inc., which moved its laboratories to Dallas from New Jersey in 1934. The young man who came to Dallas that year to head the lab was J. Erik Jonsson, who would become one of the chief architects of TI, now the largest manufacturing concern in Dallas. Jonsson also would become one of Dallas' most influential mayors.

North American Aviation opened a plant at Grand Prairie in 1940 that employed as many as 30,000 workers during the peak years of the war effort, but which was abandoned when peace came. In 1945, Texas Engineering and Manufacturing Company (Temco) occupied a portion of the plant, and in 1948, Chance Vought Aircraft Division of United Aircraft moved its entire operation into the rest of the facility. When these two companies merged a decade later with Ling Electronics, a company built "from scratch" by a brash young entrepreneur named James J. Ling, the result was Ling-Temco-Vought, now known as LTV. In the 1960s and '70s, yet another young entrepreneur, H. Ross Perot, built his Electronic Data Systems (EDS) into one of the giants of the computer industry and amassed one of the greatest personal fortunes in Texas history.

Dallas has always had a strong retail community led by exception-ally innovative merchants and developers. The Sanger Brothers and their gigantic downtown department store epitomized the "last word" in shopping for generations of Dallasites. But in 1907, an adventurous former Sanger's employee named Herbert Marcus Sr. went into business for himself, along with his sister and brother-in-law, Carrie and Al Neiman, and created what may be the most elegant and legendary name in American retailing — Neiman-Marcus.

Dallas also is recognized as the birthplace of the modern shopping center. When Highland Park Shopping Village opened in 1929, it was the nation's first master-planned, architecturally unified, multistore, off-street retail facility. Later, in the 1960s, Raymond Nasher's NorthPark set the style nationwide for fully enclosed upscale shopping malls. And in the 1980s, the local tradition of retail innovation and strength continued with the decision by J.C. Penney to move its headquarters from New York to the Dallas area, where it now ranks as one of the area's largest employers.

When Southern Methodist University (SMU) opened for classes in 1915, it was the only four-year institution of higher learning in Dallas County. But in the 75 years since, Dallas has built an enviable reputation as a center of educational and scientific achievement. In addition to SMU, with its highly respected schools of art, business, engineering, law and theology, the county is also the home of the University of Texas at Dallas, the University of Dallas, Dallas Baptist University and the seven campuses of the Dallas County Community College District. Nearby in adjacent counties are the University of Texas at Arlington, Texas Christian University, Texas Wesleyan

College and the University of North Texas.

The giant educational, health care and medical research complex now known as the University of Texas Southwestern Medical Center-Dallas had its beginnings in 1943, following the crushing loss to Dallas of Baylor College of Medicine, which moved to Houston that same year. Today, UT Southwestern, whose research scientists were honored with three Nobel Prizes in the 1980s, ranks as one of the world's leading medical centers. Its teaching and research capabilities are matched and complimented by the vast resources of Baylor University Medical Center, which includes Baylor College of Dentistry and Baylor College of Nursing, and which ranks among the largest private teaching-health care facilities in America. The Baylor complex in East Dallas traces its origins to a small sanitarium established in 1903.

Real estate development is, of course, an inevitable by-product of the type of urban growth that has transformed Dallas from a crude cluster of log huts into a city of a million people. But in Dallas, as in perhaps no other American city, the endless process of building, tearing down and rebuilding on a constantly grander scale has become both an art and a science — and real estate development has become an important Dallas industry in its own right. From the fabulous skyline that is Dallas' chief trademark, to such massive mixed-use projects as Las Colinas, developed by the John Carpenter family, evidences of this industry's impact can be found all over the Dallas area.

But the influence of such premier Dallas developers as Trammell Crow now extend from coast to coast and beyond. The rise of Crow and his company to national prominence began with his development of the now-famous Dallas Market Center, beginning in the late 1950s. In the

years since, Crow and other Dallas-based builders and developers have exported their development and commercial construction expertise to dozens of U.S. cities. And during the first half of the 1980s, they were instrumental in the greatest development boom ever seen in Dallas — a boom that virtually doubled the amount of existing office space within a six-year period.

LEFT: In 1984, a herd of longhorn cattle was driven down the Trinity River for the Republican National Convention, just as they were a century earlier.

ABOVE: The French Room in the historic Adolphus Hotel serves the finest continental cuisine in opulent surroundings. Photo by Doug Milner.

RIGHT: *Union Station, built in 1916, was renovated as part of the Reunion project in the late 1970s.*

ABOVE: *Guides dressed in period clothing conduct tours of the homes and commercial buildings restored at Old City Park. Photo by Martin Vandiver.*

Dallas may always remain an intriguing enigma among large cities, but there is nothing mysterious about the source of its greatest strength — its people. For every prominent local leader mentioned here, there are thousands of other Dallasites who have contributed to their city's amazing record of growing, improving, prospering, facing challenges and overcoming obstacles during the past century-and-a-half.

From its early days as a rawboned railroad town, Dallas has been blessed with a diverse population, a confluence of cultures and the same "melting pot" phenomenon that makes America unique. Irish tradesmen and factory workers, Jewish merchants, French and Italian artisans, German craftsmen, Chinese laborers, Scandinavian farmers, English nobility, Japanese industrialists, Southeast Asian refugees, yankee "drummers," Hispanic immigrants and former African-American slaves have all

shared in the success of Dallas and helped make it strong. From this diversity of people, talent and ideas has sprung the economic diversity for which Dallas is internationally acclaimed. From their community pride and "can-do" spirit has grown a labor force whose skills and energies are unsurpassed in the United States.

Adversity and even defeat are no strangers to Dallas, but because of its people and the strengths and values they embody, no adversity has ever been insurmountable and no defeat has ever been permanent. From the fire of 1860 to the flood of 1908 to the tragedy of the Kennedy assassination in 1963 to the financial and real estate crisis of the mid-to-late-1980s, Dallas has always bounced back, rebuilt itself, revived itself and resumed its march toward greatness.

Strangely enough, in fact, Dallas' moments of maximum triumph have often followed close on the heels of its greatest setbacks, and from all indications, the late 1980s and early 1990s will be no exception to this rule. The echoes had barely died from the resounding collapse of some of Dallas' largest and most powerful financial institutions in 1988 when the announcement came that a site just south of Dallas had been selected for the federal government's multibillion-dollar Superconducting Super Collider. And a few months after that, a major move to the Dallas area involving thousands of jobs was announced by Connecticut-based GTE Corporation.

These two seemingly unrelated events could one day assume the same significance as the arrival of the railroads, the discovery of oil in East Texas and the opening of D/FW Airport. Future historians may recall them as a crucial chapter in the story of how Dallas became the high technology capital of America.

As the 1990s begin and the sesquicentennial of Dallas approaches, the glorious mystery that John Neely Bryan set in motion on the banks of the Trinity River nearly 150 years ago continues to unfold.

CHAPTER 2

Spirit of Enterprise

By Yvonne Saliba

Why Dallas? Because there is diversity — diversity of business, of backgrounds and of expectations. A strong belief in America's free enterprise system. An openness. A penchant for opportunity. An upbeat nature. Unbridled optimism.

Dallas' pro-business government welcomes start-up businesses and large corporations alike into the local community. Photo by Martin Vandiver.

29

ABOVE: *Dealey Plaza pays tribute to the entrepreneurial drive and community spirit of G.B. Dealey, founding publisher of The Dallas Morning News. Photo by Martin Vandiver.*

TOP RIGHT: *The early bird gets the worm at Farmers Market in downtown Dallas, where farmers from throughout the region arrive before dawn to sell fresh produce. Photo by Allan Kaye.*

BOTTOM RIGHT: *The World Trade Center at the Dallas Market Center is a center of international trade and commerce for Dallas and the Southwest.*

"It was the sky which suggested that this was a place where a man could stretch out."

"A man was measured by his individual entrepreneurship and ingenuity."

"Making your own mark was not simply one of the options in Dallas — it was the required rite of every young man."

The words written by and about the late William Caruth are as true today as they were 140 years ago. Caruth left Kentucky in 1848 and settled in North Texas, becoming one of the first dozen or so white settlers to call Dallas home.

That he amassed an estate of some 30,000 acres of rich black soil ideal for cotton farming, and that the property encompassed most of the prime land edging downtown Dallas and extending north to Forest Lane, east to White Rock Lake and west to Preston Road, is but one of many marvelous success stories that color the proud heritage of Dallas.

Every city has success stories. Dallas, however, holds a particular distinction in the minds and hearts of people everywhere. If Dallas owns any particular resource above all other cities, it is the resource of people.

People who thrive on challenge, who hold frontier spirit deep in their hearts and who have molded the frontier into a sophisticated setting.

Many times and in many ways it has been said that Dallas had no reason for being. No reason for being settled, no reason to thrive in its infancy and no reason to proceed full speed into the 21st century as one of the most dynamic cities in America. No reason, but for its people.

Why Dallas? Why did John Neely Bryan persevere to establish a city on an undistinguished river bank in the middle of the North Texas prairie? Why did the Stemmons, the Gastons, the Ferrises, the Marsalises, the Sangers, Dealeys, Kiests, DeGolyers, Meadows, Thorntons, Carpenters, Braniffs, Marcuses and the Hoblitzelles, to name a few, leave their comfortable native states and come to this new frontier?

There was no navigable river. No mines. No natural resources. No oil. No harbor. No growth tied to any particular industry.

However, there was diversity — diversity of business, of backgrounds and expectations. A strong belief in America's free enterprise system. An openness. A penchant for opportunity. An upbeat nature. Unbridled optimism.

The answer has more to do with the spirit of the people than any tangible thing.

Trained as an engineer and now the director of the institute that trains entrepreneurs at Southern Methodist University, Jerry White pegs Dallas as "a breakfront between the frontier and the developed cities. Even as we leave the 20th century, there is still that frontier spirit. Brains and brawn and creativity have always been given some merit in Dallas."

There is a noise, a pace, an energy here that seems to waft through the air, bask in the sky, seep through the soil and gurgle in the water.

This curious enveloping, which has existed from the time of the earliest settlers to the days when MBAs flocked here to make their mark, is most abundantly portrayed in the stories of the entrepreneurs — thousands of people who started something where nothing existed before. And for every Sammons, Collins, Haggar, Schepps, Cullum, Cottrell, Wyatt, Cuellar and Hunt, there are tens of thousands more whose names and businesses are not household words but whose aspirations have taken hold alongside the phenomenal life of the city.

Most anyone you might meet in Dallas has had some experience with an entrepreneur. The city is quite familiar with this unique portion of our populace.

Entrepreneurship was first engaged in 1841 when John Neely Bryan began plotting and selling lots in an uninhabited wilderness. This was a calculated real estate promotion heretofore unheard of in Texas. Where land acquisitions were happenstance at best, Bryan saw a window of opportunity.

ABOVE: Dallas' comprehensive community of higher education is teaching and training the entrepreneurs and business leaders of tomorrow. Photo by Brian McWeeney.

RIGHT: The Mustangs of Las Colinas is a reminder of the rugged determination that has made Dallas succeed where others might have failed. Photo by Martin Vandiver.

Entrepreneurship was engaged in 1867 when, in a grandiose gesture for steamship travel, a 60-foot steam wheeler with a 16-foot beam chugged from Galveston to Dallas via the Trinity River. The trip took a full year.

So inspired were Dallas businessmen at the thought of this new found commercial transportation that they built their own steamship, which at 87 feet long and 18 feet across was larger than the boat that had ventured from Galveston. The Dallas steamship never made it, ultimately sunk by a stump. With it drowned the hopes of steamship travel. They had given it their zealous best shot and failed.

But never mind. City fathers already were casting eager eyes on yet another form of transportation with great commercial impact — the railroad.

Perhaps no better example of Dallas' unofficial motto — "what's good

for business is good for Dallas" — is illustrated in the negotiations that led Dallas to be chosen for not one but two rail lines.

In 1870 when surveyors for the Houston and Texas Central Railroad (H&TC) announced their route, it bypassed Dallas by eight miles. Town leaders quickly determined what it would take to move the route so it would pass through Dallas. The necessary inducements — 115 acres of land, free city right-of-way along what is now North Central Expressway and $5,000 in cash — were approved by citizens in a 167 to 11 vote.

Bingo!

However, just six days after they caught site of the first H&TC train steaming down the tracks toward Dallas, the citizens were asked to vote on yet another rail gift that would ensure the Texas and Pacific's advantageous crossing of the H&TC in the heart of Dallas. In a unanimous vote of 192 to

0, the citizens gave $100,000 in bonds and a free right-of-way.

Dallas successfully captured these vital rail links when any number of cities could have been chosen.

Much of Dallas' early success was tied to this spirit of enterprise among the citizenry. Dallas snared Southern Methodist University from Fort Worth in 1915 with an 11th-hour gift of valuable Highland Park land. Some 60 years later the city captured a visionary regional airport as one of the last such facilities to be built in the 20th century.

Major corporate relocations and government services have bolstered the city's economy, yet Dallas has always kept the hearth fires burning for individuals who have a dream and a vision beyond the walls of corporations and civil service.

An amazing number of people "from somewhere else" seem to like the lifestyle, the upbeat nature, the tenacity of the city. They also like the

fact that in Dallas, a family connection is not critical. Never has been.

Neither is gender.

Plenty of women all over America have turned personal hardship into success against great odds. But there are very few cities that had not one, not two, but three such stalwarts in the pre-feminist 1950s.

Mary Kay Ash is founder of the namesake business that made her a legend in the cosmetics industry. And the late Mary Crowley founded Home Interiors and Gifts, the incredibly successful decorating accessories company. And Ebby Halliday, a real estate agent who in the late 1940s took over the sluggish sales of experimental concrete houses and sold all 52 homes in 14 months, has built her company into the largest volume individually owned real estate company in the United States.

Women like these have bestowed upon Dallas' female populace the magnificence of the entrepreneurial spirit.

Dallas was the birthplace in the early 1980s of the Association of Women Entrepreneurs, allowing a whole new generation of women to reap the rewards of their own creative energies while nurturing, supporting and fostering each other's success.

Dallas is a city where — without one iota of fanfare about who she is descended from — a young SMU graduate took her grandmother's lunchbox treats, sweet potato chips, and founded Ruthie's Chip Corporation. Pamela Melton is the great-great-great-granddaughter of Dallas' first woman entrepreneur, Sarah Horton Cockrell.

Cockrell began her successful rise following the shooting death of her husband in 1858. A widow at 38 with four small children, she became the town's leading entrepreneur. Assuming control of her husband's holdings, she owned and operated the ferry across the Trinity River for 14 years and was a principal in the building of the first iron bridge across the river in 1872.

Cockrell owned three hotels including the St. Nicholas, the finest of the day. A partner in Dallas' first commercial flour mill, Cockrell listed her occupation as "capitalist." At her death in 1892, she owned about one-fourth of downtown Dallas as well as considerable other property. Her will was 24 pages long.

Dallas has continued this legacy of luring the entrepreneur. Enterprising people have flocked here to find their dreams, to carve their slice of the capitalist pie.

Such was the case with Comer J. Cottrell Jr., who in 1970 helped start a new industry with Pro-Line Corporation, which produces ethnic hair-care products. While the company was founded in California, Cottrell made a strategic business decision in 1980 to move the operation to Dallas.

The company's market was growing beyond the Western United States and a central location was needed. Today Pro-Line is the largest African-American-owned business in the Southwest.

While success stories are numerous, being an entrepreneur has not always had a favorable connotation. In the mid-20th century, an educated business person who was willing to go out on a limb and take on great risk when he could easily have a comfortable job in some large company was looked at with some trepidation.

Today, entrepreneurs are admired, revered — even rewarded for their efforts. Each year Arthur Young & Co., *Inc.* magazine and *The Dallas Morning News* sponsor the Dallas-Fort Worth Entrepreneur of the Year awards. The program "honors company owners and managers who have demonstrated excellence in such areas as management skills, innova-

tion, financial performance and personal commitment in their business."

Entrepreneurs honored in 1989 were:

Emerging Business — J. Paul Grayson, Micrografx.

Established Business — Jinger and Richard W. Heath, BeautiControl Cosmetics.

Explosive Growth — Michael S. Dell, Dell Computer Corporation and Bill H. Hayden, CompuAdd Corporation.

High Tech — Raju Patel, NAC Inc.

Manufacturing — Comer J. Cottrell, Pro-Line Corporation.

Minority-Owned Business — Paul R. Dickinson, H-R Industries.

Real Estate/Construction — Michael A. Myers, Myers Financial Corporation.

Retail — Gary W. Kusin and James McCurry, Babbage's.

Woman-Owned Business — Ann Popejoy, CareTeam Management Services.

Supporter of Entrepreneurship — Dr. John H. Welsh, Caruth Institute of Owner-Managed Business, Southern Methodist University.

Special Recognition — Charles T. McKinney of Charlico Inc.

Entrepreneurs also are studied in Dallas. An academic discipline has arisen that studies the case histories of successful entrepreneurs and develops a scientific approach toward researching and identifying personality types suited to entrepreneurial careers.

Although he was not an entrepreneur in the sense of "one who starts something where nothing existed before," one Dallas citizen recognized the need for education to address this new genre of business leadership. W.W. Caruth Jr., who made his own fortune out of the giant body of land that had been amassed by his grandfather and nurtured by his father, founded the Caruth Institute of Owner-Managed Business at Southern Methodist University (SMU).

As late as 1970 when the Institute was added to SMU's School of Business, few universities had such a program and little research was being done. In just under 20 years, some 6,500 students have gone through this entrepreneurship program.

The stated purpose of the Caruth Institute is "to demonstrate to students the pleasures, the thrills, the excitement, and the satisfaction of building their own businesses as well as to familiarize them with the frustrations of management and the uncertainties of the marketplace. They learn how to put themselves in a position to be lucky and overcome obstacles by their wits or through their own intelligence. They are taught to accept adversity as merely a learning experience."

LEFT: The Meadows Foundation has been a leader in community involvement by helping individuals, families and businesses reach their full potential. Photo by Scott Metcalfe.

ABOVE: Dallas' taste for fine food has made the city a natural haven for fine chefs and innovative restaurateurs. Dallas has more restaurants per capita than New York City. Photo by Benjamin Stewart.

RIGHT: Noontime in downtown Dallas finds busy business people enjoying a shirt-sleeve stroll in the Texas sunshine. Photo by David J. Sams.

FOLLOWING PAGE: Research conducted at local universities like Southern Methodist University produces information and ideas that quite often find their way into the marketplace. Photo by Scott Metcalfe.

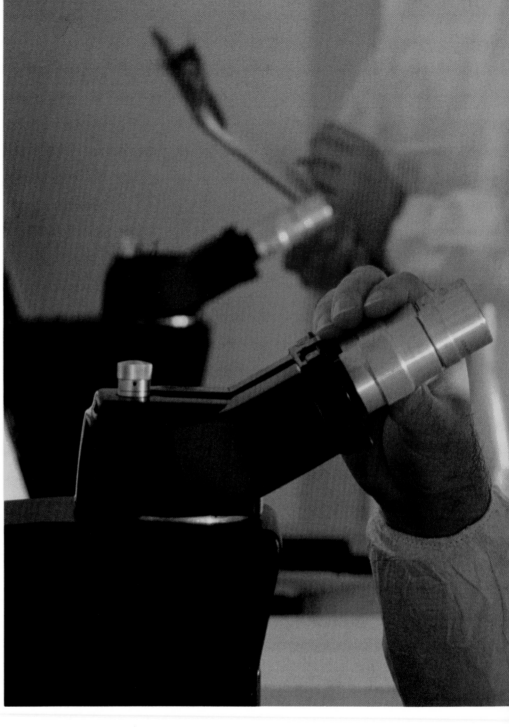

Consulting psychologist Dr. James Horger conducted research on entrepreneurial traits with Dr. Byron Williamson of SMU. They were trying to identify the type of business personalities that would provide good investment opportunities for financiers. What emerged from their research in the early 1970s is still taught today. Central to these studies are 11 characteristics of entrepreneurs:

1. Good health
2. A basic need to control and direct
3. Self-confidence
4. Never-ending sense of urgency
5. Comprehensive awareness
6. Realistic outlook
7. Superior conceptual ability
8. Low need for status
9. Objective approach
10. Sufficient emotional stability
11. Attraction to challenges, not risks

Many Dallasites possess these requisite traits of the entrepreneur. A great number of the city's largest and most innovative businesses were started by entrepreneurs. The business mix is broad, and the personalities divergent. Within the business lore of Dallas are some of the best examples of these entrepreneurial traits.

When good health is mentioned, it is easy to associate that characteristic with Norman Brinker. Founder of the Steak and Ale restaurant chain when he was fresh from college, Brinker later sold the chain to a large food company and ventured out a second time as a pioneer restaurateur. All the while he was building and developing his businesses, Brinker was refining his game of polo. Brinker plays polo all over the world and epitomizes good health.

The basic need to control and direct is inherent in the personality of Ben H. Carpenter, who took his family's ranch and built a 12,000-acre master-planned community: Las Colinas. Carpenter has said that rather than sell the land, strategically situated between Dallas and Fort Worth, and watch as others developed it, he dreamed of doing it all himself to his own exacting specifications. Today Las Colinas is acclaimed around the world as the finest development of its kind.

Self-confidence is apparent in all that Ross Perot does. From the time he was a disconsolate IBM salesman who had made his quota for the year by the end of January to the protracted legal battles he has waged with one of America's corporate giants, General Motors, Perot has relentlessly pursued his objectives — whether they be flying Christmas meals to war-torn Vietnam, taking on Texas' educational reform movement, freeing employees from an Iranian jail, or pursuing large contracts for his computer services company.

Whether it was a never-ending sense of urgency or merely the reality of the hotly competitive airline industry, Southwest Airlines chief executive officer Herb Kelleher has kept his airline flying against some of the most difficult odds. Kelleher's once fledgling commuter airline is now the 5th largest airline company in the country with revenues over $1 billion.

share of credit for the success of Dallas/Forth Worth International Airport, serving as the first chairman of the airport's board. He also was a founder of the research institute which is now the University of Texas at Dallas.

Considered to be the second richest man in Texas behind Ross Perot, Harold Simmons remains a relatively unknown and unrecognized billionaire with a low need for status. And he likes it that way. Simmons is credited with creating the "leveraged buyout." Numerous successes have followed the sale of his chain of drug stores to Jack Eckerd, and he is reported to have bought, sold or maintained control of some 36 companies over the past three decades, with an astounding 95 percent average annual return. As he was once quoted, "Once you've made your first million or two it doesn't really matter. I mean, there is only so much you can do with that kind of money." Simmons spends most evenings at home, which, in typical fashion, he paid for in cash — $7.5 million.

An objective approach to interpersonal relationships has not made Raymond Nasher one of Dallas' golden boys in terms of popularity. However, he is easily one of the most respected business men in Dallas. His NorthPark shopping center development and other real estate coups have almost been overshadowed in recent years by his art collection, which was invited to Russia by the Gorbachevs, and has been called the finest private collection of its kind in the world. Nasher is the antithesis of the Texas good ol' boy, choosing instead participation in think tanks and the advocacy of art in the workplace as his causes.

Beauty is a youth-oriented business, yet Mary Kay Ash has had the sufficient emotional stability to maintain her position at the helm of the beauty company she founded well

Despite the fact that he grew up poor, Robert Dedman had the comprehensive awareness to know that country clubs were big business. Also, he has always been aware that people who acquire great fortunes are beholden to give back to their communities. With that in mind, he has made good on his pledge to donate a portion of his income from his highly successful Club Corporation of America, the largest developers/operators of private clubs in the world, with $400 million in annual revenues.

Realistic appraisals of the real estate market have catapulted Trammell Crow to a position as America's largest real estate developer. His development of the successful Market Center concept, first in Dallas and now throughout the world, is only one of Crow's many accomplishments in the real estate industry in 86 American cities and throughout the world.

While his superior conceptual ability served him well in the founding of giant Texas Instruments, J. Erik Jonsson also put his considerable talents to work on behalf of Dallas, serving as mayor from 1964 to 1971, and as founder of the Goals for Dallas program. Jonsson is given the lion's

into her later years. She is credited
with being one of the most successful
women entrepreneurs in the country
and perhaps the greatest motivator of
people anywhere in business.

Many fashion industry experts
thought Victor Costa had committed
business suicide, when in the 1970s,
he left New York's inner circle of
fashion and headed for Dallas to set
up shop. It was the attraction to challenges, not risks that brought Costa
back to his native Texas with the
intent of making a big fashion name
for himself and his company outside
the confines of New York. Today,
Costa is known worldwide for his

stunning copies of designs from the
the high fashion coutures, and his
company sells to the finest specialty
and department stores in the nation,
with many famous women as his devotees. He remains Dallas-based.

As the 1980s slowed to a disheart-
ening pace and lending institutions
adopted a mode of contraction rather
than expansion, capital for start-up
companies and expansions of existing
ones was difficult to secure.

While no one would argue that
economic recovery is under way, some
observers see Dallas losing a measure
of its distinctive business personality.

"Whether Dallas continues to

nourish the entrepreneurial spirit remains to be seen," said Dr. Richard Tozer, a noted business consultant specializing in entrepreneurial companies. However, Tozer remains optimistic about Dallas' future, with the city's central location, diversified economy and particularly its people serving it well.

Dr. James Horger concedes the lack of financing might slow the entrepreneur down. "But it really doesn't blunt their drive; the entrepreneur will find a way to persevere with his idea."

Dallas has an abundance of up-and-coming individualists who will persist until their dreams are realized.

It is, after all, that same strain of persistence that led John Neely Bryan to continue to come up with ideas for remaining in Dallas when his various schemes for staying failed.

The same spirit of enterprise has remained alive and kicking in Dallas through some of its toughest tests since the founding days. Generations of Dallas citizens have been blessed with the ingenious ability to imagine, to innovate and to create industries where none existed before.

In the final decade of the 20th century, the spirit of enterprise in Dallas will survive challenge, indeed will continue to thrive because of the most bountiful natural resource that any city in America is blessed with — people, and their intangible aspirations to travel into new frontiers against any and all odds.

CHAPTER 3

The Heart of the City

By Bill Sloan

Downtown Dallas remains the business, financial and governmental nerve center of the city. On the streets beneath the skyline and in the buildings that comprise it, decisions are made each day that affect the lives of everyone who lives and works in Dallas.

Downtown Dallas is where the city began, and where many of its most important activities and functions still take place. Photo by Martin Vandiver.

ABOVE: *Old-fashioned surreys are the perfect way to travel through the West End Historic District. Photo by Martin Vandiver.*

TOP RIGHT: *Thanks-Giving Square with its spiraling chapel is a favorite place for lunch.*

BOTTOM RIGHT: *The Dallas Museum of Art and First United Methodist Church share a neighborhood with towers of steel and glass. Photo by Dan Hatzenbuehler.*

Downtown Dallas no longer is the "only game in town" when it comes to major concentrations of employment, luxury hotels, skyscraper office buildings and hustle-and-bustle. But it remains the heart of the city, the hub of its infrastructure, the seat of its government, the nucleus of its economy and its primary focal point for natives and newcomers alike, as it always has.

And just as important, it is enjoying a rebirth and renaissance that seemed all but impossible just a decade or so ago.

The orderly and well-organized way in which Dallas perceives itself and likes to do business has led to one of the best-defined Central Business Districts (CBD) in the country — and to one of the smallest downtowns in terms of square miles among major U.S. cities. The CBD, as outlined by the freeways that completely encircle it, contains a mere 930 acres of land, which is much less than most Texas ranches worthy of the name. But squeezed into that acreage is nearly 30 million square feet of rentable space in the multitenant office towers that make up its striking and distinctive skyline, 2,200 companies and 120,000 jobs, more than 4,700 first-class hotel rooms, at least four separate identifiable subdistricts, and enough interesting things to see and do to keep anybody busy for a day or two.

And while the term "downtown" remains synonymous with "Central Business District" in the minds of many Dallasites, there are telltale signs that the concept is escaping the concrete boundaries imposed upon it by municipal planners and overflowing into several contiguous areas beyond the freeway loop. Those most likely to become psychological extensions of downtown (if not official additions to the CBD) over the next decade include Oak Lawn to the north, already referred to as "uptown"; the area just south of the Dallas Convention Center, in the vicinity of Old City Park; and the Deep Ellum area immediately to the east.

Dallas justifiably has been proud of its downtown skyline ever since the World War I era, when *Collier's Weekly* termed it the "most imposing" of any American city "save New York." For generations since, that skyline has been catching the eye of approaching visitors from miles in all directions. A few of the structures that accentuated it back in 1917-18 are still standing today, but they are dwarfed and overshadowed by what has been built in more recent times. During the 1980s alone, the skyline soared to undreamed of heights.

But that is only part of the difference between the downtown of 75 years ago and the downtown of today. From the time of Dallas' birth until the beginning of large-scale suburban growth in Dallas County in the second half of the 1950s, downtown was the center of everything. Its cadre of giant department stores and scores of well-stocked smaller shops were a mecca for shoppers from all over North and East Texas. The marquees of its famed "Theatre Row" along Elm Street featured more big-name stars and first-run movies than any other three-block stretch of neon in the Southwest. Its glittering supper clubs, glamorous ballrooms, garish burlesque houses, popular restaurants and ample after-dark activity made it the place to go for a big night on the town.

If you required the services of a physician or dentist, no less than 400 of them had offices in the old Medical Arts Building on Pacific Avenue. If you wanted to travel, you could climb aboard a train to just about anywhere at always-crowded Union Terminal, or catch a bus at one of two busy bus stations. If you were looking for a rare book or the latest best seller, you could browse through six floors of literature at Cokesbury's, the world's largest bookstore. If you were in the market for a new car, a half-dozen auto dealerships were at your disposal. In short, whatever you needed or wanted — from a half-carat diamond to an oil change, from a side of beef to an exploding cigar — you could find it downtown. Aboard clanging streetcars and hissing trolleys, endless streams of people came from all parts of Dallas to buy goods, conduct business, enjoy leisure time and spend money.

As the years passed, however, all that changed. The streetcars went the way of the tin lizzie. The movie houses and show bars gradually disappeared, as did most of the restaurants. Big stores and small shops alike held final clearance sales, closed their doors and moved to the suburbs. And for a long time, nothing arose to replace what was fading away except more office buildings. Over the space of 15 to 20 years, the downtown that Dallas had always known vanished forever. By the mid-1970s, except for the major hotels, it was almost entirely an 8-to-5 kind of place, a place where people joked about rolling up the sidewalks at 6 p.m. and firing a cannon down Main Street on a Saturday afternoon without endangering a single soul.

Fortunately, much of this depressing scenario has changed, too, and is certain to change still further in years to come. Within the past decade, downtown Dallas has done much more than merely build skyscrapers. Despite what many pessimists said, it has proved that new life and vitality can be injected into the core of the city; that despite the appeal of suburbia, people can be persuaded to come downtown for many reasons besides just working. Today, Dallasites again are flocking downtown after business hours and on weekends. They come for many reasons: art, culture, education, sports events, concerts, theatrical productions, outstanding restaurants, sightseeing and just plain fun.

Meanwhile, as it always has, downtown remains the business, financial and governmental nerve center of

the city. On the streets beneath the skyline and in the buildings that comprise it, decisions are made each day that affect the lives of everyone who lives and/or works in Dallas. Downtown is the home of the Federal Reserve Bank of Dallas, the area's largest commercial banks and other huge corporate entities; it is the place where vast fortunes change hands and multimillion-dollar deals are made. It also is the site of the modernistic Dallas City Hall, the Dallas County Government Center, the Earle Cabell Federal Building and most of the governmental apparatus that makes and carries out the laws that govern the city's population.

There is no "government district" as such in downtown Dallas. Instead the governmental presence is interspersed with that of the private sector. County government facilities, including the Old Red Courthouse, the County Records Building and the former Texas School Book Depository, occupy much of the southwestern quadrant of the CBD. City government facilities, including the Police and Courts Building (old City Hall), the new City Hall and the Central Library, are grouped mainly in the southeastern quadrant. Also located downtown is the headquarters of the Dallas County Community College District. El Centro Col-

lege, one of the seven campuses operated by the district, occupies the old Sanger Brothers Department Store building on Lamar Street.

Since banking institutions have traditionally been scattered all over downtown, there is also no identifiable "financial district" at present, at least in a geographic sense. One may eventually emerge, however, as NCNB Texas consolidates the resources of the former RepublicBank and InterFirst Bank in the vicinity of Elm and Griffin Streets. As this book is being written, the Federal Reserve Bank is in the process of selecting a site for a new building, and this decision will have significant impact on the development of a future "financial district."

There are, however, four subdistricts within the CBD that can be readily identified today. They include:

Arts District — Designated by the city of Dallas in 1983, with the internationally celebrated Dallas Museum of Art and the Morton H. Meyerson Symphony Center as its centerpieces, the Arts District occupies 60 acres in the northeastern quadrant of downtown. The largest project of its type in the country in a central downtown location, the district is also the site of the Arts District Theater (a branch of the Dallas Theater Center) and the Arts Magnet High School of the Dallas Independent School District. The Arts District already has done much to draw the public back to the CBD as well as to stimulate commercial development in the quadrant. It will increasingly become the scene of numerous arts-related festivals and special events during the decade ahead and is expected to lead the way during the early 1990s in the resumption of high-rise development downtown.

Farmers Market — Located in the extreme southeastern corner of downtown, the market area has been quietly proving for many years that large-scale retail trade and tens of thousands of buyers can still be attracted to the central city if the right kind of merchandise is offered. In this case, the merchandise includes all varieties of fresh fruits and vegetables, ornamental plants, bedding plants and other decorative and edible items offered for sale at the municipally owned Farmers Market. Vendors display their wares seven days a week throughout the year in large, colorful, open-air sheds. A number of wholesale produce dealers are also concentrated in the area. Expanding and improving market facilities and public access for the

market's 2.5 million annual visitors will be a prime discussion topic over the next few years.

Reunion — With the magnificently restored 1916-vintage Union Station as its chief focal point, Reunion began in 1975 as a widely heralded public-private development project which resulted in a major

LEFT: Fountain Place is an appropriate name for this haven of bubbling fountains and cypress trees. Photo by Dan Hatzenbuehler.

ABOVE: Thanks-Giving Square is the site of many outdoor ceremonies. Photo by Doug Milner.

TOP: *Farmers Market brings farm-fresh produce to the heart of the city. Photo by Scott Metcalfe.*

BOTTOM: *The Hyatt Regency and Reunion Tower are silhouetted against the evening sky. Photo by Doug Milner.*

RIGHT: *The Reunion development includes Union Station (foreground) and the Hyatt Regency and Reunion Tower (center). Photo by Doug Milner.*

addition to the southwest corner of downtown. Besides the terminal, which houses the Amtrak station for Dallas, a downtown center for other types of transportation and a Visitor Information Center, the area includes the 50-story Reunion Tower, famed for its light shows and revolving restaurant; the Hyatt Regency Hotel, downtown's largest with 950 rooms; and Reunion Arena, home of the Dallas Mavericks of the National Basketball Association and site of concerts, conventions and other large public and private events.

West End Historic District — Officially designated as a historic preservation area in 1975 because of its prime examples of turn-of-the-century commercial architecture, the West End did not come into its own for nearly a decade. Although a number of buildings were restored in the district and the Old Spaghetti Warehouse restaurant enjoyed enormous success there, the area did not begin

attracting other people-oriented businesses until the mid-1980s. Today, the West End is the city's premier entertainment center — an oasis of fine dining, live music and after-dark revelry that brings thousands of people downtown each night. Two important catalysts for its success have been the picturesque West End MarketPlace, comprised of dozens of intriguing shops and eating places in an old furniture warehouse, and adjacent Dallas Alley, with its collection of lively nightspots. The West End plays host to more than 5 million visitors each year.

Far from being confined to these four areas, however, points of interest are scattered liberally all across downtown Dallas, and no sightseeing excursion would be complete unless they were included.

For many first-time visitors, the initial stop on any downtown tour is the John F. Kennedy Memorial area. In addition to the memorial itself,

this includes Dealey Plaza, site of the assassination of President Kennedy in 1963, and the former Texas School Book Depository, from which Lee Harvey Oswald allegedly fired the shots that struck JFK, and which now houses a permanent exhibit of Kennedy memorabilia known as The Sixth Floor. Adjacent to the Kennedy Memorial is a reconstructed version of the first structure ever built in Dallas: the one-room log cabin erected by John Neely Bryan, the city's founder, in 1841.

Just across Interstate 30 (R.L. Thornton Freeway) from the southern edge of the CBD is Old City Park, a charming and realistic reconstruction of small-town life in Texas during the latter half of the 19th century. Established during the mid-1970s on the site of Dallas' first municipal park, and operated jointly by the city of

Dallas and the Dallas County Heritage Society, the park contains more than two dozen painstakingly restored structures ranging from log cabins to an antebellum mansion. It includes an authentic frontier schoolhouse, church, railroad station, printshop, doctor's office, hotel, bank and general store. The park is open for tours daily.

The Dallas Convention Center is a principal destination for some 2 million visitors who attend conventions and gatherings there each year. Already containing 1.9 million square feet and occupying a vast chunk of real estate on the southern edge of downtown, the convention center is scheduled for significant expansion as Dallas builds a downtown-based convention industry ranked second only to New York in the number of delegates attracted

RIGHT: The lobby of One Bell Plaza bursts with color. Photo by Dan Hatzenbuehler.

ABOVE: The St. Patrick's Day Parade is one of many annual parades that wind through the central business district. Photo by Doug Milner.

during the late 1980s. When the latest 325,000-square-foot addition to the center is completed in 1994, it will be capable of accommodating more than 3 million conventioneers annually and will rank among the finest convention facilities in the world.

One of the most intriguing parts of downtown Dallas often goes totally unnoticed by the casual visitor, although it is literally right under his or her feet. It is an intricate and still-growing system of underground walkways that links many of the major downtown buildings and enables visitors to enjoy a casual stroll regardless of weather or surface traffic conditions. The Underground is much more than a walkway, however. It also contains numerous restaurants, fast food concessions, shops, places to relax and even a post office. Entrances to the Underground are located in numerous office buildings and several parking garages. It connects with a system of elevated walkways serving newer buildings primarily in the northeast quadrant of the CBD.

Except for the West End, downtown may seem almost totally new and modern at first glance, but it is actually a treasure chest of historic structures. These include the elegantly restored Majestic Theatre, the last survivor of Elm Street's Theatre Row, where audiences again applaud the finest in classic motion pictures and live theatrical productions; the Adolphus Hotel on Commerce Street, an architectural gem described as "the most beautiful building west of Venice" when it opened in 1912, and the object of a $45 million restoration in the early 1980s; the fortress-like Old Red Courthouse, built in 1893 and adorned with turrets and gargoyles; and the Romanesque First Baptist Church on Ervay Street, built in 1891 and now home of the world's largest Southern Baptist congregation. Incidentally, there are six churches in downtown Dallas with combined membership of 46,000.

The list of things to see and do in downtown Dallas goes on and on. It includes shopping at the world-famous original Neiman-Marcus store at Main and Ervay; pausing three blocks away at Pacific and Ervay to enjoy a moment of quiet reflection at Thanks-Giving Square, with its

ABOVE: *Dallas City Hall adds a modern slant to city government. Photo by Brian McWeeney.*

RIGHT: *The Dallas County Criminal Courts Building is among the architectural treasures of Dallas' West End Historic District. Photo by John Hethorn.*

unique spiral chapel and stained-glass ceiling; taking a nostalgic stroll through Pioneer Park Cemetery, where many of the city's early settlers are buried; riding in a horse-drawn carriage from Union Station to the West End; or hopping on an electric trolley — yes, the streetcars are back — for a trip from the Arts District to the shops and restaurants along McKinney Avenue.

Clearly, central Dallas has come a long way in its quest to become one of the most vibrant and exciting downtowns in America. And today's municipal planners and community leaders are presently cultivating two key ingredients that could enable Dallas to realize that goal during the 1990s.

The first ingredient is a resident population. In this regard, Dallas is much different from most older cities, in that almost no one lives in the downtown area. Although thousands of visitors may frequently pack downtown hotels, and about 50,000 people live within a two-mile radius, there were only about 400 full-time residents in the CBD as of late 1989, the majority of them tenants at the Manor House, downtown's only high-rise apartment building.

A 24-hour population of even a few thousand would not only enliven the environment, but set the stage for attaining the second key ingredient — intensive new retail development.

A high priority for the 1990s among Dallas' leadership is a downtown retail shopping complex which would (a) fill the void left by the departure of major department stores from old free-standing structures by enticing chain retailers back into the CBD, and (b) provide retail facilities and services, such as grocery stores, which have been long missing from the downtown scene. Several plans for such a retail complex were under study as this book went to print, but with a projected price tag of more than $40 million, each would require significant use of public funds.

Obtaining either ingredient would make it much easier to obtain the second, planners say, but there are some hopeful signs that both may come simultaneously within the next few years. An integral part of at least one of the retail center proposals, for example, also entails some residential development. And just outside the CBD, both the Deep Ellum area to the east and the State-Thomas area to the north offer promising possibilities for residential growth.

"I'll be very surprised if we don't see large-scale residential development in the central city by the mid-1990s," says Mark Stein, planning director of the Central Dallas Association. "The prospects for retail development within that time frame are also good, because there is a tremendous void of modern shopping malls all across the inner city. Downtown is the logical place for this type of facility, although construction costs will be higher than they would be outside the CBD."

While a downtown lifestyle may remain out of reach for awhile to all but a handful in Dallas, downtown itself and its myriad attractions are within everyone's reach. And as effective mass transit is developed over the next few years, both those attractions and that lifestyle should become more accessible. The 1980s were a time when Dallasites rediscovered the pleasures of their downtown area; the 1990s may prove to be a time when many of them discover the pleasure of living there.

In the meantime, even the pessimists have quit talking about rolling up the sidewalks at 6 p.m.

CHAPTER 4

Strength in Diversity

By Bill Sloan

Dallas has never been easy to categorize in a commercial or economic sense. At various times in its history, Dallas has depended heavily on a number of industries including agriculture, banking, defense, petroleum, real estate, transportation and high technology. ·

In Dallas, a center of "clean" industry, most of the few smokestacks visible are at electric generating power plants. Photo by Scott Metcalfe.

Many American cities have catchy nicknames, and as often as not, those nicknames are closely related to matters of economics and how a city earns its livelihood.

Detroit calls itself "Motown" for reasons that are perfectly clear to anyone who has seen the new cars rolling off the assembly lines there. For equally apparent reasons, Pittsburgh is "Steel Town," Las Vegas is "Glitter Gulch" and Hollywood is "Filmtown." Tulsa calls itself the nation's "Oil Capital," and Houston lays claim to "Space City." Nashville takes pride in being "Music City," and Chicago has been immortalized in literature as "Hog Butcher for the World." In many cases, one major municipal claim to fame overshadows all the rest. Beer made Milwaukee famous just as New Orleans will ever be synonymous with jazz, Indianapolis with auto racing and Kansas City with prime beef.

Dallas, on the other hand, has never been that easy to categorize in a commercial or economic sense. At various times in its history, Dallas has depended heavily on a number of industries including agriculture, banking, defense, petroleum, real estate, transportation and high technology. All have played dominant roles in the city's phenomenal story of growth. Each has enjoyed its moment at center stage in the area's economic drama, but eventually each has had to make room for other rising economic stars and supporting players. Communications, conventions and tourism, distribution and warehousing, education, fashion, health care, insurance, manufacturing, retailing, services and wholesaling all have claimed a share of the spotlight.

What do you call a city with such a multifaceted economy? How do you label it or sum up what it is all about in one or two descriptive words? Even

in a state as renowned for its bragging and boldness as Texas, it poses a genuine dilemma. Terms such as "Everythingville" or "Super City" might come close to conveying the right idea, but somehow they seem a trifle overdone.

Therefore, for understandable reasons Dallas spent its first century or so without any nickname at all. Beginning in the 1950s, thanks to a popular song and a widely read newspaper column, people started calling the place "Big D." The name seems even more appropriate now than it did then, especially if you consider that the "D" stands not only for Dallas, but for Diversity.

It is diversity, indeed, that has enabled "Big D" to grow bigger and bigger, and this same diversity is the major economic strength that continues to undergird the Dallas area as it heads toward the 21st century.

Diversity is unquestionably the most important factor in Dallas' recovery from the sharp reverses experienced by the local real estate and financial communities in the mid-to-late-1980s, at a time when the Texas oil industry was suffering through some of its darkest days.

Dynamic, determined, diversified Dallas has forged for itself a unique niche among the major cities of the world, not by focusing narrowly on any one service, product or field of endeavor, but by branching out into many. And once again during the past few years, as it has so often at other points in Dallas' past, diversity has proved a potent cure for economic adversity.

Many factors have played a part in Dallas' ability to create the broad mix of seemingly unrelated businesses that it now enjoys. Geography can be credited in some instances, and so can luck, but foresight, careful planning, willingness to take risks, an unquenchable spirit of optimism and just plain hard work have been

important contributors, too. To put it all into perspective, it is helpful to take a brief glance back through the commercial history of the city, to a time when the only nickname "Big D" truly merited was "small potatoes."

As it did with most other settlements on the North Texas prairie, the economy of Dallas originally sprang from farming. In the earliest days,

wheat, corn and a variety of fruits and vegetables were grown in what is now Dallas, but the fertile black soil of the region proved almost ideal for cotton. When the railroads arrived in the 1870s and North Texas cotton finally became readily accessible to the rest of the country, Dallas quickly established itself as the center of the nation's Cotton Belt and by 1900 had emerged as the world's largest inland

cotton market. The Dallas Cotton Exchange became one of the busiest commercial trading facilities outside New York and Chicago, and the city also became a leading center for the manufacture of cotton ginning equipment.

For the better part of a half-century, cotton was the undisputed king of Dallas' economy, but the railroads that made this possible also

ABOVE: Downtown Dallas is the business and financial heart of the region and is headquarters for major banks and financial services institutions, insurance companies, oil companies, law firms and other professional organizations. Photo by Dan Hatzenbuehler.

wrought other far-reaching economic consequences. Because of its superb rail connections, Dallas soon ranked as the most important distribution center for all types of goods in the five-state area of Texas, New Mexico, Oklahoma, Arkansas and Louisiana. By 1914 when Dallas was selected as the site for one of 12 regional Federal Reserve Banks, the city was headquarters for several thousand traveling salesmen, and its wholesalers had supplanted those in St. Louis as the chief suppliers of goods to Southwestern retailers.

Today, the cotton fields that once stretched to the far horizon on all sides of town are but a faded memory for a few oldtimers. The cotton wagons that once clogged Main Street, the cotton gins that once dotted the county, the cotton buyers who came from around the globe, and even the Cotton Exchange itself have all vanished from the scene, but the economic legacy they left behind is still very much a part of modern Dallas. Together, cotton and the railroads

brought Dallas its first international attention, its first skyscraper offices, its first large-scale manufacturing, its first big banks. As it was in cotton's heyday, Dallas remains the foremost distribution and warehousing center of the Southwest, and the commercial and financial infrastructure that began to take shape because of cotton and the railroads has continued to expand and diversify.

The agricultural bounty of Texas is still a great intangible asset to Dallas, but after the day in 1930 when the discovery well of the vast East Texas Oil Field "blew in" 100 miles to the east, "King Cotton" lost its throne. During the next few years, the petroleum industry and related enterprises injected tremendous wealth into the city, allowing it to prosper at a time when most other cities were stagnating in the grip of the Great Depression. In the process, the oil industry became a longstanding participant in the booming Dallas economy.

However, oil, like cotton, has slipped into the economic background in Dallas. Outside the state of Texas, much confusion still exists over Dallas' supposed connections with "big oil" (especially among those whose impressions are based mainly on a certain television series). And even many local observers were surprised to learn, during the downturn of the mid-1980s, that only about 2 percent of the city's employment base was in the oil industry.

The truth is that Dallas never has actually been an "oil town" in the literal sense, and it never has been as oil-dependent as other Southwestern cities. Instead, Dallas has been a center of financial resources, corporate management and technical expertise for the petroleum industry in Texas and contiguous states. While it has aided in the drilling of thousands of wells and the pumping of millions of barrels of oil in the 60 years since the East Texas Field was discovered, Dallas itself never has produced a single drop of oil for commercial use.

Perhaps oil's chief local contribution has been to propel Dallas into the front ranks of the nation's financial centers. As the Texas oil industry grew, so did the clout and assets of Dallas' financial institutions. By the early 1980s, three of the five largest commercial banks in Texas, with combined deposits of more than $13.5 billion, were headquartered in downtown Dallas. These home-grown financial giants — First National Bank, Republic National Bank and Mercantile National Bank — ranked among the 75 largest banks in the United States. Along with the Federal Reserve Bank of Dallas, a dozen other area banks with assets of between $100 million and $500 million, plus numerous strong savings and loans, these institutions made Dallas the financial capital of the Southwest.

In the meantime, other elements of the Dallas economy also were enjoying incredible growth and suc-

cess. Beginning with the opening of Dallas/Fort Worth International Airport in 1973, air travel revolutionized Dallas area business to an even greater extent than the railroads had done a century earlier. The 18,000-acre airport — the world's largest at its opening — was the result of years of debate, planning and construction, and the changes it brought could hardly have been more dramatic or far-reaching. Suddenly, Dallas was an international city. Suddenly, Dallas

TOP LEFT: Dallas is a headquarters and research center for major energy companies such as Exxon, Fina, ARCO, Caltex, Occidental Chemical, Mobil and Oryx Energy. Photo by Benjamin Stewart.

BOTTOM LEFT: Dallas' contribution to the auto industry includes parts manufacturing and final installation of components such as these Mercedes-Benz air foils. Photo by Benjamin Stewart.

ABOVE: The Federal Reserve Bank of Dallas is the heart of Dallas' banking and financial services industry. Photo by Jeff Hampton.

companies were doing business with the entire world.

Today, with 1,800 daily flights connecting Dallas with 150 U.S. and 29 international destinations, D/FW Airport ranks as the second busiest airport in the United States. Its prominence was instrumental in bringing the headquarters of American Airlines with its 20,000-plus local employees to the Dallas area, and in creating thousands of other jobs. About one out of every 12 wage earners is now employed in aviation-related jobs.

"Everyone I talk to ranks the airport as our strongest asset for future economic growth," says Tom Lewis, senior vice president of the Dallas Partnership, an outreach marketing agency funded by the Greater Dallas Chamber and 60 Dallas businesses. "It goes hand-in-hand with the geo-graphical advantage of being in the middle of the United States, and as American business moves more and more into white collar-intensive areas, these assets will loom larger and larger."

In addition to its direct affect, the airport has had enormous "spin-off" impact on the Dallas economy. For a graphic example of this, one need look no further than the city's multibillion-dollar visitor industry.

Tourists and conventioneers have been coming to Dallas for a long time, as evidenced by the fact that the city got its first "world-class" hotel — the Adolphus — in 1912. The industry got an important boost during the Texas Centennial Exposition of 1936, when millions of out-of-staters came to Dallas to take a break from the rigors of the Depression. With the development of the Dallas Convention Center in the 1960s and '70s as D/FW Airport was being built, Dallas became a leading convention destination. Since then, Dallas has played host to the biggest and most spectacular gatherings in America, including the Republican National Convention in 1984. Today, thanks to its "world-class" airport and convention center and the presence of more than 40,000 hotel rooms, Dallas ranks second only to New York among America's convention cities.

The defense/aerospace industry first assumed an important economic role in Dallas just prior to World War II, and by the 1960s, such Dallas-based companies as LTV and Texas Instruments (TI) had mushroomed into huge corporations with tens of thousands of local employees. As a front-runner in the development of the microchip, TI helped pave the way for a new industry — high technology — and helped to establish the Dallas/Fort Worth Metroplex as one of the nation's emerging high-tech centers.

Simultaneously, Electronic Data Systems (EDS) burst on the local scene in the late 1960s and grew into one of the area's largest employers in less than two decades. The phenomenal success of EDS, now a subsidiary of General Motors, gave Dallas a high profile with high tech companies

profile with high-tech companies large and small. These developments, plus the major presence of IBM in the Dallas area, have created a "ripple effect" that continues to attract other computer and technology-based firms.

Also in the area of high tech, Dallas has quietly emerged as the telecommunications center of the United States. Not only are such telecommunications giants as Southwestern Bell and GTE Southwest located in the area, but Dallas is far ahead most other U.S. cities in the application of fiber optics and other sophisticated telecommunications services. As Ed Glotzbach, general manager for Southwestern Bell, says: "Frankly, Dallas is second to none in the amount of fiber optics deployed and in such evolving innovations as integrated services digital networks (ISDNs), which put us closer to a 'paperless environment' than we've ever been."

Further supporting Dallas' great strides in technological and scientific fields, and constituting a significant portion of the area economy in its own right, is the rapidly evolving network of educational facilities and institutions. Some of the major entities within this network include the University of Texas Southwestern Medical Center, the University of Texas at Dallas, Southern Methodist University, the University of Dallas, the University of North Texas, the

LEFT: Dallas/Fort Worth International Airport is a primary reason why giant corporations such as American Airlines, J.C. Penney and Exxon have moved their corporate headquarters to the Metroplex. Photo by John Hethorn.

CENTER: Special events and attractions bring millions of visitors — and billions of dollars — to Dallas each year. Photo by Allan Kaye.

ABOVE: Electronics manufacturing and testing is a major contributor to Dallas' strength as the "Silicon Prairie."

ABOVE: *New home construction continues to be a major source of employment and economic impact as the Dallas area continues to grow from in-migration. Photo by John Hethorn.*

RIGHT: *Health facilities such as giant Baylor University Medical Center are vital to quality of life as well as the area's economic mix. Photo by Jeff Hampton.*

University of Texas at Arlington, Baylor University Medical Center, Texas Woman's University and the Dallas County Community College District. Together they offer advanced educational programs in technical areas ranging from engineering to medical research and from geology to computer science.

The sprawling campuses of the city's two university medical centers also make Dallas a national leader in health care. UT Southwestern, whose researchers won three Nobel Prizes during the late 1980s, is associated with the area's largest teaching hospital complex, and Baylor, which incorporates schools of nursing and dentistry, is one of the world's largest private health care facilities.

Fueled by the diversity of its economy, the size and quality of its airport, its pro-business attitude, its central geographic location and a boundless enthusiasm about the future, "Big D" was riding the crest of an unprecedented wave of growth and prosperity as it reached the middle years of the 1980s. Dallas was the home of several of the nation's premier real estate development firms, and it became the darling of other investors and developers across the continent. In all its history, Dallas had never experienced anything like the tidal wave of new construction they unleashed across the city and the area from 1982 through 1986. Office towers, shopping centers, apartment complexes and new homes sprouted by the thousands in all directions.

Unfortunately, the passion for growth that had always served Dallas so well in the past was about to collide with the harsh realities of the present. Even in Dallas, growth had its limits, and the diverse Dallas economy was not totally immune to the damage and dislocations that result when those limits are exceeded. Several years of feverish overbuilding by developers and investors who sometimes confused building activity with genuine growth created an oversupply of real estate products. There simply were not enough tenants to absorb all the offices and other commercial space, not enough buyers and renters to occupy all the new homes and apartments. The real estate market became glutted and sluggish, just as contractions in the petroleum, construction and real estate sectors compounded the problem.

Employment growth, which had been skyrocketing for several years, abruptly tailed off. Companies in other sectors grew cautious, and the absorption rate for commercial lease space plummeted. Instead of continuing its rapid expansion, the real estate market started to contract. Prices eroded, rental rates fell, whole office buildings and retail centers stood vacant.

That was the first shock wave. Then the foreclosures began. That was the second. By the time it ran its course and the dust settled, the Dallas financial community had suffered the worst devastation in its history and the greatest boom period of the century had deteriorated into the deepest economic crisis. Under the massive burden of non-performing real estate and oil loans, and crushed by the weight of foreclosed properties

that could not be sold, dozens of area financial institutions failed. Among them were all three of the biggest banks in Dallas and the far-flung bank holding company networks they had built.

If economic diversity stands a community in good stead during the good times, it is even more vital to stability, survival and recovery when bad times arrive. Thus, amid the "real estate depression" and financial chaos of the late 1980s, Dallas was buoyed by continued growth in high tech, health care, communications, services, manufacturing, retailing, conventions/tourism and warehousing. Because of these strong sectors of the economy, Dallas has been able to "turn the corner" and resume its march toward new heights of progress and prosperity much sooner than might be expected.

Indeed, some of the most important economic accomplishments in

the city's business history have taken place during the very depths of this "down cycle." J.C. Penney, one of the world's largest retail organizations, relocated its headquarters to the Dallas area in 1987, generating thousands of new jobs and firmly establishing the area as a major national retail center. The Penney's move also produced a noticeable "ripple effect" of economic activity. A study by one commercial real estate company showed that in addition to the 1.1 million square feet of office space absorbed by Penney's, more than 300,000 additional square feet was leased by the first wave of Penney's suppliers to establish operations here.

In 1988, close on the heels of the Penney's move, the area just south of Dallas was selected as the site for the federal government's multibillion-dollar Superconducting Super Collider, a monumental scientific project

whose potential impact on the Dallas economy over the next quarter-century is almost impossible to exaggerate. This victory, which the Dallas area won against stiff competition from other sites in other states, constitutes Dallas' biggest step yet toward its goal of becoming a top global center for high technology. In addition, the Super Collider is likely to trigger a much-needed burst of development on the southern side of Dallas, a side that has lagged far behind the explosive north in terms of economic growth and job creation.

In early 1989, only a few months after the Super Collider announcement, GTE announced the relocation of its largest division from Connecticut to the Metroplex to further enhance Dallas' reputation as a world leader in telecommunications. MCI also is moving a large portion of its telecommunications operation to the area, and Fujitsu is establishing a major manufacturing facility in the area.

Dallas business leaders believe this is only the beginning; that numerous other announcements of a similar nature will be forthcoming over the next few years. As this book was being written, the Dallas Partnership counted some 70 U.S. companies, including many large national and international corporations, that were considering moving major portions of their operations to the Dallas area. The vast majority of these moves involved corporate headquarters, as opposed to manufacturing plants or other facilities.

This continues a trend that has given Dallas the nation's fifth largest concentration of Dun and Bradstreet "Million Dollar" corporate headquarters. Dallas ranks fourth on the Fortune 500 list of industrial company headquarters with 12, and third for service-based corporations with 18. Overall, more than 1,800 corporations are based in Dallas and more than 7,500 maintain a corporate presence in Dallas County.

Ironically, as Dallas moves into the last decade of the 20th century with rekindled hope and fresh resolve, certain aftereffects of the "real estate depression" may be more of an advantage than a drawback in resuming the pace of growth to which Dallas is accustomed. As the Dallas Partner-

LEFT: Retail and wholesale trade is Dallas' leading industry, providing the region with everything from groceries and clothing to automobiles and computers. Photo by John Hethorn.

TOP: Computer boards await installation at Texas Instruments, one of the largest high-technology companies in the world and one of the first in the Dallas area.

ABOVE: The Studios at Las Colinas is the site of feature film production as well as business and corporate filmmaking. Photo by Martin Vandiver.

ship's Tom Lewis explains: "The low price of real estate may be a short-range liability, but it's emerging as an asset for the 1990s. It comes at a time when real estate prices in New York, Los Angeles and Chicago are at an all-time high and gives Dallas a competitive edge in attracting new business."

Virtually all observers agree that Dallas has "turned the corner" and put the crisis of the past few years firmly behind it. There is no question that Dallas' pride has suffered in the wake of that crisis, but there is also no doubt that Dallas is regaining its position of financial leadership.

The city's largest financial organization is once again healthy and profitable, following the federally assisted acquisition of the former banks of

ABOVE: *The hospitality industry supports the millions of visitors who come to Dallas each year for business or pleasure, but it also employs one of the area's largest workforces. Photo by John Hethorn.*

RIGHT: *A pickup truck undergoes high-tech diagnostic testing at a Dallas automotive lab. Photo by Scott Metcalfe.*

First Republic Corporation by North Carolina-owned NCNB Texas. The area financial community as a whole, meanwhile, features a lot of new names — including Bank One and First Interstate — but it has resumed the job of financing the city's future growth. Admittedly, total Dallas bank deposits, capital and assets have shrunk considerably since the collapse of oil prices in 1985, but as of mid-1989 these important measurements of the community's financial strength were on the rise again, and the banking industry's largest problems were finally behind it.

"The financial resources are going to be here, because money always flows where the opportunities are," says Bill Wallace, executive vice president of the Federal Reserve Bank of Dallas. "We have a diverse economy, and in the first half of the 1990s we'll see that economy become much more robust. My overall outlook is very optimistic. I think the learning process we've been through should be very valuable in itself."

The Dallas Partnership's Lewis agrees. "We've learned something about maturity recently that the older cities of America learned many years ago. We've had to swallow our dose of humility and we probably deserved it. But the important thing is that we've passed a supreme test of how well our diverse economy serves us in times of crisis. Even at the low point of our downturn, our employment base held up better and we had lower unemployment than any other city in the Southwest. Economic diversity is our safety net, and the safety net held."

Along with the traditional advantages it has enjoyed, the Dallas area will also benefit from dramatic changes in the economy of Texas and the Southwest over the past decade. "In moving away from an oil-based economy and replacing it with a variety of things, Texas now operates on a much more stable economic base than it did at the beginning of the 1980s," says William Gruben, senior economist at the Federal Reserve Bank. "The state is moving away from the production of goods and more into services, and since Dallas has always been ahead of most Southwestern cities in the services sector, this gives us a distinct advantage."

In order to take full advantage of the economic opportunities of the 1990s — a period in which Texas is expected to become the second-largest state in terms of population — Dallas needs only to keep expanding the infrastructure and maximizing the assets it already has, most observers agree. The expansion of D/FW Airport and the construction of two additional runways, as well as planning for a new commercial airport to serve the south side of the Dallas area in the next century, are considered very high priority items. As one business leader puts it: "You definitely have to keep feeding what's feeding you."

Beyond that, the formula for an even bigger, even better "Big D" revolves around the same economic positives that have brought Dallas from obscurity to the forefront among American cities in the space of a single century. These include its central location, its mild climate, its "can-do" spirit, its inbred optimism, its high quality of life, its skilled and diligent labor pool, its relatively low cost of doing business.

And most of all, of course, its diversity.

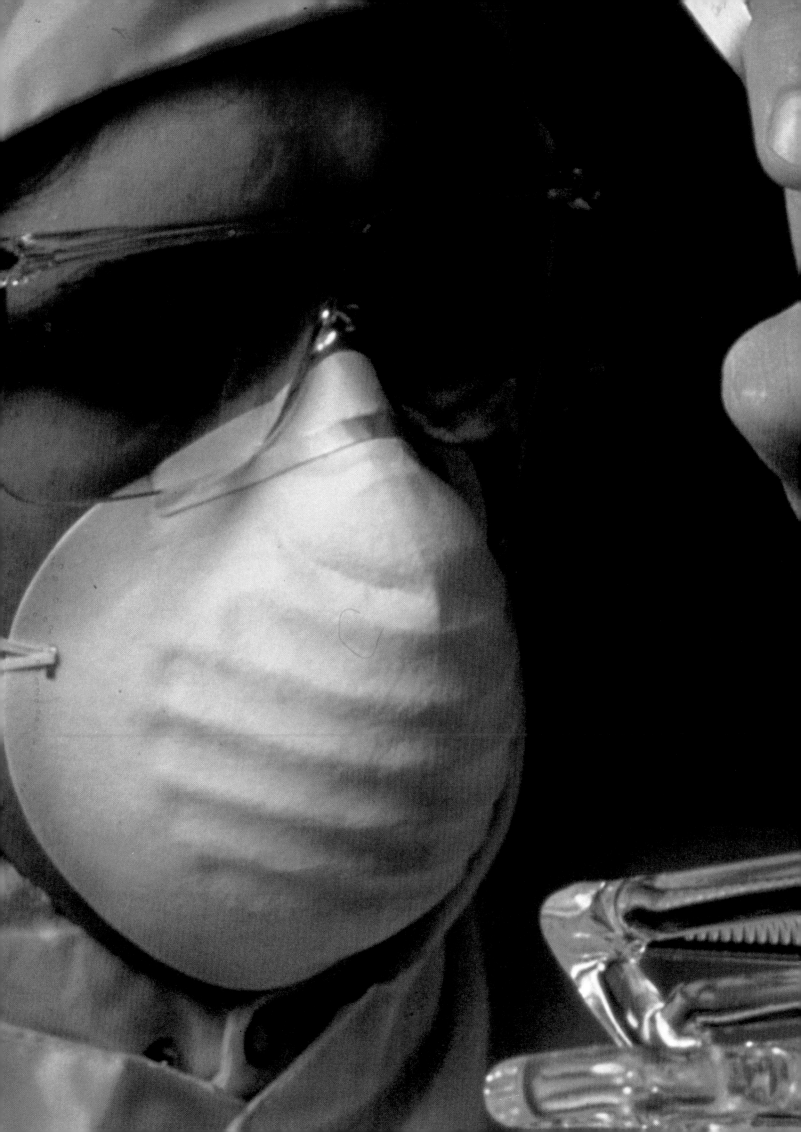

CHAPTER 5

Technology Leads the Way

By Candace L. Talmadge

Technology is all around us, intricately and even intimately woven into our daily lives. And much of the high-tech gadgetry that enables us to do many things was either developed in and around Dallas or is manufactured here.

A silicon wafer is inspected by a technician at SGS-Thomson Microelectronics.

When the lovable alien in the movie "E.T., the Extraterrestrial," sent a message home for help, he used a Speak and Spell — a high-tech child's toy made by Dallas-based Texas Instruments Inc.

E.T. realized what some earthlings are slower to grasp: Technology is bringing us together and continuing to make life much easier. To many people, technology seems nameless, faceless and talks a bizarre-sounding language packed with incomprehensible buzzwords and indecipherable jargon. They call the people who speak it "computer nerds" or "tekkies." And they assume, erroneously, that technology is remote and cold, somehow apart from their everyday existence.

But they wear digital watches.

They reach the office in an elevator that calls out, "Fourth Floor."

They drive electronic fuel-injected automobiles and call in for messages on a cellular phone.

Their kids drive them crazy playing Nintendo video games.

They figure their taxes on credit-card-size electronic calculators. And they listen each day to weather forecasts made with the help of supercomputers.

Far from being remote or intangible, technology is all around us, intricately and even intimately woven into our daily lives. And much of the high-tech gadgetry that enables us to do these things and more was either developed in and around Dallas or is manufactured here.

Ironically, technology has an undeserved low profile in Dallas, thanks in part to the city's portrayal on national television as a petroleum and agriculture center. J.R. and Bobby Ewing not withstanding, however, the Texas Department of Commerce estimates that high-tech manufacturing accounts for 7 percent of the employment in and around Dal-

las. That is seven times the mere 1 percent of local employment in the oil and gas industry. And it is more than twice the 3 percent rate of technology employment in the rest of the state.

Dallas and its surroundings, in fact, are ranked by employment among the nation's top five in three technology industry categories, according to the North Texas Commission, a regional economic development organization. These categories are computer hardware, telecommunications equipment and scientific and precision instrumentation. The Dallas area also ranks near

the top nationally in electronics and semiconductors (the brains of computers) and in defense and aerospace technology.

James N. Patrick, president of the Texas Computer Industry Council, goes even further. He estimates that two out of every five jobs in and around Dallas are directly or indirectly related to the area's thriving and diversified technology sector. More than 60 percent, or 13 of the top 20 manufacturers in Dallas are technology companies. They include some of the biggest names in the industry: TI, LTV, EDS, IBM, Rockwell International and more. These

companies provide more than 86,000 local jobs altogether.

Every LTV or Rockwell or IBM, however, supports a network of roughly 20,000 small companies, says Shawn Clark, president of Clark Marketing Agency, a Dallas firm that specializes in strategic market planning for high-tech start-up companies. These tiny businesses provide highly specialized and very often white-collar services to the big technology concerns, such as engineering analysis or developing the designs for new technology products. Annual sales for each of these small companies are between $150,000 and $10

LEFT: *Texas Instruments is one of the world's leading producers of high-tech consumer products.*

ABOVE: *Dallas is a leading area of telecommunications equipment use and manufacturing. Photo by Southwestern Bell Mobile Communications.*

ABOVE: *Voice-activated computers are among the many products under development at Texas Instruments.*

CENTER: *Dallas has been a center of high-tech research and development since the 1950s when firms like Texas Instruments and Collins Radio (now Rockwell International) began operations.*

RIGHT: *The development of defense avionics is an ongoing activity at Texas Instruments.*

million, and they also are a vital source of jobs.

It is almost impossible to trace the employment derived indirectly from the city's technology sector. But Patrick at the Texas Computer Industry Council points out that computer and software engineers buy houses and trucks, eat out, shop and consume goods and services that in turn provide jobs for many others.

"If the Dallas economy were pic-

tured as a three-legged stool, technology would be one of those legs," says Shawn Clark. Technology has been the only relatively stable business sector in Dallas during the past three years, adds Clark, who also is a consultant for the American Electronics Association.

Technology, then, clearly is critical to the structure and integrity of the Dallas-area economy. Although the industry is newer to this city than to some parts of the country, it still has a local history that spans more than half a century. Dallas' high-tech roots reach back to 1930 and the founding of Texas Instruments. During its first 10 years in business, TI provided petroleum exploration companies with seismographic maps to detect the best places for drilling new wells. In World War II, TI began applying seismograph technology to build equipment for the U.S. Navy to help detect enemy submarines. In 1952 TI started building its first electronic components, which accounted for more than half the company's $6.3 billion in revenues in 1988.

Another pioneer of the city's technology industry was Collins Radio Company, acquired in 1973 by Rockwell International and now called Rockwell Telecommunications. Collins was making radio transmitters when its founder moved a portion of its operations to a site just north of Dallas in the early 1950s.

The two companies' presence in the Dallas area is widely considered the foundation of the city's current technology industry. For starters, they both made significant contributions to furthering technology. As Rockwell Telecommunications, the former Collins Radio went on to develop advanced communications systems such as microwave and lightwave transmission networks so important to national defense and, increasingly, to business communications and productivity.

TI holds a unique place in the industry's development. Every time you use your pocket calculator or your personal computer or ride in that talking elevator, you can thank TI engineer Jack St. Clair Kilby. Kilby shares the credit for inventing the integrated circuit, which he first demonstrated in Dallas in 1958. The integrated circuit spawned microelectronics, technology that packs enormous amounts of computing power onto circuits no bigger than fingernails. These tiny devices in turn made possible personal computers, not to mention a whole array of consumer electronics that we now take for granted.

Second, and equally important, Rockwell Telecommunications and TI have functioned as springboards for other local technology companies. As the two major corporations grew, they recruited top-flight engineering and technical talent from around the country. These highly educated and valuable employees entered the big companies' ranks and stayed for decades, maturing, honing their technical expertise and developing managerial skills. Then, beginning in the late 1960s, they started leaving to build their own companies.

Dozens of successful Dallas-area technology companies were founded by former employees of Rockwell Telecommunications and TI. Plano-based DSC Communications Corporation is one example. The company is not well known to the public, but it is a major independent manufacturer of complex telecommunications equipment. Only a systems design engineer could love or understand products with odd, alphabet-soup names like SCP or DEX Megahub. But many of us are coming to appreciate how they can make our business lives simpler. Need to send a business report from Boston to Phoenix in minutes? The type of products DSC produces enable printed words and pictures to be transmitted instantaneously from one office to another across the country or around the world. They form part of the network into which you plug your fax machine.

Another Dallas technology legend founded in 1969 by former TI employees was Carrollton-based Mostek Corporation, now known as SGS-Thomson Microelectronics. In its

TOP: *The massive LTV facility in Grand Prairie produces aerospace, defense, electronics and energy related systems.*

ABOVE: *E-Systems produces defense electronics systems for the U.S. Government and other related customers.*

RIGHT: *Institutions such as Southern Methodist University and the University of Texas at Dallas make significant contributions to the high-tech research and development effort. Photo by Scott Metcalfe.*

heyday through the early 1980s, Mostek became a world leader in the production of electronic information storage devices called dynamic random access memories (RAMs). RAMs were vital to developing the first microcomputers, and it is a RAM that gives telephones their ability to redial numbers at the punch of a button. Mostek's RAMs were considered among the industry's best.

Each of Mostek's founders, who sold their company in 1979 for $380 million, has continued to create new technology companies in and around Dallas through venture capital funding. Venture capital is the lifeblood of the technology industry, the water that nourishes the seedlings of ideas and allows them to bloom. At its essence, the technology industry is a business of concepts rather than tangible items, such as real estate or herds of cattle or oil wells. This is what makes technology so difficult for many people to grasp.

Yet it is very simple. Tekkies are the dreamers, the visionaries, the tinkerers. They look at what is, and ask, "What if? How can we do this easier or faster or more efficiently?" Venture capital is what then enables them to build those bigger, better mousetraps. In the process, they sometimes create entire new industries or important new segments within an industry.

A case in point is Convex Computer Corporation. Funded by a co-founder of Mostek and started in 1982, Dallas-based Convex developed the first super-minicomputer. These computers possess enormous amounts of power. Meteorologists use them to interpret complex weather patterns for forecasting. General Motors needs them to help design new cars and simulate road tests at a huge cost saving. The price tag for a Convex super-mini is $1-2 million compared to competitors' $20 million price tag. That is the reason Convex's revenues have reached $100 million, its employees number 800 and its staff increases at the rate of 40 percent a year

Ideas, technology, funding and business smarts can combine in endless ways. Most people do not realize that Dallas is the headquarters of Satellite Music Network (SMN), the first and largest radio network distributed entirely by satellite. As of mid-1989, SMN was airing 10 types of live, original radio programming 24 hours daily to more than 1,000 affiliate stations in all 50 states, the Caribbean and Shanghai in the People's Republic of China. From its 1981 launch, SMN has burgeoned to nearly $19.2 million in annual revenues and 160 employees. The sky is obviously no limit for this Dallas-grown technology high-flier.

Closer to earth, the Dallas area is fostering a growing software industry. Five years ago, software that told

microcomputers how to draw and illustrate was little more than a concept. Yet there are now three computer graphics software firms based in and around Dallas that supply more than half of all personal computer illustration programs sold nationally. Do you need to computerize your company's financial records? Dallas-based DAC Software Inc. pioneered the first accounting software that

even the smallest of businesses can afford.

"Dallas is the wide open West for someone wanting to start with a new idea," says J. Paul Grayson, chairman and chief executive of Micrografx Inc., the first company to market illustration software for personal computers. "I found it easy to start a company here because the people were very friendly. They were cooperative

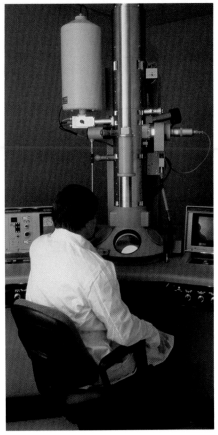

and eager to get our business."

Executives from all manner of technology companies also point to Dallas' central location as a definite plus. "There isn't anyplace in the United States I can't go, conduct a business meeting and return to Dallas all in the same day," says Conrad Masterson, president of NetWorth Inc., which makes local area networks that enable computers to communicate with each other and other machines such as printers.

Being in the middle of the country also gives Dallas technology companies an advantage over either coast in doing business both in Europe and the Far East. "If I have to, I can have a part replacement to the Philippines the next day from Dallas," Masterson adds. "The cost is high but it's doable."

We can do it. That attitude, perhaps more than any tangible factor, is what has helped nurture Dallas' tech-

nology industry and will keep it dynamic and growing. By 1995, some estimates predict that one-fourth of the city's economic output will be based on technology-driven industries, says David Henkel, director of technology industries for the Dallas office of Arthur Anderson & Company public accountants. In the 1990s, only one other metropolitan area in the country will exceed Dallas in adding more jobs — the majority of them technology related — says Donald Hicks, director of the North Texas Commission's Strategic Development Department.

"There are great opportunities for technology here," adds Shawn Clark, pointing out that in 1988, Dallas attracted most of the $24 billion in prime government contracts awarded in the Southwest. A good portion of those contracts were for military technology — the missiles, avionics systems and similar sophisticated

equipment made by TI, LTV, Rockwell and others. Hicks says that while spending on defense-related technology is cyclical, that segment of the industry also offers long-term economic growth for the Dallas area.

Not only did Dallas draw billions in government technology spending in 1988, the area also attracted high-profile corporate relocations or expansions. GTE Corporation unveiled plans to move the headquarters for its telephone operations — roughly 3,000 jobs — from Stamford, Conn., to Irving. Fujitsu America Inc. announced that it had bought 100 acres just north of Dallas in Richardson to develop an $80-million telecommunications manufacturing and office complex that would produce a minimum of 800 new jobs by 1991. And the U.S. Department of Energy chose a site just south of Dallas for its $4-billion Superconducting Super Collider research project.

Relocation has played an important long-term role in building up the industry in and around Dallas, technology executives say. As technology companies developed in the city, their activity brought other companies to this locale, reinforcing the

TOP LEFT: Dallas' INFOMART is the retail and wholesale center of Dallas' high-tech and telecommunications industry. Photo by Doug Milner.

BOTTOM LEFT: Maxim Engineers Inc., a geotechnical and structural engineering firm, uses high-tech systems to analyze structural materials.

TOP: EDS, one of Dallas' best-known corporations, designs and operates computer and communications systems for a variety of clients throughout the world.

ABOVE: DSC Communications Corporation produces telecommunications digital switching, transmission and networking systems.

industry even further. Transplants that rank among the city's top 20 manufacturers include Rockwell, telecommunications equipment maker Northern Telecom Inc., computer manufacturer IBM, office products maker Xerox Corporation, laboratory equipment manufacturer Abbott Laboratories Inc. and Boeing Electronics Inc., which makes computer-driven avionics and telecommunications systems.

Transplants to Dallas that do not yet rank among the city's largest manufacturers are still making a splash in their industry segments. Fax machines are hot, and so is Murata Business Systems Inc., the U.S. division of a Japanese fax manufacturer. Established in the Dallas area in 1985, Murata three years later became the No. 2 seller of fax machines in this country. Its top executive predicts Murata will do at least $1 billion in sales by 1995.

Perhaps the success of a telecommunications-related company should come as no surprise — at least not in Dallas. This area "is the entrepreneurial hotbed for telecommunications," says Jon Bayless, president of SRB Management Company, a Dallas venture capital firm that specializes in technology funding. "What's happening here is a combination of computers and telecommunications to provide new ways of doing business."

Change is the only constant in the technology industry. Even established corporations like TI cannot rest on past achievements. Well aware of

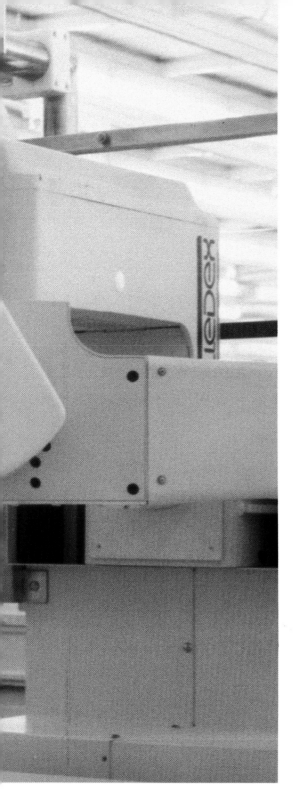

this, TI in mid-1989 unveiled the first high-speed microprocessor that can perform 29 million mathematical calculations per second, giving it the raw power of a big mainframe computer. Most of us will literally see the results of this step forward not far down the road, when we watch high definition television, which will bring a whole new world of sharper, clearer images into our living rooms.

The next high-tech success most likely will come from — or move to — Dallas.

LEFT: Automated manufacturing is both developed and used by high-tech industry giants such as Texas Instruments.

ABOVE: US Sprint is the first company to build an all fiber, all digital network. The 23,000-mile network has been carrying 100 percent of US Sprint's voice traffic since spring 1988.

CHAPTER 6

Room for Growth

By Bill Sloan

Nowhere in the modern world
has man's timeless urge to build,
tear down and rebuild on an
ever-larger scale been more
relentlessly experienced,
perfected to a higher science or a
more creative art than in Dallas.

Downtown Dallas at dawn awaits the cars, people and activity of another busy day. Photo by Dan Hatzenbuehler.

ABOVE: Construction employment accounts for approximately 5 percent of the Dallas-area employment base. Photo by Jeff Hampton.

RIGHT: A garden atrium more than 30 floors above the street adds natural interest to the Sky Lobby of Texas Commerce Tower. Photo by Dan Hatzenbuehler.

Dallas owes its very birth to a real estate development scheme, and throughout its history the business of transforming raw land into homes, stores, factories, warehouses, offices, hotels and other facilities has been an important segment of the city's total commercial activity.

While real estate development is always a by-product of economic growth, it has, in a sense, also been a key contributor to the particularly explosive brand of growth that Dallas has enjoyed. Nowhere in the modern world has man's timeless urge to build, tear down and rebuild on an ever-larger scale been more relentlessly experienced or expressed than in Dallas. And nowhere have planning, land use and construction techniques been perfected to a higher science or a more creative art.

One graphic example of this art and science can be found in the numerous master-planned mixed-use developments in the Dallas area. Dallas developers and commercial builders pioneered this concept, and it has found its most dramatic expression in the 12,000-acre Las Colinas development in Irving. Although Las Colinas was the first project of its type in the United States and remains one of the largest and most successful, it has inspired many other developers to follow the trend.

As it is in virtually all cities, however, real estate development in Dallas has tended to be highly cyclical, waxing and waning in accordance with the unbreakable laws of supply and demand. Like the concentric growth rings inside a giant oak tree, development cycles have left behind lasting physical evidence of how "wet" or "dry," how "rich" or "lean" each period in Dallas' history has been.

Even with the constant process of demolition and rebuilding, some of this evidence remains as a revealing

measurement of how rapidly or slowly development was taking place during the up cycles and down cycles of the past century or more.

It can be seen in the bulky, low-rise commercial structures of downtown's West End, representing the period between 1880 and 1900; in the mid-rise downtown structures built between 1910 and 1925; in the tidy, unpretentious tract houses of the 1930s and '40s; in the more expansive ranch-style homes and boxy skyscrapers of the 1950s and '60s; and finally, in the soaring, sprawling, reach-for-the-stars architecture of the 1970s and '80s.

With occasional exceptions, as Dallas' growth rings spread out from the heart of the city, they grow wider and wider, encompassing more and more territory. In the central city itself, meanwhile, periods of growth

have generally been expressed in terms of increasing height. While new downtown structures might have averaged less than 20 stories in the 1920s and '30s, the typical new office building in the Central Business District soared to 40, 50 or even 70 stories in the 1970s and '80s.

Fortunately for those who earn their living in the real estate and construction industries, there have been many more up cycles than down cycles since Dallas began its metamorphosis from an isolated small town to a major urban center some 115 years ago. From the 1870s on, no decade has passed in Dallas — even during the trauma of two World Wars and the hardships of the Great Depression — without a noticeable spurt of growth and development. And yet, most decades also have contained at least one dry period when

construction temporarily slowed down or even came close to a standstill.

Despite its long track record as a booming real estate market, Dallas had never experienced an outburst of development like the one that engulfed the city during the 1980s. In retrospect, it is difficult to exaggerate the magnitude of that outburst, the changes it wrought in the physical characteristics of Dallas or the far-reaching impact it had on the city as a whole.

Longtime residents watched in awe as new skyscrapers shot upward in all directions, as a flood of new shopping centers, industrial facilities and apartment complexes inundated the landscape, and as thousands of new single-family homes gobbled up vast quantities of open land.

When it was over, Dallas had more

TOP: *Stemmons Freeway is flanked by the Dallas Market Center, the Dallas Design District and other commercial enterprises.*

ABOVE: *The Southland Corporation's Cityplace development eventually will incorporate housing and retail along with office space.*

RIGHT: *Fountain Place is an oasis of water, trees and light in downtown Dallas. Photo by Jeff Hampton.*

than doubled its total office space, had the highest per capita level of retail footage of any American city and led the nation for several years in both homebuilding and apartment construction. But en route to these accomplishments, eager investors and developers also had overbuilt the real estate market in almost every major category.

Just as the boom of the 1980s was the biggest, most far-reaching, most exciting phenomenon ever to affect the Dallas real estate market, the decline that followed it was destined to be perhaps the deepest and darkest in Dallas history.

At first, many observers were optimistic that, given Dallas' strong track record for absorbing new space, the high vacancy rate would quickly disappear once the frenzy of new construction slowed down.

But in 1985, just as commercial development was showing signs of tapering off, oil prices suddenly tumbled. The economy of the entire Southwest went into a sharp decline — and so did demand for all kinds of real estate products in Dallas and other Texas cities.

When investors and developers were unable to sell or lease what they had built, many were forced to restructure their debts or default on their mortgages. This led to a rash of bankruptcies and foreclosures among developers, then to a crisis in the financial industry that was almost wholly attributable to (1) the loss of oil revenues and (2) non-performing real estate loans.

There was to be no quick fix for the crisis in the Dallas real estate market. The last third of the 1980s became a difficult "work-through" period for most concerned. Except for a few isolated build-to-suit projects, new commercial construction starts were practically non-existent for more than three years. Many banks and thrifts crumbled under the weight of bad real estate investments and uncollectable loans. Rental rates and property values plunged. Some once-thriving submarkets experienced negative absorption.

By mid-1989, though, a recovery was under way. Rents and real estate prices finally stabilized and occupancy rates slowly began to rise. Improvements were especially noticeable in the industrial and apartment segments. Absorption of industrial space for the first five months of the year was running more than double the average rate for the previous four years. Steadily improving rents and an occupancy rate that was back near 90 percent gave rise to speculation that new apartment construction was ready to resume, and that apartments would be the first sector of the real estate market to return to full health and vitality.

Most observers agree that the first years of the 1990s will see a continuation and acceleration of the real estate recovery in Dallas. Even as prices increase, a distinct "buyer's market" could remain in effect for some time, and in comparison to other major metropolitan areas, most varieties of Dallas area real estate will continue to be a bargain. This fact in itself is sparking a new surge of demand as outside companies relocate to the Dallas area and growing local companies take advantage of market conditions to expand.

"Hard economics will dictate what happens over the next few years," says John Twain, director of research for the Fults Companies, one of Dallas' largest commercial real estate leasing and management organizations. "But, Dallas is well situated nationally to benefit from relocations and expansions. The outlook for the first half of the 1990s is much brighter than it has been in the late 1980s."

While the cycles of growth and development will undoubtedly continue to some degree, the drastic up-and-down fluctuations of the past decade are considered very unlikely to recur in the 1990s. Some observers credit a new found maturity born of the adversities of the late 1980s for producing a period of more stable, predictable growth in the local real estate marketplace. Others note that the capital needed to fuel another

investor-driven development explosion similar to that of 1982-86 will be unavailable for at least several years, and in fact, may never be available again in Dallas or anywhere else.

"We will see some new building and development," Twain says, "but not on the scale of a few years ago. Investors and developers will be more cautious and not nearly as eager to commit hugh sums of money."

Ron Witten, president of M/PF Research, a market analysis firm serving the area real estate industry, agrees with this assessment. "We're seeing a continuing general recovery in our employment and economic growth, and the early 1990s will be characterized by a filling up of our existing inventories of commercial space. While we don't foresee any boom, we think the Dallas area will probably be growing faster than the nation as a whole. We'll again be running counter-cyclical to many other major U.S. cities, where development activity is slowing down. As this happens, lenders in these markets will be increasingly attracted here."

The key to a healthy real estate market is job growth, Witten emphasizes, and the employment base in Dallas is once again expanding. The Dallas/Fort Worth area experienced a net increase of close to 30,000 jobs in 1989, and indications are that the area may soon regain the level of employment growth it enjoyed during the first half of the 1980s, when some 50,000 jobs were created annually. These new jobs will come from the relocation of outside companies to the area and the expansion of companies already operating locally. Each time a job is created, new demand for commercial and residential space is created as well.

"I think Dallas has tremendous long-term advantages for real estate development," says Bob Moss of Cityplace Development Corporation, a

subsidiary of Southland Corporation, which is developing the 160-acre, master-planned Cityplace project just north of downtown. "It has the infrastructure, available sites, room to expand, low operating costs and high quality of life that make it attractive to many companies. But I also think the future growth process is going to be steady and gradual, not a boom and not a bust."

Southland's 42-story Cityplace Center East is the largest office building in Dallas outside the downtown area and was the last major office tower opened in the 1980s. The company is committed to completing the entire "city within a city" develop-

ment as it was originally conceived, Moss says. This includes some 6,000 housing units and 10.7 million square feet of non-residential space, including another 42-story office tower to be known as Cityplace Center West. By mid-1989, the first of several hundred new apartment units, built in a joint venture with Dallas-based Trammell Crow Company, were being occupied at Cityplace.

Southland's commitment reflects the long-term optimism that pervades the Dallas real estate market, but that optimism is also tempered by the new, more cautious approach being taken by developers and investors. "Obviously, we've had to revise

our original timetable," Moss says, "but Cityplace will be fully developed as market conditions warrant."

One huge advantage Dallas holds over most other major cities in the country is the continuing availability of raw land. While redevelopment projects such as Cityplace will undoubtedly play an increasing role in the city's future, there are still thousands of acres of land available that have never been developed, especially on the east and south sides of Dallas. The supply of open land of course is not inexhaustible, but while it lasts, it will be an important asset to Dallas in competing for growth and development. It also is a factor in

CENTER: *The Dallas Design District, near the Dallas Market Center, was developed for occupation by designers of clothing, furniture, accessories and other wholesale/retail items. Photo by Dan Hatzenbuehler.*

ABOVE: *The sun sets over the canals and office buildings of Las Colinas, the nation's premier master-planned mixed-use development. Photo by Scott Metcalfe.*

TOP: *The Crescent combines offices, a world-class hotel, and shops and galleries in an intimate and elegant setting.*

ABOVE: *Dallas mansions and estates reflect a variety of tastes and architectural styles, from Southwestern to Mediterranean. Photo by Scott Metcalfe.*

RIGHT: *The glut of office space created by the boom of the early 1980s made Dallas an attractive market for corporate relocations and expansions. Photo by Dan Hatzenbuehler.*

keeping average real estate costs in Dallas far below those in many other major markets.

Based on informed projections, here is a brief summary of conditions likely to influence the five principal sectors of the Dallas real estate market during the first five years of the 1990s:

Industrial Space:

Dallas' stature as a primary warehousing/distribution center — "one of the five or six key anchors in the nation's distribution network," says M/PF's Witten — kept the local industrial real estate market relatively hearty during the depths of the downturn of the late 1980s. And as that stature grows and as local warehousing/distribution activity takes on international characteristics, the demand for industrial space will grow accordingly.

First-class distribution space in the Dallas area was 90 percent leased by late 1989, as major players such as Trammell Crow and Centre Development Company bought up large blocks of existing space, and occupancy rates in the 95-percent range were expected by the end of 1990. At that point, pressure seemed certain to build for a resumption of large-scale development.

Meanwhile, Dallas' importance as a manufacturing and service center, particularly in the field of high technology, is also adding impetus for industrial development. "Just a few years ago, lots of people thought that manufacturing was going to diminish in economic importance in the United States, and maybe even be phased out," Witten notes. "But it doesn't look that way anymore. Instead, we're moving into new kinds of manufacturing, and this area is in the forefront of that move."

As has been the case in the past, most of the space added to the industrial market will continue to be of the build-to-suit variety rather than speculative, and this is yet another factor that will keep the market on a solid footing in the years just ahead.

Apartments/Condominiums:

Apartments led the Dallas real estate recovery as the 1980s drew to a close. It was the first sector of the real estate market to overcome the rampant overbuilding of mid-decade and regain its stability. By mid-1989, the overall apartment occupancy rate had climbed some 20 percent from its low ebb and was again above 90 percent. Construction of new apartment projects was beginning to resume and was expected to accelerate during the next two or three years. Rising rents were rapidly transforming the "tenant's market" of 1987-88 into a "landlord's market."

After several years in which many Dallas apartments were converted to condominiums and sold, the so-called "I-30 Condo Scandal" of the mid-1980s did much to sour investors, developers and potential buyers on the condominium concept. The scandal inflicted staggering losses on hundreds of investors, resulted in the first of many massive savings and loan failures, led to criminal charges against some developers, and left thousands of condominium units standing vacant and/or unfinished. Most of these units eventually were either converted into apartments or torn down.

The condominium market, which was virtually non-existent in the late 1980s, may make a modest comeback over the next five years if rents and interest rates increase substantially, but the odds of seeing large-scale condo development appear slim. Other likely trends during the coming decade include an emphasis on larger apartment complexes, including mid-rise and high-rise structures that can take advantage of land limitations in some areas.

Office Buildings:

Prior to 1980, the only significant concentration of office space in Dallas was in downtown, but the boom changed all that. A decade later, clusters of office towers reach skyward from a number of significant submarkets. The most important of these include Las Colinas, the LBJ Freeway corridor, the Quorum area of Far North Dallas, Oak Lawn, Preston Center, the North Central Expressway corridor and the Stemmons Freeway corridor.

After nosediving under the pressure of massive overbuilding, office occupancy rates climbed back to a more comfortable overall level of about 73 percent by the end of 1989 — their highest point since the rash of new construction began early in the decade. Absorption rates, meanwhile, were stronger than expected, although some absorption was coming from companies filling anticipated future space needs while rents were low, and thus not reflective of actual current demand.

Meanwhile, among Class A and Class B office buildings, the occupancy rate was considerably higher — above 90 percent by most estimates — and there was little space available in the large new downtown office complexes built during the 1980s. Higher lease rates may cause some tenants to seek cheaper quarters within the foreseeable future, and this may create some demand for less desirable space.

Some observers believe demand for first-class downtown office space could result in one or two new construction starts by 1990-91, with the Arts District tabbed as the most likely site.

Older buildings, particularly in the downtown area and the Stemmons Freeway corridor, will continue to pose a problem well into the 1990s. Extensive renovations will be necessary to make many of these buildings marketable, and some landmark structures have become so outmoded and inefficient by current office standards that they could face a date with the wrecking ball between now and 1995.

Retail Space:

After an unprecedented flurry of construction, followed closely by the loss of several major retail chains from the area, Dallas may remain overstocked on retail space for several years, and the recovery of the retail real estate market will likely lag behind that of other market sectors. As of late 1989, smaller strip shopping centers in Dallas had an average occupancy rate of about 75 percent and little absorption was taking place. On the other hand, conditions generally were much better in major shopping malls and most other well-anchored centers.

Campbell Center is a fine example of a multiuse development, comprising office space, shops, restaurants and the Doubletree Hotel. Photo by Doug Milner.

RIGHT: The West End MarketPlace combines shops, restaurants and entertainment in a converted turn-of-the-century warehouse in the West End Historic District. Photo by Jeff Hampton.

ABOVE: *Victorian houses restored by the Meadows Foundation are the home of nonprofit organizations in East Dallas. Photo by Scott Metcalfe.*

RIGHT: *Watching the sunset at White Rock Lake, it is easy to forget you are surrounded by a vibrant, busy city. Photo by Dan Hatzenbuehler.*

A sizeable percentage of the area's older retail facilities, especially free-standing structures located outside shopping centers, will probably disappear over the next few years. Likewise, some poorly designed and/or poorly located new facilities may never be leased as retail space, and unless other uses can be found for them, they also eventually may be demolished.

In some suburban locales, centers built "ahead of their time" in the 1980s will simply have to wait until nearby residential development justifies their existence.

Except in highly specialized circumstances, construction of major new retail facilities may be negligible for some time, but by the mid-1990s, changing patterns in housing, transportation and other elements of the Dallas lifestyle could trigger massive new activity in retail development.

Single-Family Homes

After a three-year slide in home

prices caused by widespread foreclosures and cut-rate attempts by lenders and federal agencies to rid their books of foreclosed properties, stability was returning to the single-family housing market by the end of the 1980s. Overall, prices of new and existing homes in the Dallas area had "bottomed out" and were poised to begin rising again.

Although the market for new homes remained flat for the most part, in areas of the Dallas/Fort Worth Metroplex affected by corporate relocations — including Plano and neighborhoods north and west of Dallas/Fort Worth International Airport — homes were selling at as brisk a pace as they did during the boom years.

The median price of a home in Dallas, which climbed to about $105,000 during the mid-1980s, fell by as much as 15 percent during the downturn. The value of many individual homes fell even more sharply, but prices can be expected to improve substantially during the early 1990s. As prices recover, many prospective homeowners will benefit from a short-lived "buyer's market" in existing homes, and even when the recovery is complete, Dallas home prices still will be a bargain compared to those in other major cities.

The days when new homes in the $1 million-and-up price range were being built on speculation, as they were in the mid-1980s in some of Dallas' more affluent neighborhoods, may not return for a long time, if ever. But projected job growth in the Dallas area means that additional thousands of more reasonably priced single-family homes will be needed over the next few years. Large blocks of open land to the east and south will attract many residential developers, and homebuilding will continue at a rapid pace in the far north.

CHAPTER 7

The World Comes to Dallas

By Alex M.G. Burton

Each year the city of Dallas is the destination of 15 million visitors. We are not sure where they go while they are here. But while they stay in Dallas they help the economy at a rate that makes the hospitality industry Dallas' second biggest after retail sales.

More than 2 million convention delegates visit Dallas each year, making the city one of the top three national convention sites.

Why they come is not so important to Dallas as that they come. Each year Dallas is the destination of some 15 million visitors. That is three-and-a-half times the population of Norway. Fifteen million people leave home with the intention of coming to Dallas. We are not sure where they go while they are here. But while they stay in Dallas they help the economy to the tune of about $4.5 billion annually. That makes the hospitality industry Dallas' second biggest after retail sales.

About 85,000 Dallasites are employed year-round directly in the hospitality industry. They are taxi cab drivers, hotel managers, waiters, waitresses, tour guides, people who arrange for speakers, and people who arrange flowers on the head table at the dinner where salesmen will meet their new sales manager and hear their projections for next year.

The future is strong for conventions in Dallas. There is one booked already for 2012. The National Asso-

ciation of Home Builders will see their conventional way into the next century in Dallas. Theirs is the largest convention yearly in America, and it will be held in Dallas in 1998, 1999 and 2000. They are coming, in part, due to the city's commitment by 1994 to add 325,000 square feet to the already-massive 1.9 million-square-foot Dallas Convention Center.

Not all those headed to Dallas from around the world are conventioneers, although those coming to conventions numbered 2.15 million in 1988. There were 3 million bona-fide tourists, most of whom came by car. If you care to keep score, in 1988 Dallas passed San Antonio to become the No. 1 destination in the state of Texas. (Also, 1988 was the year that Dallas passed Chicago to become the No. 2 convention city in the nation after New York.) The balance of 10 million visitors came here for about 10 million reasons: To visit friends and family, to see a rock concert, to see an art exhibit, to sell something, to buy something. The tour wholesalers of the world met in Dallas for a convention in 1988. Japanese and German tourists who want to come to America want to see Dallas first.

Where will all these visitors stay when they come to Dallas? Where will they eat?

Dallas can provide, inside the city limits, more than 40,000 rooms in 100 or more hotels and motels. As to where they will eat, there are 5,400 restaurants in Dallas, more per capita than in New York City. Only San Francisco can boast more places to eat per person. As it stands at this writing there is one eating place for every 185 people in Dallas. That means that whatever you desire in the way of food, you will find. It makes Dallasites among the nation's most discerning restaurant clientele.

The demand for quality food has grown to such an extent that the Dal-

TOP LEFT: Hotels such as the Hyatt D/FW Airport are vital to Dallas' competitiveness as a leading convention city.

BOTTOM LEFT: The Dallas Convention Center, already one of the largest convention facilities in the nation, will add another 257,000 square feet of prime exhibit space and 70,000 square feet of meeting rooms by 1994.

ABOVE: Sunlight bathes one of two atriums at The Loews Anatole Hotel, the largest hotel in the Southwest. Photo by Dan Hatzenbuehler.

ABOVE: *Sampling some of the finest cuisine prepared anywhere is a highlight of any visit to Dallas. Photo by Doug Milner.*

CENTER: *The Dallas Museum of Art features a fine permanent collection but also hosts many national and international touring exhibits. Photo by Doug Milner.*

RIGHT: *The magnificent Galleria offers shops, restaurants, a hotel, offices and entertainment in a visually exciting setting. Photo by Doug Milner.*

las County Community College District offers classes for chefs and an apprenticeship program in the more outstanding kitchens in Dallas. Dallas chefs leave their stoves and pans once every four years to compete in the Culinary Olympics. From Frankfurt, Germany, they bring home gold medals and international recognition. Not only does the quality of Dallas cooking make any visitor happy, but those who live and work in Dallas year-round enjoy it often. It is another benefit to the community from the tourism and convention business.

One factor that makes Dallas the second most popular convention spot in America is good weather. To be sure Dallas can have snow, Dallas can have floods, but the average temperature is 63 F or 18 C. The average annual rainfall is about 30 inches. While summers are hot in Texas and Dallas is no exception, air conditioning is a way of life. Malls are air conditioned, cars are air conditioned, and if you go to Six Flags Over Texas

theme park just outside of Dallas, you will feel air conditioning all around you as you stand in line for the rides. If you look up you will see air conditioning ducts in the trees.

Another factor is sophistication. The style of dress in Dallas can be as haute couture as any city in America. More than 100,000 of those who come to Dallas each year come to the fashion markets. There are nine markets a year to draw buyers from every part of America. They come here because all the show rooms are in one place. At the Apparel Mart, with 1,400 show rooms, 3.1 billion wholesale dollars trade hands each year.

Of those 100,000 buyer visits each year, each represents $477 left in the Dallas economy.

The reasons they come to Dallas are more than the convenience of one-stop shopping, and the convenience of relatively short airline trips. Hotels are cheaper in Dallas. Meals and transportation in the city are cheaper than in New York, Chicago,

Los Angeles or Atlanta.

And there is plenty to see and do while they are here. Wholesale is big business at the Dallas Market Center, but retail is big business all over town. Dallas has more shopping centers per capita than any U.S. city, including outlets of most of the great names in retailing: Macy's, Bloomingdale's, Tiffany's, Saks Fifth Avenue, Marshall Field's, Ralph Lauren, Stanley Korshak. And Dallas is the birthplace of what many consider to be the greatest of the great — Neiman-Marcus.

While shopping has become an art form in Dallas, it is no substitute for the fine arts. Visitors to Dallas can enjoy the entire spectrum of performing arts, from the thumping beats of a Deep Ellum rock band to the classical melodies of the Dallas Symphony Orchestra; from the chaotic excitement of experimental theater to the professional class of the Dallas Theater Center.

Visual arts also know no bounds. When the National Association of

Homebuilders came to Dallas in 1988, delegates were delighted to find in the city at the same time an exhibit highlighting the designs of Frank Lloyd Wright. Situated in the downtown Arts District, the exhibit included a full-size Wright-designed house built on the front plaza of the Dallas Museum of Art.

Coincidental or not, visitors to Dallas are likely to find at least one and usually several art exhibits, shows or festivals going on somewhere in the city. Often the Arts District and the Dallas Museum of Art are the site of this activity.

Near the Arts District, the West End Historic District offers freewheeling, family-oriented entertainment. It may strike some as unusual that the second-most air conditioned city in America (Houston is first) embraces so many outdoor activities, but the West End schedules events throughout the spring and summer, including parades, charity runs, an artificial beach with tons of trucked-in sand, the Taste of the West End food festi-

val (which draws tens of thousands to the 20-block area each year) and Hoop-It-Up, a major basketball tournament with hundreds of three-person teams of all ages and abilities competing.

The district's center of attraction is the West End MarketPlace, six floors of shopping, including clothing, jewelry, art, antiques and furniture, as well as food, games and even miniature golf. The MarketPlace has two areas especially for young people: an entire floor of games called Tilt, and Level V, a nightclub limited to those under 18.

The West End thrives at night with more than 30 restaurants and clubs, with five clubs in the Dallas Alley complex, including a spirited sing-along bar.

City wide, Dallas nightlife caters equally to patrons with a taste for lively crowds and to those who prefer a quiet drink in an intimate setting. Music choices are as diverse as folk music in a church and country-western in a Texas-sized honky-tonk. But Dallas is also good for a laugh — plenty of them actually, as comedy clubs such as The Improvisation and Funny Bone regularly draw top national comics.

Another reason people come to Dallas is sports. Some come to watch and others come to play. Dallas is a year-round hub for the best in professional and amateur sports: Dallas Cowboys, Dallas Mavericks, Dallas Sidekicks, Texas Rangers, GTE Byron Nelson Golf Classic, Buick World Championship Tennis, Mesquite Championship Rodeo, Pontiac Grand Prix of Dallas, Virginia Slims Tennis. And there is more.

The annual Mobil Cotton Bowl Classic is a New Year's Day tradition, capping an exciting season of college football. Another longstanding tradition is the White Rock Marathon, a premier running event that draws the

best distance runners from all over the world.

Running is a big deal in Dallas. The annual Jingle Bell Run at Christmas has thousands of runners trotting through the streets of Dallas with jingle bells on their toes. In another event, called a vertical marathon, runners start at ground level and trot up the stairs to the 72nd floor of NCNB Plaza — all in the name of physical fitness. They get to ride down.

Back on the ground, preservation and expansion guide two of the city's most beguiling attractions. The Dallas Zoo in Oak Cliff, south of downtown, is home to 2,000 wild and

LEFT: The West End Historic District is Dallas' newest hot spot for entertainment and excitement seven days and nights a week. Photo by Doug Milner.

ABOVE: Stars like Nolan Ryan, shown delivering one of his patented fast balls, have made the Texas Rangers a hot ticket for sports fans from all over the Southwest. Photo by David J. Sams.

exotic animals. Thanks to a multimillion-dollar upgrading, it introduced the first phase of the 55-acre Wilds of Africa exhibit in 1990, becoming the only zoo in the United States to recreate all six African habitats with their indigenous animals: mountain, woodland, river swamp, desert, bush and forest. Also new is a walking trail, monorail and gorilla research station.

The Dallas Arboretum and Botanical Society invites strollers to explore 25 acres of ornamental, research and demonstration gardens and 41 acres of woodlands, as well as the restored DeGolyer Estate. The Arboretum is the site of spring, fall and holiday festivals and concert series, and is situated next to beautiful White Rock Lake, a favorite among residents for sailboating, fishing, picnicking, walking and bicycling.

Another example of preservation can be found at one of Dallas' newest and most controversial museums: The Sixth Floor, a study of the life, death and legacy of President John F. Kennedy. As the name implies, the museum is on the sixth floor of the building from which Lee Harvey Oswald allegedly fired the shots that killed Kennedy. While there was local debate as to whether or not the museum should be built, visitors to Dallas have expressed a desire for such an exhibit for years. Now they have it.

A recent phenomenon in Dallas is the quasi-scientific exhibit. From June 1988 to January 1989 The Science Place in Fair Park attracted 326,000 to see a touring exhibit from the People's Republic of China that showed the ancient Chinese technologies. Thirty percent of those visitors came from out of town, and 15 percent came from out of state.

From May 1989 to August 1989, The Museum of Natural History sponsored another touring exhibit of

the artifacts and funeral art of Ramses the Great, Pharaoh of Egypt. By the time the show closed, more than a million people had come to see it. Twenty-two percent were from out of state.

It was a new sort of tourist attraction for the city, but it has set a course so the museums in city-owned Fair Park will be able to fill their endowments with tourist dollars instead of tax dollars.

What sort of an attraction for scientific tourists will the Superconducting Super Collider be?

In Europe in the Middle Ages, Frankfurt became a trading center because of its central location. Its Book Fair is still the world's oldest and largest.

In the United States as the 20th century draws to a close, Dallas enjoys the same sort of a central location. The State Fair of Texas held in Dallas every year is the oldest and largest fair held in America. But it has still not reached its potential as a site for Europeans, Asians and Americans to reach the American market at one central location.

Dallas could become the Frankfurt of the Americas. It has the location. It has the climate. It has the hotels, motels, restaurants and entertainment. It has it all.

LEFT: Flamingos and azaleas add brilliant color to the natural setting of the Dallas Zoo. Photo by Robbie Messerschmitt Knight.

TOP: The Dallas Arboretum is open year-round but also hosts a number of special events each year, including Dallas Blooms, a spring festival of tulips. Photo by Doug Milner.

ABOVE: Events and attractions such as the annual State Fair of Texas bring millions of visitors to the Dallas area each year. Photo by Allan Kaye.

CHAPTER 8

Communication Networks

By Barbara J. Wegher

Perhaps no other element plays a more important role in the continued growth, and at the same time, cohesiveness of a city business base than the art and technology of communications. This has been especially true in Dallas.

Southwestern Bell is constantly evaluating and upgrading its telephone systems to provide regional customers with excellent phone service.

Stretching across the rolling prairie, a jewel of a city rises up to meet the crystal sky. Minarets of steel and glass, accented by blinking lights or pulsing neon reflect the vibrant beat of the city below. Yet, behind the glitter of Dallas that sometimes seduces the eye and fools the senses is a city of great character and depth. A city, not of flashing lights and easy gambles, but of hard work, of industry and technology, with a strong and sophisticated infrastructure designed to support the most technically advanced businesses of the 21st century.

Perhaps no other element plays a more important role in the continued growth, and at the same time, cohesiveness of a city business base than the art and technology of communications. The Idea. The Thought. The Word. The actual mechanical means by which we transmit those elements has become a deciding factor in determining the potential and prolonged expansion of Dallas.

Since 1813 when the *Gazeta De Texas*, a Spanish tabloid newspaper, was first published, to the scant six years later when the first "singing wires" were strung across Texas' rolling plains and purple buttes, to March 18, 1878, when Colonel A.H. Belo had the first telephone lines established between his mansion and his newspaper, the *Galveston News*, Texas, and more specifically Dallas, has plunged headlong into the Communications Age.

Early in Dallas' history, the *Dallas Times Herald* and *The Dallas Morning News* were established, and both have published continuously for more than 100 years. Today, the two papers continue their high-spirited rivalry.

Unlike other large cities that have experienced difficulties in successfully maintaining two rival and largely successful newspapers, Dallas seems in no danger of losing either of its prominent dailies. Likewise, both papers receive high marks from Darwin Payne, professor of journalism at Southern Methodist University. "I think we have a very high level of journalism exhibited by these two newspapers," he says. "Just within the past year, the *News* won two Pulitzer prizes, and prior to that the *Herald* had gotten a couple. There has been expanded national coverage as a result of the establishment of numerous domestic bureaus and likewise, more in-depth foreign reporting."

And while the two major newspapers enjoy a heated rivalry and continued growth, they are by no means the only newspapers regularly read by large portions of the community. The *Dallas Business Journal* focuses its attention primarily on business stories and trends pertinent to the Dallas economy. A variety of local newspapers, including *Park Cities People*, the *Addison Register* and the *Garland News*, all report news of special interest to their respective suburban communities.

Because Dallas is made up of a rich variety of racial and ethnic groups, small presses including *El Sol* and *La Prensa* address the needs of the Spanish-speaking community. Likewise, the *Dallas Post Tribune* and the *Dallas Examiner* among a variety of others address issues of interest to the African-American community. Other smaller tabloids are published for the ever-increasing Asian and Middle Eastern communities within Dallas.

Of course, reflective of Dallas' stature as the eighth-largest city in the United States is its wide range of both television and radio stations. All three national networks — ABC,

The Dallas Morning News

BUILD THE NEWS UPON THE ROCK OF TRUTH AND RIGHTEOUSNESS CONDUCT IT ALWAYS UPON THE LINES OF FAIRNESS AND INTEGRITY ACKNOWLEDGE THE RIGHT OF THE PEOPLE TO GET FROM THE NEWSPAPER BOTH SIDES OF EVERY IMPORTANT QUESTION

NBC and CBS — are represented by local affiliate stations WFAA, KXAS and KDFW, respectively. Over the years, these stations have been highly competitive, improving the quality of local news and information programming to where Dallas' affiliates are considered some of the best in the nation.

Dallas also has six independent stations, including one representing the FOX network and two affiliated with PBS. Dallas also is home for two Spanish language stations. And like most cities, Dallas has experienced an explosion of cable and pay-per-view television, creating access to more than 20 stations.

Not to be outdone, radio stations populate the airwaves in large numbers, with stations reflecting the wide diversity of Dallas listening tastes. More than 35 stations on the AM and FM dials serve up everything from heavy metal and rock to soft rock, easy listening, country-western, rhythm and blues, soul, religious, all news and all talk.

According to media analysts, the combined efforts of all media companies — radio, cable, television and print — pump in excess of $400 million into the Dallas economy annually.

In addition to a highly competitive broadcast market, Dallas has become one of the leading advertising capitals of the United States. Advertising agency billings account for more than $930 million poured into the local economy each year. The two largest ad agencies, Tracy-Locke and Bozell, employ more than 1,000 people between their two Dallas-based offices. As a result of the high quality of work produced by Dallas agencies, companies from throughout the Southwest use their services.

The ad agency boom in Dallas has been aided by a number of factors, including the fact that Dallas is increasingly recognized for its extraordinarily high-grade commercial and industrial film production houses. That, combined with a solid graphic

ABOVE: Dallas television and radio stations make Dallas one of the most dynamic and profitable broadcast markets in the United States. Photo by Jeff Hampton.

TOP: Taylor Publishing Company is one of the region's major printers and a national leader in yearbook publishing.

LEFT: The Dallas Morning News is Texas' leading newspaper in both readership and advertising revenues.

arts community and outstanding printing establishments makes Dallas a highly attractive location for public relations firms and ad agencies.

Of course, the Dallas film community is by no means limited to industrial and commercial production. In fact, in the last five years Dallas-based production companies have funded, produced and distributed at least six big-screen productions. Two of those pictures — "Kiss of the Spider Woman," which netted William Hurt a best actor Oscar, and "Trip to Bountiful," which garnered Geraldine Page a best actress award — were produced by FilmDallas, headed by New York transplant and film wunderkind Sam Grogg. Grogg, a steadfast supporter of the local industry, says, "I personally feel that the industry here has done incredibly well. I see it continuing to grow and prosper."

In an effort to help Dallas become

a world-class and respected film center, the Trammell S. Crow Co. built the Studios at Las Colinas in 1982 for $7.2 million. The effort was designed to lure feature films and television movies away from the union-bound, high-cost studios of Hollywood. In 1983 the studios did in fact play host to Robert Altman's "Streamers," and in 1988 director/producer Oliver Stone brought his medium-budgeted "Talk Radio" to the Studios. Later the same year, he chose Dallas as the site for another film, "Born on the Fourth of July," starring Tom Cruise. Best estimates are that Hollywood filmmakers pump approximately $22 million into the Dallas economy annually. Meanwhile, local production activities generate about $186 million, with a ripple effect of three to four times that amount.

In addition to the three sound stages in the Studios at Las Colinas, there is an extensive office complex that is home to a variety of ancillary support companies needed for film production. One of these, Allied+WTBS, has processed more than three dozen feature films as well as made-for-TV movies.

Away from the studios and located at Love Field is Video Post and Transfer, one of the finest post-production tape facilities anywhere in the United States. The company boasts state-of-the-art equipment made even better by its electronics whiz-kid owner Neil Feldman. Video Post is so well respected that it draws clients from as far away as Japan, Brazil and Mexico as well as from Hollywood, and of course, from throughout the Southwest.

Not to be ignored is the increasingly significant contributions of numerous Dallas-based music recording studios and music libraries which offer quality support to both the burgeoning film community as well as advertising and public relations firms.

Another medium not normally associated with Dallas, but which has become a significant contributor to the communications industry within the last decade, is publishing. Traditionally, publishing has been closely associated with New York, Chicago and to a lesser extent San Francisco. However, publishing has been one of the significant "other" industries that has expanded and flourished even in times of general economic downturn.

The largest of Dallas' publishing houses is Taylor Publishing. Taylor, like most Dallas-based publishers, has sought and successfully competed in "niche" publishing — finding highly specialized areas of book publishing and capitalizing on them. In Taylor's case, that niche has been school and college yearbooks, an area that R.B. Marston, president and CEO, expects to expand in the coming years with the birth and education of children born to baby boomers. "The publishing industry withstood the problems of the Dallas economy," he says. "In general, we've done better than the general business climate."

Throughout the fabric of all areas of communications, Dallas has expe-

ABOVE: Microwave towers transmit millions of telephone calls in and out of the Dallas area. Photo by John Hethorn.

TOP: The Dallas/Fort Worth Teleport is used by businesses, the media and other clients to transmit live and taped audio/visual presentations to satellites for viewing around the world.

TOP LEFT: The Studios at Las Colinas are available for feature film production as well as advertising and corporate projects.

BOTTOM LEFT: The soundstages at the Studios at Las Colinas are used for everything from feature films to management training films.

rienced a significant growth in the number of minority owned and operated communications businesses. In every area of communications — advertising, public relations, printing, broadcasting, consulting — Hispanic, African-American, Asian and Native-American business people are having an increasing economic and social impact. Dallas, in fact, is the only city in the nation to have a bilingual yellow pages (other cities have yellow pages in Spanish, but not in Spanish and English), which is distributed to more than 50,000 people annually.

"The future (for Hispanic broadcast stations) is very solid. The current stations will become more prosperous and there will be more stations established in the future," says Mark Rodriquez, president of Rodriquez Communications, which

owns and operates KOJO-FM and KESS-FM.

"One of the reasons that the (Hispanic) stations are doing so well is because the percentage of the Hispanic population is growing at a consistent rate. The percentage of Hispanics is growing faster than any other population group in the Metroplex."

In order for all companies to grow whether they be communications-based or not, and to continue the trend of business relocations to the area, one critical link of the communications industry must be in place: a strong telecommunications infrastructure.

Simply defined, telecommunications is the transfer of information — whether it be voice, data or video images — by means of satellite, old-fashioned copper wires or fiber optics

ABOVE: INFOMART *at the Dallas Market Center showcases the latest in voice and data transmission technology. Photo by Allan Kaye.*

LEFT: *Companies like GTE Southwest have contributed to Dallas' distinction as the nation's leading center for telecommunications employment, research and manufacturing. Photo by Brian McWeeney.*

ABOVE: A signal transmitting tower helps cellular phone users move throughout the region with uninterrupted communications capabilities. Southwestern Bell photo.

RIGHT: Dallas vendors provide businesses and residential customers with the most sophisticated telephone systems available. Photo by Benjamin Stewart.

which utilize glass and lasers. Repeatedly, when corporations outside Dallas are surveyed as to the necessary prerequisites needed to motivate a corporate relocation, telecommunications ranks high on the list. Dallas has made sure it is up to the challenges of tomorrow's telecommunications needs by addressing the present state of telecommunications within the Metroplex today.

To this end, the Greater Dallas Chamber established a Telecommunications Committee in 1987 comprised of industry leaders, representatives of city government and leading

the AT&Ts, MCIs LDSs and Sprints. Sprint has its national headquarters in Dallas, and MCI is planning a major consolidation in the area. A large variety of smaller long distance networks are continuing to be established and grow within the city.

Finally, there are the hardware suppliers who often have a large research and development component. Over the past years, companies like Compaq and Northern Telecom have been closely tied conceptually to the computer industry and data transmission. But these companies also work on the cutting edge of combining the functions of voice/data/video transmission. Likewise, there are a substantial number of satellite and dish manufacturers and installation firms within the Metroplex.

Corporations from throughout the area have made the Dallas/Fort Worth Teleport, with its multichannel transmission capabilities throughout the Unites States, a vital part of their own internal telecommunications networks. And not to be forgotten is the massive explosion of the cellular phone industry, making Dallas one of the top 10 mobile communication markets in the United States.

The heavy concentration of all these elements has caused some experts to label Dallas the leading telecommunications center in the United States. And expected continued growth in these industries bodes well for all Dallas-based businesses.

"Certainly any major company, no matter what its business, increasingly correlates the level of the telecommunication infrastructure of the city in which it is located and its own bottom line," says Jim Bodge, director and manager of regional marketing for Southwestern Bell. "When you look at Dallas, we're right at the top. We will continue to come to the forefront as a major hub, a major focal point of the telecommunications industry in the future."

educational institutions within the city. A survey conducted by that group indicates that Dallas is well represented by the three core groups necessary for a successful telecommunications infrastructure.

The first and most easily recognized group representing telecommunications is phone companies. Southwestern Bell and GTE are firmly established within the Metroplex, with GTE relocating its telephone operations center here. Already, Southwestern Bell claims one of the most sophisticated data transmission capabilities of any phone company

with more than 1,000 miles of fiber optic lines within metropolitan Dallas alone (more than 4,000 miles in Texas) and another 50,000-plus miles of copper cable in place. Also, 100 percent of Southwestern Bell's telephone lines in Dallas are served by analog/digital switching, and the percentage only drops to 93 percent statewide. And as an employer of more than 7,000 locally, Southwestern Bell pumps in excess of $345 million into the local economy.

The second group of telecommunications businesses well represented in Dallas are long distance carriers —

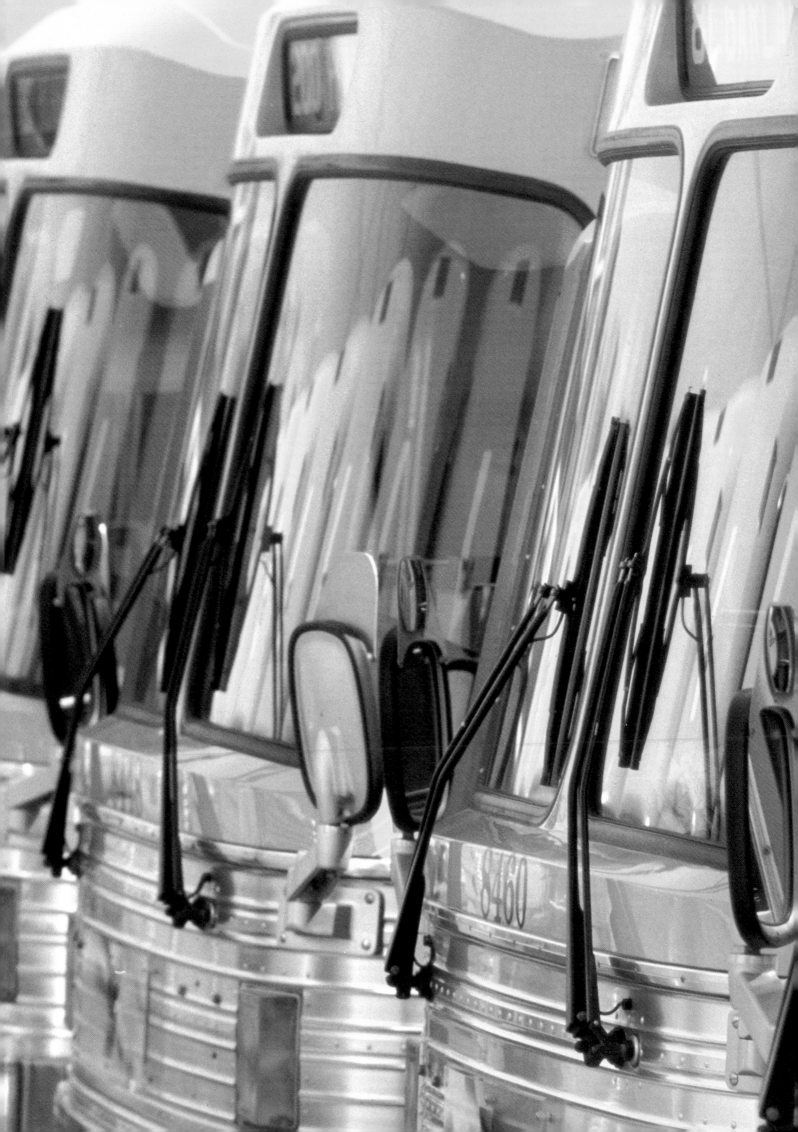

CHAPTER 9

Wings and Wheels of Progress

By Barbara J. Wegher

It was not until the coming of the railroad, the invention of the automobile and later, the airplane, that Dallas' potential as a transportation hub would become anything more than a pipe dream in the mind of an early pioneer.

Approximately 825 vehicles visit 17,000 bus stops throughout the DART service area. Photo by Doug Milner.

John Neely Bryan, Dallas' founding father, envisioned Dallas as a center for transportation. In 1841, perhaps the single most important reason for any town to thrive, particularly a landlocked one such as Dallas, was its access to waterways — the lifelines of trade, commerce and in many cases, new settlers. Bryan's dream was not to be, however. The Trinity River, despite its divine name, proved to be no godsend for the struggling hamlet. In fact, it was not until the coming of the railroad, the invention of the automobile and later, the airplane, that Dallas' potential as a transportation hub would become anything more than a pipe dream in the mind of an early pioneer.

As modes of transportation became faster and more sophisticated, Dallas, fueled by oil and real estate booms, would leap forward as one of the most important transportation hubs in the United States.

The jewel in Dallas' crown is Dallas/Fort Worth International Airport (D/FW). Much of the credit for D/FW's existence and its stature as a world-class airport goes to J. Erik Jonsson, former Dallas mayor and founder of Texas Instruments. Jonsson took his first airplane ride when he was 16 and immediately began a lifelong love affair with flight that was highlighted by the groundbreaking ceremonies for D/FW Airport in December 1968. The airport was dedicated in January 1973.

It was less Jonsson's fascination with aircraft and more his vision of the future that led D/FW to achieve its present-day stature as a world port. While many on the airport's planning committee lobbied for an airport only a little larger than 4,000 acres, Jonsson stalwartly maintained that the airport would have to be at least 25,000 acres. Eventually, a compromise of nearly 18,000 acres was reached.

In 1966, long before the first shovel full of dirt was lifted, Jonsson said, "We don't have any other choice. If we don't have the facilities to serve the big planes of the 1970s, they won't be landing here. And, a city is sure to go downhill when it has a second-rate transportation system." Always looking ahead, Jonsson, now in his 80s, actively supports future expansion of the airport.

After six long years of work, D/FW Airport officially opened on January 13, 1973. The dream became a reality. By the time the airport was finished, however, more than $2.6 billion had been invested, including the cost of the land. When completed, it was and remains the largest airport in the United States.

Oris W. Dunham Jr., executive director of the airport, is proud of what the airport has become. Like Jonsson, he is a strong advocate of continued growth and expansion. "People relocate in large part because of environment," he said. "Not only because we have aggressively

attempted to make ourselves one of the very best airports in the world, but because D/FW has made a very active contribution to the community and intends to continue to do so in the future."

In 1988 alone, D/FW handled more than 44 million passengers, 81,000 tons of mail and 200,000 tons of freight. In that year there were more than 675,000 aircraft operations at the airport. By 1989, however, the volume of airport activity, mail and cargo increased, making D/FW the third busiest airport in the world behind Chicago's O'Hare and Atlanta's Hartsfield. And in January 1989, a milestone of sorts was passed: The 200 millionth passenger boarded a plane at the behemoth airport.

ABOVE: Dallas/Fort Worth International Airport has one of the best records in the country for getting planes in and out on time. Photo by Doug Milner.

LEFT: American Airlines pilots change shifts at Dallas/Fort Worth International Airport, their home port. Photo by Doug Milner.

ary 1989, a milestone of sorts was passed: the 200 millionth passenger boarded a plane at the behemoth airport.

Today D/FW Airport services 172 destinations — 145 domestic (most within three hours) and 27 international destinations. Of these, 107 domestic and 17 international destinations are reached with non-stop service. Another 38 domestic and 10 international destinations are served directly, meaning the plane makes at least one stop but there is no plane change.

"One of the obvious advantages that Dallas has, in regard to transportation, is D/FW Airport," says University of North Texas economist Dr. Harold Gross. "It is our outlet to the rest of the world, and the world views it as their port to us. That's what's really important. More than any one factor, D/FW is repeatedly cited by businesses originally based in other parts of the country as the reason for

relocations, not only to Dallas, but the state. It has been an extremely critical factor in the diversification of Dallas' economy."

Perhaps the single most important ingredient to that sustained growth and importance of the airport is that American Airlines chose D/FW as its home port. Of the more than 150 locations served in the continental United States from D/FW, American services 85 of them. In addition, American flies to 13 points outside the United States from D/FW.

On an average day in 1987, American Airlines estimated that it handled 140,000 pieces of luggage, received 185,000 reservation calls, served 108,000 in-flight meals and snacks, hired four new flight attendants and changed 35 airplane tires. They now estimate those figures have increased by at least 25 percent as of 1989. In 1988, the airline estimated that its fleet of 424 planes consumed nearly 1.5 million gallons of fuel.

And, the airline is one of the largest employers in the Dallas/Fort Worth Metroplex, with more than 22,000 employees. The estimated dollars pumped into the Dallas/Fort Worth economy by American and its employees is estimated to be in excess of $1.5 billion per year.

And if that was not enough, American announced plans in 1988 for a massive expansion effort at D/FW Airport. Included in those plans is a new terminal, which will expand the mammoth 1 million-square-foot terminal already in use. American has already ordered 50 new aircraft and had the option with Boeing of picking up another 50 in 1989. American also boasts one of the most sophisticated computerized systems for reservations, as well as for up-to-the-minute predictions on air traffic trends and projected reservations for peak seasons, anticipating increases in specific air traffic corridors.

While American Airlines may be the largest carrier propelling D/FW Airport into the 21st century, it is by no means the only one. Twenty-one carriers — 17 domestic and four foreign — fly in and out of D/FW daily. These include American, American Eagle, Executive Express, US Air, Braniff, Continental, Delta, ASA, Metroflight, Midway, Northwest, Pan American World Airways, Piedmont, Trans World Airlines, United, Mesa Air Shuttle, Midwest Express, British Airways, Lufthansa, Mexicana and Thai Airways. International service is provided by the four international carriers and four domestic carriers.

D/FW Airport has become a significant international gateway. In addition to its role as a U.S. Customs District Headquarters, D/FW is a Fish and Wildlife Port of Entry. Also, the airport is home of Foreign Trade Zone 39. Foreign Trade Zones were established by Congress in 1934 as areas within the continental United States that are considered outside U.S. Customs' territory. Thus, goods held in those zones are not subject to U.S. taxes or tariffs and are considered part of international commerce.

As an employer, D/FW Airport itself has approximately 25,000 airline and support personnel in addition to 1,273 Airport Board employees. Best estimates are that D/FW Airport conservatively generates at least $5 billion into the local economy.

In addition to D/FW, the new Alliance Airport, the brainchild of Ross Perot Jr., is beginning to take shape. Groundbreaking ceremonies took place on July 9, 1988, and the 418-acre airport northwest of D/FW Airport is expected to provide additional support to D/FW, as well as attracting and servicing the strong manufacturing components of both Dallas and Tarrant counties. Alliance Airport was scheduled for completion in 1989 at a cost of $31 million. The airport

got a major boost in the summer of 1989 when American Airlines announced they would locate a new maintenance facility at Alliance after considering sites in Oklahoma City and other locations. The facility will be located in the 3,300-acre industrial park surrounding the airport and will create 4,500 new jobs when fully phased.

Closer to downtown Dallas (D/FW is approximately 17.7 miles from the heart of the city) is Love Field. The

LEFT: D/FW Airport services 172 destinations — 145 domestic and 27 international destinations.

ABOVE: American Airlines is one of the largest employers in the Dallas/Fort Worth Metroplex, with more than 22,000 employees. Photo courtesy of American Airlines.

ABOVE: *Dallas Love Field remains a vital airport for passengers traveling within Texas and the four contiguous states. Photo by Martin Vandiver.*

TOP: *When completed, Alliance International Center will become a major hub for general aviation and cargo distribution. Rendering by The Perot Group.*

RIGHT: *Love Field provides convenient air service just minutes from downtown Dallas. Photo by Martin Vandiver.*

airport has just recently completed a $14-million construction program designed to improve access for passengers and ground transportation. Parking was nearly doubled, and new roadways for arriving and departing passengers were constructed to facilitate passenger access to the terminal and to relieve traffic congestion. The project also included replacing the terminal's outdated exterior with a brushed silver facade, modernizing the baggage claim area and installing a new sound system, a new fire alarm system and new computerized air conditioning and heating systems.

Despite the extensive improvements, most urban planners support more changes at Love Field, including enlarging the airport and providing service to more cities at greater distances. Southwest Airlines, the airport's only commercial carrier, serves a five-state region including Texas.

Love Field has approximately 630 takeoffs and landings daily, and it is estimated that nearly 2.5 million pas-

sengers flow through the airport each year. With 150 employees and another 24,000 jobs directly attributable to Love, the airport generates at least $2 billion in benefits for Dallas yearly.

However, Love Field plays host to more than just aircraft. A variety of full-service fixed-base operators, as well as a number of other aircraft-related companies call Love Field home. It is also the new home of the Frontiers of Flight, a highly respected museum devoted to the history of flight. The collection was formerly housed at the University of Texas at Dallas. Curator Bob Kopitzke says the collection is "one of the top five aviation collections in the United States," and some place it second in importance only to the National Air and Space Museum at the Smithsonian Institution in Washington, D.C.

The museum, a composite of more than 200 private collections, claims more than 2.5 million items, including 20,000 reference books, more

ABOVE: *A Southwest Airlines jet makes its final approach to Love Field over Bachman Lake. Photo by Martin Vandiver.*

CENTER: *Greyhound-Trailways Bus Lines is headquartered in Dallas.*

RIGHT: *The Santa Fe Railroad is one of several major railroad lines that carry freight in and out of Dallas.*

than 250,000 aviation periodicals and journals and hundreds of models and other memorabilia tracing the history of flight from ancient rocket-propelled Chinese kites and early dirigibles to modern spaceships and commercial jets.

It is only appropriate that the museum be located at Love Field, because the airport itself is rich in history. The field was created in 1917 as a World War I military training base and was named in memory of an

early pioneer of flight, Lt. Moss Lee Love, who died in an airplane crash in California in 1913.

In addition to Love Field, there are at least eight other small airports in and surrounding Dallas, primarily catering to the needs of private plane owners and business jets.

While air transportation is one of the most critical keys to Dallas' continuing success as a commercial and manufacturing hub, it is by no means the only factor that figures into the transportation scheme. Greyhound-Trailways Bus Lines makes its home in Dallas, employing more than 1,500 locally. The company offers 58 daily departures from Dallas, and serves 12,000 communities in the continental United States. In 1988 Greyhound-Trailways logged nearly 7 mil-

lion passenger miles. The company also began an express package service and has implemented a new reservation and ticketing system.

Likewise, Amtrak has made a surprising comeback in Texas, operating a train three times a week from Dallas to Houston. The train is part of a longer run that begins in Chicago. Amtrak also offers the option of traveling from Dallas to San Antonio and, with a brief layover, picking up a west-bound train that continues all the way to Los Angeles. According to an Amtrak spokesman, ridership on the Dallas-Houston run is increasing steadily with 37,000 passengers in 1988, an increase of 28.4 percent over the previous year when the route ran only from Chicago via Dallas to San Antonio.

Another possible means of passenger transportation within the state of Texas is high speed rail. The Texas Turnpike Authority commissioned a feasibility study for the Texas Triangle, a proposed high speed rail system that would link Dallas/Fort Worth, Houston and Austin/San Antonio. Technology already in place in Europe and the Orient could move passengers at speeds of 200 miles per hour.

Critical to Dallas maintaining its stature as a transportation hub for much of the South and Southwest is freight rail service and trucking. The first railroads to arrive in Dallas were the Houston & Texas Central Railroad in 1872 and the Texas & Pacific Railroad in 1873. These two lines very quickly did for Dallas what the

Trinity River could not do: They brought people and supplies into Dallas, and provided a means of shipping local products out. Today eight railroads carry freight into and out of Dallas warehouses and distribution centers.

Truck freight companies serve the same purpose as the railroads, but they also work in concert with the railroads and air freight companies to move goods in and out of the area. The Texas Legislature and various interest groups are involved in an ongoing process to bring Texas intrastate trucking costs in line with national rates. Meanwhile, trucking companies are thriving in the Metroplex, due in part to the fact that trucking out of state is so lucrative, as well as the fact that Dallas' central location provides a decided advantage.

According to recent figures provided by the U.S. Department of Transportation, nearly 30 million people live within 10 hours truck transit time of Dallas. Another 76 million live within a 24-hour transit time of Dallas, and the remaining 213

million of the U.S. population live within 48 hours transit time. As a result, Dallas, with 298 million square feet of industrial warehouse space, is one of the leading warehouse/distribution centers in the United States.

Dallas, as does all major metropolitan centers, has an overabundance of cars. Sociologists often explain that Texas' love affair with the automobile began when cowboys began trading in their four-legged friends for more comfortable and faster modes of transportation. Today, there are more than 1.6 million registered vehicles (including cars, motorcycles and trucks) in Dallas County. And, within the last five years, the number of car dealerships in Dallas has jumped from 87 to 96, with 35 of those selling imports. Many of the import cars reflect high dollar models, giving Dallas a more cosmopolitan feel than when it was dominated solely by the likes of Ford and Chevy.

Compared to driving in most large cities, getting around in Dallas is a breeze. A comprehensive system of streets, boulevards, tollways, loops and highways — including four interstate highways — keeps traffic moving and congestion at a minimum. Still, work is under way to reduce congestion in some key areas, including areas of North Dallas and especially on North Central Expressway (U.S. 75). Dallas Area Rapid Transit (DART) was established in 1983 to implement a mass transit plan for the area. Thus far that plan includes a comprehensive bus system serving Dallas and many adjoining communities. Currently, DART employs 1,724 people and has an annual operating budget of $112 million.

On an average weekday, DART carries a minimum of 155,000 people; at rush hour it is estimated that DART carries the equivalent of eight freeway lanes of automobiles into the downtown area. There are more than 17,000 bus stops throughout the DART area serviced by 823 transit vehicles. Although the DART service area covers more than 700 square miles, and its normal transit vehicles total an average of 1.7 million miles monthly, the system boasts one of the best safety records of any rapid transit company in the United States. In addition to regular passengers, DART carries approximately 3.5 million people annually through its charter services.

As with most metropolitan areas, Dallas has experienced substantial growth in its suburbs. Much of the expansion has taken place to the north of the city, in the communities of Richardson and Plano. Other areas of rapid expansion include Irving as well as the Lake Lewisville area. As a result, many of the north/south corridors linking those areas with downtown, as well as east/west corridors

TOP LEFT: A causeway brings early morning commuters from the shores of Lake Ray Hubbard to the heart of the city. Photo by Doug Milner.

BOTTOM LEFT: While rush hour will increase the traffic flow on this highway, Dallas traffic is lighter than in most major cities. Photo by Scott Metcalfe.

ABOVE: On an average weekday, DART carries a minimum of 155,000 people. Photo by John Hethorn.

ABOVE: A new parking garage and covered walkways are among the improvements at Dallas Love Field. Photo by Martin Vandiver.

RIGHT: Freight and trucking companies have taken off in Dallas due to the city's central location.

extending between Dallas and Fort Worth, have increasingly become clogged, particularly at rush hours.

According to DART's most recent figures, Dallasites make about 148,000 "linked" trips per day. They estimate that figure to jump to nearly 217,000 by 2010.

However, Dallas has undertaken a project to widen and improve some of the roadways. At the same time, DART has been studying and preparing a rapid transit plan designed to reduce traffic congestion and to facilitate travel between areas of projected greater growth and the heart of the city.

At present, DART plans to build a light rail system designed to better connect outlying areas with downtown, as well as providing transit within the core of the city. DART has planned the system with public input

offered at community hearings held throughout its service area. Also, DART is setting aside $13 million annually to be used over the next seven years for such purposes as intersection improvements, new and improved signaling systems and additional lanes that will accommodate both buses and automobiles.

DART will expand express bus service to alleviate some of the congestion on such major freeways as LBJ Freeway (I-635) and R.L. Thornton (I-30), as well as adding feeder bus and van services within neighborhoods. It also will develop "circulator" systems designed to operate within major employment and activity centers such as Las Colinas, Legacy Park in Northwest Plano and Stemmons/Market Center. DART presently envisions using small buses, vans and perhaps a guided trolley sys-

tem or people movers to satisfy the needs of Metroplex residents and workers in those particular areas. Already, DART offers a comprehensive system of "lift" vehicles to help the physically impaired.

Two circulator routes that have been executed by private entities offer a contrasting look at the types of solutions that can be found. At Las Colinas, above-ground people movers carry passengers from one building to the next, while water taxis serve the same purpose on the canals and lakes below. Meanwhile, the McKinney Avenue Transit Authority is carrying passengers between the downtown Arts District and the McKinney Avenue restaurant/retail area using electric trolleys — technology that has not been used in Dallas for more than 30 years.

No matter what kind of rapid tran-

sit system is implemented, it must be "flexible," according to Dr. Harold Gross at the University of North Texas. "Dallas is in desperate need of a good rapid transit system. But whatever plan Dallas finally settles on, I have full confidence that it will, like most everything else that Dallas does, be done properly."

Perhaps the real irony is that while Dallas today is a premier transportation hub, John Neely Bryan's dream of Dallas becoming a river port was never realized. Boat traffic is the only source of transportation that was never realized by the city. Bryan's dream ended with the passage of a single boat up the unpredictable Trinity River. But thanks to the foresight and vision of later urban pioneers, Dallas is a city in large part defined by its position as a transportation center for the entire nation.

CHAPTER 10

A Place to Live

By Bill Sloan

That vast checkerboard you see from the air is actually made up of scores of individual communities and neighborhoods, each with its own unique identity, its own special characteristics, its own distinct personality.

The Dreyfuss Club at White Rock Lake is one of several popular locations for family reunions and church gatherings. Photo by Dan Hatzenbuehler.

ABOVE: *Springtime brings sunshine and buds to University Park. Photo by Brian McWeeney.*

Viewed from the window of a jetliner, Dallas and its suburbs seem to stretch out toward the far horizons in one sweeping, carefully ordered, panoramic gridwork of streets, buildings and open spaces. Except for the greenbelts along the Trinity River, the ribbon-like super highways slicing diagonally across the landscape and the occasional cluster of high-rise buildings, it all looks pretty much the same.

From 5,000 feet, Dallas epitomizes the modern all-American metropolis at its gleaming best. It is easy to pic-

ture it as one huge homogeneous mass of concrete and steel, brick and glass, wood and stone, trees and grass, cars and trucks. It also is easy to think of it as being populated entirely by stereotypical urban dwellers in pursuit of some stereotypical version of "the good life."

But if you think of Dallas in that general context, you definitely need to think again.

Like inhabitants of all large cities, Dallasites share certain common interests, concerns, problems and goals. But that vast checkerboard you

frontier times when settlers from certain European countries frequently arrived in North Texas in groups. One of the most notable cases of an early settlement with a highly ethnic makeup was La Reunion, a cooperative colony established by French, Swiss and Belgian immigrants in 1855 in what is now West Dallas. Led by Frenchman Victor Considerant, the 200 colonists hoped to establish a utopian community, but after three years of severe hardship, the experiment failed. Many residents of La Reunion returned to Europe, but others stayed to add an enriching element of culture and cosmopolitanism to Dallas. As late as 1880, the federal census showed almost 15 percent of the city's population to be foreign-born.

As it became a city, Dallas continued to be a mecca of sorts, both for foreign immigrants and migrants from other parts of the United States. In the early 1900s, a revolution in Mexico brought the first large influx of Hispanic immigrants to the city and was instrumental in the development of the "Little Mexico" area immediately north of downtown. Although parts of the original neighborhood have now been swallowed up by urban growth, strong elements of it remain intact today. And although there are now several larger Hispanic neighborhoods in Dallas, many of the county's second- and third-generation Hispanic residents still have their roots in "Little Mexico" and return there for such traditional and colorful Mexican celebrations as Cinco de Mayo.

Even in its earliest days, Dallas never was as insular or resistant to "outsiders" as some Southern towns, and over the decades it has attracted large numbers of persons of German, English, Irish, Italian, Greek, Oriental, Scandinavian and Eastern European extraction. A sizeable Jewish community has been an integral and vital part of the city for more than a century and has contributed immeasurably to Dallas' stature in fields ranging from retailing to medicine and from fashion to law.

African-American residents, too, have been important contributors to Dallas' growth and development and have always constituted a major segment of the city's population. The "Deep Ellum" area just east of downtown, which grew out of a Freedmanstown established after the Civil War, ranked as one of the nation's leading centers of African-American culture and commerce for more than half a century and is now a colorful area of artists, nightlife, restaurants and small independent businesses. Much of Dallas was built by African-American labor, and during the past quarter-century African-Americans have played an increasingly major role in the city's leadership. African-Americans now hold the top administrative positions in both Dallas city government and the Dallas public school system, as well as a number of key elective posts in various areas of government.

African-Americans reside in all parts of Dallas and Dallas County, but the largest predominantly African-American neighborhoods are found in South Dallas and Southeast Oak Cliff, where major incentives are presently in place to create more jobs and improve economic opportunity. The South Boulevard-Park Row area of South Dallas, which was officially designated as a historic preservation district a decade ago, contains some of the finest and most palatial early 20th century homes in the city. The State-Thomas area immediately north of downtown is another historic African-American neighborhood where extensive restoration has taken place.

The most recent ethnic group to arrive en masse in the Dallas area is Southeast Asian refugees who fled

see from the air is actually made up of scores of individual communities and neighborhoods, each with its own unique identity, its own special characteristics, its own distinct personality. In reality, Dallas encompasses different lifestyles, varying cultures, diverse social patterns and customs, different ideologies and religious beliefs.

Historically, Dallas has always had a high percentage of foreign-born citizens and those with discernible ethnic roots and backgrounds. Part of this diversity remains a legacy from

TOP: *An enterprising trio tests their business skills on a Dallas street corner. Photo by Scott Metcalfe.*

BOTTOM: *Al fresco dining is popular at neighborhood shopping centers. Photo by Scott Metcalfe.*

RIGHT: *Dallas apartment communities combine convenience with elegant living. Photo by Doug Milner.*

from the long, destructive war in Vietnam, Laos and Cambodia. Since the influx began in the late 1970s, more than 30,000 Southeast Asians have relocated to the Dallas area. Many have quickly assimilated into the community at large, but others have concentrated in certain areas where numerous Vietnamese restaurants, Asian food markets and other ethnic shops have appeared. This is especially true of parts of old East Dallas, but thriving Southeast Asian neighborhoods can also be found in other parts of the city and even in suburban Richardson.

Unlike the situation in some older U.S. cities, where many neighborhoods are based almost entirely on ethnicity, most Dallasites with roots in other countries have simply become part of the larger fabric of the community, although they may hold on to certain aspects of their ancestral cultures. It is next to impossible, for instance, to find an area that could be classified as an "Irish neighborhood" anywhere in Dallas County. And yet when Dallas holds its annual St. Patrick's Day parade, sons and daughters of the Auld Sod turn out by the thousands — along with countless non-Irish residents who simply enjoy the occasion.

There are, however, a few notable exceptions. For more than 50 years, the Urban Park neighborhood in Southeast Dallas has been home to scores of families of Czechoslovakian descent, who actively maintain many of their native customs and who still enjoy traditional music, dancing, food and drink. They even have their own community hall. Likewise, in a small corner of East Dallas, Greek traditions are kept alive and flourish through the Greek Orthodox Church of the Holy Trinity. One of the most enjoyable of these — and one in which all Dallasites may partake — is a Greek Food Festival each September at the church.

Indeed, churches play an indispensable role in the lives of most Dallas neighborhoods, ethnic or otherwise. Dallas is renowned as a city of exceptionally strong churches, and many of these derive their strength by serving not only as houses of worship for their congregations, but as focal points for neighborhood-based activities and as busy public service organizations. Hundreds of churches across the city provide child care facilities,

emergency services, aid for the elderly and handicapped and many other forms of assistance to area residents.

But, rather than having been created along ethnic, cultural or religious lines, the vast majority of the most visible Dallas and Dallas County neighborhoods are the result of geography, terrain, timing of their construction, architectural style groupings, master planning, organized real estate promotions, socio-economic considerations — and sometimes pure accident.

Most of the principal identifiable residential sections within the city of Dallas were the brainchild of a real estate developer. Oak Lawn, for example, is now sometimes referred to as "Uptown" because the recent

proliferation of high-rise office buildings has transformed it into a north-ward extension of the Central Business District. But parts of it remain residential, and homeowners continue to fight to keep it that way. Oak Lawn originated in the 1890s as a "beautiful, majestic" residential addition with a golf club as its principal attraction. Today's Oak Lawn generally can be defined as the entire area between downtown on the south, the Park Cities and Love Field area on the north, Central Expressway on the east and the Stemmons Freeway corridor on the west. While there still are pockets of single-family homes in Oak Lawn, many of the area's residents live in the posh high-rise apartments and condominiums that line beautiful Turtle Creek.

Oak Cliff, a term now used to describe all of that vast area of Dallas lying west of the Trinity River, began as a totally separate community from Dallas. A town called Hord's Ridge was established there in the 1840s but virtually disappeared after challenging Dallas in an election to pick the county seat. In the late 1880s, developer Thomas L. Marsalis began building Oak Cliff as a model city on 2,000 acres of land, and it was hailed as the "Brooklyn of the Southwest." It was incorporated in 1890 as a city in its own right, but became part of Dallas in 1903 by virtue of an annexation election, which carried by just 18 votes.

Since then, Oak Cliff has existed mainly in the minds of the thousands of proud, independent Oak Cliff lovers who live there, but parts of it still retain a pleasant small-town atmosphere. Within Oak Cliff lie such fascinating neighborhoods as Winnetka Heights, an outstanding collection of historic homes dating from Oak Cliff's earliest days, and Kessler Park, an area of huge trees, rugged terrain and great natural beauty. Oak Cliff also is the home of some of the city's most beautiful parks and the Dallas Zoo.

Beyond the western boundaries of Dallas — or Oak Cliff, if you prefer — are the major suburban cities of Grand Prairie, birthplace of the county's multibillion-dollar aerospace industry, and Irving, home of fabulous 12,000-acre Las Colinas, one of the world's largest master-planned, mixed-use developments. To the south are other fast-growing suburbs including Cedar Hill, Duncanville, DeSoto and Lancaster.

In its modern context, the term East Dallas refers to an entire quadrant of the city. But in the 1880s, East Dallas, too, was a separate incorporated town, which actually encompassed more land area than the city of Dallas itself. East Dallas was established in 1882 with wealthy businessman William H. Gaston as the driving force behind its creation and with great period mansions along Ross Avenue as its main emphasis. Eight years later, it also was annexed by Dallas and during the next three or four decades became one of the fastest growing sections of the city.

Munger Place, developed in 1905 and now a designated historic district in old East Dallas, boasts one of the nation's finest collections of large prairie-style homes and a fiercely loyal neighborhood spirit among the "urban pioneers" who have restored them to their original elegance. The Swiss Avenue Historic District, situated a few blocks away in an area developed between 1910 and 1925, contains dozens of restored examples

of even larger, more elegant residential architecture.

East Dallas is also the home of Bryan Place, a neighborhood of new homes and townhomes built since the mid-1970s by developer Dave Fox. As the only residential development located within easy walking distance of downtown offices, Bryan Place is a favorite of both young urban professionals who enjoy living in the shadow of the skyscrapers and

LEFT: Munger Place, one of Dallas' oldest neighborhoods, has witnessed a revival in recent years. Photo by Doug Milner.

ABOVE: Old East Dallas is a popular neighborhood for young families with a penchant for restoration. Photo by Brian McWeeney.

retirees who appreciate its convenience.

Lakewood, where large-scale development began in the 1920s, is located just east of old East Dallas and derives its name from its proximity to White Rock Lake, a sailboat-studded reservoir surrounded by huge trees, scenic drives, bike trails, picnic areas and parks. Some of Dallas' finest and most expensive homes are located on Lakewood's winding, picturesque streets and around the Lakewood Country Club's rolling golf course. Two of Dallas' best-known mayors, Robert L. Thornton Sr. and Wallace Savage, were products of Lakewood, a neighborhood whose residents place it second to none in the city.

Lying south, east and north of Lakewood and also drawing on the appeal of White Rock Lake are other attractive, upscale residential neigh-

borhoods, including Lake Highlands, the Cloisters, Forest Hills and Casa Linda. Lake Highlands, in particular, has become a magnet for "upwardly mobile" young professionals. Just to the south and east is Casa View, a large, pleasant, middle-class neighborhood of well-kept family homes.

On to the south is Pleasant Grove, which began in the 1890s as a crossroads hamlet and a one-room schoolhouse near what is now the intersection of South Buckner Boulevard (Loop 12) and Lake June Road. Almost a century later, Pleasant Grove has become a term sometimes used to refer to the entire southeastern quadrant of Dallas, although the Pleasant Grove neighborhood actually constitutes only a small part of that quadrant. Today's Pleasant Grove is home to thousands of hardworking, middle-income and bluecollar families and offers some of the

city's most affordable housing in both old and new subdivisions. Although it is very much a part of Dallas, Pleasant Grove retains some of the appealing attributes of a small town.

A number of other identifiable neighborhoods also lie within Southeast Dallas, each with its own character and identity. Urban Park, one of the best-maintained older neighborhoods in the city, features winding streets, large native trees, a fascinating mixture of architectural styles including some historic homes, and several thousand proud homeowners. Buckner Terrace is an attractive, affluent, white-collar neighborhood with homes priced up to $150,000 and one of the strongest neighborhood organizations in Dallas. The Rylie-Kleberg area in the city's extreme southeastern corner contains several working-class residential developments, but it still contains much open land and remains semirural to a large degree.

Stretching around the eastern perimeter of Dallas is an unbroken string of suburban cities. At the northern end of that chain is Garland, the county's second-largest municipality with a population of more than 180,000; Sunnyvale and Rowlett, offering attractive homesites overlooking Lake Ray Hubbard; Mesquite, an old farming town transformed into a major "bedroom city"; Balch Springs, a developing residential community; and Seagoville, where the flavor of a quiet country town lives on.

Moving north, the "island city" of Highland Park is an enclave of mansions and manicured estates, many valued in the millions of dollars. Today Highland Park ranks as the wealthiest and most prestigious of Dallas suburbs, but it was only a chunk of bare prairie lying well beyond the northern boundaries of Dallas in 1906 when John S. Armstrong and Hugh E. Prather hired the

same landscape architect who designed Beverly Hills in California to lay out a model all-residential community there. By the time it was incorporated in 1913, Highland Park had established itself as the place to live in Dallas County for those who could afford it, and it has retained that status ever since.

Adjoining Highland Park and surrounded by Dallas on three sides is University Park, the home of Southern Methodist University and some of the most sought-after residential real estate in Texas. The typical home in this other half of the so-called "Park Cities" is between 40 and 60 years old and much smaller and less ostentatious than its Highland Park counterpart. But, no home in the county has a higher per-square-foot value. Many upper-middle income wage earners aspire to live in University Park, but only a relative few manage to do it.

North of the Park Cities are the ultra-expensive estates of Preston Hollow, the most exclusive residential area within the city of Dallas. Although it owes its start as a neighborhood to a lack of space that had developed by 1930 in Highland Park, today's Preston Hollow residents

ABOVE: Dallas has 197 playgrounds, five public golf courses and five public tennis centers. Photo by Doug Milner.

TOP LEFT: "Mt. Vernon," the mansion built by oilman H.L. Hunt, is one of many sumptuous estates lining the shores of White Rock Lake. Photo by Dan Hatzenbuehler.

BOTTOM LEFT: Elegant mansions and fine automobiles are the norm in Highland Park. Photo by Doug Milner.

make no apologies to anyone where their neighborhood is concerned. On average, a Preston Hollow home costs just as much as a Highland Park home and probably comes with considerably more land. Estates of two, three or more acres dominate here and give the area an atmosphere of regal remoteness.

Finally, out beyond Preston Hollow and stretching for miles from west to east along either side of Lyndon B. Johnson Freeway (Interstate 635) lies the populous, affluent vastness of what Dallasites during the past 20 years have come to call simply "North Dallas." That term frequently

ABOVE: Town Hall in Highland Park is a center of activity and government for this "island" community. Photo by Scott Metcalfe.

RIGHT: Lily pads float lazily on Turtle Creek which winds its way through one of Dallas' most lushly vegetated neighborhoods. Photo by Allan Kaye.

reaches beyond the corporate limits of Dallas proper to embrace the chain of burgeoning suburban communities along the city's northern perimeter.

But in a very real sense, "North Dallas" is more than a locale. It is a lifestyle, a philosophy, a psychological mind-set that recognizes no neatly drawn boundaries. It is a synonym for newness and glamour, a symbol of prestige and social arrival, and for many the epitome of "where it's at." Not all who live in North Dallas consider themselves a part of this phenomenon, of course, but it pervades the atmosphere nonetheless. It extends into the suburbs of Addison, Farmers Branch, Carrollton, Richard-

son and Plano, all separate cities, but each gaining incalculable benefits from the "North Dallas" phenomenon.

Until the early 1970s when large-scale commercial and residential development began in the LBJ Freeway corridor, little of North Dallas existed. Since then it has been the scene of explosive, unprecedented growth, and the area around the intersection of LBJ and the Dallas North Tollway, with the famed Galleria office/hotel/shopping center as its centerpiece, has virtually become a second "downtown." The pace is quicker here, the demeanor more harried, the tone more urgent, the action more frenetic, the traffic heavier. Some residents of the "old" Dallas find it all slightly dizzying, perhaps even a little unnerving, but North Dallasites seem to like it this way.

Of course, all residents of North Dallas are not carbon copies of each

other, and neither are all North Dallas neighborhoods. Homes in the northern quadrant of the county are available in a wide variety of styles and prices, ranging from older, relatively modest tract houses to multimillion-dollar castles built within the past few years. While the land is mostly flat to gently rolling, such neighborhoods as Bluffview, just south of Northwest Highway, are known for their dramatic terrain and natural beauty. Age groups and social preferences are a major factor in many North Dallas neighborhoods. The Village, an apartment area near Skillman Avenue and Northwest Highway, is populated mostly by young singles, and the personality of the area reflects that fact.

Far from being the sprawling homogenous mass it may appear from the air, Dallas represents an incredibly broad spectrum of ways to live and places to live. Regardless of whether you decide to make your home on the north, south, east or west side — or somewhere in between — Dallas offers a neighborhood where you can feel at home and a lifestyle you can enjoy.

Within the limits of your resources and imagination, you can find almost every conceivable type of living quarters and environment — from an apartment at the high-rise Manor House in the heart of downtown to a lakeside townhome with marina privileges, from a Turtle Creek condo with the skyline as a backdrop to an acre with a vegetable garden in some far suburb, from a stately Victorian home in a preserved Oak Cliff neighborhood to a loft in a converted "Deep Ellum" warehouse, from a mini-ranch in Mesquite to a mansion in Highland Park. Whether you prefer stimulation or relaxation, opulence or simplicity, bright lights and joyful noise or the muted chirp of crickets in the dusk, the choice is yours.

CHAPTER 11

Strong Bodies

By Robert Vernon

Dallas hospitals do an estimated $1.2 billion in business each year. Growth can be attributed to the aggressive approach the Dallas medical community has taken toward improving its standing in research and treatment.

Pathologists in local hospital laboratories seek the answers to some of life's most puzzling questions. Photo by Doug Milner.

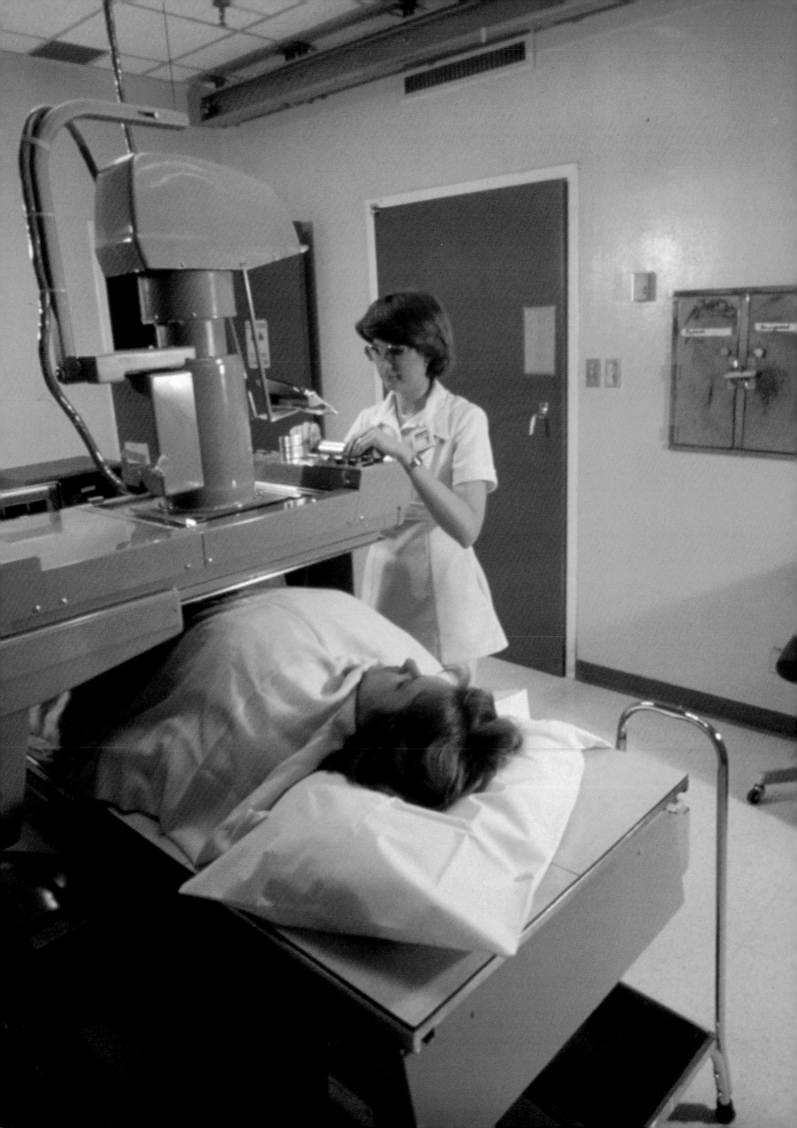

"The sick people of this city have a right to demand more accommodations. Humanity demands it. . . . I shall never tire until something is done in the interest of the poor sick people in my care."

Dr. John Carter, city health officer, excerpted from an impassioned plea to the City Council in 1887.

To say that Dr. John Carter was steamed is probably an enormous historical understatement. In 1887, Carter was part of a frustrated Dallas medical community trying in vain to provide adequate medical care to the city's growing population.

At the time, the city's lone hospital, a two-story building at Wood and Houston streets in the heart of the city's red light district, treated mainly indigents and was considered unclean and unsafe by a large number of Dallas residents.

Carter and other physicians watched in dismay as many of the area's sick and injured opted to make the long trek to Galveston to be treated at the State Medical College.

In many ways, it appeared to Carter as if medical care in Dallas had not progressed much beyond the treatment that Dr. John Cole, who set up the city's first medical practice in 1843, dispensed from horseback.

Apparently Carter's plea did not fall on deaf ears, as Parkland Hospital opened its doors seven years later. High praise was heaped on the hospital, which newspapers reported to be "the most substantial, capacious and elegant hospital in the state." Two years later, St. Paul's Sanitarium was accepting patients. Then came a nurses training school, and in 1903,

LEFT: Dallas medical facilities use the latest technology available for the diagnosis of disorders and the treatment of patients. Wadley photo.

TOP: Baylor University Medical Center is Dallas' largest general hospital and the largest private general voluntary hospital in Texas, not to mention the second largest in the nation. Photo by Jeff Hampton.

ABOVE: Dallas medical professionals put their patients' health, comfort and well-being first.

Texas Baptists bought the 14-room Good Samaritan Hospital with the help of a $50,000 contribution from Colonel C.C. Slaughter and opened the Texas Baptist Memorial Sanitarium.

A little more than a century later, Carter's fervent plea continues to echo through the halls of medicine in Dallas, serving as an inspiration always to strive to provide better medical care because, as Carter said, "humanity demands it."

Carter would be pleased to see what has happened in the 100 years since he stood before city fathers. Where only one hospital stood in those days, 80 exist in the Dallas/Fort Worth area today.

Dallas hospitals do an estimated $1.2 billion in business each year, and according to a recent study by the Texas Hospital Association commissioned by *The Dallas Morning News*, that figure could grow two-and-a-half times within five years — a staggering $4.2 billion by referrals.

Growth can be attributed to the aggressive approach the Dallas medical community has taken toward improving its standing in research and treatment.

The first step was taken in 1949, when Southwestern Medical School was made a part of the University of Texas system. Currently, the school is one of the nation's leading medical and research institutions. Eight of the nine medical members from Texas in the National Academy of Sciences and three recent Nobel Prize winners are on staff at UT Southwestern Medical Center-Dallas.

Parkland Memorial Hospital established the first pediatric trauma center in the nation and the first Level 1 trauma center in the state. Parkland also features one of the top 10 civilian burn units in the nation.

Baylor University Medical Center is the largest hospital in Texas and the second largest in the nation. Only

Pittsburgh's Presbyterian-University Hospital performs more liver transplants than Baylor. The National Institutes of Health ranked Baylor as one of only five U.S. centers for excellence in adult liver transplants along with Pittsburgh, the University of Minnesota, the University of California at Los Angeles and the Mayo Clinic.

Methodist Medical Center has one of the largest organ donation centers and is among the six largest kidney transplant centers in the nation. Methodist also boasts a trauma center

that, like Parkland's, has been certified as Level 1, giving Dallas two of the three Level 1 trauma centers in Texas.

At Humana Hospital-Medical City Dallas, the International Craniofacial Institute, founded in 1986, treats patients from around the world. It also is renowned for work in pediatric neurosurgery and pediatric orthopedics.

Presbyterian Hospital of Dallas is moving in elite circles with the acquisition of the Leksell Gamma Unit, otherwise known as a "Gamma Knife," for non-invasive neurosurgery.

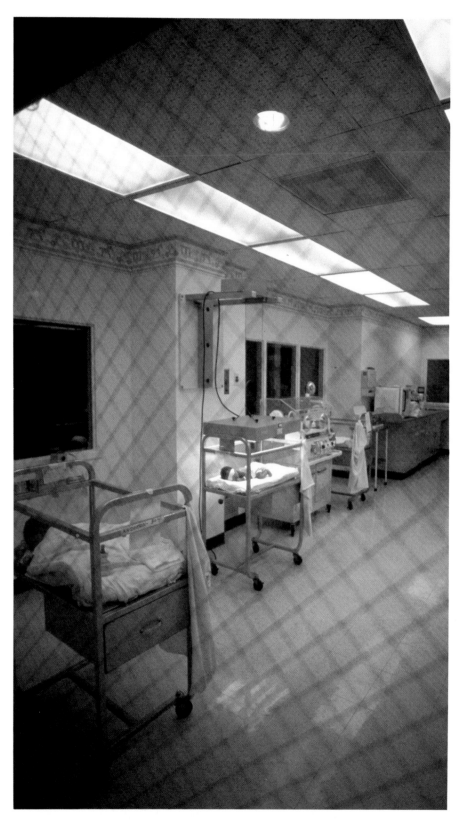

Presbyterian's "Gamma Knife" is one of only five units in operation worldwide.

Though Fred Meyer, head of the Greater Dallas Chamber's Medical Task Force, calls the health-care business in this city "one of the best-kept secrets in town," the word is getting out.

Much of the thanks for Dallas' newfound celebrity in the medical world comes to rest at the doorstep of UT Southwestern.

In 1985, two of the center's researchers, Dr. Michael Brown and

CENTER: Patients at local medical centers are the beneficiaries of countless hours of medical research and analysis. Photo by Doug Milner.

ABOVE: Thousands of new residents enter the world through Dallas maternity wards each year. Photo by John Hethorn.

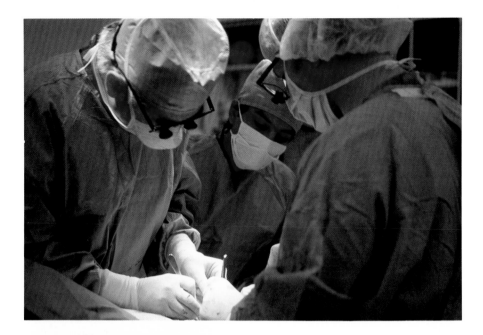

Dr. Joseph Goldstein, won the Nobel Prize in medicine for their discovery of a genetic defect that causes elevated cholesterol levels. The white-hot spotlight of the international medical community suddenly was focused on Dallas. Three years later, Brown and Goldstein added to the stature of the medical school when a cholesterol-controlling drug that was developed from their research reached the marketplace.

In 1988, Dr. Johann Deisenhofer, who has a dual appointment as professor of biochemistry at UT Southwestern and an investigator for the Howard Hughes Medical Institute, became the third Nobel Prize recipient on staff when he won the award in chemistry for his work in describing the structure of a protein needed in photosynthesis.

Add these developments to the international attention heaped on UT Southwestern following Dr. Scott M. Grundy's work at the school's Center for Human Nutrition, and it is easy to see why Dr. Kern Wildenthal, president of UT Southwestern Medical Center, believes Dallas will soon be internationally prominent in the health care arena. The key to that prominence, Wildenthal says, is UT Southwestern Medical Center.

And he is probably right. When construction is completed on Zale-Lipshy University Medical Center, a $40-million, 160-bed research hospital for complicated referral cases, the combination of the hospital and the medical school will form the hub of a dynamic, innovative and high-profile medical community in Dallas.

One study commissioned by UT Southwestern suggests that in the next five to 10 years, current expansion at the medical center will create nearly 3,000 additional jobs in medical services and retail industries, as well as approximately $126 million in additional overall economic activity.

And so it grows. In 1987, the Susan G. Komen Foundation announced its affiliation with UT Southwestern Medical Center and Baylor University Medical Center to establish a breast cancer research, treatment and education center.

With the medical community on the upswing, the business community has been quick to respond.

Phillips Petroleum Company has teamed with Wadley Technologies Inc., parent company of Dallas' largest private blood bank, in a $5 million joint venture to develop commercial applications for blood research being conducted at Wadley.

Unlike a century ago, no city health officer would have to go before the city council today to beg for better medical services. Truth is, city officials probably would turn the tables and ask what they could do to help.

Why? There's no mystery here. The answer is: Money, and lots of it.

A study conducted by Southern Methodist University revealed that referral patients and accompanying family members spend more than $8,000 per hospital admission.

What can that mean for a city's economy? Consider that in 1986, Dallas hospitals did approximately $166.1 million in business with patients from outside the Dallas area. Sounds good, but in comparison, Houston hospitals reaped roughly $300 million from patients who came from outside Harris County. Dallas, which attracts approximately 25 percent of its patients from outside the area compared to 35 percent for Houston, still has a ways to go.

In many ways, it is difficult to compare the industry of medicine in the two cities. The Houston medical

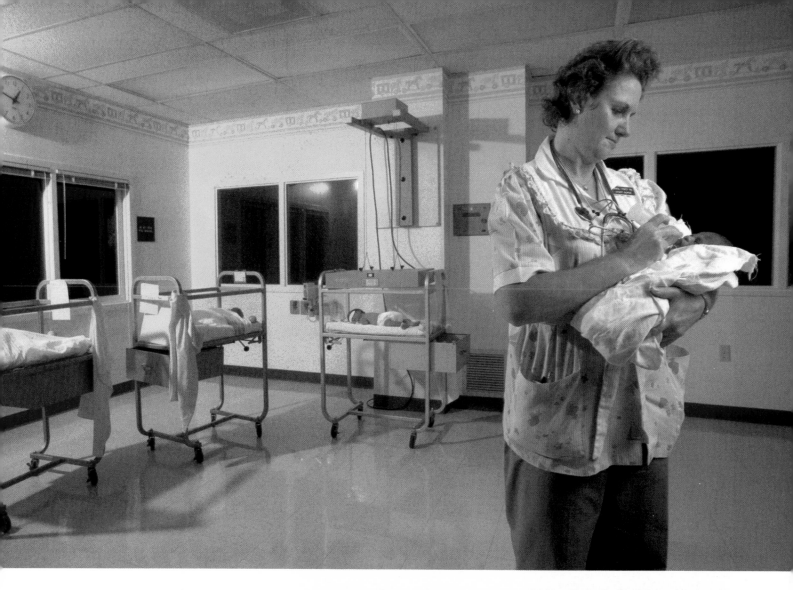

community was built over a period of 40 years. The growth of the 546-acre Texas Medical Center with its concentration of facilities has been carefully planned and monitored by city officials and medical administrators.

Dallas, meanwhile, has featured a more decentralized approach, with hospitals spread throughout the county. This scattershot setup grew out of a desire for community convenience, but it has made cooperation and support between institutions more difficult.

The Chamber's Medical Task Force represents an unprecedented move toward cooperation on the part of Dallas' medical community. Through the task force, comprised of medical experts and business leaders, Dallas is launching a concentrated effort to market its entire health-care product to doctors and their referral patients throughout the region, the state and indeed the world. Rather than competing for larger pieces of a

TOP LEFT: Dallas surgical teams are able to perform the most complex procedures available anywhere, with the area becoming a major center for organ transplantation. Photo by Scott Metcalfe.

BOTTOM LEFT: Patients at Dallas medical centers benefit from an enthusiastic and energetic volunteer force. Wadley photo.

TOP: A newborn baby gets a little tender loving care at Methodist Medical Center. Photo by Doug Milner.

ABOVE: Community events like the annual Jingle Bell Run raise funds for Wadley Blood Center and other medical facilities. Wadley photo.

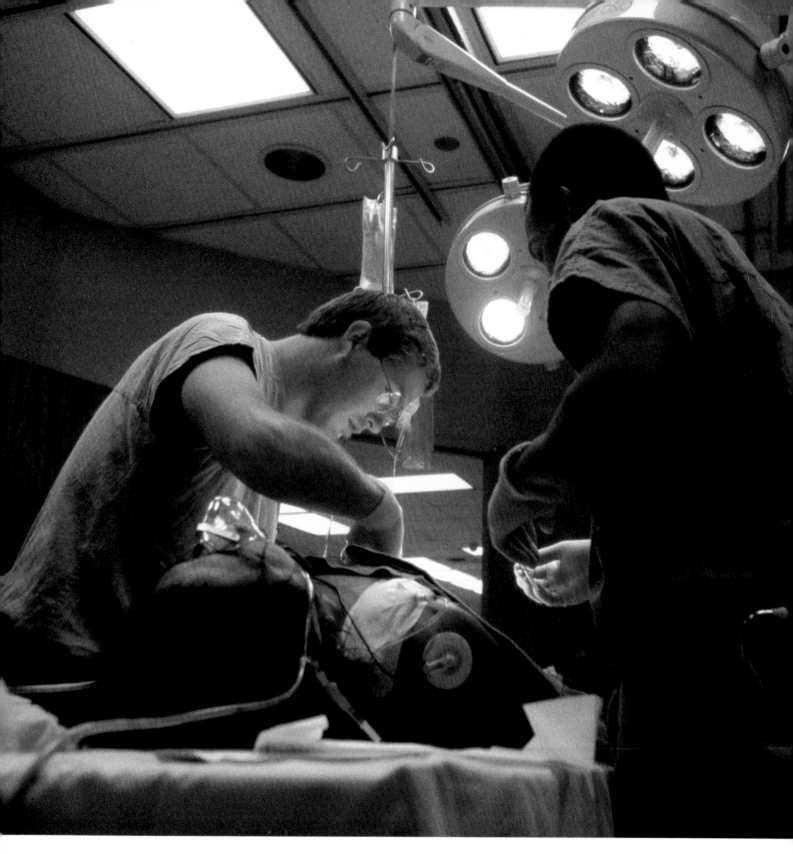

ABOVE: A patient undergoes preliminary treatment
in the emergency room at Baylor Medical Center.
Photo by Doug Milner.

RIGHT: Wadley Institutes of Molecular Medicine is
a leading center for blood and tissue research as well
as for patient treatment and education. Wadley photo.

limited pie, health facilities are now
working to increase the size of the pie,
thus giving everyone a larger piece.

That is not to say that the competitive atmosphere has not helped
spur the growth of Dallas as a major
medical center. Each facility has
mounted aggressive efforts to move to
the medical forefront. In addition to
spending money for advanced medical
technology, administrators have

sought the finest medical talent and
tried to entice them to pack up their
stethoscopes, tongue depressors and
rubber gloves and move to Dallas.

These efforts have been met with
considerable success. In 1984, Dr.
Goran Klintmalm came to Dallas
from the University of Pittsburgh
Medical School, where he worked
with the nation's most renowned liver
transplant pioneer, Dr. Thomas Starzl.

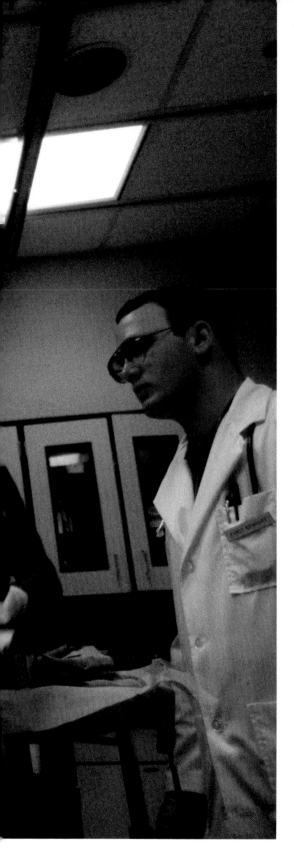

Klintmalm became the director of transplantation for Baylor's Department of Surgery.

Dr. William Steves Ring, a prominent Minnesota heart surgeon and one of the nation's most active heart transplantation specialists, joined the staff of UT Southwestern Medical Center in 1988 as professor and chairman of thoracic and cardiovascular surgery. He came to Dallas with the goal of building a world-class heart transplant program.

Dr. Ian R. Munro, a highly respected specialist in the field of craniofacial surgery, left the stagnating world of socialized medicine in Canada to work with Dr. Kenneth Salyer at Humana Hospital-Medical City.

Dallas also has a strong foothold in the world of preventive medicine.

Since the publication of his first book, *Aerobics,* in 1968, Dr. Kenneth H. Cooper has been at the forefront of the battle to prevent disease. An international fitness star of the highest magnitude, Cooper is credited with helping launch the jogging boom of the 1970s.

At his Institute for Aerobics Research, Cooper has helped spread the gospel of healthy lifestyle in a continuing battle against heart disease.

The same can be said of Dr. Scott Grundy, whose name looms large in the field of nutrition research.

At the Center for Human Nutrition at UT Southwestern, Grundy and his researchers search for ways to reduce cholesterol through a scientific approach to nutrition, and reduce the number of heart attacks in the process.

"We are among a handful of nutrition research centers in the country that have the capacity to do this," Grundy says.

Whether it is prevention or treatment, the Dallas medical community continues to rise in stature. But to take the next step in big medicine will require big business.

The involvement of the business community is vital to improving and expanding the medical industry in Dallas.

The potential is there, and so is the desire.

CHAPTER 12

Bright Minds

By Robert Vernon

Education represents the front line in a community's or region's battle to ensure future excellence and growth in business, government, health, social services, recreation — almost every vital aspect of life.

Dallas Hall was the first building erected on the Southern Methodist University campus when the school opened in 1915. Photo by Doug Milner.

149

It is an opportunity Dr. Robert Rutford has always wanted; the type of challenge that during even a very long professional career might come only once. If and when the opportunity does present itself, there is generally only one chance to grasp it and get it right.

Rutford has the opportunity, and he does not plan to mess it up.

On June 28, 1989, the Texas Legislature passed a bill to expand the University of Texas at Dallas (UTD) to a four-year university. It was a move that could have a dramatic impact on higher education not only in Dallas, but all of the Southwest.

Under the legislation, the university, which previously offered only upper-level and graduate courses, was allowed to admit freshmen and sophomores beginning in the summer of 1990.

For Rutford, president of the university, it is the opportunity of a professional lifetime. The prospect of a four-year university is the most exciting challenge of his career.

"The list of questions about how to expand a four-year undergraduate program is as long as you'd like to make it," he says. "But the opportunity to do it right — to become a model program for the next century — that's exciting.

"Here is an opportunity to design a core curriculum and to provide an innovative and high-quality educational experience from the ground up. As a young university, there are fewer turf problems, and it will be easier for us to take a fresh look at new curricula and imaginative approaches for teaching and scheduling."

Indeed, while Rutford faces an enormous challenge, Dallas is a place where such challenges are viewed as golden opportunities — especially when they concern education.

After all, education represents the front line in a community's or region's battle to ensure future excellence and growth in business, government, health, social services, recreation — almost every vital aspect of life.

For that reason, education is a

subject that is not taken lightly in Dallas. Nor is it taken lightly in Texas, a state that in the late 1980s inacted massive reforms to improve the quality and equality of public education.

At the core of the Dallas-area's educational community are the public school systems, and especially, Dallas Independent School District (DISD). With more than 132,000 students at more than 200 facilities, DISD is the eighth-largest public school system in the United States. Dallas has one of the best "large" public school systems in the country, but to DISD administrators, that is not good enough; they are working to make DISD one of the best public school systems — period.

Dr. Marvin Edwards, who became superintendent of schools in 1988 after serving in the same capacity in Topeka, Kansas, immediately set ambitious goals for raising student achievement scores and reducing the dropout rate. By the middle of his second full year as superintendent, there already was measurable improvement in both areas.

Ever since the first public schools opened in Dallas in the mid-1800s, innovation has been a regular practice in local schools. Of special note is DISD's magnet high schools where students have the opportunity to take concentrations of career-oriented courses in fields such as arts, business and health sciences.

While these programs address student career goals, DISD has established a curriculum that meets the needs of the community at large as well.

"I think the curriculum has been dynamic over the years across the country based on what our society needs," says Edwards. "We're already teaching more math and science than was the case in the past." Other studies reflecting the increasing emphasis on technology and a global marketplace are computer science, foreign languages and cultural awareness.

TOP LEFT: The Dallas Independent School District serves more than 132,000 students at more than 200 facilities. Photo by Doug Milner.

BOTTOM LEFT: A sculpture at the old Dallas Public Library building illustrates the enlightenment that comes from the pursuit of knowledge. Photo by Scott Metcalfe.

ABOVE: Dallas teachers strive for excellence in the classroom. Photo by John Hethorn.

TOP: The Central Library downtown is the heart of the Dallas Public Library System.

ABOVE: Through extracurricular activities such as athletics, students learn teamwork, discipline and physical skills. Photo by David J. Sams.

RIGHT: The Learning Resource Center at Northlake College, part of the Dallas County Community College District, is an example of the excellent educational facilities available to Dallas-area students. Photo by Dan Hatzenbuehler.

Another innovation, one that has earned national recognition and has become a model for such programs all over the country, is Adopt-A-School. Managed by the Greater Dallas Chamber, businesses adopt schools for which they supply tutors and volunteers, physical resources, supplies and monetary support. In 1989, 1,371 business partnerships were in place, with $2.9 million in funds, materials and in-kind services donated to Dallas schools.

Dallas businesses also support the DISD's magnet high schools and Skyline Career Development Center.

Working alongside DISD are kindergartens and Montessori schools, private schools and suburban public school districts. Some of the latter — schools in Richardson, Highland Park, Plano, Mesquite, Irving and Garland, to name a few — are considered some of the best public school systems in the United States.

Private schools run the gamut of curricula and sponsorship, from church-related schools such as First Baptist Academy in downtown Dallas, to private college preparatory schools with longstanding traditions of excellence such as St. Mark's School of

Texas and Jesuit Preparatory School, both for boys, and The Hockaday School for girls.

These primary and secondary schools undergird a system of higher education that is second to none. Dallas first became a center of higher education in 1915 when Southern Methodist University (SMU) opened on a hill north of the city. The school became possible when Dallas business leaders gave 133 acres and several thousand dollars of seed money to establish a major university in the area.

Over the years the city grew out to meet and surround SMU, and the university itself has grown to become one of the nation's premier centers of learning. With enrollment of 8,600, SMU offers more than 80 undergraduate majors. The university's Edwin L. Cox School of Business is one of the nation's top-ranked business schools. Also receiving national praise are the School of Engineering and Applied Science, the School of Law and Perkins School of Theology.

SMU also is well known for its sophisticated research capabilities. In July 1989, Dr. Eugene Herrin, a geophysicist in SMU's Institute for the Study of Earth and Man, received a $15-million grant to build a seismic

system for monitoring nuclear weapons tests.

The grant came from the Defense Advanced Research Projects Agency (DARP). It is by far the largest in the school's history. In fact, it topped its own previous grant, which was a $3.8-million, two-year federal contract to Herrin to develop this very project.

"It's very interesting work scientifically, and it can really make a difference to the country," says Dr. George Reddien, dean of SMU's Division of Graduate Studies and Research.

The seismic system uses computers to analyze the ground motion caused by nuclear explosions. The system is capable of detecting and locating seismic events down to Richter magnitude 4 a quarter of the way around the world. It also can order the events, from those most likely to be nuclear tests to seismic disturbances caused by other factors, such as mining or demolition.

The data is transmitted to a human analyst, who can more quickly determine if a seismic event is a nuclear blast and if it meets the size limits determined by treaties signed by the United States and the Soviet Union in 1974 and 1976.

The roots of the SMU project can be traced to a 1987 plan by the techni-

cal wing of the United Nations' Council on Disarmament. The plan outlines the construction of a global seismic network to help ensure compliance with treaties that restrict nuclear weapons testing. The SMU system represents the major United States contribution to the UN network.

The federal grant for SMU came as very important positive news during a time when the university has been evaluating its purposes and goals. Leading that evaluation has been Dr. A. Kenneth Pye, the ninth president of the institution.

Pye came in during a period of

descending enrollment, a significant budget deficit, and an athletic scandal that left SMU without football for two years.

"I am here in administration for the scholars of the institution to have the resources they need to devote themselves to problems worthy of solution," Pye said when he took over the president's post in August 1987.

"The challenges of SMU are well-equalled by the opportunities. There's no reason why — if we decide what we want to do and limit what we can do well to what we can afford — we cannot be spectacular."

Pye's attitude is shared by the administrators of numerous institutions in the area, which together form an educational community that could best be described as "spectacular."

The Dallas area has one of the most dynamic and diversified higher education communities in the United States. Within 150 miles of Dallas can be found: Austin College (Sherman), Baylor College of Dentistry, Baylor University (Waco), Collin County Community College District, Dallas Baptist University, Dallas County Community College District, East Texas State University (Commerce),

LEFT: Cadets in the ROTC program at Plano High School learn discipline, patriotism and the meaning of serving one's country. Photo by Doug Milner.

ABOVE: As superintendent of the Dallas Independent School District, Dr. Marvin Edwards is working to provide Dallas children with the best education possible. Photo by Carolyn McGovern.

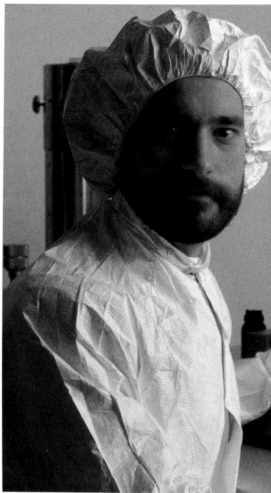

ABOVE: *Higher education knows no bounds in the Dallas area. Photo by Scott Metcalfe.*

CENTER: *Research conducted at Dallas-area colleges and universities benefits the area's booming high-tech industry. Photo by Scott Metcalfe.*

RIGHT: *Perkins School of Theology at Southern Methodist University trains tomorrow's ministers, counselors and spiritual leaders. Photo by Doug Milner.*

Midwestern State University (Wichita Falls), Southern Methodist University, Tarrant County Junior College District (Fort Worth), Texas Christian University (Fort Worth), Texas College of Osteopathic Medicine (Fort Worth), Texas Wesleyan University (Fort Worth), Texas Woman's University (Denton), The University of Texas at Arlington, The University of Texas at Dallas, The University of Texas Southwestern Medical Center at Dallas, the University of Dallas and the University of North Texas (Denton).

These schools work independently, and together through organizations such as the Association for Higher Education of North Texas, to meet the needs of students as well as to provide degree programs geared toward the professional and business demands of the region.

A perfect example of this is high technology. Beginning with Texas Instruments and Collins Radio (now a part of Rockwell International) in the late 1950s, the Dallas area now is one of the world's leading centers of high-technology manufacturing and employment. In fact, the area is the No. 1 center for telecommunications industry employment, and overall, the region has earned the title of "Silicon Prairie."

That being the case, there is an ever-increasing need for individuals

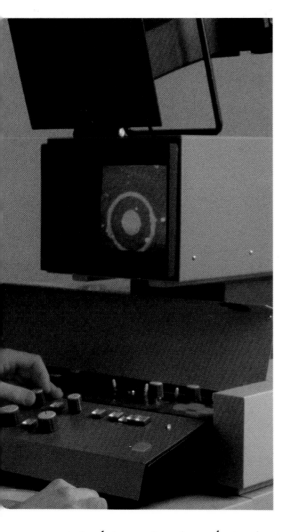

trained in engineering, electronics, computers and other technical disciplines. Which brings us back to the University of Texas at Dallas (UTD) and its recent designation as a four-year undergraduate university.

UTD has a strong technical and scientific orientation, dating back to its origins in 1961 as the Graduate Research Center of the Southwest. That institution was founded by Erik Jonsson, Cecil Green and Eugene McDermott, who dreamed of a first-class higher education and research institution for the bright, young talent at their growing company, Texas Instruments.

Now more than ever, there is a great need for graduates to work in the high-tech business community. In the mid-1980s, a business-led task force took a hard look at the area's high-

technology resources and determined that the local demand for engineers was on the rise, while the supply was not.

UT Arlington and SMU both produce engineering graduates, but they cannot meet the demand in the area's burgeoning high-tech business climate.

Despite the absence of the "brain centers" like those at Stanford University and the University of California at Berkeley, which helped establish the Silicon Valley, or the Harvard-MIT connection that spawned Boston's famed "Route 128," the task force found that the North Texas area was still sprouting highly concentrated high-tech patches. With a little nurturing, it was believed that these patches too would grow and create something special in North Texas.

So, the push was on to put UTD in a position to fill the need. It is an appointment that UTD faculty members are not taking lightly.

"It is clear that our challenge is to provide technical and educational leadership for the high technology, information-based industries of Dallas/ Fort Worth, Texas and the nation. Regionally, preeminence is too modest a goal," wrote Blake Cherrington, dean of the Erik Jonsson School of Engineering and Computer Science at

UTD, in a letter published in the UTD engineering and computer science newsletter.

"To provide superior service to the community, we must be leaders and not followers in the creation of knowledge — new principles and practices that will form the basis for industries of the future — and we must be leaders in transmitting new knowledge to the professionals who will provide leadership for the state and the nation.

"To fulfill this mission, we will strive to develop graduate research programs and undergraduate instructional programs of the first rank — programs of the same quality, if not the same magnitude as Stanford, Berkeley, Illinois and MIT. From this, all things will follow."

But to recruit the best and brightest undergraduates, school officials realized that a curriculum focused entirely on engineering, mathematics and computers might be a hard sell to those highly motivated students that also wanted a side order of Russian history or Shakespeare to go along with their main course of calculus and systems engineering.

As a result, UTD officials have approached several four-year colleges and universities without engineering programs to propose a "three-two"

ABOVE: *While they may dress casually, Dallas students take their studies very seriously. Photo by Scott Metcalfe.*

RIGHT: *UT Dallas' Callier Center for Communication Disorders is one of the leading research centers studying disorders ranging from deafness in infants to loss of hearing in the aged to recovery of speech and language by stroke patients.*

solution. Under a "three-two" plan, a student would spend three years at a partner institution taking courses to satisfy its degree requirements, usually in science or mathematics, as well as meeting the prerequisites for entry into electrical engineering. The student's last two years would be spent at UTD studying electrical engineering.

After five years, the student qualifies for a bachelor of arts or bachelor of science degree from the partner institution, and a bachelor of science in electrical engineering from UTD.

The first three-two agreement

was ratified in January, 1988, with Austin College in Sherman. In August, 1988, Texas Woman's University agreed to a three-two arrangement. In April 1989, Abilene Christian University joined the three-two program, and at this writing plans were under way for an agreement with the University of Dallas.

The real challenge, says UTD President Robert Rutford, will be to accomplish all of UTD's goals and yet to maintain the same focus on excellence upon which the school was founded and currently operates.

That is no small task, for UTD already has a solid national reputation in mathematics, basic science, computers and engineering.

And it is those areas and upon that reputation that UTD is planning to expand.

"We will not be all things to all people," Rutford says. "Our emphasis will be science, mathematics and engineering. If you want to major in Russian history, UTD will not be the place to do it."

"The concept here is not another UT Austin or Texas A&M; it's a Texas-style MIT," says Peter O'Donnell, one of the leaders of the movement to expand UTD to a four-year undergraduate institution.

That sentiment is echoed by Texas Gov. Bill Clements, who says: "I suspect that in due course, in the next several years, that will turn into literally another Cal-Tech or MIT or an institution of that caliber."

Indeed, coupled with a new engineering school, which opened in the fall of 1986 and graduated its first students in 1989, the newly bestowed status could give UTD a big boost toward becoming one of the most academically rigorous universities in the country.

As a result, UTD is being viewed as the Southwest's answer to the highly selective schools on the east and west coasts. That is a huge leap

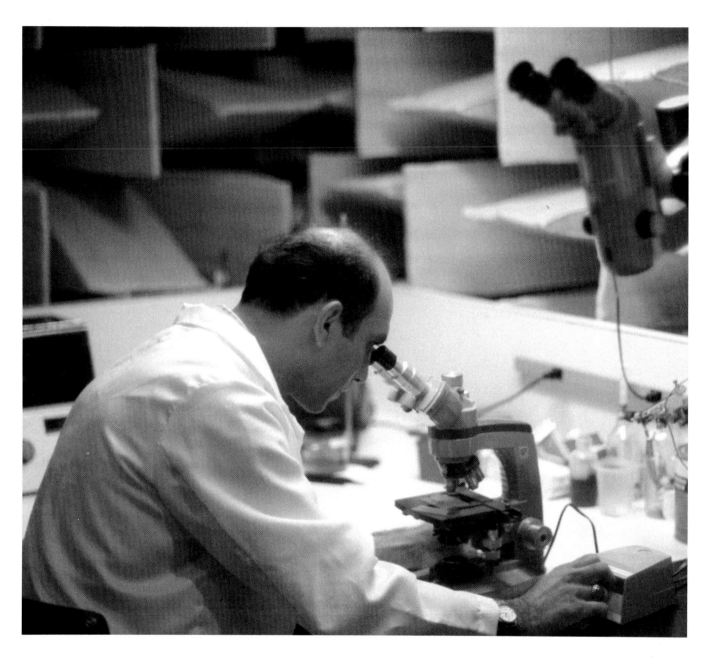

for a school conceived and founded as a private graduate-level research institute way back in 1962.

Even so, Rutford is quick to point out that such a momentous leap will not come in a single bound. It will, he says, take many smaller jumps. And as for the "Texas-style MIT" label, well, Rutford is glad everyone is so optimistic, but frankly, he grimaces every time he hears it.

"UTD does not intend to simply copy MIT's approach, but to aspire to create a highly competitive program that emphasizes the sciences," he said in an interview with *The Dallas Morning News*. "It is unfortunate that we got stuck with that label. MIT is not a bad school to emulate, but one has to understand that MIT is 100 years old, has a large endowment and strong programs not just in science and engineering. To expect UTD to emulate it in one, five or 10 years is just not possible."

Certainly, it is a tremendous task, but one that Rutford and other concerned observers believe will eventually happen. By way of example, O'Donnell points in the direction of the University of Texas Southwestern Medical Center.

"They just kept after it, and they have become one of the best medical schools in the country," he says.

Indeed, the task is large, but so is the commitment, and Rutford is not about to let anyone at UTD forget it.

"I have told our faculty members that we are going to be a four-year undergraduate school, and anybody who doesn't want to come along should get out now."

The commitment is clear. So too is the message.

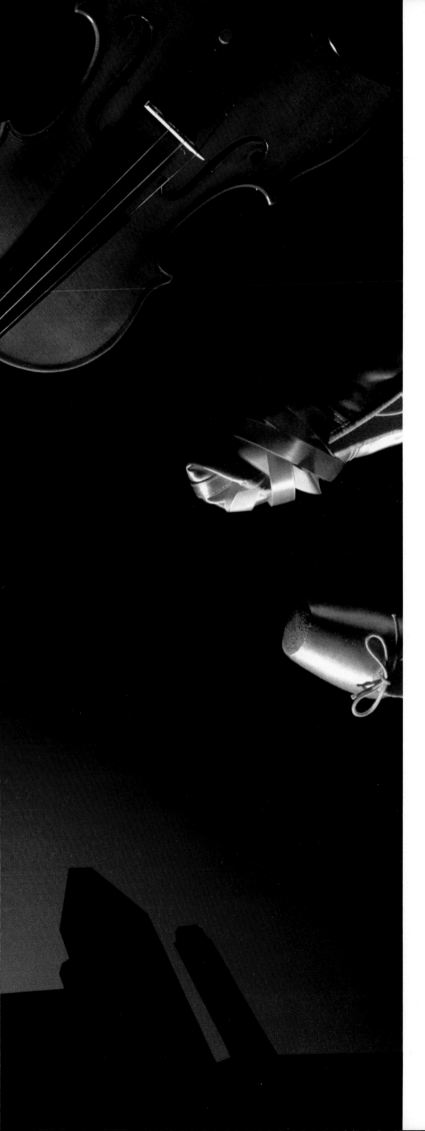

CHAPTER 13

Artistic Flair

By Glenn Mitchell

Interest in the arts as a civilizing and unifying influence has remained a Dallas hallmark, beginning with an abiding interest in the highest forms of musical, dramatic and visual arts, and continuing through entertainment at its most casual and personal.

Opera, theater, music, fine arts, dance — Dallas has it all in large quantities and world-class quality.

In 1855, barely more than a decade after Dallas' founding, the young town already boasted Field's Opera House, the first of the city's 19th-century performing arts venues. In that same decade, immigrants from France led by Victor Prosper Considerant founded La Reunion, a colony of artists and craftsmen near Dallas.

Field's is long forgotten, and Reunion lives on in name only with Reunion Tower and Reunion Arena downtown. Interest in the arts as a civilizing and unifying influence, however, has remained intact, beginning with an abiding interest in the highest forms of musical, dramatic and visual arts, and continuing through entertainment at its most casual and personal. That interest has been enforced by a respect for the past and a fascination with the future.

Given Dallas' long love affair with the fine arts, it is appropriate that the city's first artistic establishment was an opera house, at least in name. A century later, in 1957, the creation of the Dallas Opera catapulted the city into international notice. The company presented the American debuts of singers Joan Sutherland, Jon Vickers and Placido Domingo, and director Franco Zefferelli, and it was the sponsor of Maria Callas' first U.S. triumphs. In addition to the standard repertoire, the Opera mounted the first American production of a Vivaldi opera of the Baroque period, and in 1988 gave the world premiere of Dominick Argento's "The Aspern Papers," which it commissioned. The demand for opera was also responsible for the formation in 1982 of the Lyric Opera of Dallas, which specializes in musical theater, operetta and light opera.

The elder statesman of the city's musical enterprises is the Dallas Symphony Orchestra, which marked its 89th anniversary in 1989 by moving to the Morton H. Meyerson Symphony Center, designed by renowned architect I.M. Pei. The symphony, conducted by Eduardo Mata, frequently plays host to world-renowned soloists and guest conductors, and during the past decade has gained recognition through a major recording contract and tours of Europe and South America.

Other classical music organizations include Voices of Change, a new music ensemble, which delights devotees of modern chamber and vocal music, the Fine Arts Chamber Players, the Dallas Chamber Orchestra and the Dallas Bach Society.

In addition to the wealth of performances by Dallas artists, the list of

touring musicians that grace Dallas stages is augmented by Allegro Dallas (formerly the Dallas Civic Music Association) and the Dallas Classic Guitar Society, which sponsor recitals by leading soloists and ensembles. The International Theatrical Arts Society (TITAS) has added to performances by such Dallas companies as the Dallas Black Dance Theatre and Dancers Unlimited by importing troupes ranging from the

ABOVE: *The Dallas Museum of Art is the site of numerous art festivals and shows. Photo by Brian McWeeney.*

TOP LEFT: *The Dallas Opera is known for its world-class productions.*

BOTTOM LEFT: *Dallas is a regular stop for national and international touring ballet companies.*

ultra-modern Alvin Ailey American Dance Company and Pilobolus to the classically trained stars from the Bolshoi Ballet.

Dallas' enthusiasm for film is best represented by the annual USA Film Festival, which gives filmgoers an opportunity to see independently produced features, shorts and documentaries. Of the 55 films at the 1989 festival, a dozen were national or world premieres in a major, week-long event. Area universities and the Dallas Museum of Art are among other institutions that offer rich, diverse series of foreign and domestic films.

The Southwest Film and Video Archive contains 8,000 films, hundreds of videotapes and the Tyler Collection of once-lost African-American-produced films of the 1930s and 1940s.

Dallas' theatrical cornerstone is the Dallas Theater Center (DTC), which debuted in its Frank Lloyd Wright-designed theater on Turtle

Creek in 1959. Among the high water marks of DTC's colorful history was the world premier of Preston Jones' "A Texas Trilogy."

Dallas runs the gamut from established, actor equity companies to smaller, experimental theaters. The varied list includes Theater Three, Dallas Repertory Theater, Greenville Avenue Pocket Sandwich Theater, Pegasus Theater, Undermain Theater and Deep Ellum Theater Garage. This line-up is enhanced by Dallas Summer Musicals, touring Broadway shows and the Majestic Theatre Broadway Series.

No theatre city worth its salt would be without a summer Shakespeare Festival, and Dallas' is the second oldest free festival in the United States after New York's. The festival's productions have included traditional stagings of the great comedies, romances, histories and tragedies, plus such inventive updatings as "Two Gentlemen of Verona (Texas)."

Popular festivals join classical ones in the open air. Outdoor musical entertainment is a fixture of Dallas spring and summer evenings, whether it is a rock'n'roll show at the Starplex Amphitheater in Fair Park, a classical concert by the Dallas Symphony with listeners reclining comfortably on the grass with blankets and picnic baskets, or a night of jazz in the Arts District at the Dallas Museum of Art's annual Jazz Under the Stars series.

The downtown Arts District is the focal point of the arts in Dallas. It is already the home of the Morton H. Meyerson Symphony Center, the DTC Arts District Theater and the Dallas Museum of Art. Adjacent office buildings, churches and open spaces are also the site of numerous activities year-round: noontime concerts, annual Latin music, gospel and jazz concert series, art displays, festivals and theatrical and dance per-

formances. Talented students from the nearby Arts Magnet High School add a welcome dimension to the area's performances.

The Dallas Museum of Art (DMA), the anchor of the Arts District, moved from Fair Park to its present home in 1984. The museum owns significant collections of Pre-Columbian and African art and a large sampling from the American post-war period. Major exhibits which have toured the DMA include the Georgia O'Keeffe centennial and "An American Vision: Three Gener-

ations of Wyeth Art." The DMA was the only North American venue for "Images of Mexico: The Contribution of Mexico to 20th Century Art."

Dozens of galleries provide exhibition space for artists of both regional and international renown.

Dallasites who enjoy music, theatre and the visual arts can choose not only from established enterprises, but also from those on the cutting edge. Deep Ellum, the area just east of downtown along Elm Street, was a center of black blues and soul music in the early part of the 20th century. Then in the early 1980s after years of neglect and abandonment, the storefronts and warehouses became a bohemian area of artists' studios, music clubs and theaters.

The artists who work in Deep Ellum stage several festivals each year during which visitors can spend a day strolling through the area visiting galleries and street displays, or watching the artists at work in their studios. In addition, Deep Ellum's music clubs are the heart of the city's new music scene.

LEFT: Dallas' Shakespeare Festival often takes the Bard where he's never been before. Photo by Doug Milner.

ABOVE: The Morton H. Meyerson Symphony Center is the new home of the Dallas Symphony Orchestra.

TOP: *The Music Hall at Fair Park is the home of the Dallas Summer Musicals and other live productions. Photo by Benjamin Stewart.*

BOTTOM: *Children enjoy face painting at an outdoor arts festival. Photo by Benjamin Stewart.*

RIGHT: *Scarborough Faire brings Renaissance-style arts, crafts and activities to the countryside near Waxahachie. Photo by Allan Kaye.*

Deep Ellum's mixture of history and modernity blends in with the revival at an adjacent location — the Exposition Street and Fair Park area, further east from downtown. Fair Park has been the site of the annual Texas State Fair since 1887. The large, impressive Art Deco exhibit halls in the park were built in 1936 when Dallas hosted the six-month Texas Centennial Celebration. The structures were restored to their original splendor for the Texas Sesquicentennial Celebration in 1986.

While the State Fair comes and goes each October, Fair Park is the year-round home of several impressive museums. The Science Place looks equally to the past and future, with exhibitions ranging from robot dinosaurs and the China of 7,000 years ago, to super colliders. The Museum of Natural History gives a portrait of Texas' natural history during the past 100 million years (the museum also played host to the nationally touring "Ramses the Great" exhibit in 1989). The Museum of African-American Life and Culture, also based in Fair Park, stages exhibitions around the city.

Old City Park, located on a verdant 12-acre site just south of downtown, features 35 structures built in North Central Texas between 1840 and 1910 which have been carefully moved and restored to their original appearance.

The newest and most dramatic addition to the recording of Dallas history harkens back to the city's bleakest day, November 22, 1963. Called simply The Sixth Floor, this exhibit is located on the sixth floor of the former Texas School Book Depository from where Lee Harvey Oswald allegedly shot and killed President John F. Kennedy. Specially produced videos and carefully researched exhibits as well as a recorded walking tour cover in detail the early period of the Kennedy Presidency, his trip to Texas, the assassination and its aftermath, the investigation and the Kennedy legacy.

The city's concern for preserving its past is equalled by its hope for the future. Opportunities for children to enjoy art are as diverse as those for their parents. The Dallas Arboretum teaches youngsters about nature through tours and other activities. The Gateway Gallery children's wing at the Dallas Museum of Art offers exhibitions and activities aimed at young visitors, while the Van Gogh

program takes art appreciation and instruction into the Dallas Independent School District (DISD).

In addition to presenting a series of plays for young people, the Dallas Theater Center conducts classes in theater instruction for children ages three to 18 in its Teen/Children's Theater project. The Children's Arts and Ideas Foundation offers a summer program teaching visual arts, drama and music, and sponsors the Creative Alternative Programs through the DISD. The Dallas Public Library has a special children's section, and The Science Place at Fair Park offers summer programs for children.

Taking a very active role in these and other projects to promote the arts is the Dallas business community. Through the Business Committee for the Arts, the Northwood Institute and other organizations, businesses are encouraged to participate in artistic endeavors that not only benefit them but the community at large.

Corporations such as Frito-Lay and AT&T have long histories of artistic sponsorship, while Raymond Nasher, whose private sculpture collection just completed a two-year worldwide tour, is a prime example of individual commitment to Dallas' cultural foundation. The annual Obelisk Awards recognize these contributions.

Field's Opera House was suited to its time, but Dallas has never lost sight of the future while stopping to revere the past. Dallas' concern for celebrating what is lasting in the arts is equalled by its excitement over what is to come.

LEFT: Despite its western image, Dallas rocks as much as any modern city. Photo by Benjamin Stewart.

ABOVE: Majestic Theater has been the home of vaudeville, motion pictures, opera, Broadway and other productions for 70 years. Photo by Dan Hatzenbuehler.

CHAPTER 14

The Dallas Look

By Yvonne Saliba

Fashion observers consistently applaud all strata of Dallas society for a well-groomed and well-informed citizenry. The buyers who shop Dallas markets have coined an oft-used industry phrase: "If it doesn't sell in Dallas, it won't sell."

The windows of Neiman-Marcus' downtown store are a great place to get a look at the latest trends in fashion. Photo by Steve Vaughan.

171

Just as voters look to the New Hampshire primaries as a bell-cow of the political mind-set, American arbiters of style have come to look at Dallas as the proverbial clotheshorse of the nation. Dallas is as style conscious and fashion forward as any city in the nation — not as avant-garde as California or as formal as New York — but a harbinger of what will be worn and accepted as fashion in the heartland of America.

This passion for fashion is woven intricately throughout the history of the city, beginning with the Caddo Indians who occupied the North Texas area before the white settlers. They lived in permanent villages and had a domesticated culture.

The Caddos are renowned for having been preoccupied with their appearance. One French researcher, Jean Louis Berlandier, noted, "They never cease admiring themselves in their little looking glasses, which they never lay aside." The Caddos have also been described as having been vain people who also were preoccupied with ornaments and the paints with which they decorated their bodies.

Dallas, too, always has had the sense that appearances are important. Though the first settler, John Neely Bryan, wore the standard dress of deerskin pants, a shirt and moccasins (even on his wedding day), he was the epitome of 19th century decorum when he posed for a formal portrait with his wife Margaret Beeman. On that occasion, he dressed in a dark suit, starched white shirt and bow tie; Mrs. Bryan wore a dark dress with white collar.

The contingent of Europeans that organized the utopic community of La Reunion brought with them the manners and the habits of their native French, Swiss and Belgian cultures.

These artists, weavers, shoemakers, jewelers and craftsmen were unable to make it as agrarians, so many of them joined Dallas' mainstream population in 1858. Dallas came to know first-hand via these settlers the "chic" that has always been associated with Europeans, especially the French. That they had an affinity for fine things, even in the roughneck early days, is evidenced by the fact that by the beginning of the Civil War, Dallas had seven mercantile houses, a jeweler, shoemaker and milliner for its population of 500. Today, Dallas is said to have more shopping centers per capita than any other city in the United States — more than 800, including 16 regional shopping malls.

The arrival of the railroads in the 1870s made Dallas a key distribution point for goods going south, east and west. A century later, apparel is a billion-dollar industry employing close to 100,000 people statewide, and Dallas is its impetus for being.

Those early "terminus merchants," peddlers and merchants who followed railroad construction crews, were fore-runners of latter-day retail giants. Sanger Brothers, the first of the large retailers, opened in 1872 on Elm Street downtown. By 1873, the number had grown to 29 dry good stores. The first "skyscraper" in Dallas was built by Joseph Linz in 1899 for his jewelry store. And though sold to Gordon's of Houston in 1965, Linz remains a prominent Dallas jewelry store.

The giant merchandising industry of Dallas had a foothold in the warehouses of the 1890s, from which "drummers" sold goods by wagon throughout the Southwest. Descendants of that same profession — salesmen — today occupy some 2.2 million square feet at the Dallas Apparel Mart. The Apparel Mart is a private company, part of the Dallas Market Center, whose owner is Trammell Crow in partnership with Dai-Ichi, a Japanese life insurance company, and Equitable Financial Companies of New York.

The fashion industry as we know it today in Dallas, both from the per-

spective of retail and wholesale, began remarkably with two unrelated events in 1907.

Neiman-Marcus, the retailer that did more than any other to establish Dallas' fashion presence on the world scene, opened in downtown Dallas that year. Billed as "a new and exclusive place for fashionable women," the store was founded by Herbert Marcus Sr., his sister, Carrie Neiman, and her husband, Albert Neiman. The store achieved an international reputation via its founding hallmarks of attention to detail, outstanding and flamboyant merchandising and personalized service.

The store caught the fancy of the buying public and established itself among the aristocracy of retail stores in America. The Marcus family remained active in the store even after it was sold to the Carter Hawley Hale chain in 1968. Stanley Marcus, the son of Herbert, is considered one of the true retailing legends of the 20th century; the industry's "Stanley" award is named in his honor.

LEFT: Christmas decorations and accessories are the emphasis in this bank of showrooms at the Dallas Market Center. Photo by Michael Haynes.

ABOVE: With more shopping centers per capita than any city in the United States, Dallas is a shopper's paradise. Photo by David J. Sams.

Stanley Marcus' son, Richard, was the last family member to head the Neiman-Marcus operation. He left the business in 1988.

The other equally significant happening in 1907 was when August Lorch established Texas' first ready-to-wear jobbing house, manufacturing clothing for New York firms. The Lorch Company, which closed in 1989 after a devastating fire, was guided in its growth by August Lorch's son, Lester. Lester is also the founder of the group of manufacturers and wholesalers that organized in 1942 and is now known as the Southwest Apparel Manufacturers Association.

With Neiman-Marcus' stylish presence as a retailer, and the manufacturing seeds planted by Lorch in 1907 and by Higginbotham-Bailey-Logan in 1914, Dallas was well on its way to becoming a fashion center.

In 1926, a young Lebanese immigrant named Joseph Marion Haggar founded what was to become Dallas' largest apparel firm. The textile and merchandising prowess of Haggar revolutionized the menswear industry. Haggar Apparel Company remains Dallas-based and is owned by the founder's sons, Ed and Joe Haggar, as well as several of his grandchildren.

In the men's clothing industry, Haggar is recognized for stabilizing retail pricing, decentralizing the manufacture of his garments and for being the first in his field to advertise nationally. Haggar is also credited with adding the term "slacks" to modern usage as a term for trousers worn during "slack" times.

Retailing first flourished in downtown Dallas. However, in 1935 Volk Brothers made a prophetic move to the suburbs, and that exodus has characterized Dallas retailing ever since. Volk Brothers (which became Colbert's in 1970) chose Highland Park Village for its location. When it was developed in 1931, the center was

the nation's first planned suburban shopping center, complete with off-street parking. Still thriving, Highland Park Village houses expensive boutiques and is considered a prime location.

The media sat up and took notice of Dallas' fashion status in a 1937 article in *Fortune* Magazine. "Perfect clothes are as much the cultural expression of Dallas as art is of Toledo," the article proclaimed.

An opulent expression of Dallas' fashion gold mine is the Texas Fashion Group Collection at the University of North Texas. This resplendent collection contains much of Carrie Marcus Neiman's personal wardrobe, as well as gowns designed by Cristobal Balenciaga for Claudia Heard de Osborne, a Texas woman with strong ties to Dallas. De Osborne, who had lived in Spain during her marriage to an heir to a Spanish sherry fortune, wore complete and opulent ensembles by Balenciaga, one of Spain's greatest fashion designers. He later achieved international fame as a couturier in Paris .

If Dallas' national reputation was first created by Neiman-Marcus, it has been nurtured through the years by the hundreds of retailers who have created a virtual shopping mecca here. Sophistication, style and elegance are ordinary traits of most Dallas women, who easily out-glamorize their counterparts in most cities. And that trait is world renowned. People in Dallas spend money on clothes, and historically they have had the goods right at their fingertips.

Names such as Sanger-Harris, Titche-Goettinger, Dreyfus and Son and E.M. Kahn no longer are names on retail marquees here, but their early influence continues to be felt. Many have been absorbed into larger conglomerates; Sanger-Harris is now

LEFT: *Wholesale buyers get an orientation and directions to the massive World Trade Center. Photo by Michael Haynes.*

TOP: *Highland Park Village is known as the nation's oldest shopping center, and today it still is one of Dallas' most elegant. Photo by Scott Metcalfe.*

ABOVE: *Another Fall line is debuted in Dallas.*

Foley's, and Titche-Goettinger became Joske's which itself became Dillard's.

There has been rapid growth in the wholesale industry as well. The Monday of the October 1949 apparel show is remembered as the first day the Dallas Market had a million-dollar day without its salesmen traveling. During the 1950s and '60s, Dallas grew to be the third largest apparel manufacturing center in the United States. The gigantic Apparel Mart opened its doors in 1964 and has seen significant expansions in its size.

The 1970s brought the beginning of the influx of major names in American retailing to Dallas. Also, high fashion designers based in New York's garment district began to show their collections at the Dallas Market. There is an impressive retail contingent now represented in Dallas, and virtually every major fashion house shows its collection to buyers in Dallas.

Catalog shopping became a way of life for upscale Americans thanks to the founding in 1970 of The Horchow Collection by Roger Horchow of Dallas. The catalog spawned an entire new industry. Horchow was acquired by the Neiman-Marcus Group in 1989. Interestingly, Horchow began his career at Neiman-Marcus. Also a large catalog force, the Neiman-Marcus *Christmas Book* has a worldwide circulation of 3.4 million.

Many allied fields have thrived due to the great retailing and wholesaling industries. Dallas' modeling industry ranks fourth in the nation, for example. Needlework has also been called the new "cash crop" in Texas farming communities, and as many as 100 Texas towns have a least one sewing contractor business. Some 700 sewing plants operate statewide. Four trade publications cover the fashion industry in Dallas, and both daily newspapers provide consumer trends coverage in weekly sections.

One company that has had marked impact on the Dallas economy has been the J.C Penney Company, which relocated to Dallas in 1987. Employing some 7,200 people, Penney's move to Dallas has had a positive ripple effect on many segments of business that operate as suppliers to the retailing giant. Penney's currently occupies more space in regional shopping malls than any other U.S. retailer.

The 1980s were a time of great transition in retailing in Dallas. While 1985 marked the height of shopping center development (with some 5 million square feet of retail space added), Dallas went from the hottest spot in the nation for retailing to one of the weakest. The wholesaling industry also had its strength tested when tenants of the Apparel Mart demanded rent and yearly percentage increase rollbacks — ideas that had been plausible during periods of great growth in the 1970s and early '80s, but which seemed bad for business as the decade came to a close.

ABOVE: *Store buyers inspect merchandise during a housewares show at the Dallas Market Center.*

TOP: *There is a saying in the fashion industry: "If it doesn't sell in Dallas, it won't sell."*

LEFT: *The Apparel Mart is one of eight buildings that comprise the 9.2-million-square-foot Dallas Market Center. Photo by Doug Milner.*

names such as Lou Lattimore, Marie Leavell, Lester Melnick, Jas. K. Wilson, The Carriage Shop and Andra's continue the strong Dallas fashion tradition.

Many of Dallas' largest manufacturers remain virtually unknown on their home turf but are very successful in the volatile fashion industry. These include Jerell, Sunny South, RLM, Jones and Brenner. One of the successful newcomers is the firm whose roots are the Frankel family of Jerell — the Leslie Lucks label.

Some of the best-known designers in Dallas include Victor Costa, who creates copies of the couture at a fraction of the price; Barboglio, the sister duo which is a division of Lorch; Sandra Garratt, whose knitwear separates pioneered the trendy modular dressing field, first with her Units label, and later with Multiples. Her design laboratory is located in the historical Deep Ellum district of Dallas. Companies such as Prophecy, a leader in career apparel for women, and lingerie firms like Henson Kickernick of Greenville and Russell Newman of Denton continue to keep the Dallas apparel industry a growing force in the area.

Dallas has two major fashion collections, which are important both to the cultural and creative spirits. The Dallas Historical Society houses its 20th-century costume collection at the Hall of State in Fair Park; the Fashion Group houses its couture collection at the University of North Texas in Denton. Even the Salvation Army in Dallas has a traveling retrospective style show of fashions which have been donated down through the years. Dallas also has a best-dressed list, drawn largely from members of the exclusive Crystal Charity Ball committee.

A non-profit group called the Fashion Industry Council was formed in 1989 "to stimulate awareness and appreciation of the sociological and

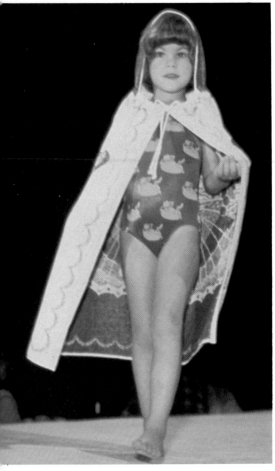

But just as it had begun on a high note, the 1980s closed with the opening of yet another regional shopping mall in Lewisville, northeast of Dallas, and the promise of yet another regional mall in Far North Dallas, which would bring the total to at least 18 by the close of the century.

New retail and wholesale establishments continue to come to Dallas, bringing their updated looks from all corners of the world. Clothier Koala Blue, owned by singing superstar Olivia Newton-John, chose Dallas for one of its expansion sites outside Australia in 1989; and trendy New York retailer Barney's was looking at Dallas sites as the decade closed.

Dallas continues to be the home base for some of America's finest specialty shops, and even in the merger and acquisition mania of the '80s, many remain home-grown and home-owned. Among them are women's boutique Delann's, men's clothier Culwell & Son and others. Fine

cultural contributions made by the fashion industry." Membership includes executives in both retail and wholesale, the market center, designers and others in related fields.

Sociological and cultural contributions notwithstanding, the final plaudit for the so-called "Dallas Look" belongs to the men, women and children of the area. Fashion observers consistently applaud all strata of Dal-

las society for a well-groomed and well-informed citizenry. The buyers who shop Dallas markets have coined an oft-used industry phrase: "If it doesn't sell in Dallas, it won't sell."

Dallas without question is considered one of the best-dressed cities in America, with a gloriously fashionable past and an illustriously stylish future.

ABOVE: *Another day of shopping comes to an end in Dallas. Photo by Jeff Hampton.*

TOP LEFT: *At the Dallas Design District, tomorrow's fashions and accessories are being designed today. Photo by Dan Hatzenbuehler.*

BOTTOM LEFT: *Apparel for all ages is shown and bought for retail sale at the Dallas Market Center.*

CHAPTER 15

A City That Competes

By Russ Pate

Both Dallas the team and Dallas

the city share a consuming desire

to be the best they can be. It is a

Dallas trademark that began

long before the Cowboys were

conceived. Or, for that matter,

before football players wore

helmets and shoulder pads.

A Dallas Cowboy dives over the line for six more
points. Photo by Doug Milner.

181

By the late 20th century, professional football had replaced major league baseball as America's most popular team sport. Though nobody can say when the change occurred, it is a safe bet the Dallas Cowboys were directly involved.

The guess here is that the moment came in the mid-1970s, after Cowboys quarterback Roger Staubach completed one of his miraculous, last-minute touchdown passes to vex the arch-rival Washington Redskins and give Dallas yet another division championship. The denouement was so dramatic and utterly remarkable that no one called the local CBS television affiliate to complain about the football broadcast running over its allotted time, which meant "60 Minutes" and all other Sunday evening TV programming would be pushed back.

No one cared. Not even Mike Wallace or Dan Rather or Morley Safer. The whole country had been transfixed by what it had witnessed.

Baseball had been the national pastime in the rural, agricultural America of the early 1900s. You'd finish your Saturday morning farm chores and head for the fairgrounds, judging pigs and tasting pies before stretching out on a red-and-white tablecloth to watch the local team play hardball with an outfit from the next county. A doubleheader, if they could squeeze in a second game before darkness.

Baseball had a leisurely pace just right for the times. Why it even had a "seventh inning stretch" — patrons perked up before the home half of the seventh inning — a ritual suggesting that the senses needed stirring lest anyone nod off before the game ended. Quaint.

By the late 20th century, however, America had transformed itself from a rural to urban society, from an agricultural-based to service-oriented economy. Yesterday's farm owner/operator had evolved into today's corporate manager, whose world revolved, not around plows and threshers, but personal computers, fax machines, cellular telephones and other implements of instant communication.

Football had a frenetic pace ideal for the times. Modern life in metropolitan areas had become the equivalent of football's "two-minute" offense. Rushing to the line of scrimmage and through the plays was not unlike rushing onto the freeway, into the downtown parking garage and up the elevator to your office. Rush, rush, rush. Life in the fast lane.

Of the 28 teams competing in professional football at the beginning of the 1990s, the Dallas Cowboys rank as the most closely watched and widely followed — despite recent gains from the Chicago Bears and San Francisco 49ers, among others. Dallas' popularity with pro football fans can be traced to the franchise's performance from the mid-1960s to the mid-1980s — two decades of sustained excellence.

America's Team caught America's fancy. From the stars on their helmets to their penchant for last-minute heroics, the Dallas players had a mystique about them that helped create a constituency of fans from coast to coast. The Cowboys received the prime assignments from the TV networks, including a Thanksgiving Day game at home in Texas Stadium, where they invariably carved up some opponent then drove home for more turkey. The Cowboys accounted for the most NFL merchandise sold — jerseys, pennants, drinking mugs and other memorabilia.

Everybody adored Dallas (with the obvious exception of the members of the Official Dallas Cowboys Haters' club). A popular joke was that the roof on Texas Stadium had been left uncovered so God could watch his favorite team play. A variation went like this: Why was Texas Stadium left uncovered? So God could watch his other son (meaning coach Tom Landry).

But the Dallas Cowboys were as much about substance as style, as much about guts as glitter. Twice in the 1970s, Dallas won the Super Bowl. On three other occasions, Dallas reached the championship game and suffered narrow, heart-wrenching defeat.

In the process, the Cowboys presented their fans with a parade of

personalities:

• Roger Staubach, the Naval Academy grad who returned from duty in Vietnam and led Dallas to its greatest triumphs. A dedicated athlete and father, Staubach was the straightest of straight arrows, which only went to show that nice guys can finish first. Captain America, they called him.

• Don Meredith, the native Texan whose aw-shucks affability masked the heart of a warrior. Meredith later added to the Dallas Cowboys' aura by joining the broadcasting booth for ABC's "Monday Night Football," gaining legions of fans for being the man who dared to prick Howard Cosell's ego. Dandy Don, they called him.

• Bob Hayes, the world's fastest human, as he proved in the 1964 Olympics in Tokyo. Hayes made the difficult transition from track-and-field to the football field without breaking stride and became the team's most spectacular player. Bullet Bob, they called him.

• Then there was the Dallas defense, a collection of the gifted —

The Dallas Cowboys prepare for another Sunday battle. Photo by Allan Kaye.

Bob Lilly, Mel Renfro, Randy White, Ed Jones — and the overachievers — Lee Roy Jordan, Cornell Green, Cliff Harris, Harvey Martin. Doomsday, they called the Dallas defense, which played as ominously as the name suggests.

ABOVE: *The Dallas Cowboys Cheerleaders are as well known around the globe as the football team they represent. Photo by Allan Kaye.*

RIGHT: *The Mobil Cotton Bowl Classic on New Year's Day pits the Southwest Conference Champion against another nationally ranked team. Photo by Jeff Hampton.*

Perhaps the most memorable characteristic of the Dallas Cowboys teams, though, was their competitiveness. Their will to win. Dallas' never-say-die attitude allowed the Cowboys to fashion some improbable comeback victories over such perennial playoff foes as Washington and Minnesota. Hail Mary, indeed.

The Cowboys, in that respect, mirrored the city they represented. Dallas, the city, was as determined and results-oriented as the team in the silver-and-blue uniforms. Like the Cowboys, Dallas could be resourceful enough to find an avenue for success when all roads appeared blocked. A deep-rooted optimism permeated Dallas, a "can-do" spirit.

Both the team and the city knew the benefits of innovation. Tom Landry, the Cowboys' coach/mastermind for 29 years, created a space-age offense with shifting sets and multiple formations that kept opposing defenses dazed and confused. On defense, Landry created a "flex" scheme that disrupted the opponents' blocking patterns. Mentally, he always found an edge, an opportunity to exploit.

Dallas the city was equally innovative. Its leaders correctly forecast the long-term benefits of aviation — "The air is our ocean," city fathers liked to say — and created Dallas/Fort Worth International Airport, one of the largest and most efficient complexes in aviation. With the subsequent decision of American Airlines to relocate its headquarters operation to the Dallas area, D/FW Airport became one of the world's major hubs.

Dallas leaders also recognized the value of an educated populace. They worked with the Texas Legislature to extend the University of Texas system into North Texas, ensuring that a steady stream of college graduates would flow into the local work force. The benefits were obvious to established Dallas companies, start-ups and companies relocating to the area.

Both Dallas the team and Dallas the city share a consuming desire to be the best they can be. It is a Dallas trademark that began long before the Cowboys were conceived. Or, for that matter, before football players wore helmets and shoulder pads.

Under new majority owner Jerry Jones, a former Little Rock, Ark., oilman/insurance executive, the Dallas Cowboys are retooling for more greatness in the 1990s. Ironically, it was just as the overheated Dallas economy suffered a meltdown in the mid-1980s that the Dallas Cowboys saw their winning years come to a halt.

That both Dallas the team and Dallas the city would suffer reversals of form at the same time smacks of more than coincidence. Maybe Cowboys fans, faced with their own business dilemmas, could not fill Texas Stadium with the same positive energy, the same good vibrations, as before. Maybe the Cowboys players, stuck with some of the same bad investments and sour deals, could not summon forth the same effort as before. Or maybe both the team and the city were overdue to undergo what economists call a "correction."

But that is all about to change. Both the city and its most famous asset — the Dallas Cowboys — are back on track. If happy days are not quite here again, they surely are right around the corner.

In Troy Aikman, a strapping son of neighboring Oklahoma, Dallas has what looks to be its most strong-armed and stout-hearted leader since Roger Staubach. And in Jimmy Johnson, the Cowboys have a new head coach who elevated the University of Miami's football program to two national championships in the 1980s.

This duo figures to rekindle the excitement and enthusiasm endemic during Dallas' glory days. Sunday afternoons, regardless of whether the Cowboys played at home or away, was the one time that Dallas' dealmakers stopped dealing. For three hours — sometimes more if the TV broadcast ran long — the only game in town was at Texas Stadium. And that was a Big Deal.

But with all due respect to what the Cowboys have meant to Dallas, they are no longer the only game in town. The Dallas sports year begins on January 1 with the Mobil Cotton Bowl Classic and in essence never stops. A carrousel of top-drawer sporting events spins all year long. Round and round they go, bobbing up and down in competition for the sports dollar. Meanwhile, with an abundance of good weather in Dallas, the participatory athlete finds no end to recreation he or she can pursue, from running, jogging or cycling on your own to organized leagues for softball, soccer, rugby. Dallas is a sports person's paradise, whether your game is doing or watching — or both.

The Cotton Bowl Classic — which pits the champion of the Southwest Conference against a top-rated national contender — and the preceding Cotton Bowl Parade showcase the city to a national television audience on New Year's Day. Dallas' trump card as a bowl site is its hospitality. The Cotton Bowl's ambassadors of goodwill like Jim "Hoss" Brock, Jim Williams, Dan Petty, Jim Ray Smith and the father-and-son team of Field and John Scovell are well-known faces on the national sports scene. Athletic directors and university presidents recognize that an invitation to the Dallas bowl game guarantees a good time for its players and fans alike. They know that though Dallas has become an international and sophisticated city, it has not forgotten how to be warm, friendly and neighborly.

The Cotton Bowl began in 1937, with Texas Christian University (TCU) from nearby Fort Worth defeating Marquette University from Milwaukee. Through the ensuing years some of the greatest names in the history of college football — Sammy Baugh, Bobby Layne, Doak Walker, Jim Brown, Earl Campbell, Erick Dickerson, Roger Staubach,

Dan Marino and even Troy Aikman — have appeared in the Cotton Bowl Classic.

In perhaps the most famous Cotton Bowl game, the 1971 Classic, the University of Texas saw its 30-game winning streak snapped by Notre Dame. The Irish, avenging a loss to the Longhorns a year earlier, prevented Texas from winning its second consecutive national championship. The defeat prompted Texas coach Darrell Royal to philosophize: "There ain't a horse that can't be rode; there ain't a rider can't be throwed."

The Cotton Bowl was the brainchild of J. Curtis Sanford, a Dallas oilman, who promoted the first game as a private enterprise, putting up

$6,000 of his own money to cover expenses. Sanford dreamed of creating a bowl game on the state fairgrounds in Dallas that might rival the Rose Bowl in California. History has borne out Sanford's vision. The Cotton Bowl is well established as one of the highlights of the New Year's Day footballathon.

How appropriate that the Cotton Bowl began as an entrepreneurial endeavor. Entrepreneurial spirit has been alive and well and living in Dallas — some would say thriving — ever since the city was founded. Whether the chips are high-tech (Texas Instruments) or salted (Frito-Lay), Dallas business executives have always been on the cutting edge of change.

ABOVE: The Dallas Mavericks have become one of the premier franchises of the National Basketball Association. Photo by Doug Milner.

BELOW: Dallas has golf courses to challenge professionals and amateurs alike. Photo by Brian McWeeney.

RIGHT: Buick World Championship Tennis brings international tennis action to Reunion Arena. Photo by Doug Milner.

No one person more so than Lamar Hunt. Hunt, son of H.L. Hunt who made a fortune in the East Texas oil boom, wrote his master's thesis on sports entrepreneurship. Meaning that he is a master. Lamar Hunt's ventures included the Dallas Texans of the American Football League (now the NFL's Kansas City Chiefs) and World Championship Tennis. He also brought professional soccer to the area — the Dallas Tornado and its headliner, Kyle Rote Jr. — and had a hand in professional team bowling.

Yet another Dallas-based sports entrepreneur is Terry Murphy, creator of a street basketball competition called Hoop-It-Up. After reading about the concept in a *Sports Illustrated* feature story, Murphy, a magazine publisher himself, set about launching the street competition that's now played in more than two dozen U.S. cities. Hoop-It-Up is one of the highlights of the ongoing events in Dallas' West End Historic District, a popular destination for visitors to Dallas.

While the Cotton Bowl officially marks the beginning of the sports year in Dallas, New Year's Day finds the pro basketball season well under way and the Dallas Mavericks playing to sellout crowds at Reunion Arena on the western edge of downtown.

Like football, professional basketball has the fast pace that mirrors life in the urban metropolis. Languishing in the late 1970s, the National Basketball Association experienced a boom of its own in the 1980s as fans embraced the ebbs-and-flows (called "runs") of most pro games and the incredible displays of sheer athletics from the participants, arguably the best "pure" athletes in modern sports.

The Dallas Mavericks profited from this surge in the sport during the 1980s. But they also created their own identify as they evolved from a scrappy bunch of has-beens and never-weres, into a championship contender. Much of the credit goes to the Mavericks' front office, including general manager Norm Sonju and vice president of player development Rick Sund. They never oversold the product, carefully built from within and through the draft, improved steadily and became the ticket of choice with many Dallas sports fans.

By the time the CBS cameras arrived at Reunion Arena for a Mavericks' playoff game against the Los Angeles Lakers, network officials could not believe their eyes and ears. Dallas fans had gone bonkers over the team. Like the Cowboys, the Dallas Mavericks had forged a bond with the city. Veteran players like Rolando Blackman and Brad Davis became as visible and popular as any of the Dallas Cowboys. And the Mavericks played to 99 percent of the seating capacity at Reunion — not for a few games, but for an entire season.

Two other events showcased both Reunion Arena and Dallas' ability to host big-time sports. Both came in 1986. First, Dallas hosted the NBA's All-Star weekend, an extraordinary occasion highlighted by 5'6" Spud Webb (who grew up in the Dallas area) winning the slam-dunk competition against athletes more than a foot taller. Less than two months later, the NCAA conducted its Final Four basketball weekend in Dallas — a tournament won by Louisville — and coaches, players and school administrators from all parts of the country left hailing Dallas for its hospitality and heaping praise on Big D.

The Mavericks share the bill at Reunion Arena with the Dallas Sidekicks of the Major Indoor Soccer League (MISL). The Sidekicks, paced by their scoring sensation Tatu, captured the league championship in 1986-87, winning a thrilling final series against the Tacoma Stars. Soccer has made great strides in the area, especially with support engendered through numerous youth programs. Dallas annually hosts an international competition for some of the world's best youth teams.

By spring, professional tennis has made its pass through Dallas, with both the Virginia Slims tournament for women and World Championship Tennis for men. Virtually every great player in the "open" era of tennis has appeared in Dallas. The WCT tournament also was the site for what some tennis historians regard as the best match of all time, a WCT final between Australian greats Ken Rosewall and Rod Laver.

Professional golf, too, moves through Dallas in the spring. The GTE Byron Nelson Classic, played at the Four Seasons Hotel and Resort complex in nearby Irving, is one of the most successful events on the PGA Tour and the only one that bears the name of one of golf's greatest legends.

Proceeds from the GTE Byron Nelson Classic support camps for troubled youth sponsored by the Salesmanship Club of Dallas. For years the tournament has generated more than a million dollars annually for the camps' operating funds. That is because the Nelson is a happening,

a must-see event. Mike Massad Sr., chairman of the Salesmanship Club's executive golf committee, chuckles when he relates the story of the fast-track young Dallas executive who once told him, "Gosh, Mr. Massad, a person just has to go to the Nelson. It's the place to see and be seen. Everybody who's anybody in Dallas will be there."

The Tournament Players Course at the Four Seasons, with its "stadium golf" concept featuring large spectator mounds, helps attract mammoth crowds. So does the Pavilion tent, which represents Dallas' own rite of spring. It is where boy meets girl, girl

meets boy, and business cards and phone numbers get exchanged in nano seconds. It is such an extended party that the story, perhaps apocryphal, is told about the young Dallas woman, who after an extended stay in the Pavilion tent, headed to the nearby ladies' porta-potty, beyond which she noticed several golfers and their caddies marching down the first fairway.

"Y'all," she said upon her return to the Pavilion, "There's some sort of game going on out back there."

Genteelness gives way to brawn — and oil and gasoline — across town on the grounds of Addison Airport

where some of the best professional and amateur drivers compete in the series of races that makes up the annual Pontiac Grand Prix of Dallas. This weekend of racing is fast becoming one of the most popular stops on the annual racing circuit, and like the Byron Nelson, it has become a popular gathering spot for Dallas' social set.

By summer, the focus on Dallas sports turns to major league baseball. The Texas Rangers' American League franchise has held forth in nearby Arlington Stadium since the early 1970s, when the Washington Senators decided to depart the nation's capital. After years of struggling at

the bottom of the standings, the Rangers had begun to show significant progress by the end of the 1980s. Homegrown talent like Ruben Sierra had reached stardom, fresh troops like Julio Franco and Rafael Palmeiro had arrived to bolster the attack, and Texas native/legend Nolan Ryan had decided to end his storied career in a Rangers' uniform. For the first time in memory, talk about playoffs and pennants did not seem farfetched.

In addition, a change in the Texas Rangers' ownership had put the management reins in the hands of George W. Bush, son of the President of the United States. If the team ever found itself needing a notable person to

ABOVE: The Texas Rangers are the pride of the Dallas/Fort Worth Metroplex. Photo by Brian McWeeney.

TOP RIGHT: Don Gay shows his world-champion style at the Mesquite Championship Rodeo. Photo by Doug Milner.

BOTTOM RIGHT: The annual Tour of Texas bicycle race winds its way around White Rock Lake. Photo by Allan Kaye.

throw out the ceremonial first ball, the owner could simply phone home. "Hello, Dad? Mom?"

The Dallas sporting season, not surprisingly, also showcases the area's western heritage. The Mesquite Championship Rodeo is one of the best facilities on the professional rodeo circuit, thanks to the team effort of the Gay family, whose ranks include Don Gay, a many-time national rodeo champion.

Willow Bend Polo & Hunt Club, meanwhile, showcases the talents of accomplished riders and horses in a season-long series of polo matches. You do not have to be a Dick Francis devotee to enjoy an afternoon at Willow Bend.

After summer comes fall, when football rules. Not only are the Dallas Cowboys a headline attraction, but area fans avidly follow the fortunes of Southern Methodist University and nearby schools like the University of North Texas and UT-Arlington. And on Friday nights, regardless of whether you live in Dallas, Highland Park or one of the suburbs, high school football games dominate the social calendar.

Fall leads into winter, of course, which means the holiday season begins and New Year's Day approaches and that means one thing, hoss: it's time for the Cotton Bowl kickoff. And then the carrousel of Dallas sports begins another revolution.

CHAPTER 16

Shining Future

By Jeff Hampton

"Dallas has so much going for it. I think our future is very bright. There is a spirit here that says anything is possible if you work hard. We just keep looking forward and working hard. There's just an indomitable will to succeed." — Dallas Mayor Annette Strauss.

The Hall of State at Fair Park is a monument to the proud heritage upon which Dallas' shining future is being built. Photo by Martin Vandiver.

191

ABOVE: *The ability to reach lofty goals takes the kind of leadership and determination for which Dallas is famous. Photo by Robbie Messerschmitt Knight.*

RIGHT: *Proposed expansion of Dallas/Fort Worth International Airport is vital to the region's future and competitiveness as a business center.*

From his office in a downtown Dallas skyscraper, J. Erik Jonsson enjoys a panoramic view of the city below. From his window he can see beyond downtown to the commercial and residential areas stretching to the far horizon. There is irony in this setting, because Jonsson is a man who never has been limited by visual horizons. He has always looked beyond — into the next month, the next year, the next decade, even the next century.

Jonsson is what historians call a "visionary." In 1930 he joined a small company called Geophysical Services. Seeing its potential, he bought the company and built what is known the world over as Texas Instruments. In the early 1960s he established the Graduate Research Center of the Southwest to serve the research needs of his company. Today that institution is the University of Texas at Dallas, one of the leading institutions in the are and a major contributor to the area's high-tech prominence.

In the mid-1960s, Jonsson envisioned a major airport that would serve both Dallas and Fort Worth and would help the region become a major inland port. Ask executives of companies like J.C. Penney, Exxon, GTE, MCI and others why they moved operations to the Dallas area, and Dallas/Fort Worth International Airport tops the list.

Jonsson also was the man responsible for leading Dallas out of the gloom of the Kennedy assassination. As mayor, Jonsson was architect of the landmark "Goals for Dallas" program, which helped the city get back on track and served as a model for similar programs in other cities.

Now in his 80s, Jonsson has plenty to look back on with pride. But as a visionary, he still is looking ahead. Most recently, he has been an outspoken advocate of further expansion of D/FW Airport and lends his support to other issues that he considers of vital concern to the future of the region.

"The way of the prophet is very rough," Jonsson admits. "It's a very risky business, but I don't mind being wrong occasionally."

Jonsson has seldom been wrong during the course of his distinguished career. He attributes his record to the way he looks at the future, and not necessarily what he sees. "There is a difference between guessing, and thinking and estimating."

Jonsson says the key to planning Dallas' future is to "clarify what we are trying to do here. You do it on paper first; you establish goals and then you take inventory of the resources you have or need to meet those goals. Once you have established a plan, you execute it. Then you check how the plans are going regularly and often."

So what are the issues that Jonsson sees as strategic to the future of the Dallas area?

"I am beginning to worry about our water supply," he says. "We probably won't be at a crisis stage for another 20 years, but if you wait till then to look for solutions to water needs, it is too late. It is going to cost you more."

Ironically, Jonsson is thinking about the area's water supply during a rainy spring in which the area surpassed its normal annual precipitation in less than six months.

"If you don't have enough water, then people will move away, and that's not the kind of solution that interests most people," he continues. "It's when you are having flooding and overruns that you need to begin considering what to do about shortages. We need to have a lot of ground water."

That kind of timing is vital to the success of any project, including building a great city, Jonsson says. "In your planning, you have to think about how long you have to work on it. Everything we plan has to have a time scale attached to it."

A prime example is proposed expansion of Dallas/Fort Worth International Airport. A study by KPMG Peat Marwick indicates that at the current rate of growth, the airport will reach capacity by 2010.

"There comes a point in the life of an airport when you have one too many airplanes in the traffic pattern," says Jonsson. "The question follows as to when you should make room for that one extra plane. Do you wait until you have that one more plane, and it is no longer safe, to consider solutions? Of course not. You can't wait until you reach that saturation point."

Much to the credit of Jonsson and other farsighted individuals, public attention already has been focused on D/FW Airport and the need to add two runways before one of the region's greatest resources becomes just another major bottleneck.

"The impact study shows that D/FW would become as congested as Chicago O'Hare, Atlanta Hartsfield, Newark, New York's Kennedy and LaGuardia, and Washington National unless the proposed east and west runways are built," says Richard Douglas, president of the North Texas Commis-

ABOVE: *Major highway additions and improvements are under way to assure mobility for years to come. Photo by Scott Metcalfe.*

RIGHT: *Maintaining adequate public services such as police and fire protection will remain a primary concern of city leaders and residents alike. Photo by Dan Hatzenbuehler.*

CENTER: *The Dallas Independent School District is working to give the youth of Dallas the best educational opportunities possible. Photo by Benjamin Stewart.*

sion, a regional economic development agency which commissioned the study. "If this is allowed to happen, the economic consequences for the Dallas/Fort Worth Metroplex would be severe.

"Right now, D/FW is the most efficient mid-continent airport in the United States," he continues. "The airport's annual average delay is currently half the delays experienced at other major U.S. airports. Without the proposed runways and ancillary facilities, service at D/FW will noticeably deteriorate over the next two to five years as traffic stacks up."

While airport expansion is a relatively new public issue, ground transportation has been of concern to many people for some time. Compared to other major cities, Dallas does not have a transportation problem; traffic moves freely and fairly unencumbered. But in a business-oriented city such as Dallas, any time spent in traffic is too much. It is no wonder cellular phones are so popular here.

Improving traffic flow is the goal of Dallas Area Rapid Transit (DART), which already has implemented a comprehensive bus plan and now is working on getting a rail system up and running for the area.

Complementing DART's work are improvements and additions to the area's freeway system. Central Expressway, a U.S. highway that surprised engineers and planners by becoming a major north/south artery, is being widened from four to eight lanes from downtown Dallas into Plano 20 miles

to the north. Phased construction will minimize the inconvenience to the 150,000 motorists who use the roadway daily.

Another element of the local infrastructure of vital importance to the region's future is public education. It is through the educational system that tomorrow's leaders are trained — for business, professions, trades, community service and government leadership.

Dallas has the eighth-largest public school system in the country, and administrators of the Dallas Independent School District (DISD) are working hard to see that the system progresses from being one of the best "large" school systems to one of the best school systems, regardless of size.

DISD Superintendent Dr. Marvin Edwards has placed special emphasis on improving student test scores and reducing the dropout rate, as well as making sure teachers are sufficiently trained and compensated. As he sees

it, there is much at stake — for the individual students but for the entire region as well.

"I don't think enough people in the community realize how important schools are to people moving in. It's at the top of the list," says Edwards. "No matter how well you do on things such as arts and entertainment and transportation, if you don't have excellence in your schools, you're going to miss some opportunities to attract new industry, new families and a variety of students."

Also affecting an area's future viability are taxes and public services such as police and fire protection. As the only major U.S. city with a triple-A bond rating from both Moody's and Standard & Poor's, Dallas is able to finance major improvement projects through bond issues, allowing residents to enjoy a reasonable tax rate.

But still, there are questions to be raised as the 21st century approaches.

"How do we deal with change in the population growth? How do we redefine our tax structure? How do we continue to reduce our costs of providing services?" asks Richard Knight.

As manager of the largest city in the United States with a council/manager government, Knight and his

staff must present recommendations to a council representing an increasingly diverse constituency. These recommendations cover a broad spectrum of issues — productivity, public safety, human services, equal economic opportunity, race relations.

"I still think that this is a great city, but we have some problems to solve internally," he says. "We have to be able to recognize our diversity and build on it to fuel the machinery of prosperity. We are a mosaic of different colored tiles. While we are all Americans, we are all different."

To answer these questions and solve these problems, it will take the cooperation of many people, not just government, Knight adds. "Charity begins at home, and people need to look closely at what they can do. I'm an advocate of individuals making personal contributions to the system."

It is just that kind of personal contribution and leadership that has brought Dallas to the forefront of U.S. urban centers and will carry it on to new greatness in the 1990s and beyond.

"Dallas has so much going for it. I think our future is very bright," says Mayor Annette Strauss. "There is a spirit here that says anything is possi-

ble if you work hard. We just keep looking forward and working hard. There's just an indomitable will to succeed."

Dallas does succeed, and it will continue to do so in a variety of different areas.

High Tech — Already a major center of high-tech business and employment, Dallas will continue to experience growth in this industry during the next 10 years, says Les Alberthal, president and chief executive officer of EDS. "One of the most important things high tech has done is provide a significant level of diversity in the Dallas economy," he says. "High tech is not an industry that has matured and flattened out."

Conventions and Tourism — The Dallas area is one of the top three convention destinations in the United States, and the No. 1 visitor destination in Texas. "I think it's important for us to strive to be No. 1," says Greg Elam, Vice President of Communications and Meeting Professional in Residence for the Dallas Convention and

Visitors Bureau. "To accept being No. 2 or 3 is not Dallas' style. We'd rather be going uphill than downhill."

Health Care — "The overall quantity, quality and variety of treatment available in Dallas is as good as what you can find at Texas Medical Center in Houston, the Mayo Clinic or anywhere else," says Dr. Kern Wildenthal, president of the University of Texas Southwestern Medical Center at Dallas. The Dallas Medical Action Group, a new coalition of the area's major hospitals, is letting the world know what Dallas has to offer.

LEFT: Greenspaces and parks such as the Dallas Arboretum add immeasurably to the quality of life. Photo by Doug Milner.

TOP: SouthFork Ranch, the home of television's Ewing clan, is a popular tourist stop as well as a full-service convention, meeting and party facility. Photo by Allan Kaye.

BELOW: Harris Information Terminals is one of the many firms making Dallas a leading high-tech development, employment and manufacturing center.

ABOVE: Dallas still has plenty of wide open spaces to attract future businesses and residents. Photo by Martin Vandiver.

RIGHT: Dallas is a city built on business, but there is always time for fun. Photo by Allan Kaye.

TOP: Innovative projects like Bryan Place are bringing new life and residents back to the inner city. Photo by Jeff Hampton.

Banking and Finance — The late 1980s was a rough period for Dallas' financial sector, but a new day has dawned. "It's hard not to look back, but we have to look ahead," says John Adams, chairman and chief executive officer of Texas Commerce Bank, Dallas. "I think we'll see new growth again, and I think the leadership that is evolving is more qualified and diversified to take advantage of opportunities."

Real Estate and Construction — "The Metroplex office market bottomed out in 1988," says John Crawford, president and chief executive officer of Crawford & Company Real Estate Services. "While the extraordinary growth of the early 1980s is behind us, the early 1990s will bring slow but steady growth and is expected to continue to grow at a rate surpassing the national average."

Oil and Gas — With Exxon adding its name to the list of prominent corporate transplants in the late 1980s, Dallas remains a strong headquarters and business base for the oil and gas industry. "Despite what happened (with the oil crash of 1986), Dallas still has a major petroleum industry. Companies such as American Petrofina, ARCO, Maxus and now Exxon are still significant employers in the Dallas area," says Jan Collmer, chairman of the Greater Dallas Chamber.

Retail and Wholesale — The continued success of the World Trade Center, a huge and diverse mix of retail establishments and the corporate leadership of firms such as J.C. Penney Company are paving the way for Dallas' continued growth as a major fashion and general merchandising center.

Manufacturing and Distribution — Central location and a well-planned transportation network will continue to attract manufacturing and distribution operations to the area. "Everything is made here in Dallas by someone," says Collmer, also president of Collmer Semiconductor. "Heavy machinery, food, consumer items, electronics — the list of manufacturers is long."

International Business — "On the international front, our focus is sharper and a strong foundation for growth is being laid," says Hugh Robinson, chief executive officer of the Tetra Group. "The Dallas/Fort Worth market continues to increase its contributions to Texas' No. 2 status as a major exporting state."

Economic Diversity and Business Opportunity — "This vast metropolitan center ... has become the most diverse and dynamic economic base in the U.S. The so-called Metroplex ... is today's dream location for business." So said the editors of *Fortune* Magazine in an October 1989 cover story that named Dallas the No. 1 business center in the United States.

Overall Quality of Life — "A city of excellence — that's what we are targeting today for the 1990s," says Richard D. Upton, president of the Greater Dallas Chamber. "I believe

that the 1990s will be Dallas' decade of greatness. We do face challenges in the '90s, and the issues we are facing you don't develop good solutions to overnight."

Dallas must be a city that practices and not just preaches an agenda of inclusion, Upton says. "The South Dallas Development Corporation (SDDC) is part of that in that it is bringing opportunity to minority businesses and minority people." The SDDC promotes private sector involvement and investment in South Dallas-based businesses, as well as providing capital injections and "gap" financing for businesses in need of temporary assistance.

Businesses must support the school board and the superintendent, he says, and the crime/punishment issue should be a concern to everyone. "Those people who want to be rehabilitated should have the opportunity," he says. "We need them in the labor force."

Other key issues that Upton says must be addressed include continued rehabilitation of the central city, improved transportation, access to capital, enhancement of small business development and regional cooperation. "If Dallas is going to be successful, the Metroplex is going to have to be successful."

That "all-for-one and one-for-all" attitude carries over into leadership.

"To solve many of the issues we now face as a city and as a region, people are going to have to start meeting their responsibilities as leaders," Upton says. "Leadership changes all the time, and the great thing about Dallas' past is that people stepped forward with the fortitude to face those challenges. And there were some tough ones in the past.

"Tomorrow's successes are going to be built on coalitions. I think leadership today is a matter of bringing many people together."

Erik Jonsson agrees. "I think the only possible way to get anything done is by consensus, which means you take a little, but you give a lot. And I'm not just talking about one

person; you need a whole gang of people in there not afraid to roll up their sleeves and do the work."

Dallas has just such a gang — at city hall, in the county courthouse, in downtown office towers, in small neighborhood shops, in classrooms, on factory floors, in suburban neighborhoods and on quiet country lanes. Together, they are building on Dallas' proud heritage to guarantee a shining future.

LEFT: Shopping centers like The Galleria add to the quality of life and make Dallas a major destination for tourism and conventions. Photo by Scott Metcalfe.

TOP: Dallas keeps reaching ahead while keeping a firm grip on its past. Photo by David J. Sams.

ABOVE: Dallas City Hall is the seat of the city's pro-business government. Photo by Allan Kaye.

PART TWO

Partners in Dallas

Photo by Martin Vandiver

"EDS has evolved from a local company to an international one with its reach literally extending around the globe. But despite its incredible growth, the company has continued its long-standing commitment to the Dallas area."

— EDS

"Encouraging Dallas' continued growth, while maintaining its high quality of life and top ranking as the nation's No. 1 business center is at the top of the Greater Dallas Chamber's agenda. A mission very similar to its charter agenda some 80 years ago."

— Greater Dallas Chamber

"We have established our identity in this market as the first source for news and information. Our listeners know that when a big story breaks, they can count on Newsradio 1080 to provide complete news coverage and the latest updates."

Michael Ewing, Vice President and General Manager — KRLD Newsradio 1080

"In 1990 KTVT begins its 35th year of broadcasting as one of the crown jewels of Gaylord Broadcasting Company. And the station continues to fulfill its creed: Operate a professional station well and serve the public in the best way possible."

— KTVT-TV Channel 11

"Dallas has the reputation of being a high tech city, and with ACS being a large, full-service data processing company, we knew that locating here would bring us the resources that we needed to succeed."

Darwin Deason, Chief Executive Officer — Affiliated Computer Systems

"Two of the wisest decisions American ever made were to move our headquarters to the Dallas/Fort Worth area and build a major connecting hub at Dallas/Fort Worth International Airport."

Robert L. Crandall, Chairman and President — American Airlines

"KDFW's slogan — Believing in Texas — underscores its continuing commitment to leadership and excellence in television broadcasting service to Dallas and the region."

— KDFW-TV Channel 4

"The Zig Ziglar Corporation is demonstrating every day that a dream fueled by desire and determination and that is organized into a specific plan of action can far exceed its original concept."

— Zig Ziglar Corporation

"Westinghouse has always been an innovator, and STAR 105.3 has an incredible opportunity to continue that legacy in Dallas. The deck is stacked in our favor. Everything a successful business needs to prosper is here."

Sue Rhoades, General Manager — KQZY Star 105.3

"The Southwestern Bell network in Dallas is regarded as one of the nation's best, and digital high-tech capabilities have made Dallas a major center for telecommunications and corporations counting national and even worldwide communications as their heartbeat."

— Southwestern Bell

"WFAA-TV Channel 8 is building on its reputation of quality programming, a news operation that is second to none and an enviable track record of successful and meaningful community service."

— WFAA-TV Channel 8

"Northern Telecom and the community are a remarkable team, solidly investing in one another's potentials. As a strategic force in the telecommunications industry, we remain committed to creating solutions and opportunities."

— Northern Telecom

"Dallas' entrepreneurial climate has made it possible for young businesses like Wordtemps to find support and success. Wordtemps personifies the spirit of Dallas — life is good and great things are possible."

Valerie Freeman, President — Wordtemps Inc.

"KMGC and its Dallas audience have created a radio station truly unique in the nation with its upbeat blend of adult Lite Rock and contemporary Lite Jazz. It's a reflection of the vibrant, contemporary Dallas lifestyle."

Bill Clark, President of Shamrock Broadcasting — KMGC Magic 102.9

"Our mission is to be the premier service company in the world, and that is to be achieved through our commitment to quality and care. We feel very firmly that this guiding philosophy will continue to help us achieve our goal."

George H. Scragg Jr., Vice President — Aviall

"From the day we traveled our first route, we have believed that air travel should be inexpensive, hassle free and fun."

Herbert D. Kelleher, Chairman, Chief Executive Officer and President — Southwest Airlines

"Perhaps more than any other single entity within the Metroplex, Dallas/Fort Worth International Airport continues to spur economic growth for the region as well as propel itself into the position of one of the preeminent airports in the world."

— *Dallas/Fort Worth International Airport*

"GTE grew up with the Southwest. It has rejoiced in the good times and suffered in the bad — and never stopped working to improve communications for its customers."

— *GTE Southwest*

"Dallas is the second-largest presence in the US Sprint operation, and the city has become quite a telecommunications center because it offers all the resources for a high tech community to flourish."

Roger A. Vernier, President, Central Business Marketing Group — US Sprint Communications

CHAPTER 17

Networks

Dallas' transportation and communications firms, as well as its business networks, keep people, information and power circulating throughout the region.

EDS (Electronic Data Systems)

EDS' futuristic Information Management Center in Plano serves as the network command site for managing the company's global communications.

Perhaps no company better symbolizes Dallas' much-acclaimed "can-do" attitude, entrepreneurial spirit, commitment to excellence and enthusiastic acceptance of a challenge than EDS. Founded in 1962 with only a handful of employees, EDS (Electronic Data Systems) now employs more than 56,000 people, has operations in all 50 states and 27 countries and registers annual revenues of more than $5 billion.

One of the reasons for EDS' dramatic success is that it is a company with a vision, a company that knows where it wants to go and has the determination and professional expertise to get there.

Another is that EDS' senior management group is virtually unique in modern American business: Most of its members have spent almost their entire careers with the company and have matured together as businessmen and women who are extraordinarily knowledgeable about their industry (information technol-

ogy services), enthusiastically committed to fulfilling their customers' needs and intensely loyal to the company and devoted to each other.

The management group at EDS charts the company's success not on the basis of short-term financial gains but on how well customers are satisfied and how well EDS is helping them attain their strategic goals. Significantly, 85 percent of EDS customers — an industry record — renew their relationships with the company year after year. As a result, EDS has been able to continue its remarkable growth and success for more than a quarter of a century.

In addition to taking care of its business, EDS strives to be an outstanding corporate citizen.

Each year, EDS supports more than 100 local organizations that work to enhance the quality of life in Dallas through their cultural, charitable, civic and educational efforts. Among them are Children's Medical Center, the Dallas Museum of Art

and the Dallas Symphony.

In 1989, EDS provided extensive resources and technical expertise to The JASON Project, an exciting and innovative new program designed to increase the interest of American schoolchildren in science. The project, run by Dr. Robert Ballard, the scientist who discovered the *Titanic* and the *Bismarck*, provided an incredible educational opportunity for more than 250,000 schoolchildren: It took them along on an undersea exploration as it happened, via robotics and telecommunications. The students, who witnessed the event at 12 museums in the United States and Canada (including The Science Place in Dallas), got a chance to learn simultaneously about oceanographic exploration and the ever-expanding world of modern communications. EDS made a sizable financial commitment to the project and took charge of the critical technical operations involved in transmitting a clear color picture from the pitch-black

bottom of the Mediterranean Sea to museums thousands of miles away.

EDS sponsored two other major events in 1989: the popular "Ramses the Great" exhibit in Dallas and "EDS Stars and Spikes," a series of volleyball matches between American and Soviet Olympic teams.

In 1990, EDS will lend its support and sponsorship to another major undertaking — an exhibit at the Smithsonian Institution entitled "The Information Age: People, Information and Technology."

Over the years, EDS has shared its management expertise as well as its financial resources with the community. Through the Dallas United organization, EDS "loaned" a company executive to help the Dallas Police examine the application of systems management and other administrative processes within the department. The company also has shared its management resources with the Plano Independent School District and the Dallas County Department of Human Services.

EDS also plays a leading role in various civic organizations. Company Chairman, President and CEO Les Alberthal is a member of the Dallas Citizens Council and serves on the board of directors of the Greater Dallas Chamber of Commerce, the Texas Association of Taxpayers and the Better Business Bureau of Metropolitan Dallas. Other EDS executives serve on the boards of the Dallas Sym-

phony Association, the Collin County Crisis Center, the Plano Chamber of Commerce, the University of Texas at Dallas and the United Way.

In addition to having an active senior management team, EDS promotes employee involvement in the community through its corporate volunteer program. By matching local needs with employee interests and talents, the volunteer program has

EDS Chairman, President and CEO Les Alberthal.

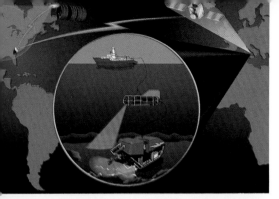

The Jason
Project

*More than 250,000 schoolchildren in the United
States and Canada participated in The JASON
Project, sponsored by EDS and run by Dr. Robert
Ballard. The ship used in the exploration was the Star
Hercules.*

provided assistance to a host of charitable and cultural organizations. More than 600 employees have contributed their time, energy and skills to those in need.

One of the most dramatic community service projects EDS and its employees were involved in last year was Operation Buddy Search. EDS volunteers set up a computer registration system for Vietnam veterans attending a memorial dedication ceremony and then used the system to help the veterans locate old "buddies" from their service in Southeast Asia. In many cases, the vets did not even know if their former colleagues were still alive.

EDS believes that its most valuable asset is its employees, and the company's commitment to their professional growth and personal well-being is legendary. That commitment has ranged from the company's much-publicized rescue of two employees from Iran to less dramatic, but nonetheless significant examples of putting employees first.

Each year, EDS spends more

than $80 million on education to keep employees in technical areas abreast of the latest developments in information technology and to ensure that those in non-technical areas have the best training available for professional growth.

EDS' commitment to employees also extends to their health and fitness. At each EDS location, health and fitness coordinators are available to provide physical assessments and guidance on setting up personal workout regimens. At EDS' Dallas, Detroit and Washington-area locations, employees also have access to exercise facilities. In Dallas and Plano, for example, EDSers can swim, play golf or tennis, work out on weight equipment or treadmill machines and take classes in aerobics and scuba diving.

From the beginning, EDS executives have sought to build their industry by providing examples of vision and leadership, and they have been awarded a host of honors for their efforts. Les Alberthal, for example, has been voted one of America's 10

best large-company executives by the *Gallagher Report*. The officers, directors and managers at EDS belong to a wide range of professional organizations and participate enthusiastically in the activities and leadership of such groups. But the most significant way EDS demonstrates its commitment to the information technology services industry is by consistently turning in outstanding annual performances and by being the recognized leader in the field.

EDS is synonymous with entrepreneurial spirit and drive.

A generation ago, few people knew what systems integration or facilities management meant. EDS pioneered both concepts and saw them as promising and innovative ways to serve companies' burgeoning information-services needs.

EDS was the first company to implement the concept of regional information-processing centers — facilities housing powerful mainframe computers that could process the work of many customers at a central location — at a time when companies still bought their own computers and did their own data processing. In 1988, EDS expanded the concept even further, building the world's first Information Management Center at the company's new facility in Plano. The futuristic, 153,000-square-foot center, which officially opened on March 29, 1989, serves as a network command center for coordinating and directing the voice, video and data communications of more than 6,500 EDS customers in Europe, Asia, North America, South America and Australia.

EDS was an innovator from its inception. At a time when most data-processing contracts were for 60 or 90 days at hourly rates, EDS introduced the long-term, fixed-price computer-services contract that is now the industry standard.

In 1963, EDS signed its first data-processing contract with an insurance company. It was the first time an insurance company had gone "out-

EDS photos.

EDS employs about 56,000 people worldwide — 11,000 of them in North Texas. At top is the Forest Lane campus in North Dallas; below is the Information Management Center, one of the facilities at the company's sprawling Legacy Park site in Plano.

side" for its data processing. Today, EDS is the largest insurance data processor in the United States.

In 1968, a Dallas bank became EDS' first financial institution customer. Today, EDS is the world's largest provider of data-processing services to banks and savings and loans. Much the same thing occurred in the credit union marketplace: Starting in 1974 with eight credit unions, EDS is now the world's largest provider of credit union data-processing services, supporting more than 3,000 such institutions.

In 1978, there were only three EDSers in the company's first Washington-area office as EDS made its first attempt to market facilities-management and systems-integration services to the federal government. Today, about 6,000 people work in EDS' government marketplace.

In 1983, EDS had no customers

EDS supports a wide range of civic, charitable and cultural endeavors. Here, EDSers join employees of other Dallas area companies in a walkathon to raise money for the March of Dimes. **EDS photo.**

in the auto industry. Today, it provides complete data processing and communications service to General Motors Corporation, the largest industrial company in the world.

EDSers now can be found working on information-processing projects in virtually every major industry around the world.

For 27 years, EDS has boldly gone where no company has gone before. Whether it was building the world's first Information Management Center, transmitting live video signals form the bottom of the Mediterranean Sea to museums a continent away or rescuing two employees from an Iranian jail, EDS has been willing to take calculated risks and put itself on the line to improve the human condition. Over and over again, EDS has proven that it has a heart and a soul, as well as a good business mind.

The company and its management consistently are recognized as leaders in the information technology services industry. For the past two years, in fact, EDS has been named the top diversified service company in the country in *Fortune* magazine's annual Corporate Reputations Survey.

EDS has evolved from a local company to an international one with its reach literally extending

around the globe. But despite its incredible growth, the company has continued its long-standing commitment to the Dallas area. EDS employs nearly 11,000 men and women in North Texas and is a source of long-term, dependable financial stability and economic energy for the area's economy.

In addition to maintaining its campus-like facility in North Dallas, EDS has established a major presence in Plano as part of the Legacy business park that the company initiated and is now actively developing.

EDS: A company that is preeminent in its industry. A company that places customer satisfaction first. A company that nurtures its employees and treats them with respect and dignity. A company with an experienced management team and consistently excellent financial performance. A company that helps new and established businesses around the world reach their strategic goals. A company dedicated to community service and to the Dallas area. A company that boldly goes where no company has gone before.

GREATER DALLAS CHAMBER

A high quality of life and a strong business climate have always been top priorities for Dallas citizens, even for the first people who settled in the area in the 1840s. Maintaining a healthy business climate and providing a strong central organization were the goals of citizens years later when they established the Dallas Chamber of Commerce in 1909.

By then, 68 years after its crude beginnings, Dallas was a major center of mercantile and trade, but the city's shortcomings had become evident.

City planning and money were desperately needed to improve the railroads, the Trinity River flood plain (after a massive flood in 1908) and other elements of the infrastructure. To catalyze these and other improvements, the Chamber was chartered by merging four existing organizations: the Commercial Club, the 150,000 Club, the Freight Bureau and the Trade League.

Fifteen of Dallas' most influential business leaders — men like Alexander Sanger of Sanger Brothers and G.B. Dealey of *The Dallas Morning News* — formed the Chamber's first board of directors. For the first time, Dallas had a strong foundation for growth and the unified front to build the city into a prospering business hub. Although the directors had their own businesses to look after, each was willing to attend meetings — sometimes daily — to organize Dallas' civic and business machinery.

And their volunteer work paid off. The Chamber established the City Plan and Improvement League in 1910 to make much-needed improvements in several key areas. George E. Kessler, a nationally renowned city planner, was brought to Dallas to lead the effort.

The problems facing him were startling; most imperative was restructuring the Trinity River flood plain. His plan involved massive changes to the city: shifting the river from its natural course and channeling it between protective levees; creating sanitary sewers; restructuring city storm sewers; rebuilding railway lines; and constructing new viaducts and traffic arteries to accommodate the new river channel and railway lines. These were changes that would

The Greater Dallas Chamber has been a catalyst for progress and change for more than 80 years. Photo by Martin Vandiver.

affect the city's growth and structure for years to come.

Another major concern of the Chamber was bringing higher education to the area. In 1911, the Chamber failed in an attempt to lure the Methodist Church's Southwestern University away from Georgetown, Texas. However, impressed by the city's commitment, the church voted to establish a new university in Dallas after the city and business leaders donated $300,000 and 666.5 acres. Southern Methodist University opened in 1915, and several years later, the Chamber's board of direc-

tors stood in the receiving line to congratulate the first graduates.

Throughout the years, the Chamber — through a supportive and active membership — has continued to thrive alongside the city. Many major corporations that call Dallas home — LTV, Texas Instruments, Electronic Data Systems, GTE Southwest, J.C. Penney and Exxon, to name a few — do so thanks in part to the work and influence of the Chamber.

Involved heavily in bringing aviation to Dallas and putting the city on the country's air traffic map, the Chamber was instrumental in the development of Love Field as a major airport and in the construction of Dallas/Fort Worth International Airport in the 1970s. Today the airport is the second-busiest in the world, and the Chamber is active in efforts to increase the airport's capacity to meet air traffic projections in the 21st century.

As the 1990s unfold, the Chamber is positioned to help the city and the entire region meet the challenges of the future. Through its Public Affairs and Community Development departments, the Chamber is actively addressing issues of vital importance to the region's future: governmental affairs, transportation, aviation, education, minority affairs, natural resources and leadership development. Some programs, such as Dallas United and Adopt-A-School, have received national honors for voluntary involvement and are emulated in other cities.

National and international business development as well as business retention are the primary concerns of The Dallas Partnership. Since the Partnership was formed in 1987, a wide variety of companies and organizations have announced relocations or major expansions in the area, including J.C. Penney, Fujitsu, GTE, MCI, American Airlines,

the Associates Corporation of North America, Mesa Limited Partnership and the Superconducting Super Collider.

Dallas also has become what *Fortune* magazine called "the most diverse and dynamic economic base in the U.S. The so-called Metroplex ... is today's dream location for business."

Dallas is a dream location for conventions and tourism, thanks to the efforts of the Dallas Convention and Visitors Bureau. In 1988, *Business Travel News* named Dallas the No. 2 convention city in the United States behind only New York based on the 2.1 million convention delegates Dallas hosted in 1987. Conventions and tourism contributes about $4.5 billion to the local economy each year.

Central to all these efforts are more than 7,000 Chamber members who are both served by and work with the organization. Members benefit from a variety of activities, including networking events and business development seminars, governmental briefings and a variety of informative publications. The Chamber's Independent Business Council provides numerous programs and activities that promote business growth and professional development for small and medium-sized businesses.

Chamber members also have the opportunity to make a difference by serving on committees and task forces that govern and promote the efforts and concerns of the Chamber membership and the business community at large.

Encouraging Dallas' continued growth, while maintaining its high quality of life and top ranking as the nation's No. 1 business center is the main priority for the Greater Dallas Chamber's agenda. A mission very similar to its charter agenda some 80 years ago.

KRLD NEWSRADIO 1080

The Dallas lifestyle of the 1990s dictates that a person cannot be too rich, too thin or too well-informed. And although Dallas residents can satisfy the first two requisites on their own, for the third they must rely on a crucial assist from the media.

In Dallas radio, that means the one preeminent outlet for news and information: KRLD Newsradio 1080. All news, all day.

Residents of the Dallas/Fort Worth Metroplex have learned to tune in award-winning KRLD as their first source of news for breaking stories from city hall, county and federal courts, police headquarters or traffic control.

With its experienced crew of radio news professionals, KRLD has unmatched resources to assign to top stories of the day in the Dallas/Fort Worth area — whether it is a cultural event like the opening of the Ramses Exhibit or the Morton H. Meyerson Symphony Center, a new government contract for LTV or General Dynamics, a corporate relocation for an American Airlines, GTE or Caltex Petroleum, a natural catastrophe or a five-alarm fire.

Complementing KRLD's local coverage are the station's hourly reports from CBS News, which present a roundup of news develop-

Residents of the Dallas/Fort Worth Metroplex have learned to tune in award-winning KRLD as their first source of news for breaking stories from city hall, county and federal courts, police headquarters or traffic control.

ments worldwide. As an affiliate of the CBS Radio Network, KRLD offers its listeners exposure to news and commentary by such accomplished broadcasters as Dan Rather, Charles Kuralt and Charles Osgood.

KRLD also airs 15 daily reports by *The Wall Street Journal*, experts in business and financial analysis. Altogether, KRLD's blend of local and national news, weather and sports is unmatched in Texas.

"We have established our identity in this market as the first source for news and information," says Michael Ewing, vice president and general manager of KRLD, a Command Communications station. "Our listeners know that when a big story breaks — locally, nationally or internationally — they can count on Newsradio 1080 to provide complete news coverage and the latest updates.

"KRLD has an established franchise within this marketplace," he continues. "For most Americans, radio is still the first source for news.

And that's where our job begins. We're in business to be fast, first, factual and to do the most comprehensive reporting."

KRLD has covered Dallas' growth and maturation into "Big D" since signing on in 1926. The station pioneered "remote" broadcasts in North Texas, providing live coverage of a diverse range of community events around Dallas and Fort Worth, from high school football games to gala opening nights in the Venetian Room at the Fairmont Hotel.

"This station's reputation is based on a long track record of superior performance," says Ewing. "Like any broadcast station, our success ultimately depends on our credibility with listeners. We never lose sight of the fact that we have to supply more news, and a better and fresher perspective, than our competitors. That is the challenge we face each day."

In addition to its franchise in news, KRLD has several other calling cards.

One is sports. Since 1972, KRLD has been the flagship station for the Dallas Cowboys. KRLD sports directors Brad Sham and the late Frank Glieber have taken Cowboys fans along to the dizzying heights of two world championship seasons. The team of Brad Sham and Dale Hansen provides play-by-play coverage and analysis as the reformulated Dallas Cowboys under coach Jimmy Johnson try to refuel their fans' dreams of glory.

KRLD recently has expanded its sports coverage to include live broadcasts of virtually all the major professional events. "In the past year, we've had the baseball playoffs and World

Since 1972, KRLD has been the flagship station for the Dallas Cowboys. The team of Brad Sham (left) and Dale Hansen (right) provides play-by-play coverage and analysis as the reformulated Cowboys try to refuel their fans' dreams of glory.

Series, the NFL playoffs and Super Bowl, the NCAA Final Four, the Dallas Mavericks, the NBA Finals, the Indy 500, WCT and Virginia Slims tennis, and the Byron Nelson and Colonial," Ewing notes.

"Our listeners tend to be sports-oriented individuals. A high percentage of them are college-educated, and they follow their alma maters in NCAA football and basketball. They also tend to have a keen interest in the Cowboys, Mavericks and other professional teams. Sports blends well with the interests of the news-format radio listener."

One other sports note: The station also provides live coverage of the Texas Longhorns' football and basketball games, meaning the ears of Texas are on KRLD. Brad Sham and Chuck Cooperstein broadcast UT football, and Sham also handles Longhorn basketball play-by-play.

Yet another KRLD leading feature is its gardening reports by best-selling author Neil Sperry. Widely

With its experienced crew of radio news professionals, KRLD has unmatched resources to cover the top stories of the day in the Dallas/Fort Worth area.

known and recognized as Texas' top authority on gardening and horticulture, Sperry hosts a popular call-in show that airs Saturday and Sunday mornings.

"Neil commands a large and loyal following throughout Texas," Ewing observes. "His program consistently attracts the largest audience during its time period. It's become a phenomenon into itself."

While Sperry is a man for all (growing) seasons, and KRLD's sports programming offers a game for all seasons, the basic fare at KRLD remains its in-depth news coverage. As the newsmakers and opinion leaders in Dallas/Fort Worth will tell you themselves, when you need to know, simply turn the radio dial to Newsradio 1080. And leave it there.

KTVT-TV CHANNEL 11

Gaylord Broadcasting President James R. Terrell (L) with KTVT Vice-President and General Manager Ed Trimble.

In 1955, the television business was still very much in its infancy. Most television stations relied solely upon the three major networks for the vast majority of their programming. The idea of signing on the air as a non-affiliated station was considered to be a highly speculative and very risky gamble. It was that year when KTVT, Channel 11, became the first "independent" television station in the Dallas-Ft. Worth area. In fact, KTVT, until 1959 known as KFJZ-TV, was only the third television station in the United States to declare its independence. In 1962, KTVT became a Gaylord Broadcasting property and by 1964 was operating in full color, broadcasting from the tallest tower in the state of Texas, located in Cedar Hill, just southwest of Dallas. By 1966, KTVT became

the only television station in Dallas-Ft. Worth to operate two major production studios, one in each city. The year 1985 marked the station's move to its new state-of-the-art facility, considered by industry leaders to be one of the country's foremost broadcast facilities.

In 1990, KTVT begins its 35th year of broadcasting as the dominant independent television station in the Dallas-Ft. Worth market, and as the flagship station of the Dallas-based Gaylord Broadcasting Company. KTVT continues to fulfill the creed of its founder and Chairman of the Board, Edward L. Gaylord, to operate a professional station well and serve the public in the best way possible. According to company President James R. Terrell, "Gaylord Broadcasting stations are proud to be consid-

ered leaders in the broadcast industry, and particularly proud to be a part of the Dallas-Ft. Worth area's dynamic growth and bright future."

KTVT enters the new decade as the area's primary source for the highest quality programming on free and independent television. Its program schedule offers something for every viewer, from family favorites such as "The Cosby Show" and "Growing Pains," to hit situation comedies such as "Cheers" and "Night Court." From major motion pictures to Texas Rangers Baseball and Dallas Mavericks Basketball, to locally-produced chil-

KTVT

GAYLORD BROADCASTING COMPANY

dren's programming, a concept pioneered in Dallas-Ft. Worth by KTVT.

But KTVT's strong viewer loyalty is not based entirely upon the station's programming efforts. Channel 11 has proven itself to be a concerned citizen within the community it serves. Not only has the station lent its financial support to many of the area's service organizations, but it has also provided these organizations support through free production services and air time. Since 1988, KTVT has been involved in an ongoing public awareness campaign called "For Kids' Sake." This campaign is designed specifically for parents to spend more time with their children. The station has produced countless "For Kids' Sake" public service announcements featuring local dignitaries and sports figures. "For Kids' Sake" is a joint effort between the station, concerned advertisers and the community. Supported by active involvement and many televised specials throughout the year, "For Kids' Sake" has achieved many goals. Into the next decade, KTVT follows the tradition of "For Kids' Sake" with an all-new public service campaign, "Time To Care."

In the words of Ed Trimble, KTVT's Vice-President and General Manager, "Quality programming, a commitment to broadcasting excellence, and a sincere desire to help the community we serve, are the foundations on which KTVT enters the 1990's."

KTVT's State-of-the-Art Production Control A

AFFILIATED COMPUTER SYSTEMS INC.

When electronic data processing entrepreneur Darwin Deason formed Affiliated computer Systems Inc. of Dallas in July 1988, in one sense he had come full circle.

Twenty years earlier, Deason had founded a company with the same name. From a virtually cashless beginning, Deason built the first ACS to a company of more than $300 million. It became the largest company in the nation providing computerized banking, financial data processing services and electronic funds transfer. In 1975, Dallas bank holding company Mercantile Texas Corporation bought ACS and later renamed it MTech. Deason stayed at the helm as chief executive.

In April 1988, however, the former Mercantile Texas Corporation, known now as MCorp, was searching for a way to raise capital. It put MTech up for sale and the company was bought by crosstown rival Electronic Data Systems for $465 million. Deason chose to resign the day after the merger was completed.

Three months later, Deason returned to the bank data processing industry. Once more, he was at the helm of a startup company. The new ACS took shape when Deason and other investors acquired the data processing subsidiary of First Texas Financial Corporation. Joining Deason was Charles Young, former MTech president of Corporate Services and president of the new ACS. The purchase included the TransFirst electronics benefits transfer business plus its MoneyMaker network of 900 automated teller machines and First Texas Computer Corporation.

Electronic funds transfer may sound technical and complex, but what it accomplishes is very simple. Through linked computers, an electronic funds transfer system can move money almost instantaneously across town or around the world. The electronic method of transfer is much faster, more efficient and far more secure than physically moving cash from one location to another.

Most people are familiar with automated teller machines (ATMs), which perform electronic funds transfers for the retail customers of banks or savings and loans. ACS acquired MoneyMaker, the nation's 12th-largest ATM system, which operates the largest network of off-premise ATMs in the nation. There are now more than 1,000 MoneyMaker machines in retail locations throughout Texas.

The deal, however, put ACS into more than just one segment of the electronic funds transfer industry. ACS also acquired a burgeoning electronic benefits transfer business. The technology is basically the same as that used in an ATM network, but it is applied to distribute government benefit amounts or private benefits such as insurance payments. ACS also has 2 million customer accounts for over 300 Financial institutions.

Deason had come full circle, but he was by no means all the way back to square one. The new ACS began with far greater financial strength than Deason's first venture. The second time around, ACS was launched with a strong recurring revenue base and balance sheet. That financial strength has enabled the young company to grow both internally and through further acquisitions.

Deason moved swiftly to put key players in place and doubled the number of ACS employees to 700 in just five months, primarily through aggressive acquisitions. ACS bought MICR Specialty, a Houston firm that specializes in preparing statements based on checking transactions. It snapped up Electronic Data Management Company., a Dallas software firm that provides applications software and related data processing services mainly to airlines and long-distance telecommunications

companies.

In early 1989, ACS purchased 131 bank data processing contracts that had belonged to failed First RepublicBank Corporation, an acquisition expected to generate more than $10.8 million in revenue. The deal boosted ACS' financial data processing contracts to more than 250. It also gave ACS, for the first time, access to banks in key Texas markets.

ACS entered the Oklahoma market by purchasing United Data Services Inc. (UDSI) and its sister company, United Check Processing Inc. (UCPI) in Oklahoma City from Mutual Security Life Insurance Company of Indiana. UDSI provides bank data processing and automated teller machine services throughout Oklahoma, while UCPI offers data processing for financial institutions. At

Precept, an ACS company, manages the shipping and distribution of financial services forms, records and equipment.

the same time, ACS bought Abilene-based First Independent Computers, a cardholder processing service company whose parent company, Credit Card Software, is based in Florida.

ACS' next move was to acquire the correspondent bank data processing business of NCNB Texas National Bank. The purchase of the NCNB unit, based in Waco, brought ACS 39 more customers and increased to more than 350 the number of Southwest financial institutions for which it provides data processing services. Heading further west, ACS bought Computab Inc., based in Honolulu and the largest data processing services firm in Hawaii.

From the outset, ACS and Deason proved as adept at winning contracts as they were at acquisitions. The company scored a major coup in December 1988 by signing a 10-year agreement to provide data processing and telecommunications services to Dallas-based Southland Corporation, the nation's largest operator of convenience stores.

The agreement made ACS a data processing utility for Southland. The contract, by far the biggest in ACS' short history, meant a substantial increase in ACS' annual revenues and allowed ACS to acquire 89 employees already in Southland's data center.

ACS operates MoneyMaker, the nation's 12th-largest ATM system and the largest network of off-premise ATMs.

A year after it was formed, ACS signed a $30 million contract with the Maryland Department of Human Resources to create a sophisticated electronic network to distribute social services benefits. The five-year pact provided for ACS/TransFirst to design a system to distribute public assistance and child support payments as well as food stamp benefits to 300,000 Maryland residents. These benefits would be available through ATMs. It was the largest contract awarded to date to the ACS/TransFirst unit.

Aggressive, experienced and savvy leadership and management have been major factors in ACS' rapid expansion during its first year. But ACS also is poised to take advantage of markets that offer exciting growth opportunities. In benefits transfer, for example, ACS estimates that less than half of 1 percent of the 2.5 billion social services checks distributed nationally each year are delivered electronically. The field is wide open for those who know how to play the game, and ACS is the leader in this new industry.

ACS' pact with Southland is an example of how the use of computers

ACS' electronic benefits transfer business distributes government benefit amounts or private benefits such as insurance payments.

and computer-related services is changing among major U.S. corporations. Companies no longer want to become bogged down in the nuts and bolts of setting up and running data processing centers, and businesses are turning to specialists such as ACS to provide computer utilities, much like the phone company provides communications and gas or electric companies provide their services.

Location also has played a major role in ACS' fast growth. "There was no question in my mind that Dallas would be the location for ACS," says chief executive Deason. "Dallas has the reputation of being a high tech city, and with ACS being a large, full-service data processing company, we knew that locating here would bring us the resources that we needed to succeed."

ACS employees are motivated by the challenge of local competition, Deason continues. "Seeing that Dallas is a city of large processors, we are able to get out into the market and hustle. 'Good things come to those who are patient, but normally it's the leftovers from those who hustle.' This is a company philosophy we work by and is a major reason ACS has grown as quickly as it has — and will keep growing."

ACS also can return something substantial to its headquarters city by offering job opportunities.

"We have a great potential in electronic benefits transfer," Deason points out. "ACS is a pioneer in processing technology, so ACS employees get full-scale, on-the-job training. With that, and the fact that we are capable of processing for commercial, retail, financial and government, we have several job opportunities for the community."

Darwin Deason, founder of Affiliated Computer Systems Inc.

AMERICAN AIRLINES INC.

When American Airlines Inc. moved its corporate headquarters operation from New York City to Dallas/Fort Worth in 1979, there were some skeptics who wondered aloud whether such a large corporation with a strong presence on the East Coast could fly into town and become a local entity of power and vision.

Today, more than a decade later, American and its parent, AMR Corporation, have proven beyond everyone's expectations that they are the kind of corporate citizens that some metropolitan areas can only dream about attracting. To wit: American is the largest and most profitable airline in the free world, flying out of Dallas/Fort Worth International Airport to destinations throughout the United States, Europe, the Orient and South America. It serves 115 U.S. cities and 41 international points.

The corporation, which employed some 89,000 people worldwide at the end of 1989, has more than doubled in size since 1980; and in the D/FW area alone, AMR has more than 22,000 employees — making it the second-largest employer in the Metroplex and a towering presence in the community. Indeed, it would be hard to speak of American Airlines without mentioning Dallas/Fort Worth in the same sentence.

What some people may not know is that American's roots in the area actually go back more than 60 years to an amalgam of tiny aviation companies — one of which employed Charles Lindbergh — that in 1930 became known as American Airways. It was headed by a young Texan named C.R. Smith, who would go on to serve at the helm of American Airlines (as it was reincorporated in 1934) for more than 30 years.

American has always been an industry leader, creating such textbook marketing innovations as the family fare (1948); the first stewardess college (in 1957, near what today is D/FW Airport); SABRE, the industry's first computerized reservations system (1964); the hugely successful Super Saver fare (1977); and AAdvantage, the world's first frequent-traveler program (1981).

From the early days when AA engineers helped design the most famous passenger plane ever built — the Douglas DC-3 — the airline has always flown the best, most modern aircraft available. Today, its fleet consists of 480 airplanes ranging from the mammoth Boeing 747SP used on the airline's D/FW-Tokyo route to the sleek McDonnell Douglas MD-80

American has always been an industry leader, creating such marketing innovations as the family fare, the first stewardess college, the industry's first computerized reservations system, the successful Super Saver fare and the world's first frequent-traveler program.

American is the largest and most profitable airline in the free world, flying out of Dallas/Fort Worth International Airport to 115 U.S. cities and 41 international points.

flown on many of American's domestic routes. On order for delivery over the next three years are the state-of-the-art McDonnell Douglas MD-11, the Boeing 767-300ER and the Fokker 100. The fleet's average age of 9.2 years at year-end 1989 will drop to eight years by year-end 1993, giving American one of the country's youngest aircraft fleets.

But airplanes and marketing ideas alone do not make American the most continuously successful air carrier in the United States. Paramount to its far-reaching growth plan — put into place several years ago by chairman and president Robert L. Crandall and his top officers — is expansion into many new worldwide markets and the airport facilities and other improvements to support that expansion.

One of the biggest local news

stories of 1989 involved American's $400-million maintenance and engineering center to be built at Alliance Airport in Fort Worth. The first phase of the giant facility will be open by late 1991 and will employ 2,500 people, further strengthening AMR's presence in the area. Ultimate employment could exceed 4,500.

The company also is continuing to expand its headquarters in the Centreport complex near D/FW Airport. Housed there, in addition to the airline's corporate staff, are management employees for AMR Services, a company that provides ground services such as baggage handling and maintenance for other airlines; AMR Information Services, which offers American's computer system to other organizations, as well as a large telemarketing operation called American Airlines Direct Marketing Corporation; AMR Investment Services, a company offering mutual funds and other investment products to corporate and institutional investors, primarily in the areas of pension fund and short term cash management; and AMR Eagle Inc., a company that operates seven American Eagle commuter airlines with more than 1,400 daily flights throughout the United States and the Caribbean.

American's dynamic growth plan has zeroed in on the international market, and its long-term strategy calls for flights from D/FW, Chicago and New York and other hubs to every major city in Europe, as well as service to the major cities of Asia.

With this type of aggressive, futuristic thinking, it is no wonder that American Airlines was selected "Airline of the Year" for 1988 by *Air Transport World* magazine — the only airline to win the award twice — and was named the No. 1 airline in the world in 1987 by North American frequent flyers. American topped the list of airlines in *Fortune* magazine's 1987 "Most Admired Corporations" and was named the best domestic airline for the seventh consecutive year in 1988 by the readers of *Executive Travel* magazine. Moreover, Crandall was named the best chief executive of a major U.S. airline for five consecutive years by the *Wall Street Transcript,* for a total of six times between 1981-87. He also earned *Financial World* magazine's Bronze Award as the leading airline CEO in 1988. And in 1988 the prestigious *Gallagher Report* named Crandall one of the top 10 managers in U.S. business.

In addition, American was named the best trans-Atlantic airline in 1988 by readers of London's *Executive Travel* magazine, beating out British Airways for the first time; and American's passenger sales force was tapped No. 1 in the transportation

---

American Airlines has always flown the best, most modern aircraft available. Today, its fleet consists of 480 airplanes ranging from the mammoth Boeing 747SP used on the airline's D/FW-Tokyo route to the British Aerospace 146-200 seating 81 passengers.

industry by the readers of *Sales and Marketing Management* magazine in June 1988.

AMR's kudos for community work in the Metroplex are almost too numerous to mention. Most recently, the corporation has been heavily involved with the opening of the Morton H. Meyerson Symphony Center in downtown Dallas. It has been a tireless supporter of the Dallas Symphony Orchestra, the Dallas Opera, many museums and theaters, and a number of athletic events over the years. AMR employees are always among the top contributors to the United Way, and probably every major volunteer organization in the Metroplex lists AMR employees in their rosters, a sign that these transplanted Texans are here to stay.

Chairman Robert Crandall has repeatedly emphasized AMR's commitment to Dallas/Fort Worth and to Texas. He stresses his company's faith in the Metroplex: "It has many advantages, including a positive business climate, a reputation for leadership and achievement, and the operational benefits of being at the center of the nation and of our route system."

KDFW-TV CHANNEL 4

KDFW-TV's longtime Vice-President and General Manager, Bill Baker, associated with station from 1952 until 1990.

December 3, 1949, was a very historical day in Dallas. In sports, it was truly memorable because the wild and brash Doak Walker/Kyle Rote-led SMU Mustangs took on the Notre Dame Fighting Irish in the newly expanded Cotton Bowl. More than 73,000 fans saw a remarkably exciting game in person.

Those who were not able to attend were still able to watch one of the biggest games in the history of college football via the infant medium of television, thanks to the newest station in the area. For on that December day, KRLD-TV Channel 4 signed on for the first time with the broadcast of the contest and thereby became the first station in Dallas to televise a live football game involving a Southwest Conference team.

Today, Channel 4 is now KDFW-TV and has grown dramatically from the old Channel 4 that in the beginning signed on at 5 p.m.

KDFW-TV, one of the Times Mirror Broadcasting Group stations, is a wholly owned subsidiary of the Times Mirror Company whose corporate headquarters are in Los Angeles.

Jeff Rosser serves as vice president and general manager of KDFW Channel 4, and Carl (Bud) Carey is president of Times Mirror Broadcasting which is headquartered in New York City. For 40 years, KDFW's studios have been at 400 North Griffin in downtown Dallas, just a stone's throw away from the emerging Dallas Arts District.

During those 40 years, Channel 4 has broadcast more than its share of truly memorable events. In 1963 a Channel 4 camera (the only one operating at the time) captured for history the chilling murder of alleged Kennedy assassin Lee Harvey Oswald by Jack Ruby in the basement of the Dallas City Jail. No sports fan will ever forget the stoic Tom Landry's painful out-of-character grimace in 1966 when his upstart Dallas Cowboys lost to Green Bay in the final seconds of the NFL championship game. The list goes on.

Always on the cutting edge of television technology, that legacy was enhanced in the mid '60s with the addition of the Channel 4 Color Cruiser, a state-of-the-art mobile production facility; it was the best-equipped mobile unit in the country at that time. Not only was the unit under contract to CBS, but both ABC and NBC "borrowed" it for various entertainment and sports remote broadcasts. Even to this day, Channel 4 remains a broadcast technology leader, with the latest in remote satellite facilities at its immediate disposal.

However, all the broadcast technology in the world does not assure long-term success without quality programming. And Channel 4 has provided the Dallas/Fort Worth area with quality entertainment and sports programs from CBS and excellent local programming, not to mention award-winning news presentations. Channel 4 was the first local station to recognize the significance of the killings that blossomed into

Channel 4's helicopter and live vans in addition to the latest in remote satellite facilities, keep KDFW-TV a leader in broadcast technology.

the sensational T. Cullen Davis murder trials, and initiated a tireless two-year investigation that resulted in the arrest and conviction of Charles "Tex" Harrellson for the 1979 San Antonio murder of Federal Judge John Wood.

The jewel in the award-winning news crown at Channel 4 occurred in 1986 when anchor Clarice Tinsley broke the story of the city of Dallas' inefficient ambulance service, complete with dispatcher tape. For her investigative work, Tinsley received the coveted Peabody Award.

There is, however, another equally important side to Channel 4: community service. The station prides itself in its consistent contributions to the community it serves. KDFW-TV has produced public service announcements for many community organizations in and around Dallas. These organizations include The American Red Cross, The American Cancer Society, Mental Health Association, Edna Gladney Center, Dallas Civic Music Association, People with AIDS Coalition, Senior Citizens of Greater Dallas and the Historical Preservation League.

Channel 4's studio in the shadow of the downtown Dallas skyline.

Channel 4 News co-sponsored a colon-rectal cancer series including free home test kits. More than 80,000 kits were distributed along with information concerning the disease. Since many of those kits returned with positive results, countless lives were saved through early detection. The news department also was involved in producing a breast cancer screening program in which mammograms were made available to women over 35 at greatly reduced costs. These are only two of many examples of Channel 4's partnership in the health and welfare of our community.

In April 1989, Channel 4 sponsored Walk America at White Rock Lake. More than 8,000 Dallas citizens, including the Channel 4 news team and 60 of the station's employees, walked the 9 miles around the lake twice, (which turned out to be a very challenging 18-mile course) with proceeds benefitting the March of Dimes.

Channel 4 also sponsored Hoop It Up, the largest three-man basketball tournament in the country. More than 100,000 participants and spectators took part in the two-day event held in the West End with Special Olympics benefitting from the proceeds.

Other community service events sponsored all or in part by Channel 4 include Hearing Impaired Day at Scarborough Fair, the springtime Renaissance festival held south of Dallas; Montage, an Arts District street festival that drew more than 60,000 people and benefitted the 500 Inc; the Hearty Party, a low-cholesterol food festival that benefitted the American Heart Association; and others too numerous to mention.

In short, KDFW's slogan, "Believing in Texas," underscores its continuing commitment to leadership and excellence in service to Dallas and the region.

ZIG ZIGLAR CORPORATION

Zig Ziglar, founder, and Ron Land, president of the Zig Ziglar Corporation.

John Jones was in New York City. He wanted to go to Boston, so he went to the airport and bought a ticket. Having a few minutes to spare, he walked over to some scales, stepped on them, inserted a coin and down came his fortune: "Your name is John Jones, you weigh 188 pounds and you are going to catch the 2:20 to Boston." He was astounded because all of this information was correct. He figured this must be a trick, so he stepped back on the scales, inserted another coin and down came his fortune: "Your name is still John Jones, you still weigh 188 pounds and you still are going to catch the 2:20 to Boston." Now he was more puzzled than ever. Sensing a trick, he decided to "fool" whoever or whatever was responsible. He decided to go to the men's room and change his clothes. Once again he stepped on the scales, inserted his coin and down came his fortune: "Your name is still John Jones, you still weigh 188 pounds — but you just missed the 2:20 to Boston."

From Zig Ziglar's best-selling book *See You at the Top*

For more than 35 years, Zig Ziglar and the corporation he founded have been spreading a unique message of hope to people around the world. Based in Dallas, the company has grown dramatically from 16 employees in 1980 who shared a dream of spreading the tools of hope and success. It is now a multimillion-dollar corporation touching the lives of millions of people as it distributes a multitude of dynamic sales and motivational tools.

In a manner of speaking, the goals and dynamics of the Zig Ziglar Corporation closely parallel those of Dallas. Both share a vibrant commitment to success and exciting plans that include realistic goals for future growth.

The Zig Ziglar Corporation is demonstrating every day that a dream fueled by desire and determination and that is organized into a specific plan of action can far exceed its original concept. Time and time again, Ziglar has shown individuals and companies the keys to success, first individually, and then collectively.

Eventually, the concepts and ideas helped the Zig Ziglar Corporation evolve into "The Training Company." This operation employs more than 80 people and markets a highly specialized line of more than 40 tools to train corporations "from the front desk to the back door."

But the key to success cannot be found only in the workplace. As Ziglar himself is fond of saying, "No man can call himself a success if he fails at home." Ziglar helps many people apply the aspects of his positive ideals into their own personal lives, while providing plans and tools that fall into three categories: Materials for Corporate Training, Materials for Personal Growth and Materials for the Family.

The Zig Ziglar Corporation's materials have a strong foundation in books written by Ziglar. *See You at the Top* is the first and most popular. It has evolved "Born to Win," a dynamic three-day seminar held bimonthly in Dallas that draws participants from all over the world. The seminar itself has been developed into a highly significant and meaningful video presentation used by many *Fortune* 500 Companies.

Many other success tools have evolved from these original ideas. These programs include; "Improving People and Performance," designed to build teamwork and personal self-esteem; "Effective Business Presentations," which develops public speaking and business communications; and "Top Performance," a management training tool. These and other programs are designed specifically for businesses and those who wish to succeed, regardless of their chosen field.

One of the biggest problems facing society today is disintegration of the family unit. Ziglar confronts this all too frequent tragedy in his book, *Courtship After Marriage*. The book offers a positive and loving plan that helps couples overcome the stresses found in every marriage that if left unchecked, often result in divorce.

The Zig Ziglar Corporation is committed to family success as deeply as it is to personal and business success. A 4-tape video program, "Raising Positive Kids in a Negative World," is helping parents do just that. Another aid in helping parents help their children become better citizens is the audio presentation

Zig speaks on personal and professional success motivation to a very attentive audience.

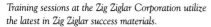

Training sessions at the Zig Ziglar Corporation utilize the latest in Zig Ziglar success materials.

"Clean, Straight and Sober! How To Raise Drug-Free Kids In A Drug-Filled World."

In short, Zig Ziglar and the company he founded are supplying people with the tools they need to succeed, regardless of environment or circumstance. Ziglar calls his formula the "Tri-Dimensional Tools to Personal Success," because it focuses on the physical, mental and spiritual traits of every human being.

But as tremendously successful as the Zig Ziglar Corporation has been, like Dallas, it has a dynamic plan for growth. No less than 45 multimedia projects that will compliment the current corporate mission are on the drawing board for the next five years alone. They range from auxiliary programs to compliment existing sales/motivational programs, to syndicated radio and newspaper projects, to support programs for public education, to self-esteem and success foundations for elementary school children,

such as the developing program "I Can."

And these are only a drop in the bucket of human character and potential realization which is the cornerstone of the Zig Ziglar Corporation.

What the Zig Ziglar Corporation offers is hope, and even more than that: The Zig Ziglar Corporation also offers proven plans for success, regardless of the personal challenge. Some, like John Jones, may be suspicious of the information that is being given, regardless of how obvious it might be. But maybe, the John Jones' of the world will realize they "still have a plane to catch." Dallas realizes this fact. And so too, do the successful and committed people-builders — Zig Ziglar Corporation.

STAR 105.3, KQZY

Star 105.3 Vice President/General Manager Jenny Sue Rhoades takes the wheel of "Vanna Black," the station's digital remote broadcast van.

The brightest broadcaster in Dallas and the Lone Star State has deep roots in the origins of radio itself.

To Westinghouse Chief Engineer, Dr. Frank Conrad, it seemed like a bright idea — even if his friends did not agree. In 1912 (and with a $5 dollar bet at stake), Conrad built what turned out to be a small radio receiver so he could hear time signals from the U.S. Naval Observatory in Arlington, Virginia. Five dollars richer, and pleased with his new hobby, Conrad shortly thereafter built a transmitter and began broadcasting everything from recorded music to live vocal and instrumental "on-air concerts" on what he called "8XK Radio."

Someone else had a bright idea too. Westinghouse Vice President H.P. Davis obtained a radio license, and on November 2, 1920, 8XK Radio became KDKA Radio with its first public broadcast: the Harding-Cox presidential election returns.

The rest, to borrow a phrase, is Westinghouse broadcast history.

Today, bright ideas continue to permeate each of Westinghouse Broadcasting's four divisions: Group W Television, Group W Productions, Group W Satellite and Group W Radio, parent company of Dallas/Fort Worth's STAR 105.3.

While esteemed sister stations KDKA (AM), WBZ (AM) and KYW (AM) may mark the company's historical distinction, Group W's FM properties set a pace for both format innovation and excitement. Nowhere is that more evident than in the Metro-plex at STAR 105.3 (KQZY FM).

"It's rock'n'roll for the rest of us," says a beaming Vice-President and General Manager Jenny Sue Rhoades. "That's the perfect definition for STAR 105.3. Adults love Phil Collins, Cher and Whitney Houston, but they don't want rap or heavy metal mixed in. The STAR is an adult hit music station for the '90s, and that's very exciting."

The ingredients for STAR's bright future in Dallas are certainly in place — from the fresh blend of today's music, to the warm and friendly personalities, to the long-term stability offered by the pioneering spirit of parent Group W. Rhoades, and all of Dallas for that matter, have good reason to be excited.

Channeling enthusiasm and a "can-do-anything" attitude into her staff, Rhoades continues to build STAR 105.3 into one of this area's leading adult radio competitors.

If community visibility is any gauge of that goal, STAR 105.3 is at the top. From balloon festivals to Mardi Gras parades to collecting shoes for the homeless, STAR 105.3 shows a dynamic presence in all areas of the Metroplex.

"STAR 105.3 makes sense for the Plano Parks and Recreation Department because the station makes the Plano community a special part of its efforts," says Sue Padden, superintendent of Special Programs for Plano Parks and Recreation.

"Plano is family-oriented," adds Rhoades. "It makes sense to target one of the fastest-growing communities in the Metroplex."

STAR 105.3 also maintains high visibility in Fort Worth. The station sponsors events such as the Fort Worth Zoo's annual fundraiser, "Zoo

Even Elvis refuses to miss Star 105.3's Halloween Mardi Gras every fall in the West End.

Star 105.3's listeners, and "balloon-o-philes" gather at the Plano Balloon Festival, and prepare for the big send-off.

Doo," along with the Fort Worth Symphony's "Oktoberfest."

But on the streets of Dallas, a special autumn festival brings out the "beast" in the city. The event, which features two days of ghoulish festivities, is appropriately called "STAR 105.3's Halloween Mardi Gras." Thousands of costumed participants jam the West End Historic District for street dances, carnivals, parades and live music.

"With all we do in and for the community, our staff must be in great physical shape," muses Rhoades. "And as for our listeners, if they can't come to an event, they can still keep in touch via Vanna Black."

That is the name given to STAR 105.3's black digital remote satellite broadcasting van. "We've broadcast from all over the Metroplex," says Rhoades, "from hot-air balloons to parade floats."

For STAR 105.3, Group W's 70 years of broadcasting experience and innovation clearly sets an exciting pace for the future. "Group W wrote the first chapter on broadcasting," says Rhoades, "and now, they are busy writing a whole new chapter." This "new chapter" was introduced recently when the company made the largest radio acquisition in the industry's history. Group W is the most significant non-network radio group in America, boasting 20 stations with 12 in nine of the top 10 markets.

"STAR 105.3 has an incredible opportunity to continue the Group W legacy in Dallas," says Rhoades. "The deck is stacked in our favor. Everything a successful business needs to prosper is here — from spirit and attitude to education, employment and an economic outlook that far exceeds most large cities in the entire world."

If Dr. Conrad could only see what his $5 bet developed.

SOUTHWESTERN BELL

In June 1881 there were only three telephones in the city of Dallas. Fire Chief W.C. Conner, who had the first phone near old city hall, could call only two other numbers: the fire department's station house and the water department.

Today, no one knows how many telephones or related telecommunications devices exist, since almost any legitimate device can be used on telephone company lines. However, what is known is that there are more than 1 million access lines and the number grows daily.

Since the first days of the telephone company in Dallas, and despite very humble beginnings, the telephone has played an indispensable role in Dallas' growth. Today, the Southwestern Bell network in this area is regarded as one of the nation's best, and digital high-tech capabilities have made Dallas a major center for telecommunications and corporations counting national and even worldwide communications as their heartbeat.

But back in the 1880s, phone service was primitive at best. The first poles — compared to today's underground distribution facilities — were seedlings from the Trinity River bottoms hauled to town over muddy, unpaved streets under the direction of then-owner D.M. Clower.

The first exchange was managed by J.S. Burton, who also ran the Western Union office on the side. The Dallas exchange had several locations and several owners in those early years, eventually being purchased by Southwestern Bell in the late 1880s. By 1885 about 500 customers had service, and the first long distance lines were being strung to a few other cities in Texas.

By the turn of the century Southwestern Bell moved its main downtown exchange to Jackson and Akard Streets, now 308 S. Akard across from the modern Bell Plaza

complex. A focal point in downtown Dallas, Bell Plaza houses the Texas Division headquarters of Southwestern Bell.

There was competition around the turn of the century from the Dallas Automatic Telephone Company, but the company did not last too long. Six years after Dallas Automatic began, it merged with Southwestern Bell in 1918. By 1925, more than 50,000 telephones were tied into the Dallas network.

Today, Southwestern Bell employs more than 7,000 people in Dallas and is one of the largest and most active corporate citizens in Texas. In addition to a much greater number of employees, the services offered are dramatically different from those in the "good old days."

The old-style crank phone has given way to electronic switching, voice message services, integrated switched digital networks and other high tech innovations. A call across the country and around the world is

as commonplace today as a call across town was not too many years ago. And technological advances enable the transmission of any type of communication, from voice to print to electronic data.

D.M. Clower, J.S. Burton and other historical figures would hardly know the company today. But it is an extension of what they and other telephone pioneers began as well as their company's legacy: a commitment to providing service when, where and in whatever form customers want, which remains unchanged.

Dallas, like the businesses serving it, is still growing, and like Southwestern Bell, it is looking to a bright future as the 21st century prepares to unfold.

Bell Plaza, a focal point in downtown Dallas, houses the Texas Division headquarters of Southwestern Bell, which employs more than 7,000 people in Dallas and is one of the largest and most active corporate citizens in Texas.

WFAA-TV CHANNEL 8

The studios of WFAA-TV Channel 8 in downtown Dallas at dusk.

Having begun its fifth decade of broadcasting in September 1989, WFAA-TV Channel 8 is continuing to build on its reputation of quality programming, a news operation that is second to none not only in North Texas but across the country, and an enviable track record of successful and meaningful community service.

Affiliated with the ABC Television Network, Channel 8 is able to present critically acclaimed network programs such as Emmy award-winners "thirtysomething," "The Wonder Years" and "China Beach." The station backs up these programs with proven winners like "Donahue," "The Oprah Winfrey Show" and "Entertainment Tonight." Locally produced programs include "8 Country Reporter" and "Peppermint Place" which have both been successfully syndicated throughout the state and around the world.

Considering that Dallas/Fort Worth is the eighth-largest media market in the country, the fact that Channel 8 has been at or near the top in all local newscast areas for more than 20 years is truly astounding.

Channel 8's primary anchors boast more than 60 years of cumulative news/weather/sports reporting in the Dallas/Fort Worth area alone, not to mention total aggregate experience. The on-camera mix of news anchors such as Tracy Rowlett, Chip Moody, weatherman Troy Dungan and sports anchor Dale Hansen, who also spends time as a member of the Dallas Cowboys' play-by-play radio broadcast team, sets the standard for other broadcast journalists to follow.

But Channel 8's news anchors are only the tip of a very impressive iceberg. Boasting one of the largest local news staffs in the country, WFAA-TV has won more awards and critical acclaim than all other local stations combined. News 8 covers breaking stories like no other television station, while investigative journalism remains the cornerstone of the Channel 8 news foundation. Spot news coverage and in-depth investigative work have resulted in numerous awards, including the coveted George Foster Peabody Award, Columbia Dupont Award, countless Dallas Press Club "Katies" and many Associated Press and United Press Awards for reporting excellence.

Channel 8's commitment goes beyond what viewers see on the television screen. Channel 8 is deeply involved in the community, contributing to the quality of life in North Texas. Involved with 40 separate events in 1989, some of the more notable include:

"Channel 8's Santa's Helpers": Weatherman Troy Dungan is the annual chairman of this Dallas/Fort Worth Christmas tradition which does its best to see that no disadvantaged child wake up on Christmas morning to an empty tree.

"Health and Fitness": This special event brings viewers and medical/health professionals together for free demonstrations, health tests and giveaways.

"A World of Difference": Channel 8's Phyllis Watson examines the differences in the community by explaining the ethnic, racial and religious prejudices in a series of prime time specials. Watson, who does not hide her compassion and feelings from the camera, lends her special warmth to the project.

Special Events: Both sportscaster Hansen and news anchor Moody host benefit golf tournaments for local charities which have become media events in their own right. Also, when the Morton H. Meyerson Symphony Center opened in September 1989, Channel 8 joined 50 other local corporations and arts patrons in sponsoring a month of classical and arts-related entertainment.

Channel 8's theme, "The Spirit of Texas," sums up the station's commitment to quality programming, excellence in keeping North Texas informed, and serving the community it has been a part of for more than 40 years.

NORTHERN TELECOM

In 1987, on a spring night in Washington D.C., precisely on schedule at 8 p.m., the telephone rang in a small reception room at the U.S. State Department. Trade Representative Clayton Yeuter picked up the receiver, and from halfway around the world in Japan, a voice rang out loud and clear: "Hello, Mr. Ambassador. This is Ed Fitzgerald."

With those words, Northern Telecom Chairman and CEO Ed Fitzgerald and the ambassador celebrated the initial phone call placed over the first non-Japanese digital central office switch in Japan. It also marked another milestone in Northern Telecom's growing influence in the global telecommunications market.

Northern Telecom Inc., the U.S. subsidiary of Canada's behemoth Northern Telecom Limited, is the second-largest telecommunications manufacturer in the United States and a major contributor to the overwhelming growth of the telecommunications industry worldwide.

With its 2,400 local employees, Northern Telecom ranks among the top 50 employers in the Dallas area. By 1991, all of Northern Telecom's Metroplex employees will be housed in a new $100-million, four-building office center on 18 acres north of Dallas.

Northern Telecom entities in the Metroplex include: BNR (Bell Northern Research), Northern Telecom's primary research center, which employs nearly 700 people in the area; Meridian Business Systems, which employs 440 locally and some 4,500 others nationwide; Data Communications and Networks, a marketing arm employing approximately 1,100 locally and another 723 nationwide; and Integrated Network Systems, a marketing office that sells central office switching systems to telephone companies throughout the Southwest.

Northern Telecom is involved in the manufacture and sale of a wide variety of hardware systems for the telecommunications industry, including computerized switching systems used by telephone companies and major corporations.

However, Northern Telecom is a significant player in more than just telecommunications hardware; it is a leader in research that will fuel the technological breakthroughs of tomorrow. For instance, BNR is developing digital cellular radio as

well as a variety of other 21st century products. The company's dedication to such research will continue to support the company's prominent position within the highly competitive industry.

That strong research and development program, combined with a streamlined, cost-effective marketing focus, helped the company collect $5.4 billion in revenues in 1988, with revenues anticipated at $30 billion by the year 2000.

Much of Northern Telecom's

growth has been based on the worldwide acceptance of the company's digital telecommunications products for the telephone central office as well as for transmission and business voice/data communications. Northern Telecom expects further expansion and deeper market penetration in such diverse markets as Western Europe, the Pacific Rim, Africa and the People's Republic of China. And, Northern Telecom expects its market to expand in North, Central and South America.

Says Des Hudson, president of Northern Telecom World Trade: "Given the sheer size of the global market we serve, World Trade is structured now to achieve $1 billion in international business in the early 1990's." Thus, the company is uniquely positioned to reach this goal

Artist rendering of Northern Telecom/BNR facility slated for occupancy in late 1991.

through its world network of subsidiary operations, strategic alliances, joint ventures and licensee relationships.

And while Northern Telecom is busy securing and expanding its position as a world leader in the field of telecommunications, it also is vitally interested and involved in the community in which it works.

Northern Telecom located its various branches in the Metroplex for many reasons, including the strong employment base, an outstanding quality of life offered its employees and a variety of educational institutions committed to such areas of study as science and engineering.

"Northern Telecom is pleased to be able to return the favor with ongoing contributions toward the betterment of its communities and residents," says Donald Peterson, group vice president of the Meridian Business Systems subsidiary. "From creating new jobs to funding community needs, the company remains dedicated to making differences in life quality as well as high technology.

"Northern Telecom and the community are a remarkable team, solidly investing in one another's potentials. As a strategic force in the telecommunications industry, we remain committed to creating solutions and opportunities."

Whether Northern Telecom is forging forward in new markets or satisfying the needs of existing customers, the company is consistently developing, manufacturing and selling products for public and corporate networking.

Says Geore Brody, Assistant Vice President, Richardson Lab Director, BNR: "For us, there is no question that the major opportunity before the telecommunications industry today is to develop innovative solutions that tie together different manufacturer's equipment in public, private and hybrid networks."

WORDTEMPS INC.

Valerie Freeman is the founder and driving force behind the highly successful Wordtemps and its divisions, Freeman & Associates and Prime Timers.

In 1982 when Valerie Freeman saw a tremendous need in the Dallas community, she did something about it. The company she founded, Wordtemps Inc., specializes in the temporary placement of people skilled in computer technology.

Wordtemps is one of the first businesses of its kind in the United States. In addition to staffing Dallas businesses with computer literate personnel, Wordtemps also maintains a technology training center equipped with the most current software and hardware. Staying up-to-date on tech-

nological innovation is the key to the tremendous success of the company.

"Companies need a core of full-time people, but they also need the capability to staff up at times toward that end," Freeman says. "Wordtemps provides people with top skills and intelligence."

Wordtemps offices operate in Dallas, Fort Worth, Plano and Irving, and further expansion is on the books for the 1990s. Two divisions of Wordtemps Inc. are Freeman & Associates, a permanent placement firm founded in 1981, and Prime Timers, founded in 1987.

In starting Prime Timers, Freeman set out to help destroy the mistaken perceptions which plague older workers in the business world. Prime Timers provides temporary and full-time placement and computer cross-training for displaced mature workers and retirees.

Valerie Freeman balances business activities with an active role in Dallas civic affairs. She serves on the boards of the Greater Dallas Chamber and the Dallas Women's Foundation. She is a past president of the National Association of Women Business Owners. Freeman has received numerous professional awards, including recognition as the 1989 Small Business Person of the Year by the Sales and Marketing Executives of Dallas.

Freeman lauds work done by the U.S. Small Business Administration in encouraging and teaching entrepreneurs such as herself. On her office wall is a citation from the White House, recognizing her election in 1986 to the White House Conference on Small Business. It reads:

"The greatest innovations for new jobs, technologies and economic vigor today come from a small but growing circle of heroes — the small business people." It is signed by President Ronald Reagan.

KMGC MAGIC 102.9

Disney's Magic, in the air and seen everywhere in the Dallas/Fort Worth Metroplex, is KMGC-FM at 102.9 on the dial. Listeners call the station "Magic"; known for its unique adult music mix of "Lite Rock and Lite Jazz" as well as its imaginative, Disney-style approach to morning radio programming and community event entertainment.

Roy E. Disney (Walt Disney Company vice chairman) and his family founded Shamrock Broadcasting Company more than a decade ago with the purchase of KMGC. Now one of the nation's largest and most respected broadcast station groups, the privately held organization boasts 18 truly original stations in 13 cities. "Our growth, and our family's greatest pride is in the innovation, commitment and service our stations bring to their communities," says Disney.

In the Metroplex, Magic's banner and air personalities can be seen wherever the station's targeted, upscale audience gathers; fun events that foster a sense of community. The annual July 4th "Magic Freedom Fest" at Fair Park for example, draws more than 100,000 for a free, all-day family tradition of food, fun and community pride, complete with major concerts and fireworks.

Tom Landry bids farewell to 29 years as head coach of the Dallas Cowboys, "America's Team," at the 1989 Magic Pro Football Classic. Photo by Phil Huber, Sports Illustrated.

Sports Illustrated captured a once-in-a-lifetime Magic moment on film, when KMGC brought all-time Dallas Cowboys greats to town to take on the George Allen-coached Washington Redskin legends. For the man who symbolized the spirit of Dallas, it was his last coaching assignment at Texas Stadium. The locally televised game and concert that followed was the climax of the emotional "Farewell to Tom Landry Day." Tributes from around the world, 100,000 fans lining Landry's downtown parade route and a City Hall podium packed with luminaries of the football world made for one of the most memorable days in Dallas' history.

Magic is at the heart of dozens of fun area-wide fundraisers: running events like December's downtown Jingle Bell Run; arts events for the Dallas Theater Center, the Fort Worth Ballet and public television; a lively assortment of tournaments, concerts, festivals, parties and even a "Bachelor Auction" for Cystic Fybrosis that holds the national fundraising record.

On the air, KMGC is in its 10th year of contemporary adult programming. Extensive ongoing market research and a highly creative staff have transformed Magic into a truly one-of-a-kind radio station. Like the countless creations associated with the Disney name, 102.9 FM is an original.

"While Shamrock Broadcasting is an independent, privately held company," explains CEO Stanley Gold, "the values associated with the Disney name are very much a part of our company culture: integrity, innovation and excellence."

Today's Magic showcases the popular, zany morning team of "Tommy and the Beamer," Texas broadcast veterans whose characters, skits, original songs and listener calls are indeed "the most fun in the morning." Upbeat air personalities, a

Magic celebrates the Fourth of July with the Metroplex at the annual Magic Freedom Festival.

full local news staff, airborne traffic reporters, meteorologists and the city's best broadcast movie reviewer round out KMGC's creative air staff.

"Innovation is the key to audience success," says Ross Reagan, KMGC general manager. Reagan is a 28-year broadcasting veteran who joined Shamrock at its inception and who, as a corporate vice president, coordinated the company's programming development.

"Ten years ago, stations impressed advertisers by programming for large, massive audiences," he says. "Today's advertisers want to cost-effectively reach the specific prime consumers of their products. KMGC specifically researches and programs for the upscale, young adult listener. And we've consistently, year after year, delivered one of the city's largest high-income, 25 to 44 consumer audiences."

"KMGC and its Dallas audience have created a radio station truly unique in the nation with its upbeat blend of adult Lite Rock and contemporary Lite Jazz," says Shamrock Broadcasting President Bill Clark. "It's a reflection of the vibrant, contemporary Dallas lifestyle."

AVIALL

Quality service is the hallmark of Aviall, one of the world's largest independent aviation maintenance companies. Their business includes worldwide parts distribution, turbine engine overhaul and repair, and a fixed-base operation located at Dallas Love Field.

Aviall, employing more than 3,500 employees worldwide, is a subsidiary of Miami-based Ryder System, Inc. which expanded its land-based transportation interests into the aviation industry with its purchase of Aviall in 1985.

In 1989, Aviall was divided into two divisions: The Airline Services Division, headed by Marshall B. Taylor, serving the needs of the commercial airlines; The General Aviation Services Division, headed by John L. Wallace, serving business and general aviation; regional airlines and governmental entities.

Major engine manufacturers supported by Aviall include Pratt & Whitney, Pratt & Whitney Canada, General Electric, Rolls-Royce, Allison Gas Turbine, Garrett General Aviation Services and CFM International. Aviall operates eight regional turbine shops in the U.S., a compo-

Quality service is the hallmark of Aviall, one of the largest independent aviation maintenance companies in the world.

nent repair facility and four major turbine engine overhaul facilities, the largest two of which are located in Dallas.

Today, the two largest components of Aviall's business are airline engine overhaul and repair and business aviation new parts distribution. Currently, the General Aviation Services Division distributes over 80,000 line items from over 200 leading manufacturers through more than 80 branches on 5 continents," says George H. Scragg Jr., vice president of business aviation services. The Airline Services Division supports a wide variety of major and regional airlines, including well known names such as Alaska Airlines, America West, Midway and Dallas based Southwest Airlines. In addition, this division also distributes parts and supplies from over 130 manufacturers to virtually all airlines in the free world.

Recently Aviall received authori-

zation to repair and overhaul the Pratt & Whitney Canada PW100, the dominant new engine presently powering a wide variety of commuter aircraft. "We expect over $300 million in revenues from this engine program alone within the next 10 years," says Scragg.

Aviall's fixed-base operation on Dallas Love Field is nationally recognized. It encompasses 600,000 square feet of buildings spread over 56 acres at the airfield. "Aviall is consistently ranked among the top 20 fixed-base operations in the country, and since there are thousands of them, it's a great testimony to the quality of our service," says Scragg.

"Every time an aircraft operator comes here and we serve him well," he continues, "it gives us the opportunity to demonstrate our company's commitment to quality service. As a result of that commitment, Aviall has become a 'generic' name in corporate aviation and one of the largest service companies catering to the aviation industry in the world," he says.

A major part of Aviall's operation is its business aviation parts business, which distributes about 80,000 line items through over 80 branches on five continents.

That overall commitment to quality and customer service also has helped enable the company to become the world's largest distributor of aircraft parts. Another major reason why Aviall has been so successful is that it provides a cost-effective means by which aircraft parts manufacturers can distribute their products anywhere in the world.

Another critical factor contributing to Aviall's outstanding growth has been its near-ideal geographic location. "First, geographically, as far

Aviall was recently awarded the overhaul contract for the Pratt & Whitney Canada PW100, the dominant engine utilized by a wide variety of commuter aircraft operators.

as convenience and accessibility for shipping are concerned, Dallas just couldn't be a better spot," says Scragg.

And with revenues now approaching $1 billion the company will continue to need a large number of high quality people. "The quality of life here in Dallas should help us find and attract these people," he says.

Regarding Aviall's purchase by Ryder System, Scragg says the fit has been exceedingly good. "Ryder manages by the same philosophy and principles that we have always been governed by: We're a very people-conscious company, and the two organizations have benefitted from the synergy. We believe that our people are our best asset and that quality service comes from quality people."

One of the ongoing challenges

Aviall faces is growth. "Because we enjoy a leadership position in several of our markets, it has become more difficult to continue our previous rate of growth in those market segments," says Scragg. "However, with selective acquisitions, the increasing use of business aircraft and the rapid expansion of regional airlines, our future continues to look very bright."

Aviall will continue in the future, as it has in the past, to make major investments in its people, technology and facilities.

"The Ryder System mission," explains Scragg, "is to be the premier service company in the world, and that is to be achieved through a commitment to quality service. At Aviall, we are confident that this guiding philosophy is helping us achieve this goal."

SOUTHWEST AIRLINES

The word that seems to best capture the spirit of this unique company is "maverick." Southwest Airlines' maverick attitude is the reason millions of customers still enjoy everyday low fares and frequent flights between popular business and leisure cities served by the airline.

"From the day we traveled our first route, we have believed that air travel should be inexpensive, hassle free and fun," says Southwest Airlines chairman, CEO and president Herbert D. Kelleher, one of the airline's founders.

Southwest Airlines calls Dallas Love Field home. During its 18 year history, the airline survived many controversies and obstacles. During the mid-1960s, Rollin King, a pilot and independent businessman, approached Herb Kelleher with an idea for creating an airline that offered improved air service between Dallas, Houston and San Antonio. These three cities were among the fastest growing in the nation, and it became evident that the potential

As founder and now chairman, CEO and president of Southwest Airlines, Herbert D. Kelleher is the man behind the success of the innovative, maverick airline.

business between these markets was virtually untapped.

King and Kelleher filed with the Texas Aeronautics Commission, and on February 20, 1968, they were granted permission to fly between these three Texas cities. The next day, suit was filed by competing airlines already serving these markets, arguing that additional service was not warranted. Three years of litigation followed, and eventually the case was heard before a higher court. The suit was finally decided in Southwest's favor, and while subsequent injunctions followed, all were overturned in favor of Southwest.

Lamar Muse joined the King and Kelleher team, and together they realized they had to hold on to their "egalitarian" vision with a tenacity beyond reason if they were to be successful. They selected an executive management team with several years of varied airline experience and formulated a plan to market a refreshing alternative for Texas travelers.

By early June 1971, the advertising campaign finally broke. It consisted of teaser ads containing provocative headlines such as, "The 48-minute Love Affair," "At Last a $20 Ticket You Won't Mind Getting" and "A Fare to Remember." The newspaper ads featured flight attendants in hot pants, cash registers that issued tickets, drinks called Love Potions and peanuts called Love Bites. Approximately 25,000 calls were generated by the initial campaign. "If it hadn't been for this unique campaign, it's possible Southwest might not have survived the early years," says Kelleher. Finally, on June 18, 1971, the first Southwest Boeing 737 took off from Dallas Love Field.

Of course, Southwest's competition did not take matters lying down and immediately matched the $20 fares. The battle attracted national media attention for several months

and only endeared Southwest to the consumers as the gutsy little underdog that had survived against powerfully entrenched competition.

In 1972 Southwest turned a profit and has been profitable ever since. Southwest Airlines became a leader in the airline industry because the airline listened to customers and fulfilled their needs. Through a period of trial and error Southwest adopted the winning combination of low fares, frequent flights and fun, setting it apart from the rest of the industry.

Southwest's big break came in 1974 when all the other major airlines moved from Love Field to the new Dallas/Fort Worth International Airport. Kelleher went to court twice to fight for the right to stay at Love Field and won, this time going all the way to the U.S. Supreme Court. Although Kelleher won this round, he later had to compromise when Texas Congressman Jim Wright moved to attach a rider on a trade bill that eventually banned any interstate flights between Love Field and anything but the four states contiguous to Texas.

Southwest finally became an interstate carrier after deregulation in 1979 with service between Dallas Love Field and New Orleans, Louisiana. Now Southwest serves 31 airports in 14 states including Texas, New Mexico, Oklahoma, Louisiana, Arkansas, Tennessee, Alabama, Missouri, Michigan, Nevada, Arizona, California, Indiana and Illinois.

Southwest led the charge for deregulation and became a true champion of opportunity. Southwest continues today with the same tradition of providing convenient short haul service to business and leisure customers who want to take advantage of frequent flights and low fares. The airline is now the ninth-largest carrier in the nation. Historically, when Southwest enters a market, a new traveling public emerges. Southwest low fares provide affordable air travel for millions of people, who otherwise would not have the opportunity to fly.

Corporations increase the number of employees traveling and business travelers increase the number of trips they take because of Southwest's low fares. More than two-thirds of the traffic in this country is in city pairs located less than 500 miles apart, and Southwest is the only short-haul specialist left in the industry.

The airline's low cost structure is the main reason it can offer significant savings to its customers. Standardization to one aircraft type is a key factor. Southwest currently has a fleet of 93 Boeing 737 aircraft, with an average age of just over five years. The planes are used up to 11 hours a day. Customers deplane and the aircraft is reloaded in 15 minutes or less for most flights. Most of the flights are under one-and-a-half hours, and the airline does not serve meals, although snacks are offered on their few flights over 90 minutes.

In 1978 Lamar Muse left Southwest Airlines to start his own company, and Muse Air was launched in July 1981. Muse tried to compete with Southwest between Dallas and Houston, and later he expanded from Houston to California and Florida. In June 1985 Kelleher, who now was president and chairman of Southwest, purchased Muse Air in a defensive move against Continental Airlines, which had expressed interest in Muse. The Muse name was changed to Transtar in February 1986, and by August 1987 it ceased operation.

Southwest currently has approximately 8,000 employees, more than one-third of which are based in Dallas. Since 1973 employees have enjoyed a profit-sharing plan, and they take pride in knowing they own 15 percent of the company. Kelleher attributes the success of the airline to

Southwest Airlines' friendly, attentive employees are encouraged to take the business seriously, but not themselves.

the employees, "Because they take the business seriously, but not themselves." Customers are given more personal, friendly attention.

In 1986 Southwest chose the Ronald McDonald House as it's primary charity. Employees across the Southwest system play an active role in fundraising projects such as celebrity basketball games, golf tournaments and other special promotions. In addition they routinely cook dinner for the families staying at the houses and help the house managers with other special needs or requests.

Southwest won national recognition for its "Home for the Holidays" program, which provides tickets for a select number of senior citizens who would otherwise be unable to afford travel to visit their families during the Christmas holidays.

In January 1988, Love Field celebrated it's 70th anniversary with the opening of a new parking facility and remodeled exterior. Southwest is truly an integral part of this history since it was instrumental in keeping Love Field open.

Since 1974, Love Field has added approximately $2.9 billion per year to the Dallas economy without expending a single taxpayer dollar. The area surrounding Love Field has been revitalized from a depressed, rundown area to a prosperous, growing section of Dallas. Southwest currently is building a new $17.5-million three-story headquarters adjacent to its flight simulator training facility and existing maintenance hangar.

Love Field has served as a model for Southwest's expansion to other convenient airports and terminals such as Houston Hobby, Chicago Midway and Detroit City Airport.

Since 1980, Southwest has doubled the number of cities it serves and in 1988 posted profits of $58 million on operating revenues of $860 million, compared to $2 million in 1971.

The future looks bright for Southwest Airlines as it continues to prosper and share the benefits with it's customers. In 1990 Southwest will take delivery of the first Boeing 737-500s off the line.

DALLAS/FORT WORTH INTERNATIONAL AIRPORT

Perhaps more than any other single entity within the Metroplex, Dallas/Fort Worth International Airport continues to spur economic growth for the region as well as propel itself into the position of one of the preeminent airports in the world.

Conceived by visionary J. Erik Jonsson in the 1960s, the airport was one of the first examples of the major role a regional airport could play in the overall economic development of an area.

Sprawling over nearly 18,000 acres, the airport boasts six runways, with two more planned for the future. Recently, DFW Airport jumped past Los Angeles International Airport to become the second-busiest airport in the world in terms of volume of passengers, operations, cargo and mail handled. For example, in 1988 the airport handled more than 81,445 tons of mail and nearly 202,000 tons of cargo. Also that year, more than 44 million passengers passed through

the airport. There also were more than 675,000 aircraft operations in 1988, including 496,000 airline, 20,000 general aviation and more than 1,300 military operations.

The airport, which is home to American Airlines, services 150 U.S. and 31 international destinations. There are 113 boarding gates located within the four existing terminals.

DFW Airport's growth in many regards has paralleled the growth of American Airlines, which has based

Dallas/Fort Worth International Airport is the world's second busiest, handling more than 675,000 aircraft operations, 44 million passengers, 81,445 tons of mail and nearly 202,000 tons of cargo each year.

its operations at DFW since 1979. The carrier is presently negotiating with the airport to more than double the size of its existing 918,782-square-foot terminals. The construction cost of $1 billion is more than the cost of building the entire airport between 1968 and 1974.

Delta Air Lines' second busiest hub is located at DFW and that carrier is also considering plans that would expand its growing operational presence.

DFW Airport also is a major Metroplex employer, with 1,326 Airport Board employees and another 25,000 individuals employed either by the airport or companies operating at the airport. These employees help the airport contribute an estimated $6.2 billion annually to the regional economy.

A critical factor which helped DFW Airport become a major international hub is its original concept. Erik Jonsson prophetically realized that in order for the airport to grow, and thus for the entire region to grow, sufficient acreage would have to be acquired. At the time, the largest airport in the United States was Dulles near Washington, D.C. with 10,800 acres.

Jonsson realized that the combination of sufficient land for growth, the airport's central geographic location within the United States and a mild climate year-round would contribute to DFW's success.

However, the time has come for new visionaries with bold and well-conceived plans to begin planning for DFW Airport's future.

Joe Dealey Jr., director of public affairs for the Airport, says one of the keys to DFW's dominance among international airports is its size. "DFW has in its nearly 18,000 acres of real estate a precious commodity that virtually no other airport in the world possesses, and that is the land upon which can be built improvements to make DFW competitive as the airlines forecast increasing numbers of both flights and passengers. In 1990, DFW anticipates receiving permission from the Federal Aviation Administration to construct two additional air carrier runways of 8,500 feet and 9,900 feet long,

respectively. Complementing this construction will be the lengthening by 2,000 feet of two of DFW's four existing north-south parallel runways, and possibly the construction of what may prove to be the most impressive airline terminal in the world (the previously mentioned American Airlines terminal)."

Dealey is a strong proponent of airports such as DFW becoming more complimentary as opposed to competitive with other major airports. "We need to be thinking in terms of complementary versus competing airports if this country is not to become gridlocked in the skies."

At DFW alone, it is estimated that by the year 2005 the number of operations and passengers will double, meaning that more than 1.25 million flight operations and more than 100 million passengers will be handled by the airport. "If we are to meet that challenge," says Dealey, "we must take steps, today. We need to be just as visionary as Erik Jonsson."

DFW Airport's computerized Airtrans shuttle system moves passengers quickly and efficiently throughout the 18,000-acre airport.

GTE SOUTHWEST

life to almost everyone, the people providing telephone service hung in there, doing the best job they could, even when they scarcely knew from minute to minute whether they would have jobs or not.

This is touchingly described by long-retired assistant vice president Ray Red, who was a plant engineer in the 1930s. He says they did "good" work. "I guess you'd say our spirit was one of hungry pride."

Well, the barbed wire rusted away a long time ago, and its successors — copper cable, microwave, etc. — are now rapidly being replaced by fiber optic cable.

No one calls "central" any more. Many people dial international long

Some stories never end — but every story has a beginning.

Part of GTE Southwest's beginning was out on the plains of West Texas, where telephone calls tended to travel down the top strand of a barbed wire fence. Telephone service in rural areas was pretty primitive in the first part of this century.

Or, perhaps it was just the telephone equipment that was primitive. The service — the part that is per-

From left, Pete Butler and Tim Spanella, communications technicians for GTE Southwest; Troy Hignight, special projects coordinator; and Earl A. Goode, GTE Southwest president. GTE Southwest serves Texas Stadium, home of the Dallas Cowboys, and has never missed broadcasting a single second of playing time in the stadium's history.

formed by people — was the best that the technology of the times allowed.

Even during the Depression of the 1930s, which served a hard-knock distance calls themselves, and what used to be "rural" areas have turned into Las Colinas and Dallas/Fort Worth International Airport.

But the pride of the people at GTE Southwest has not changed. The company just has better equipment to serve its customers in Texas and parts of Arkansas, New Mexico and Oklahoma — some 1.3 million access lines.

And the pride is justified. GTE grew up with the Southwest. It has rejoiced in the good times and suffered in the bad — and never stopped working to improve communications for its customers.

Today, with electronic and digital offices, not to mention a host of computerized programs, GTE can do more work better in less time than ever before, including checking all lines each night so that problems can be fixed before customers even know they exist.

This does not mean that GTE has forgotten how to get out in the weather, however. GTE's employees work in dust storms, ice storms, rain storms and snow storms — whatever it takes to restore service to customers when something goes wrong.

And GTE has equipment that will "listen" when life-threatening conditions occur. With enhanced 911 service, callers' phone numbers and addresses are displayed on a screen. So if for some reason a customer cannot tell the dispatcher where to send help, they can still respond in seconds when seconds really count.

And this is only the beginning of what GTE Southwest will be able to offer in the way of telecommunications services. It is a long, long way from that top strand of barbed wire, but the end is nowhere in sight.

From left, Mike Massad, chairman of the golf committee of the GTE Byron Nelson Classic; Rex Timms, GTE Southwest vice president-public affairs; and Herb McJunkin, president of the Salesmanship Club of Dallas. The three are shown at the education center of the Salesmanship Club Youth and Family Centers Inc. Through the Salesmanship Club assistance is provided to emotionally disturbed children and their families in the Dallas area. These projects and programs of the Salesmanship Club are made possible by funds raised through projects like the GTE Byron Nelson Classic.

US SPRINT

The goal of US Sprint is direct and clear-cut: to become the world's best telecommunications company. And, considering the dedication and entrepreneurial spirit of its employees and the fact that it already ranks third in the long distance market, that objective is realistic.

US Sprint is the energetic off-spring of two industry pioneers, GTE Corporation and United Telecommunications, which in 1986 merged their respective long distance companies, GTE Sprint and US Telecom. To this marriage GTE Sprint brought a large customer base and brand name awareness; US Telecom brought America's largest fiber optic network, which uses state-of-the-art, high-quality voice and data/video telecommunications transmission. Indeed, US Sprint is the first company to build an all fiber, all digital network. The 23,000-mile network has been carrying 100 percent of US Sprint's voice traffic since Spring 1988.

The Kansas City, Mo.-based corporation, which employs some 14,000 people in 49 states, has three major divisions, including the Central Business Market Group based in

US Sprint technicians monitor and channel voice and data transmission traffic through the company's 23,000-mile fiber and digital network.

Dallas. This group manages sales and service for middle market business accounts in a 10-state area.

Locally, US Sprint employs about 2,100 at a three-building regional headquarters complex in Las Colinas and at the National Service Center on Stemmons Freeway.

Dallas is the second-largest presence in the US Sprint operation, and the city "has become quite a tele-communications center because it offers all the resources for a high tech community to flourish," says Roger A. Vernier, president of the Central Business Marketing Group. In fact, more than one-third of Texas' high tech employment is in this area, and Dallas ranks second in telecommunications manufacturing employment in the United States. Today, there are approximately 500,000 US Sprint customers in the Dallas/Fort Worth area, some 100,000 of them business customers.

The thriving US Sprint-Dallas relationship goes back to 1974 and Southern Pacific Communications Co., a forerunner of the company. It initially followed the railroad's right-of-way in creating the first Sprint network. In 1983, the company was acquired by GTE and became the first specialized common carrier to serve all 50 states. Additionally, U.S. Telephone, originally based in Dallas, was incorporated in Texas in 1979 and marketed as U.S. Tel; it became US Telecom in 1985. US Sprint was born in July 1986.

US Sprint is the first company to build an all fiber, all digital network. The 23,000-mile network has been carrying 100 percent of US Sprint's voice traffic since Spring 1988.

From the outset, US Sprint has been dedicated to clients' needs, with each of the company's operating units gaining its share of the market by stressing strong customer service and orientation. US Sprint continually updates its product range in order to remain on the cutting edge of an extremely competitive business. It has a full range of products and services in the long-distance market, and a family of WATS and 800 products, as well as data, videoconferencing and international services.

In short, US Sprint is lean, aggressive and always seeking new opportunities in an ever-changing, exciting and challenging industry.

US Sprint is constantly upgrading and modifying its network to provide business and residential customers with the best telecommunications service available.

Photo by Martin Vandiver

"From the time that Dallas was a small, small village, First Baptist Church has been in the heart of it, has contributed to it and has grown with the leadership and population of the city."

Dr. W.A. Criswell, Pastor — First Baptist Church of Dallas

"Dallas has always had a good business atmosphere, a good transportation system and an excellent work force. This is part of the reason why Dallas has traditionally been one of the insurance centers of the nation."

John D. Melton, President — Blue Cross and Blue Shield of Texas Inc.

"While Presbyterian is one of the youngest hospitals in the Dallas area, it has set a progressive pace in the local health care community and has established new standards for excellence and innovation."

— Presbyterian Healthcare System

"Education is, quite simply, our last, best hope for the future. By bringing quality educational opportunities within means for virtually every citizen, Dallas' community colleges serve a vital need — for individuals but also for the greater community we share."

Dr. Lawrence W. Tyree, Chancellor — Dallas County Community College District

"With its legacy of excellence in patient care, together with superb diagnostic and treatment capabilities and the promise of impressive new facilities, Methodist Medical Center truly is building on its fine reputation."

Methodist Medical Center of Dallas

"In its first 100 years, the University of North Texas has anticipated regional and state needs. The university has the potential to play an even larger role in the years ahead."

Dr. Alfred F. Hurley, President — University of North Texas

"We have decided to specialize in a niche in the medical industry. As a result of that commitment to excellence, both the surgeons and patients, as well as the health care industry at large, benefit."

John Carlyle, Senior Vice President and Chief Financial Officer. — Medical Care International

"At the heart of Dallas' dynamic health-care community is the city's only medical school and academic medical center. The Nobel Prize-winning institution stands for excellence in teaching, patient care and research."

— The University of Texas Southwestern Medical Center at Dallas

"Children's mission is healing sick children by employing expert medical treatment and technology supported by research, medical education and child advocacy."

— Children's Medical Center of Dallas

"At Parkland Memorial Hospital, dedication to patients goes beyond providing quality medical care. It means caring about the overall well-being of patients and attempting to make them whole."

— Parkland Memorial Hospital

"Humana Hospital-Medical City Dallas is dedicated to providing world-class medicine to Dallas, a world-class city. In partnership with Dallas, we are advancing healthcare into the next century."

Ira Korman, Ph.D. — Zale-Lipshy University Hospital

"We're very critically aware of care, so we have a good group of people — they really want to be in health care. Many of our doctors enjoy practicing at Doctors because of the friendly, unhurried atmosphere and top-notch staff."

Chris DiCicco, Chief Executive Officer — Doctors Hospital

"Whether by conducting research, attracting leading scholars, educating the work force or infusing millions of dollars into the local economy, U.T. Dallas enriches the life of the region."

— University of Texas at Dallas

"Through innovations in approach as well as knowledge and technology, Humana Hospital — Medical City Dallas has transformed healthcare in North Dallas. Through the Institutes, the hospital has made a difference all over the world."

— Humana Hospital-Medical City Dallas

"Adhering to a fundamental belief that the foundation for growth is built on a prospering customer base, FoxMeyer sees itself as a service company first."

Mark Pulido, Executive Vice President — Foxmeyer Drug Company

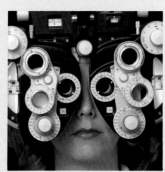

"From its inception, Kaiser Permanente has been an industry leader in developing innovative and cost-effective approaches to health care. Many of the principles it pioneered have become accepted norms within the managed care industry."

— Kaiser Permanente

"DISD is the eighth-largest public education organization in the United States, operating more than 220 educational facilities. Together, the DISD and Dallas are creating competent, well-rounded citizens for the 21st century."

— *Dallas Independent School District*

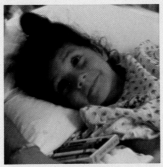

"Baylor University Medical Center is an intrinsic part of Dallas' heritage and leads the way in making health care an important part of Dallas' future."

Baylor University Medical Center

"We want to be known as the medical center that's committed to very important values related to human life and caring for people who are in need of services."

Anthony L. Bunker, President — St. Paul Medical Center

"We are justifiably proud of the University of Texas at Arlington's creative and enduring achievements over the past decades. Its location in the middle of the thriving Dallas/Fort Worth region, coupled with its outstanding faculty, students and staff, signals a most promising future."

Dr. Hans Markm Chancellor — University of Texas System

"Dallas provides the right kind of environment for our company, for our vision is to become the nation's health-care provider of choice and employer of choice."

Kenn S. George, Chairman and Chief Executive Officer — Epic Healthcare Group

CHAPTER 18

Quality of Life

Medical, educational and religious institutions, as well as recreation and leisure-oriented companies, all contribute to the quality of life enjoyed by Dallas' residents and visitors to the city.

FIRST BAPTIST CHURCH OF DALLAS

In 1871, the one-room building of First Baptist Church was part of the Dallas skyline. Today, the largest Southern Baptist church in the world is still part of that skyline, sitting squarely on the same piece of ground it originally occupied. It is, in fact, the only downtown Dallas church which can boast of such. But it has grown a little; it now occupies four acres.

The church not only has grown, but it has watched and been a part of the city's growth. First Baptist Church has provided outstanding spiritual leadership for the city for more than a century. Grounded in its belief in the Holy Scriptures, First Baptist Church teaches its members to be good citizens, loyal in support of civil government and ethical in business transactions.

With its well-preserved historic sanctuary and other attractive buildings, its excellent day-care center and schools and its excellent libraries and recreational facilities, First Baptist Church is an asset to downtown Dallas. Downtown churches, as well as community churches, are essential to the growth of the city.

The church was founded in 1868, but the first one-room building was not erected until 1871. In 1890, a large red brick church was completed on the same piece of land. Today, though remodeled, that same building houses the church's beautiful sanctuary.

Each day more than 2,000 people pass through the church. On Sundays it takes three services to accommodate the 4,100 people who attend. The staff of 325 presides over an area of five city blocks with the square footage of a 70-story building.

But it was not always like that. The man responsible for much of the tremendous growth of First Baptist was 34 years old when he preached his first sermon in the sanctuary on August 24, 1944. At that time, the church was at a standstill since the pastor of 47 years, George W. Truett, had lain ill for more than a year.

Dr. W.A. Criswell delivered a rousing sermon that day and was called to be pastor on September 27, 1944. He has served in that position ever since.

Criswell believes that the purpose of the church is "to build a lighthouse for Christ in the great Metroplex area; to point men and women to Jesus who is the hope of the world."

Proclaiming the inerrancy of the Bible, church leaders say they have had a tremendous impact on spreading the Word of God to not only the community of Dallas but to the world through worldwide missionary efforts, television and radio broadcasts and

through First Baptist Academy and Criswell Center for Biblical Studies.

Numbers attest to the tremendous growth of the church during Criswell's tenure. In 1945, there were 7,804 church members; today there are 28,196. Sunday School enrollment has grown from 3,940 in 1945 to 11,824; the number of downtown buildings from two to 11 and square footage from 221,750 to 1.39 million; the number of church-supported missions from 0 to 29; and the operating budget from $377,171 to $11.25 million.

In addition, Criswell College was begun in 1971 and has grown to include 400 students and 20 professors. The Criswell Radio Network, KCBI, broadcasts on 100,000 watts, and KCBI International goes out on 30,000 watts. Students in the kindergarten through 12th grade at First Baptist Academy number 808. There are 20 different choirs and seven musical groups.

Perhaps the church's most famous member is Evangelist Billy Graham.

Recently, the church purchased Gaston Avenue Baptist Church and plans to move the Criswell Center for Biblical Studies to that site to make room for other programs at the downtown location.

But despite spiraling growth and somewhat cramped quarters, church leaders say it is imperative that First Baptist remain a downtown church.

"From the time that Dallas was a small, small village, First Baptist Church has been in the heart of it, has contributed to it and has grown with the leadership and population of the city," says Criswell. "There are many thousands of us to whom Dallas has been endeared because of the marvelous ministry of First Baptist Church.

"Through the years numbers of the gifted civic leaders who have contributed vastly to the growth and

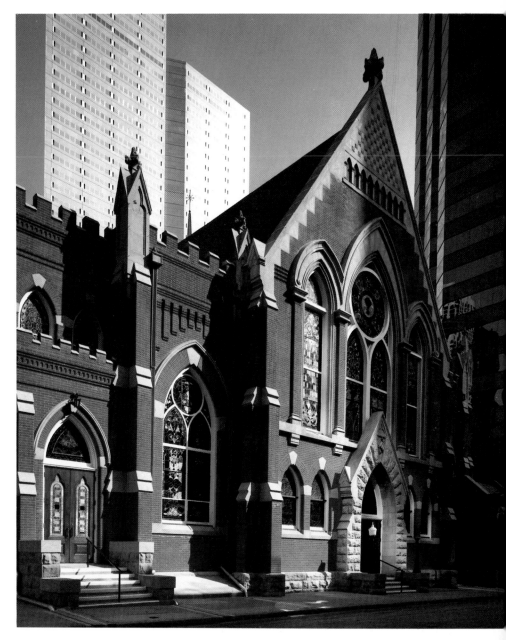

influence of Dallas have been the same leaders who have built this marvelous congregation of the Lord. Through these years many of the great leaders of America have been our guests, tremendously gifted men such as President Woodrow Wilson, and in these recent years President Gerald Ford and President George Bush. All of these things are but harbingers of the greater contribution of the church to the greater growth of the city of Dallas. From the beginning we have been here together, and to the end we shall be comrades and

Inset photo: First Baptist Church constructed in 1890 and still standing today on the same piece of property

Left: Inside view of the Main Sanctuary of the First Baptist Church, Dallas

Above: Side view of the First Baptist Church off old San Jacinto Street in downtown Dallas

fellow-pilgrims in the marvelous providences that lie before us all.

"We love you and stand by you, wonderful city of Dallas."

BLUE CROSS AND BLUE SHIELD OF TEXAS, INC.

An ability to meet huge challenges and cope with vast socioeconomic changes has been one of the keys to the success of Blue Cross and Blue Shield of Texas, Inc. And today, as a large and experienced health care insurer in Texas, the company stands ready to meet the challenges of the future in the rapidly changing, increasingly complex field of health insurance.

Certainly, no other insurance firm in the state can match the expertise and know-how amassed over more than 60 years by this Richardson-based organization, which literally "wrote the book" on group health protection.

Blue Cross and Blue Shield of Texas traces its origins to late 1929 and one of the greatest financial crises in American history: The stock market collapsed, sending the U.S. economy into a tailspin. Millions of wage earners were suddenly out of work.

The situation was desperate enough for those who were well and able-bodied, but for the sick and injured, it was far worse. There was no such thing as health insurance at the time. As a result, hospitals and their patients were left financially crippled. Without jobs, money or insurance, patients had no way to pay their hospital bills, and many hospitals found themselves on the brink of bankruptcy.

Baylor Hospital in Dallas was no exception. Although it was among the city's largest health care facilities, there were fears that without some sort of financial miracle, the hospital would be forced to close its doors within a few weeks. That miracle occurred in the form of a bold new idea proposed by Dr. Justin Ford Kimball, a former Dallas school superintendent who had been named vice president of Baylor University in charge of its Dallas units.

In 1923, Kimball had pioneered a unique "sick benefit" plan for Dallas teachers, under which each teacher could contribute $1 per month to a cooperative association, and in turn would receive $5 per day for each work day lost to illness after the first week for 21 days. At the time, a teacher who was seriously ill received only half pay for two weeks, and then was dropped from the payroll entirely. For that reason, Kimball's plan had been endorsed by virtually 100 percent of Dallas teachers and had worked well in the six years since its adoption.

From its headquarters in Richardson, Blue Cross and Blue Shield of Texas holds a commanding presence in the group health insurance industry. A stalwart of the past, the company is positioned as an innovator for the future.

Now, as the situation at Baylor grew more desperate by the day, Kimball decided an extension of his plan might not only save the hospital from economic disaster but enable the sick to pay for health care during the chaotic conditions imposed by the Depression.

After discussing the idea with other Baylor administrators, Kimball spelled out his plan to Dallas school teachers. Using what may have been the world's first actuarial tables for health benefits, and based on his previous experience with the teachers' "Sick Benefit Fund," Kimball offered a plan providing up to 21 days of care at Baylor for a cost of just 50 cents per month.

Approximately 1,000 teachers — or three-fourths in the Dallas school system — signed up immediately. Before Christmas 1929, Miss Alma Dickson, an Oak Cliff teacher, suffered a broken foot and became the first patient to receive hospital care under the plan. Soon, other employee groups began adopting the so-called Baylor Plan, and within a few years it had become nationally famous and was used as a model for other prepaid health care plans across the country.

In 1939, eight years after Kimball explained the Baylor Plan to a convention of the American Hospital Association, that group established standards for all prepaid health plans, and the Blue Cross symbol became a registered trademark.

Also in 1939, the Texas Legislature approved a statewide group hospitalization service plan, and a company known as Group Hospital Service, Inc. was chartered to administer the plan. It offered coverage at a rate of 75 cents per month for men, 85 cents for women and 15 cents for minor dependents. After its first year of operation it was serving 171 member hospitals, representing 75 percent of the available beds in Texas.

In 1941, the company became a Blue Cross Plan, and two years later the Baylor Plan was discontinued and its responsibilities assumed by Blue Cross (Group Hospital Service).

Since that time, Blue Cross and Blue Shield of Texas, the latter a companion plan instituted in 1945 to provide benefits for physician care, have been integral parts of the evolution of the prepaid health care concept. At the same time, Blue Cross and Blue Shield of Texas serves as a carrier for the federal Medicare program, processing millions of Medicare claims annually through one of the insurance industry's most sophisticated computer systems.

The health care and health insurance industries face one of the most critical periods in their history in the 1990s — a period that may be as difficult and trying in its own way as the Great Depression. The quality

In the core of the company's advanced information system network, the quietness and efficiency belie the incredible volume of claims processed each day. Millions of claims pass through its operation annually.

This 1934 poster from Minnesota in the then-modern art deco style was the nation's first glimpse of a blue cross to identify one of the new hospital prepayment plans. (Courtesy of Blue Cross and Blue Shield of Minnesota.)

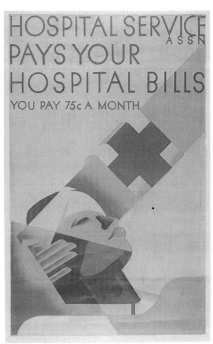

and cost of long-term care for an aging U.S. population and a drastic escalation in overall health care costs are among the most pressing concerns facing patients, medical professionals, employers and insurers. But Blue Cross and Blue Shield of Texas will be able to rely on its long and successful track record, its superior technology and the skills of its 3,100 employees to meet these and other challenges.

"Our experience and capabilities will help us deal with whatever comes for our industry," says John D. Melton, president since 1981. "We're by far the most experienced health insurance company in the state and have the strongest relationship with doctors, hospitals and other health care professionals. In handling the bulk of all Medicare claims in Texas, we also have extensive experience in working with the federal government. Because of all this, Blue Cross and Blue Shield of Texas is uniquely qualified to face the future."

Melton emphasizes the need for cooperation in the public and private sectors to find answers to such thorny problems as cost containment and accessibility of health care for the American public. "All our efforts are focused on cost containment and the affordability of health care insurance."

One example of cost containment employed by Blue Cross and Blue Shield of Texas is "pre-admission certification," a process in which the company's own medical professionals carefully evaluate every non-emergency case in which a physician recommends inpatient treatment. "Our goal is to eliminate unnecessary hospital stays, and to hold those that are necessary to the shortest possible time," Melton explains.

The next decade is likely to bring many far-reaching changes in the way health insurance is administered and paid, but one thing that will not change is the presence of Blue Cross and Blue Shield of Texas at the forefront of the health insurance industry. From its 550,000-square-foot headquarters in Richardson, which the company occupied in 1981 and where 2,400 employees report to work each day, Blue Cross and Blue Shield of Texas will continue the leadership role it has played in years past.

"Some other big insurance companies are selling their health care divisions, but group health insurance is our only business," Melton says. "We are committed to this market for the long term — for today and for tomorrow."

PRESBYTERIAN HEALTHCARE SYSTEM

A Commitment To Caring

Behind every decision and activity at Presbyterian Healthcare System is a single principle: a dedication and commitment to a stated mission of providing excellent health care to the people and the communities it serves. This mission is not qualified by race, creed or economic status. And although this System exists primarily to treat the sick and injured, its scope of activities does not end there. Presbyterian accepts the responsibility of addressing its constituency in terms of the total person, encompassing physical, mental, social and spiritual wellness.

As one of the four major hospital systems in the Dallas area that are owned by or closely associated with a large church body, Presbyterian Healthcare System has a tradition of service that includes quality health care, service to the community, responsible management, volunteerism, leadership and innovation.

This tradition of service began when several Dallas civic leaders, including Frank H. Kidd, M.D., a respected Dallas physician; William

M. Elliott, Jr., former senior minister of Highland Park Presbyterian Church; and Toddie Lee Wynne, Sr., a far-sighted civic leader and businessman, agreed in 1954 on the need for a quality, full-service, not-for-profit hospital in North Dallas. From that vision, supported and encouraged by many sectors of the Dallas community, Presbyterian Hospital of Dallas came into being in 1966.

At its inception, Presbyterian's approach to its mission of providing quality health care was marked by a forward-looking attitude that has resulted in a medical staff which includes the most qualified and sophisticated physicians and health care professionals as well as facilities equipped with the latest in medical technology. That dedication to maintaining state-of-the-art quality in the care of its patients has remained a strong influence in its growth and maturity.

Presbyterian Hospital of Dallas opened its doors in May 1966. Today, as a part of Presbyterian Healthcare System, it is one of the most important tertiary care facilities in the Southwest, sprawling over a 75-acre campus.

Nurses and other healthcare professionals provide a comforting, as well as healing, atmosphere for hospitalized children.

In fact, the evolution of Presbyterian into its present form is a study in the application of thoughtful, long-range planning based on a clear understanding of current and future trends in health care. The health care environment entered a state of rapid change in the 1980s, and promises to remain very challenging for the foreseeable future. In response, the leadership of Presbyterian Healthcare System has made major commitments to the kind of managed growth and development that will best enable it to continue fulfilling its mission.

The Presbyterian vision of the future relies on an integrated system of health care, in which the various elements within the system all make specific contributions to the full spectrum of human health care needs. Within this concept, the physician plays the central role, taking responsibility for diagnosing and managing the application of the appropriate expertise and services that best meet the patient's needs. In the shifting

approach to patient care, Presbyterian recognizes that more emphasis is being placed on outpatient care characterized by providing the appropriate level of care in the appropriate setting, including wellness programs, preventive medicine, skilled nursing care and home health care.

For the 1990s, the Presbyterian Healthcare System is well-positioned with staff and facilities to serve North Dallas and its satellites to the north, east and southeast. In addition to Presbyterian Hospital of Dallas, the System includes Presbyterian Hospital of Kaufman and Presbyterian Hospital of Winnsboro. The System also includes Presbyterian Village North, a retirement community in North Dallas; PrimaCare Centers, urgent health care centers throughout the Metroplex; Presbyterian Medical Offices North; Presbyterian's and Children's Healthcare Center of North Texas, located in Plano; the Finley Ewing Cardiovascular Fitness Center; the Community Mental Health Center; the Radiation Oncology Center; and the Presbyterian professional buildings.

Consistent with its commitment to innovation and leadership, Presbyterian Healthcare System has established a sound record of introducing new, effective approaches and techniques to the pool of health care services. The System made headlines with its acquisition of the first lithotriptor in the area. This machine enables doctors to use non-invasive sound waves to rid the body of kidney stones. Presbyterian remains the only hospital in the southwest area with a Gamma Knife, a sophisticated non-invasive surgical technique using highly focused beams of radiation to eliminate certain types of brain lesions that would otherwise be inoperable. Presbyterian's neonatal intensive care unit was the first in North Texas to offer extracorporeal membrane oxygenation (ECMO), a tech-

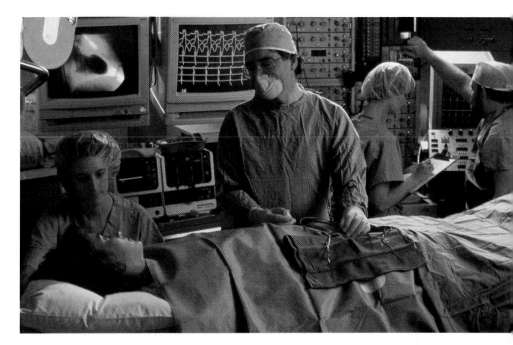

Highly skilled teams perform sophisticated procedures in a variety of settings within Presbyterian Healthcare System.

nique that offers hope for newborns who are dying of respiratory failure.

Other technological advances at Presbyterian include electrophysiology, the science of mapping the heart. Used primarily as a diagnostic tool, it allows physicians to determine the existence and causes of certain irregular heart rhythms. Similarly, Presbyterian's Southwest Diagnostic Imaging Center offers a wide range of X-ray procedures and non-radiation diagnostic tools, such as magnetic resonance imaging.

Today's Presbyterian Healthcare System is much more than facilities and equipment. Additionally, Presbyterian Healthcare System — as a member of a hospital consortium — offers CareFlite, a regional helicopter ambulance service. It has also led the way in the creation of new approaches to various health problems. Its Sleep/Wake Disorders Center, with facilities that allow doctors to monitor patients as they sleep, treats sleep disorders and conducts

research into one of the least understood human functions. At the Margot Perot Building, a variety of services for women is provided, from specialties in infertility and high-risk pregnancies to the latest treatment for breast disease. Presbyterian's "Easy Street," a fully-equipped physical rehabilitation unit, replicates real-life physical situations that allow patients to regain mobility and return to independent living.

As a commitment to wellness, Presbyterian also operates Optifast, a weight-management program, and has instituted a dynamic medical education program at the new Fogelson Forum, a continuing education center for professional staff that will also offer classes and seminars for the public. Presbyterian has even recognized its responsibility to promote wellness by banning smoking in any of its facilities.

With a solid commitment to quality health care supported by a devoted staff and excellent physical facilities, Presbyterian Healthcare System dedicates itself to serving the people in the community, ever aware that there is no one more important than the patient.

DALLAS COUNTY COMMUNITY COLLEGE DISTRICT

On any given day throughout Dallas County, more than 80,000 students are pursuing their personal dreams.

The traditional student — intent on studies which will lead to that coveted bachelor's degree. For another, a one- or two-year technical program and the promise of a solid, well-paying future. And for many, many others — at every age and stage of life — the challenge of new learning . . . for personal enrichment, intellectual fulfillment, career advancement.

This is the Dallas County Community College District.

The DCCCD has been changing lives as well as the community for more than two decades, and its remarkable record of growth reflects the spirit and diversity of Dallas itself. From a fledgling El Centro campus opened in 1966 with just over 4,000 students, the district has burgeoned to the largest undergraduate institution in the state, annually serving more than 160,000 students, and it is one of the top-ranked community college systems in the nation. Along the way, it has opened doors and minds for more than one million students in the Greater Dallas community.

Committed to learning as a life-long experience, Dallas County Community Colleges structure pro-

Graduates of numerous technical and health occupation programs are in high demand by Dallas' hospitals and medical centers.

grams to a wide variety of student needs and goals. Students working toward a bachelor's degree can build a solid academic foundation. Each campus offers a full range of courses in the humanities, natural and social sciences, business, communications and mathematics that can be transferred easily to a four-year institution. Two-year associate of arts and sciences degrees are awarded, and the colleges are fully accredited by the Southern Association of Colleges and Schools.

For students seeking rapid entry into a dynamic, marketable career field, the DCCCD has answers and options. Responding to Dallas' diverse economy and the demand for skilled workers in a variety of fields, the county's community colleges provide more than 120 one- and two-year programs that are constantly updated to meet both the needs of students and those of the business community. Programs in such high-demand fields as accounting, data processing, office careers, legal assisting, nursing and other vitally needed health occupations are offered. Up-to-the-minute training in engineer-

ing, electronics and telecommunications provides an educational conduit for those seeking futures in North Texas' thriving high-tech industries.

Students with short-range learning goals also find their place at Dallas' community colleges. A virtual cornucopia of non-credit continuing education courses attract more than 40,000 eager learners of every age and interest each semester. In addition, cultural, entertainment and other special events make DCCCD campuses the virtual hub of community life in many suburban areas.

The DCCCD is literally a microcosm of the community. Seven strategically located campuses — Brookhaven and Richland in North Dallas, Cedar Valley to the south, Eastfield to the east, Mountain View to the southwest, North Lake in the northwest, and El Centro in the heart of downtown Dallas — encircle Dallas County, providing convenient access from home or work. A tuition rate doggedly held to the lowest possible level — less than $200 per semester for a full course schedule — plus financial aid options that include grants, loans, scholarships and coop-

A relaxed campus atmosphere where students receive personal attention and individual encouragement is characteristic of Dallas' community colleges.

erative work/study programs, bring higher education within reach of virtually every Dallas-area resident.

Convenience and moderate cost are but two of the major benefits that bring students to the community college doorstep in growing numbers. Flexible day, night and weekend classes allow them to custom tailor a schedule to the needs of family and work. In addition, numerous award-winning telecourses designed by the DCCCD's Center for Telecommunications, one of the largest producers of telecourses in the country, and offered via PBS and cable stations bring learning home for students with time, physical or other constraints.

The quality of the DCCCD faculty and a personalized approach to learning that accepts each student where he is, then finds creative ways

to take him where he wants to be, are key both to the success of its students and to the DCCCD. More than 95 percent of academic transfer faculty hold a master's degree or higher, and close to 20 percent have doctorates. The dedication to excellence of DCCCD faculty has been noted repeatedly through such prestigious awards as Piper Professorships given for outstanding academic, scientific and scholarly achievement, as well as Fulbright Fellowships and other distinguished recognitions.

Expert counselors work hand-in-hand with both faculty and administrators to provide guidance and support on an individual level. Underscoring its strong commitment to quality counseling as well as quality staff and facilities, the DCCCD recently implemented an advanced computer assessment program to augment the efforts of staff in helping students with specific learning needs. CASES (Computer Analysis System for Educational Success) was custom-designed by DCCCD counseling and computer experts and is one of only two such programs in the nation.

More than just *looking* to the future, the DCCCD is aggressively *reaching* for the future, expanding its role as a vital link to the Dallas of tomorrow. To reinforce its partnership in economic development, the district recently opened its new Bill J. Priest Institute for Economic Development, a $7.8 million business and job training complex that brings together under one futuristic roof its business and training outreach services. Named in honor of founding DCCCD chancellor Bill J. Priest, the institute houses five major programs, including the Business and Professional Institute, the Edmund J. Kahn Job Training Center, regional offices of the Small Business Development Center, the Center for Government Contracting and an innovative Business Incubation Center.

The DCCCD's future also is looking *up*, with plans now completed for the 1990 expansion of the Center for Telecommunications through construction of a new $2.5-million facility on the Richland campus. Utilizing three ITFS (Instructional Television Fixed Service) channels, the new facility will deliver live, interactive instructional programming and teleconferencing not only to DCCCD campuses, but also to area schools and to businesses and industry locally and nationally via satellite. On its North Lake campus, the DCCCD also is completing a new center to consolidate its numerous construction and construction management programs.

Building. Growing. Changing with the needs of the people of Dallas. The Dallas County Community College District now enters its 25th year of service with one basic commitment unchanged: that every citizen — no matter what his age, social or economic circumstance — deserves the educational opportunity to go as far as his talents, his ambition and his dreams can take him.

Two-year associate degrees are awarded annually by the DCCCD in a full range of courses in the humanities, natural and social sciences, business, communications and mathematics, as well as in more than 100 technical fields.

METHODIST MEDICAL CENTER OF DALLAS

Methodist Medical Center opened in 1927 with 100 beds, a staff of 90 and an element that is very much in evidence today: a commitment to providing high-quality health care. That commitment is being sustained by the most ambitious expansion program in the 60-year history of Methodist, now rising on the hilltop site overlooking downtown Dallas.

The focal point of the $75.5-million development is the 11-story patient tower now under construction, a 326,000-square-foot building designed with efficiency and patient comfort in mind. All patient rooms will be private, and with this new facility, all patient service areas at Methodist will be less than five years old.

Already completed is the nine-story Pavilion II Outpatient Center, which combines diagnostic, treatment and day surgical capabilities with a 100,000-square-foot professional office complex. This new facility, with its sophisticated medical technology and conveniently arranged services for outpatient care,

Methodist Medical Center is in the midst of a $75.5-million expansion program, including an 11-story patient tower and the nine-story Pavilion II Outpatient Center.

is another example of how Methodist is responding to patient needs.

The building program also includes a new central power plant, parking garage expansion, new connecting corridors and skyways and extensive renovation and landscaping of the entire grounds.

The new facilities will support and strengthen this dynamic medical center, cited by *Good Housekeeping* magazine as one of the 14 best general hospitals in the United States.

Methodist Medical Center is internationally renowned as an organ transplant center. More than 900 kidney transplants have been performed at the Center since 1981, and the program has grown to be the largest in Texas and one of the 10 largest in the nation. This expertise has also placed Methodist's surgical teams at the forefront of pancreas transplantation, one of the most complex and rare organ transplant procedures. Another integral part of the outstanding success rate of these transplant programs is Methodist's technologically advanced laboratory for tissue-typing.

The Medical Center also provides a wide range of services for patients with heart disease. More than 250 heart surgical cases, including open heart/coronary bypass pro-

cedures were performed at the Methodist Heart Center in 1988, as well as hundreds of other specialized cardiac-related procedures. Important new diagnostic equipment offers computer-enhanced images of the heart and arteries, making blockages easier to diagnose and allowing physicians and surgeons to view different angles of the heart simultaneously.

New technology is also important in the comprehensive treatment of cancer patients. The Methodist Cancer Center will have an all-new facility with the most sophisticated radiation therapy equipment available, greatly expanding the center's capabilities in cancer care. Chemotherapy, diagnostic expertise and surgical services combine with radiation therapy to provide comprehensive techniques for cancer treatment. Emotional support and concern for the patient's total well-being will also remain a key focus of the center.

Methodist's service to the health-related concerns of women is recognized widely. Maternity patients

Methodist Medical Center is internationally renowned as an organ transplant center. The hospital's kidney transplant program has grown to be the largest in Texas and one of the 10 largest in the nation.

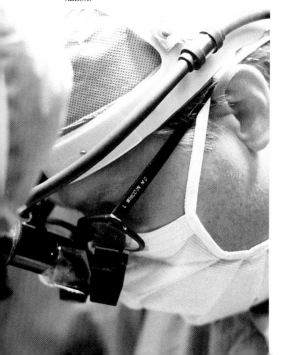

have numerous birthing options, plus the security of a facility with the highest attainable rating in obstetric and neonatal services. The Women's Center at Methodist also serves the community through education, counseling, physician referral, a resource library and special diagnostic and screening programs.

These are just some of the many programs and services that are a part of a leading regional health care system — Methodist Hospitals of Dallas.

Methodist Medical Center offers a full range of services, from obstetrics and neonatology to advance cardiac care and organ transplantations.

Charlton Methodist Hospital serves the growing communities of the southwest Dallas area, including Duncanville, DeSoto, Lancaster and Cedar Hill. Southeastern Methodist Hospital serves a large population in the Pleasant Grove area, Mesquite, Balch Springs, Seagoville and other communities. Each hospital offers general medical, obstetrical, chemical dependency, day surgery and emergency services.

The mission of the three Methodist Hospitals of Dallas is to serve people in defined areas by meeting their health care needs effectively and in a manner that reflects "a commitment to Christian concepts of life and learning." Affiliated by covenant

with the North Texas Conference of the United Methodist Church, Charlton and Southeastern join Methodist Medical Center in serving Dallas and the entire region.

As one of the four historic, church-related teaching and referral hospitals in the city, Methodist Medical Center also works with the other medical institutions to establish Dallas as an international health care referral center. Because of its legacy of excellence, together with superb diagnostic and treatment capabilities, Methodist is a leader in this effort. And with the promise of impressive new facilities, Methodist Medical Center truly is building on its fine reputation.

UNIVERSITY OF NORTH TEXAS

There's a spirit at the University of North Texas in Denton that matches the vibrant "can do" spirit of Dallas and the entire North Texas region.

It is the spirit that prompts the University of North Texas to be fully responsive to the needs of each of its students for a high quality education. It is the spirit that has made North Texas the largest university in the region and the fourth-largest university in the state. It is the spirit shared by more than 25,000 students and by nearly 100,000 alumni, more than 40,000 of whom live and work in the North Texas region.

And the easy accessibility of North Texas from Dallas, Fort Worth and Dallas/Fort Worth International Airport makes it truly the university of the North Texas region.

Innovative, forward-thinking programs have long been a hallmark of the faculty of the university. The Classic Learning Core anticipated the need for university graduates who

Students enjoy the picturesque, tree-studded North Texas campus, where a tradition of friendliness and informality fosters friendships that can last a lifetime.

The 412-acre University of North Texas campus in Denton is easily accessible from Dallas, Fort Worth and Dallas/Forth Worth International Airport.

have a superior background in the liberal arts. The Meadows Excellence in Teaching Program is creating an elite corps of master teachers who will serve Texas school children for years to come. The internationally acclaimed One O'Clock Lab Band and other music and fine arts programs, the Institute of Petroleum Accounting, the Emergency Administration and Planning Institute and the Computer Education and Cognitive Systems Department are just a few examples of how the university anticipates the needs of the North Texas region.

In the sciences, North Texas has made remarkable progress in this decade. The Institute of Applied Sciences has become a regional, state and national force in water quality research, remote sensing technology and archaeology. The Center for Materials Characterization has the only particle accelerator in the nation dedicated solely to materials science, as well as the most powerful electron microscope in a five-state region. Research in refuse-derived fuel puts North Texas at the forefront nationally in seeking solutions to air pollution and waste management.

The Center for Economic Development and Research serves as the focus for the university's commitment to become a major economic development resource for the North Texas region. The center furnishes research and technical assistance to local and regional communities, business and industry, as well as accurate information about economic conditions and trends across the region.

Helping American industry gain access to academic research expertise and facilities is one of the primary goals of the North Texas Research Institute. NTRI is a not-for-profit corporation created to market the university's research capabilities and seek research partnerships with companies from across the United States.

The Texas Academy of Mathematics and Science gives the state's brightest high school students the chance to complete their last two years of high school and first two years of college concurrently.

All these programs and more exemplify this "can do" partnership that will be 100 years old in 1990, when the University of North Texas celebrates its Centennial Year.

MEDICAL CARE INTERNATIONAL

There is a revolution under way in outpatient medical care and surgery. Leading the way is Dallas-based Medical Care International, a seven-year-old organization that is both the fastest growing and the largest owner and operator of free-standing outpatient surgical centers in the United States. As of December 1988, the company had 223 operating rooms in 51 surgical centers located in 23 states from coast to coast. Together, Medical Care International centers performed 155,000 surgeries in 1988, up 16 percent from the 133,000 performed in 1987.

Medical industry analysts estimate that in 1988 at least 40 percent of all surgeries were performed on an outpatient basis. That figure is projected to increase to at least 50 percent by 1990, while the total number of surgeries in the United States is expected to increase only by about 2 percent each year. Overall growth in outpatient surgeries is, of course, reflected by growth in the use of free-standing medical surgical centers such as those owned by Medical Care International. By the end of 1990, at least 10 percent of all surgeries will be performed in such centers compared to 6.5 percent in 1987.

Medical Care International, however, has surged well beyond the national averages, having experienced 20 percent growth during each of the past five years. In 1988, the company posted more than $100 million in net revenue. Industry analysts generally agree that the company is on an extremely fast and well conceived growth curve.

The company has been highly successful for a number of reasons. "We have focused our attention on the needs of particular surgeons who are specializing in fields that do not lend themselves to inpatient care," explains John Carlyle, senior vice-president and chief financial officer. "Doctors specializing in ear/nose/

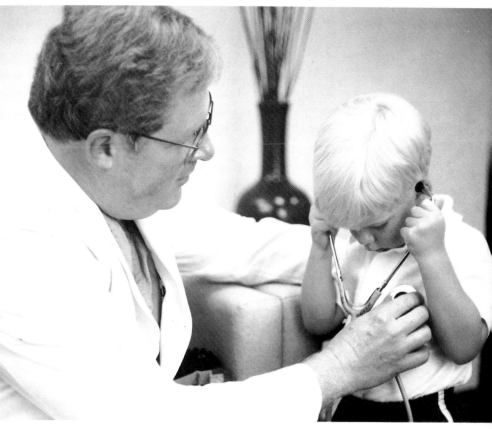

Dallas-based Medical Care International leads the nation in quality outpatient medical care and surgery.

throat, gynecological, ophthalmic, orthopedic, plastic and podiatric procedures often are finding themselves 'bumped' out of hospital operating rooms because their patients do not require inpatient care, thus they do not significantly contribute to that hospital's bottom line. At our facilities a surgeon is never bumped."

Because Medical Care International's free-standing centers serve outpatients only, there are no ancillary facilities such as laundries or food services. Buildings are smaller (usually no more than 10,000 square feet), and 24-hour operation is unnecessary. Thus, Medical Care International centers can deliver services comparable to hospital-based operating facilities at almost half the cost of inpatient treatment and 30 percent less than hospital based outpatient surgery.

The result of such savings is a boon to the entire health care industry, in that it makes a significant contribution to capping the rising cost of

health care. Medical Care International also is committed to the needs of patients as well as those of surgeons. This commitment is exemplified by specialized nursing staffs, allowing surgeons to "block" successive amounts of time for successive surgeries, operating rooms equipped with state-of-the-art medical equipment and superior patient recovery rooms.

Says Carlyle: "We have decided to specialize in a niche in the health care delivery system. We don't want to divert our efforts into other areas; we just want to be the very best in this one particular area. As a result of that commitment to excellence, both the surgeons and patients, as well as the health care industry at large, benefit."

THE UNIVERSITY OF TEXAS SOUTHWESTERN MEDICAL CENTER AT DALLAS

At the heart of Dallas' dynamic health care community is The University of Texas Southwestern Medical Center. It is more than a nationally respected school or expanding hospital complex. The Nobel Prize-winning institution is a driving force for excellence in teaching, patient care and research that reaches far beyond the Dallas/Fort Worth region.

The medical center's three schools educate today's brightest minds: well-prepared physicians who will care for the sick, scientists who will chart new frontiers of knowledge and allied health professionals who are essential in the skilled delivery of care.

Three Nobel laureates currently active on the faculty make UT Southwestern unique among the nation's medical centers. Dr. Michael Brown and Dr. Joseph Goldstein earned the 1985 Nobel Prize in Medicine for discoveries in cholesterol metabolism that already have had an impact on the prevention and treatment of heart disease. Dr. Johann Deisenhofer shared the 1988 Nobel Prize in Chemistry for the first description of the structure of a complex protein in which photosynthesis takes place.

With a research faculty of more than 700, UT Southwestern has a creative, multidisciplinary environment in which new findings move quickly from the laboratory to the patient's bedside. More than 1,300 research projects totaling more than $80 million a year are yielding better diagnosis and treatments for problems ranging from cancer, heart disease, arthritis, diabetes, prematurity and Alzheimer's disease to burns and other types of severe injury.

Dallas Biomedical Corporation, formed by UT Southwestern with venture capitalists, bridges the gap between laboratory and marketplace, developing commercial applications of campus research.

From humble beginnings in 1943 in wartime barracks, UT Southwest-

UT Southwestern has three active Nobel Prize winners on its faculty: (from left) Johann Deisenhofer (Chemistry, 1988), Michael Brown (Medicine, 1985) and Joseph Goldstein (Medicine, 1985). Gittings Photo.

ern has blossomed in size and scientific stature. Today, the main campus is the focus of a large medical complex including four teaching and referral hospitals: Parkland Memorial Hospital, Children's Medical Center, St. Paul Medical Center and the new 160-bed Zale Lipshy University Hospital. This private, non-profit facility will enable faculty to accept patients from all over the world who need their special expertise.

Generous community support has helped propel UT Southwestern's expansion. A new 30-acre campus site given by the MacArthur Foundation will allow construction of more than 2 million square feet of new research and educational facilities over the next two decades. The first building, the Mary Nell and Ralph B. Rogers Magnetic Resonance Center, will open in early 1990. This will soon be followed by the Simmons Biomedical Research Building, to include laboratories of the Harold C. Simmons Comprehensive Cancer Center.

Under the leadership of President Kern Wildenthal, UT Southwestern is at the forefront of science — caring for today's patients, teaching tomorrow's physicians, and discovering new answers for the 21st century.

UT Southwestern Medical Center, Zale Lipshy University Hospital, Parkland Memorial Hospital and Children's Medical Center of Dallas interconnect to form the heart of Dallas' academic medical center. Landis Aerial Photo.

CHILDREN'S MEDICAL CENTER OF DALLAS

Children's Medical Center is a private, non-profit, 168-bed hospital which provides the most advanced medical care available to children from birth through age 18. Established in 1913, it has grown with Dallas to become an internationally known pediatric referral center. It occupies a unique place in Dallas health care as the one area hospital specializing in treating children only.

Children's mission is healing sick children by employing expert medical treatment and technology supported by research, medical education and child advocacy. It offers a full range of pediatric inpatient medical and surgical care, intensive care services and outpatient services in more than 40 specialties.

As Dallas' only resource for complete pediatric health care, Children's is very active. Each year more than 10,000 children are admitted to the hospital, 7,000 surgeries are performed in its state-of-the-art surgical facilities, more than 1,000 children receive life support in its ICU, and 90,000 outpatient consultations are conducted through Children's specialty centers.

Children's patients benefit from leading-edge programs in cardiology, gastroenterology, genetics, hematology/oncology, infectious diseases, intensive care, nephrology, organ transplantation, sleep disorders and surgery.

During its 77 years, Children's has developed a reputation for advancing the frontiers of pediatric medicine, with milestones such as prototype intensive care, the first day-surgery program in the Untied States, groundbreaking pediatric MRI technology, sleep disorders diagnosis and management, preventive cardiology programs, and heart, liver and kidney transplant centers ranking among the country's largest.

Children's specialists utilize the latest treatments, therapies and understanding of disease discovered through scientific research. Through its affiliation with UT Southwestern, its staff conducts ongoing research of a national scope in many subspecialty areas. Notably, Children's maintains one of only 14 national pediatric research centers sanctioned by the National Institutes of Health.

Strict guidelines govern the training and selection of Children's health care professionals. As the pediatric teaching hospital for UT Southwestern, Children's offers a three-year pediatric residency program for physicians and supports academic fellowships in many subspecialties. Qualified resident physicians provide 24-hour care at a level that only a teaching hospital can offer. Many of the more than 600 physicians on Children's medical staff received their training in this program and remain in the community to provide a network of care. Children's also ensures outstanding nursing care by maintaining a high ratio of nurses per child and by requiring each of its 400 professional nurses to complete rigorous training in pediatrics.

Children's embraces child advocacy in its efforts to provide quality health care for all children. Child development specialists, teachers, social workers and chaplains work to make sure the emotional, educational and social needs of Children's patients are considered as carefully as their medical conditions.

Hospital officials work continually to enhance legislation expanding access to quality health care for children. Children's public education programs encourage children and their families to adopt healthy lifestyles. And a multimillion-dollar expansion under way will give Dallas a 266-bed pediatric hospital ranking among the top 10 in the nation.

Children's Medical Center pledges to continue to enhance the services it provides in order to safeguard the most important component of Dallas' future — its children.

Children's Medical Center plays an integral part in Dallas history as the area's premier pediatric health care resource. As a private, non-profit organization, Children's measures success in terms of children healed and returned to their families to enjoy healthy lives.

PARKLAND MEMORIAL HOSPITAL

Parkland Memorial Hospital not only is one of the best hospitals in Texas, but it ranks among the top 25 in the United States. It is the primary teaching hospital of the University of Texas Southwestern Medical Center at Dallas.

Prominent citizens and non-paying patients alike enjoy a quality of care that has advanced the hospital's reputation to a world-class status. Originally established in 1894 to serve only Dallas County's indigent residents, Parkland remains the county's only public hospital.

Parkland's Trauma and Burn centers enjoy wide-ranging recognition, but the hospital perhaps is best known in the medical community as a premier training center for physicians. Young doctors have trained under the direction of such medical leaders as Donald W. Seldin, M.D., considered the dean of American medicine in the Southwest, and Charles R. Baxter, M.D., noted for his pioneer work in skin-graft surgery. The hospital's medicine, surgery and ob/gyn programs continue to contribute to the new body of knowledge in improved patient care.

The relationship between Parkland and UT Southwestern is mutually beneficial for patients and advancement in medicine. A research discovery by UT Southwestern physicians Joseph Goldstein and Michael Brown earned them the Nobel Prize in medicine in 1985. These physicians, like other highly productive clinicians and researchers also attend at Parkland.

This atmosphere of state-of-the-art medicine attracts significant numbers of private patient referrals to Parkland's many centers of medical excellence, which specialize in neurosurgery, diagnostic cardiology and treatments for osteoporosis, abnormal heart rhythms, heart disease, stroke, epilepsy and deadly and disfiguring forms of skin disease.

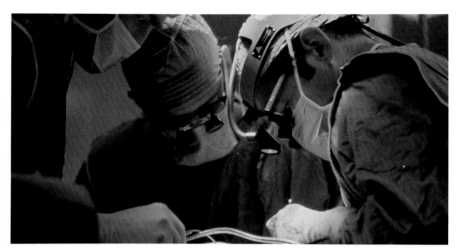

A rich history of accomplishments make Parkland, together with the medical school and adjacent campus entities, one of the greatest single assets of the city of Dallas and the county. Its history includes a number of firsts that continue to benefit the community and beyond.

Since establishing a Regional Burn Center in 1962 that pioneered skin graft techniques, infection control and nutritional support for burn patients, Parkland has treated more burn patients than any other civilian burn center in the world. A reorganization of Parkland's Emergency Department into six distinct areas in 1962 served as a model for the nation.

Since the first kidney transplant in Texas was performed at Parkland in 1964, more than 1,000 kidney transplants have been performed here; Parkland's rate of success in kidney transplants among African-Americans is unparalleled in the United States. The hospital's Pediatric Trauma Unit was developed in 1983 to become the first of its kind in the nation and served as a model for other units across the country.

Parkland is a busy place, handling more than a half-million patient visits per year in its outpatient clinics and emergency room. It is the nation's third-largest birthing hospital, delivering nearly 15,000 babies annually.

Surgery is just one end of the spectrum of medical excellence at Parkland Memorial Hospital. It excels in many areas of medical treatment and research, including neurosurgery, diagnostic cardiology, heart disease, stroke, epilepsy, transplantation and diabetes. Its burn and trauma centers are world-renowned, offering state-of-the-art critical care to accident and burn victims.

As a public hospital, Parkland has remained and will continue to remain true to its multiple missions of education, research, community service and providing medical care to Dallas Country residents regardless of ability to pay. However, it also must stay abreast of the shifting trend toward competition in the health care arena.

It is for that reason that Parkland's Board of Managers has taken an aggressive role in helping to establish University Hospital as part of the medical campus that includes Parkland, UT Southwestern and Children's Medical Center. The 160-bed facility, together with Parkland, is a place for Southwestern physicians to refer private patients. Many of Parkland's medical services will not be duplicated at University Hospital, and this coordination of effort enhances the campus' reputation as a major medical center.

It is with this commitment to the future that Parkland Hospital is beginning its second century of dedication to health care and community service.

ZALE LIPSHY UNIVERSITY HOSPITAL

Dallas' newest hospital, Zale Lipshy University Hospital, adds a new facet to what was already an internationally recognized center for medical care, education and research.

The University of Texas Southwestern Medical Center at Dallas had endured for decades as the only leading academic medical center in the nation without a private referral and teaching hospital. Such a hospital, to which patients with complicated disorders may be referred for state-of-the-art diagnosis and therapy, is a key element in attracting and retaining outstanding clinical faculty. Such a hospital also brings the doctors of tomorrow face-to-face with the more challenging problems of their specialties.

The state of Texas could not fund such a hospital, so the unique combination of Dallas business and Dallas medicine came to the rescue. From 1984 to 1989, more than $30 million

was donated to build this key component in UT Southwestern's comprehensive picture of medical excellence.

The private 160-bed teaching and referral facility is staffed by UT Southwestern medical faculty and residents, as are Parkland Memorial Hospital and Children's Medical Center. Physically, the new hospital is linked floor-by-floor with the rest of the medical complex through the new Charles Cameron Sprague Clinical Science Building, where clinical faculty will have offices, laboratories and classrooms.

The specialized departments and services of University Hospital coordinate with those of the other institutions in the medical complex. For example, there is no emergency room or obstetrics division at the new hospital because Parkland provides these next door. Nor does the institution offer pediatric care, not with superb care only a building away at Children's Medical Center.

Procedures that require highly sophisticated and expensive equipment already available at Parkland — such as nuclear medicine, cardiac catheterization and dialysis — are purchased from the county hospital. Some of these services have been

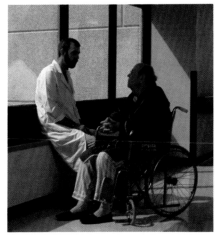

University Hospital was built for patients referred to UT Southwestern faculty experts.

expanded because of University Hospital's opening, which will benefit patients at both hospitals.

The hospital offers nine floors of medical excellence. On one floor, 12 oversized operating rooms accommodate state-of-the-art equipment for eye, ear, nose and throat surgery, gynecological surgery, urology, neurosurgery, orthopedic surgery, chest and vascular surgery and special general surgery.

Another floor has 20 intensive care beds — each equipped with a space-age bedside terminal that monitors the patient's vital signs, updates records automatically and frees nurses for one-on-one personal care. Yet another floor provides spacious, comfortable rooms for psychiatric patients, focusing on affective disorders, schizophrenia, eating disorders and Alzheimer's Disease.

The hospital's rooms are adorned with museum-quality textiles donated through the generosity of the McDermott Foundation, and many rooms feature breathtaking views of the downtown Dallas skyline.

Zale Lipshy is the newest university hospital in the country. It is destined to be one of the finest.

University Hospital is the new private teaching and referral hospital at UT Southwestern Medical Center.

DOCTORS HOSPITAL

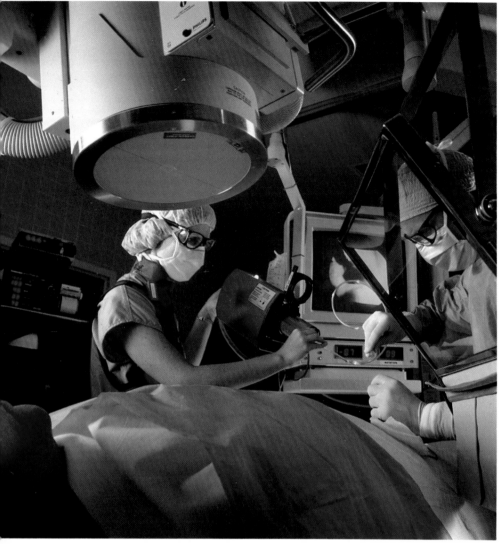

Doctors Hospital is surrounded by the beautiful trees of East Dallas and sits on a rise overlooking White Rock Lake and the Dallas skyline. The peacefulness of the geography has a positive impact on the tertiary care hospital, lending a good-humor to physicians, workers and patients alike.

"I like the atmosphere here," says Katherine Mitchell, R.N., director of surgery. "I think the whole place exudes friendliness."

"This is also one of the best staffs I've worked with in 15 years," she says. "They really care. They're dedicated to their work, and they strive to do a good job for the patient."

The 278-bed hospital was founded in 1959 by a group of area

Doctors Hospital is becoming well known for its cardiac work, especially the cardiac catheterization program which allows physicians to determine, without major surgery, what steps are necessary to restore heart health.

physicians, says Chris DiCicco, CEO. "They were looking for a quality service and a place to take care of their patients," he says, adding that the original hospital did not have an obstetrics unit or an emergency room. In the past 3 years Doctors Hospital has grown as the community around it has grown. What was once a hospital offering only standard surgery and medical procedures is now a regional care center with 24-hour emergency care, obstetrics and much more.

In 1984, the hospital's founders sold the hospital to National Medical Enterprises (NME), and Doctors Hospital became one of 52 Healthcare Centers operated by NME, DiCicco said. The company also runs numerous nursing homes and many rehabilitation centers for chemical and physical dependencies.

NME kept the philosophy of caring and personal attention that Doctors Hospital was founded on, and expanded and added services, including an obstetrics unit and a very advanced cardiac catheterization program. The company also has remodeled extensively, added outpatient facilities and additional intensive care units.

"We're very critically aware of care," DiCicco says, "so we have a good group of people — they really want to be in health care." Many of the hospital's doctors enjoy practicing at Doctors because of the friendly, unhurried atmosphere and top-notch staff, he says.

The hospital is becoming well-known for its cardiac work, especially the cardiac catheterization program which allows physicians to determine, without major surgery, what steps are necessary to restore heart health.

The hospital also performs valvuloplasty, a new treatment for patients suffering from constricted heart valves.

To further cardiac care, DiCicco says the hospital plans a state-of-the-art cardiac rehabilitation center which will include a swimming pool and a running track.

As Doctors Hospital expands, administrators and staff alike hold to one main goal: to continue the tradition of outstanding medical care in a hospital dedicated to the personal care of its neighborhood and East Texas.

UNIVERSITY OF TEXAS AT DALLAS

From its beginning, The University of Texas at Dallas was destined for distinction. In the 1950s, civic and industrial leaders Erik Jonsson, Cecil Green and the late Eugene McDermott dreamed of a first-class higher education and research institution for the bright, young talent at their growing company, Texas Instruments Inc.

Pursuit of the dream began in 1961 when the men established the Graduate Research Center of the Southwest, later renamed the Southwest Center for Advanced Studies. In 1969, the men donated their institution to the state of Texas, and The University of Texas at Dallas was born.

U.T. Dallas has gradually fulfilled its founders' dream. Outstanding programs in the natural sciences and mathematics begun at the Southwest Center provided a strong foundation on which to build a great university. U.T. Dallas added programs in arts and humanities, management, human development, general studies, social sciences, engineering and computer science.

The university built a distinguished faculty that included the first Nobel Laureate to serve on a Texas university faculty, two Texas Academy of Sciences "Scientist of the Year" award winners, and scholars who annually attract more research funds than the faculty at any other academic institution in the region.

Internationally respected scholars with specialties in areas such as marketing, the natural sciences, performance art, geography, the learning needs of infants and the space sciences make U.T. Dallas the regional leader in academic research. As the U.T. Dallas founders understood, this research is critical to the region's economic health. Local business and industry benefit from the research of top scholars at U.T. Dallas. Their research adds millions of dollars and hundreds of jobs to the

Antarctic explorer and U.T. Dallas President Robert H. Rutford stands before the Multipurpose and Engineering Start-Up Facility, which houses the university's Erik Jonsson School of Engineering and Computer Science and the university administration.

North Texas economy.

Having a top faculty means U.T. Dallas students learn from leaders in their fields of interest. Those students, through most of U.T. Dallas' history, have generally been non-traditional students — older students, students employed full time and supporting families, single parents needing new skills to enter the work force and employed professionals seeking advanced degrees. U.T. Dallas serves these students by providing convenient day and evening classes.

In 1989 the Texas Legislature approved expansion of the undergraduate program to include freshmen and sophomores. While the student body may change, the essential mission of the institution remains: To provide quality graduate programs (especially for employees of nearby high tech companies), build a highly respected faculty, and create knowledge through research. Whether by conducting research, attracting leading scholars, educating the work force or infusing millions of dollars into the local economy, U.T. Dallas enriches the life of the region. The founders' dream of quality research and education in North Texas has become a reality. U.T. Dallas is providing quality leadership for tomorrow's Texas.

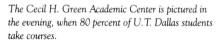

The Cecil H. Green Academic Center is pictured in the evening, when 80 percent of U.T. Dallas students take courses.

MEDICAL CITY DALLAS

Forget your old concepts about hospitals. The cold, clinical atmosphere — sterile, stuffy surroundings — detached, aloof health-care professionals going through the motions...

Medical City Dallas is different, and you will realize that the moment you walk through the door.

You are greeted with the expansive beauty of a magnificent atrium and skylights, beautiful courtyard resplendent with a garden and fountains and a mall with specialty shops, restaurants, a flower shop, beauty salon and barber shop, a bakery, a bank and more. Several floors of physician offices frame the mall, with more located in the adjacent medical towers.

This is a very non-institutional environment — by design.

Specially selected original artwork adorns each room, and the color schemes and furnishings are all carefully coordinated for a warm and inviting atmosphere.

Friendly, attentive and caring health-care professionals follow through with the promise of the surroundings. They know that making

With its spacious atrium lined with shops and restaurants, Humana Hospital — Medical City Dallas breaks down preconceptions about what a hospital should look like.

you and your visitors feel at home is an important part of the healing process.

Medical City Dallas is anchored by 350 physician offices and Humana Hospital — Medical City Dallas. Because of the close proximity of the physician offices to the hospital, patients have the added assurance that their physicians are literally steps away from their bed — an important factor in providing high quality medical care.

A Hospitality Program of special services makes the hospital experience comfortable, pleasant and convenient for patients. And because visitors are important to a patient's well-being, hospitality is extended to families and friends with the Passport Program. These services offer a host of benefits ranging from courtesy pagers for relatives of ICU patients to special visitor discounts on food and merchandise.

"My compliments to the chef," are words frequently heard at Medical City Dallas. And, indeed, leading chefs are brought in regularly to add variety and quality to the menu. Because of these consultants, patients enjoy culinary delights that are anything but typical hospital fare.

These are just a few of the programs and services that contribute to the uniqueness of Humana Hospital-Medical City Dallas.

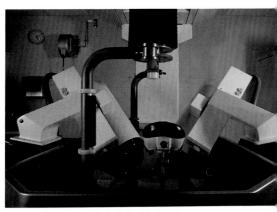

Humana Hospital — Medical City Dallas uses innovative diagnostic technology, including bi-plane catheterization in the Cardiovascular Center of Excellence, and a Magnetic Resonance Imaging Center.

Medical City's staff is among the finest ever assembled, and it is backed by the most advanced medical technology available today.

The hospital's cardiovascular and neuroscience centers are both nationally recognized Humana Centers of Excellence. And the Humana Advanced Surgical Institutes has earned an international reputation for craniofacial and pediatric orthopedic surgery, as well as pediatric neurosurgery.

Total cardiac care is also offered at Medical City Dallas. A cardiac intensive care unit offers a level of round-the-clock, personal care that sets the standards for medical centers; diagnostic capabilities are second to none, using medicine's most conclusive technology including bi-plane catheterization. Special rehabilitation programs and facilities provide specialized, supervised care including monitored exercise testing and training and stress management. Cardiopulmonary Services provide special help for patients with heart and/or lung problems.

This Center of Excellence functions as a referral center for specialists and hospitals around the country.

Medical City Dallas is a source of excellence for more than 60 medical

specialties. Obstetrics, pediatrics, plastic surgery, oncology, orthopedics, hematology, cardiology — there is virtually no specialty that has not distinguished itself with the medical community.

Nationally known for pioneering projects in neurological diagnosis for both adults and children, the Neuroscience Center of Excellence deals with all phases of the nervous system.

There are three basic specialty divisions: Medical Neurology, Neurological Surgery and Neurological Laboratories. All three divisions work together to provide patients with the very best diagnosis and treatment available today. The center has made outstanding contributions in the treatment of sleep and seizure disorders.

Medical City's family-centered care involves the whole family in the preparation and birthing process. The hospital offers ongoing patient classes on prenatal, early pregnancy, cesarean section, breast feeding, postpartum care and a special course for siblings.

Care at Humana Hospital — Medical City Dallas is family oriented. And nowhere is that more evident than throughout the Pediatric Center where parents are involved in the treatment team as much as possible.

Women choosing to have their babies at Humana Hospital-Medical City Dallas can take extra reassurance in the total back-up capabilities, including a Level III Neonatal Intensive Care Unit for newborns with special medical needs.

The Cradle Club is a unique program of parental education and service available to women in the community who are delivering at Humana Hospital-Medical City Dallas. And it is free.

The Pediatric Center caters to the unique needs of children and their parents by focusing on both the psychological and physical aspects of hospitalization. The Pediatric Center has an unparalleled level of service and quality with more than 100 pediatricians on staff, many with pediatric subspecialties.

And, Parent Prestige Services are offered, including: free puzzles and games for young patients and a Medical City Dallas Health Heroes Club Activity Kit; parents can order flowers, special gifts, birthday parties, special outings — virtually any request to make a child more comfortable will be entertained. Parents may even stay in one of two hotel-style rooms on the same floor, or in their child's room. For even greater convenience, in-room meals and snacks are available for parents.

Thousands of Dallas-area youngsters are learning interesting and fun ways to stay fit and healthy as members of the Health Heroes Club. Children receive exciting activity books, newsletters and more. Each year The Health Heroes-Captain Rick Hearty, Stay C. Fit and The Blaster — host a Kids' Healthcare Fair. Membership in the club and all materials are free.

Major crisis or minor emergency, Medical City's 24-hour Emergency Center is ready to help. And patients have the great reassurance of knowing that every available medical resource stands ready in case of need.

Medical City Dallas is anchored by 350 physician offices and Humana Hospital-Medical City Dallas.

Medical City has highly qualified physicians on duty at all times, and specialists in more than 6-fields on call day and night. The Emergency Center also offers specialists in children's emergencies and orthopedists to diagnose and treat sports injuries.

More than 160 radiological medical professionals work with leading edge technology to make Medical City an unparalleled resource for diagnostic excellence. Digital radiography, Magnetic Resonance Imaging and CT Scans are included in the hospital's array of high-tech capabilities.

Need a personal physician? Use Medical City's physician referral network, Humana On Call. The best time to choose a physician is before one is needed. Continuity of care under a physician who knows your medical history is essential to good health. Whether you need a specialist or a family physician, Humana On Call will discuss your needs and match you with a doctor on staff who best meets those needs.

The very best way to understand Medical City's combination of a friendly, non-institutional atmosphere and highly sophisticated, highly advanced medical care is to stop by and get acquainted.

FOXMEYER DRUG COMPANY

Though relatively new to the area, FoxMeyer Drug Company's impressive history of growth marks the 10-year-old company as an important corporate citizen in the Dallas business community.

In fact, FoxMeyer has earned a reputation that goes far beyond Dallas. What started as a regional company with under $100 million in sales is today a multibillion-dollar corporation recognized as the fastest-growing drug distribution company in the United States.

Ranked third among the nation's largest pharmaceutical firms, Fox-Meyer operates primarily in the Midwestern and Southern states to serve independent drug stores, hospital pharmacies, food and drug combinations, chain drug stores and mass merchandisers.

Past acquisition of drug distribution companies gives FoxMeyer the high-volume buying power to be a price-competitive wholesaler in all

Wholesale pharmaceutical distribution to drugstores, chains and hospitals have helped FoxMeyer Drug Company become the nation's third-largest drug wholesaler and the largest subsidiary of Pittsburgh-based National Intergroup.

Registered pharmacist and CEO Bob King is leading FoxMeyer Drug Company's continued growth as one of the country's top drug wholesalers.

markets, and plans are to continue building market share in all regions. Already, customer orders for more than 25,000 products are transmitted daily to FoxMeyer's central data processing center in Wichita, Kan. and then relayed to one of 12 regional distribution warehouses for near-immediate delivery.

But the corporate philosophy says that the job does not end with the completion of a delivery. Adhering to a fundamental belief that the foundation for growth is built on a prospering customer base, FoxMeyer sees itself as a service company first. Its commitment to the field translates into personal attention and programs that help customers respond to the changing marketplace.

Fully half of those customers are among the nation's independent drug stores, which look to FoxMeyer for the tools they need to survive head-to-head competition with the larger

chain store down the street. In addition to offering economies-of-scale pricing, promotions and inventory programs, FoxMeyer also provides a full range of unique marketing, advertising and training programs that help the independent drug store move goods out the front door.

The most comprehensive of these is FoxMeyer's exclusive Health Mart franchise program, which gives independents the kind of integrated merchandising, marketing and image development support usually only afforded by chain outlets. Health Mart stores increase sales and profits by incorporating a common identity that includes total store layout, a circular and television advertising program, private label products, training

seminars, market research, customized plan-o-grams, merchandising and management consultation, and a complete grand opening package.

With almost 600 independently owned stores in the program, Health Mart is recognized as the fastest-growing drug store franchise chain in the country.

In the health care industry, FoxMeyer's service-driven philosophy is the basis for Health Care Pharmacy Providers (HCPP), which acts as a third-party administrator and plan manager for prescription drug benefits offered by HMOs, PPOs, insurance companies and employers. HCPP gives these managed health care plans a single, cost-effective administrative source that includes comprehensive support services such as claims processing and management information systems. HCPP promises to be another high-growth segment in FoxMeyer's continuing market expansion.

FoxMeyer also offers customers a single-source approach to the home health care market, combining product sales with the training, advertising and operations guidance needed to establish leadership in this booming new market category. A fully accredited continuing education program is included for store personnel.

FoxMeyer's growth began in 1978, when it acquired FoxVliet Drug Company and later Meyer Brothers Drug Company to create the FoxMeyer name. The company went public in 1983 and in the mid-1980s grew through a series of acquisitions that took annual sales to nearly $1 billion.

In early 1989, FoxMeyer completed its acquisition of Louis Zahn Drug Company, a $209-million wholesaler with largely independent pharmacy customers in Indiana and Illinois. The acquisition gave Fox-Meyer the majority share among all drug wholesalers in the Chicago-centered region.

Since 1986, FoxMeyer has been the largest subsidiary of National Intergroup Inc., a diversified Pittsburgh-based company whose other holdings include Ben Franklin Stores Inc. and The Permian Corporation, an oil distributor. National Intergroup also holds investments in steel and aluminum manufacturing.

Health Mart Care-A-Van, a 28-foot mobile screening unit, travels throughout the United States monitoring customers' cholesterol, blood pressure, heart rate, vision and height/weight ratios. Care-A-Van is just one of the many valuable services offered to independents through FoxMeyer's comprehensive Health Mart franchise program.

Independent drugstore owners can take advantage of FoxMeyer's exclusive Health Mart franchise program, which offers integrated merchandising, marketing and image development support. Health Mart is recognized as the fastest-growing drug store franchise chain in the country with almost 600 independently owned stores.

KAISER PERMANENTE

Dallas is headquarters for the Texas Region of Kaiser Permanente, the nation's largest prepaid group practice medical care program — serving the health care needs of more than 6.5 million members nationally and more than 120,000 members locally. Kaiser Permanente began on the West Coast in the 1940s with about 25,000 members and expanded its operation to Texas in 1979, initially serving about 2,000 members.

The not-for-profit organization is composed of two major and equally important arms. In Texas, they are Kaiser Foundation Health Plan of Texas which enrolls members and manages the business aspects of the program; and the Permanente Medical Association of Texas, a physicians group which provides medical care exclusively for Kaiser Permanente members. Together, they form Kaiser Permanente, a partnership between professional business managers and professionals of medicine — sharing responsibilities for delivering quality, comprehensive health care at a predictable, economical cost.

The prepayment of monthly membership dues is one of the guiding principles of Kaiser Permanente. The original members of the program, who were West Coast construction and shipyard workers for industrialist Henry J. Kaiser, paid five cents per day per worker through payroll deductions for their health care. The prepayments provided the base income needed to efficiently run the medical operations founded and operated by Dr. Sidney R. Garfield.

Today, the prepayment concept is still working. Kaiser Permanente provides affordable quality health care for members in 16 states and the District of Columbia. Members represent all regions of the country, all industries and all socio-ethnic groups.

Kaiser Permanente employs close to 7,000 physicians and 60,000 non-physician employees nationwide. National and Northern California regional headquarters are located in Oakland. Other regional offices are located in Pasadena, California; Denver; Atlanta; Honolulu; Shawnee Mission, Kansas; Washington, D.C.; Raleigh, North Carolina; Hartford, Connecticut; Portland, Oregon; Cleveland; and Dallas.

The latest financial statement indicates revenues in excess of $6 billion annually, net income of $100 million and assets of $2 billion. If Kaiser Permanente were a "for profit" company, it would rank within the top 100 of *Fortune* 500 companies.

From its inception, Kaiser Permanente has been an industry leader in developing innovative and cost-effective approaches to health care. Many of the principles it pioneered such as quality assurance, emphasis on preventive care and outpatient surgery have become accepted norms within the managed care industry (commonly called HMOs).

Kaiser Permanente has prospered despite the vagaries of the health care industry, because the program has remained committed to its guiding principles in organizing, financing and delivering quality health care. Those principles are:

Group practice medicine — physicians working as a team, consulting one another in treatment of patients.

Prepayment — members pay a fixed monthly rate, set annually, for all covered services.

Organized facilities — health care facilities which are planned, developed, equipped and staffed as an integral part of a regional health care program.

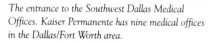

The entrance to the Southwest Dallas Medical Offices. Kaiser Permanente has nine medical offices in the Dallas/Fort Worth area.

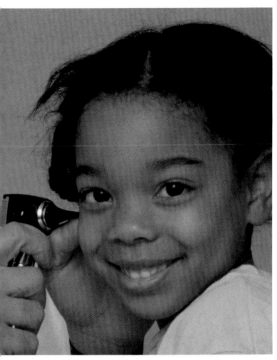

Kaiser Permanente covers a wide range of services including pediatric care.

Voluntary enrollment — members enroll by choice.

Preventive care — prepaid benefits cover periodic health checkups, inoculations, tests and health education programs.

Physician responsibility — program physicians are organized into independent medical groups and manage their own activities.

Kaiser Permanente believes in long-term solutions with incentives to seek care when it is first needed, not delayed due to concern for out-of-pocket costs. The objective is the wellness of members, not the over-utilization of Kaiser Permanente's services for the program's gain.

Benefits include comprehensive physician and hospital services, maternity and well-baby care, X-rays, laboratory and other diagnostic tests, immunizations, routine checkups, allergy testing, skilled nursing care, emergency and home health care as well as alcoholism treatment and detoxification for drug abuse.

Texas Region

The Texas Region of Kaiser Permanente has more than 125 physicians and 1000 staff serving 120,000 voluntarily enrolled members in the Dallas/Fort Worth area.

There are six Kaiser Permanente offices in Dallas County and three in Tarrant County. Locations are: Medical City Dallas Medical Office, Southwest Dallas Medical Office, Irving Medical Office, Plano Medical Office, Garland Medical Office, Mesquite Medical Office, Arlington Medical Office, Hurst-Euless-Bedford Medical Office and Central Fort Worth Medical Office.

Inpatient services are provided at leading community hospitals. Kaiser Permanente members are usually hospitalized at Methodist Medical Center in Southwest Dallas, Humana Hospital-Medical City Dallas in North Dallas, and Harris Methodist in Fort Worth.

Local members of the Kaiser Foundation Health Plan of Texas Board of Directors are: Adelfa B. Callejo, attorney at law; Sibyl Hamilton; John D. Miller, member, national board; Raymond D. Nasher, chairman of the board, Raymond D. Nasher Company; and H. Ron White, attorney at law.

Margaret H. Jordon, R.N., M.P.H, has been vice president and regional manager of Kaiser Foundation Health Plan of Texas since March 1986. She came to Dallas from Kaiser Foundation Health Plan of Georgia Inc., where she served as associate regional manager. Jordon began her career with Kaiser in Oakland in 1981 as coordinator of licensing and accreditation.

Richard P. Hoffmann, M.D., became president and executive medical director of the Permanente Medical Association of Texas in July, 1984. He also serves as chairman of Kaiser Permanente's Executive Medical Directors Group.

From 1978 to 1984, Hoffmann worked with the Colorado Permanente Medical Group, Denver, in various capacities including chief of medicine, director of quality assurance and as a member of the board of directors.

Eye examinations are just one of the many services offered by Kaiser Permanente of Texas.

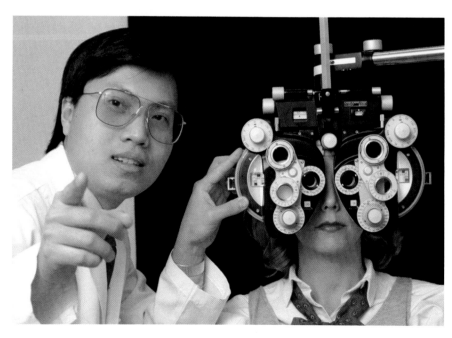

DALLAS INDEPENDENT SCHOOL DISTRICT

Over the last 115 years the Dallas Independent School District has evolved from modest beginnings into the eighth-largest public education organization in the United States, operating more than 220 educational facilities. Today, with a AAA Moody Bond rating as its financial hallmark, the district employs nearly 16,000 people (8,400 of them teachers), operates on an annual budget exceeding $632 million, and is responsible for the education of more than 132,000 students.

Being a dynamic urban school system, the DISD is rich in ethnic diversity. It serves students from no fewer than 80 different cultures. That diverse ethnic mix provides many windows of opportunity that further enhance the international and multicultural development of Dallas, which is emerging as a geographic and commercial center for this part of the world. Such a fact is not lost on the many national and multinational firms who see Dallas as a potential base for future operations.

One of the major challenges of a school district is to provide students with the intellectual skills necessary to become successful and productive members of society. The DISD is committed to that ideal. Students will soon begin studies to become trilingual, including computer literate. More than 60 percent of its graduates enroll in colleges, and approximately 35 percent of its career-directed magnet high school students directly enter the workforce upon graduation. All students are expected to hone the competitive, academic, artistic and career tools that are vital to their success in today's society.

One area in which the DISD has had great success is its partnerships with area businesses, civic organizations, private and higher education schools, religious institutions and

Innovative programs such as DISD's magnet high schools offer students a choice of schools and course work in their selected career fields.

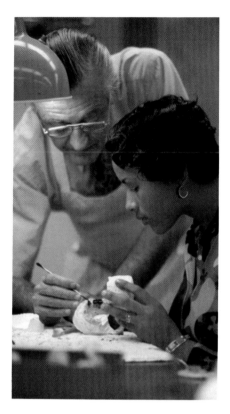

Innovative programs such as DISD's magnet high schools offer students course work in their selected career fields.

parent groups. Many students are given the opportunity, through several nationally recognized programs, to interact directly with the community. High achievers become interns with small business companies, private foundations or many of the multinational corporations that call Dallas home. Corporate Dallas adopts many of the district's schools, lends its executives and blue ribbon advisors, provides scholarships and other achievement incentives and considers the overall success of Dallas' youth to be a part of its long-term agenda.

As a result, the DISD is returning to the community state-of-the-art educational advances which lead to even greater expectations of excellence from both student and educator. Together, the DISD and Dallas are creating competent, well-rounded citizens for the 21st century.

BAYLOR UNIVERSITY MEDICAL CENTER

Since its founding in 1903, Baylor University Medical Center has served patients from Texas, the Southwest and around the world. "Hospitals are a natural product of Christian religion," said Dr. George W. Truett, a Baptist minister and an original Baylor trustee. His vision of "a great humanitarian hospital" prompted Dallas Baptists to sponsor a new medical facility at a time when Dallas had less than 100 hospital beds.

Licensed for 1,455 beds, Baylor University Medical Center today comprises five connecting patient hospitals and more than 20 medical specialty centers on a campus covering more than 20 city blocks.

Baylor's commitment to medical education, research and excellence in patient care has remained constant for more than 80 years. Always an

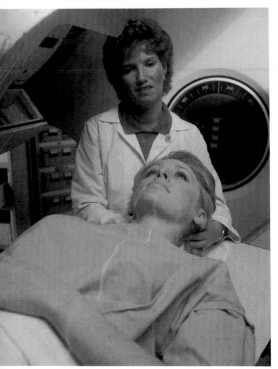

Radiation therapy is one of several treatment modalities that may be prescribed at Baylor University Medical Center's Charles A. Sammons Cancer Center.

innovative leader in health care, Baylor was the birthplace of Blue Cross.

Later in the 1940s, the American Association of Blood Banks and the International Society of Hematology began at Baylor. More recently, Baylor was the first in Texas to utilize magnetic resonance imaging for clinical purposes, the first in the United States to perform a gallstone lithotripsy procedure, and the first in Texas to perform a heart-lung "domino" transplant.

Approximately 240,000 patients are treated at Baylor University Medical Center each year. In addition to acute patient care, specialized care is provided through individualized centers.

Baylor is nationally and internationally known for its multiorgan transplant program. The adult liver transplant program is the second-largest in the United States. Active programs in heart, kidney, heart-kidney, liver-kidney and bone marrow transplantation have also gained national recognition.

Baylor's Diagnostic Center for Digestive Diseases combats digestive disorders through an active treatment and research program. It is one of only two centers in the world specializing in diseases of the digestive tract.

Baylor's H.L. and Ruth Ray Hunt Heart Center is recognized as one of the top heart centers in the country. Since opening in 1976, more than 70,000 patients have been diagnosed and treated for heart disorders.

The Charles A. Sammons Cancer Center treats more cancer patients than any other center in North Texas. It serves as the focal point of oncology (cancer) activity at Baylor. A multidisciplinary team uses the most advanced methods in diagnosis and treatment. Research and education also are important components of the center.

Baylor University Medical Center is Texas' second largest private teaching and research hospital and the third-largest church-related hospital in the United States. Located east of downtown Dallas, Baylor's campus covers more than 20 city blocks.

Baylor also has specialized centers in metabolic diseases, infectious diseases, neonatology, medical imaging, orthopedics, eating disorders, chemical dependency, diabetes, psoriasis, eye disorders, physical medicine and weight management.

Baylor University Medical Center serves as a major teaching facility for physicians, nurses and other allied health professionals.

Each year, approximately 50,000 nurses, physicians and other allied health professionals receive up-to-the-minute information on new medical technology, advances and research through the A. Webb Roberts Center for Continuing Education.

Active clinical and basic research programs at Baylor enable physicians and scientists to learn more about different diseases and better treatment methods. Baylor has made significant contributions to medical science through the killing of potentially life-threatening viruses in blood with lasers, artificial bone discoveries, breakthroughs in digestive diseases and infectious diseases, and many other firsts.

The Baylor Research Foundation, a 23,000-square-foot laboratory, opened in 1988. More than 150 research projects are under way in eight major areas targeted for study.

As advances in science and technology continue to challenge and improve medicine, Baylor University Medical Center's mission remains to provide quality patient care, to advance medical research and to educate health professionals — all within a Christian setting.

A medical residency program trains 148 new physicians each year in 12 different specialties. More than 13 fellowship programs also are available for physicians seeking highly specialized training. Baylor School of Nursing also is located on campus, offering an in-depth nursing education program through Baylor University in Waco, Texas.

Other educational programs at Baylor include schools for radiation therapy, radiology and respiratory therapy. Emergency medical technicians are trained through Baylor's emergency room, and internships in perioperative nursing, hospital administration, dietetics and pastoral care are offered.

Baylor also is committed to community education. Active participation in health fairs and community events, a speaker's bureau and free seminars for consumers all serve to educate the public. Baylor sponsors "HealthSource," a health information report on a local television news program. A sun intensity index also is used by weather forecasters to advise consumers how to avoid sunburns. And, a variety of support groups sponsored by Baylor help patients and their families deal with illness.

Child life therapy is an important aspect of Baylor's family-centered pediatric program.

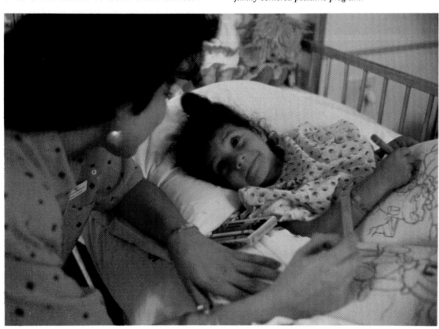

ST. PAUL MEDICAL CENTER

The history of St. Paul Medical Center is the story of an illustrious partnership which began as the 19th century was coming to a close. At that time, Dallas was already on its way to becoming one of America's important urban centers, and the city's economy and population were flourishing.

Recognizing the need for qualified health care, a group of city leaders appealed to the Daughters of Charity of St. Vincent de Paul who had a 263-year reputation for serving the sick and needy throughout the world. At a time when health care and hospitals were fairly new concepts, this religious community of women already was known for its impeccable facilities.

Answering the call, the Sisters came to Dallas and organized what would become one of the Southwest's finest, full-service health care institutions. Today, nearly a century later, the partnership with the Dallas community still is going strong. Fueled by the same commitment, St. Paul Medical Center continues its dedication to meeting the physical and spiritual needs of the citizens of Dallas, while serving each patient with humanity, respect and dignity.

That mission — to serve both the

St. Paul Medical Center, a 600-bed tertiary care facility, is the oldest private, not-for-profit hospital in Dallas.

physical and spiritual needs of humanity with a special emphasis toward providing for the poor — has provided the basis for a partnership between Dallas and St. Paul Medical Center.

"The tremendously successful relationship enjoyed between the Medical Center and the people of Dallas is something we can all take pride in," says Anthony L. Bunker, president of St. Paul.

Through contributions from the citizens of Dallas, St. Paul Sanitarium was completed in 1898. The stately, five-story red-brick building at the corner of Bryan and Hall streets had a 110-bed capacity.

The Daughters of Charity opened their first clinic for the poor in 1906 with a budget of $7.50. By 1924, the Marillac Center opened, providing health services and food to Dallas' sick and homeless. And in 1937, St. Paul opened a five-story clinic to care for the indigent.

Today, almost $5.5 million of St. Paul's annual budget is set aside to assist the poor. As many as 12,000

indigent people are treated annually through the St. Paul Outpatient Clinic.

"We want to be known as the medical center that's committed to very important values related to human life and caring for people who are in need," says Bunker. "Our goal is to have people see those values when they come into our medical center."

In addition, he says, "St. Paul Medical Center has been a very progressive health care organization in the Dallas area. We've been an innovator in giving the community many alternatives in traditional health care delivery."

Important firsts at St. Paul Medical Center include Dallas' first school of nursing, the first intensive care unit, the first successful heart transplant in Dallas, the first coronary care unit, the first accredited Pathology Department, the first hospital-based Social Work Department, the first approved Cancer Center, the first nuclear medicine department as well as the first full-service hospital to provide a day-surgery option for its patients.

In the medical center's tradition of learning and health care excellence, St. Paul continues to operate its private residency teaching program. With a total of 65 participating residents, St. Paul's program continues to be at the forefront in many surgical and medical specialties.

St. Paul Medical Center, now one of the premier medical centers in the Southwest, employs more than 1,800 people, 700 staff physicians and is licensed for 600 beds. St. Paul moved in 1963 from its original location to an 18-acre tract adjacent to the University of Texas Southwestern Medical Center at Dallas.

In 1988, St. Paul established the UT Southwestern/St. Paul Medical Center Heart Transplant Program. St. Paul's program is part of the University of Texas Southwestern Heart Transplant and Cardiothoracic Surgery Program, a consortium of five area facilities in which St. Paul participates as the only facility where adult heart transplants are performed.

"I believe we have the leading medical resource in the community in terms of cardiovascular care," says Bunker. "Not only do we provide a full spectrum of cardiac testing and care, but St. Paul is one of only 35 centers for heart transplantation in the country."

Recognizing the need for comprehensive as well as preventive medicine, St. Paul Medical Center established four Centers of Excellence.

The St. Paul Woman's Center provides a range of services from pregnancy and childbirth to parenting classes. The Diabetes Center offers its patients comprehensive educational classes as well as the most advanced care available on both an inpatient

Sr. Brenda Domingue is a member of the Daughters of Charity, the Catholic order of women founded nearly 400 years ago by St. Vincent de Paul in France. Today, the Daughters of Charity National Health System is the largest not-for-profit health care system in the country.

In its tradition of innovation and modern technology in health care, St. Paul Medical Center has opened 15 labor-delivery-recovery (LDR) rooms. LDRs provide expectant families a comfortable room in a home-like atmosphere for the entire birthing process.

and outpatient basis.

The St. Paul Arthritis Center provides everything from aquatics therapy to a fully developed day program, allowing individuals the luxury of comprehensive therapy as well as a physician's counsel in one complete, individualized session.

St. Paul had Dallas' first approved Cancer Center and today the center offers services including early detection programs, as well as diagnosis, treatment and rehabilitative services for all types of cancer. In a joint program with Children's Medical Center, St. Paul provides pediatric radiation oncology for the children of North Texas.

In addition, St. Paul retains capabilities in the areas of lab services, the latest in ultrasound, nuclear medicine, computerized tomography (CT scanner) and magnetic resonance imaging (MRI). These services help complete St. Paul Medical Center's multidiscipline approach to the delivery of health care.

In St. Paul's tradition of community awareness and involvement, the St. Paul Medical Center Foundation, an independent, not-for-profit corporation, was formed in 1964 to further the mission of St. Paul Medical Center. The foundation's 40 board members include physicians, community leaders and socially involved citizens.

So, whether it is new technology, new facilities or programs designed for assistance or education, St. Paul Medical Center's fundamental dedication is to the whole health of the individual. And as Dallas continues to grow, St. Paul will remain steadfast in meeting its future health care needs and, in doing so, will provide Dallas and the surrounding communities the benefit of longer, healthier, more productive lives.

THE UNIVERSITY OF TEXAS AT ARLINGTON

The University of Texas at Arlington is a comprehensive graduate and research institution located in the heart of the Dallas/Fort Worth metropolitan area, where it serves the unique needs of this thriving center of business, technology and the arts.

"The signals we read from the Dallas/Fort Worth area clearly indicate — for the next decade and beyond — that this region's challenge will be to prevail in expanding world markets," says UTA President Wendell Nedderman.

"We are confident that UTA's partnership with the Dallas/Fort Worth community — the creative power of our faculty and graduates — will shape new dimensions of economic opportunity for the region as we develop new knowledge and technologies. But to savor the value of these achievements, we must sustain our belief that the university exists to produce graduates who are literate, wise and cultured — good citizens and community leaders."

U.T. Arlington is the sixth-largest university in Texas, with 24,000 students and the second-largest component of The University of Texas System. It was founded nearly 100 years ago as Arlington College and became a senior college in 1959.

UT Arlington was founded nearly 100 years ago as Arlington College and became a senior college in 1959. Since then, it has matured into a leading research institution that has attracted scholars of international stature.

UT Arlington is the sixth-largest university in Texas, with 24,000 students and the second-largest component of The University of Texas System.

Since then, U.T. Arlington not only has quadrupled its enrollment, it has matured into a leading research institution that has attracted scholars of international stature.

Among these scholars are noted mathematician Dr. George Fix, who formerly was chairman of the mathematics department at Carnegie Mellon University; Dr. Sandra Myres, one of the nation's pre-eminent frontier historians; Dr. Eirik Furubotn, one of the world's leading microtheorists in economics; Dr. John McElroy, former deputy director of NASA's Goddard Space Flight Center; Dr. Linton Powell, one of the world's foremost authorities in Spanish keyboard music; and Dr. Vincent Bruno, a leading authority on ancient Greek art.

These are just a few of U.T. Arlington's roughly 900 full- and part-time faculty members. The University offers 50 baccalaureate, 55 master's and 18 doctoral degrees. It is best known for its College of Engineering and its College of Business Administration, which has earned national recognition for its accounting program. But U.T. Arlington is rapidly acquiring a solid reputation for its School of Architecture and School of Nursing.

The faculty, students, and alumni of UTA have made significant contributions to the community. For example, U.T. Arlington's Institute of Urban Studies is working with Dallas leaders to develop housing alternatives for victims of catastrophic illnesses. The School of Nursing, recognizing the shortage of trained medical investigators to probe "questionable" deaths, has established the nation's first forensic nursing program. NASA is supporting U.T. Arlington's new $1.7 million Aerospace Research Center to accelerate aeronautical design development in the Dallas/Fort Worth area. And U.T. Arlington faculty members played important roles in persuading the Federal Government to locate the Superconducting Super Collider just south of Dallas and the UTA campus.

U.T. Arlington alumni also have distinguished themselves. They include radio personality and author Alex Burton; Dallas City Council member Lori Palmer; Vice President of Texas Instruments' Defense Systems & Electronics Group Dr. Glenn Gaustad; singer Ray Price; Dallas Mavericks owner Donald J. Carter; actor Lou Diamond Phillips; and astronaut Army General Robert Stewart.

EPIC HEALTHCARE GROUP

Employee ownership makes the difference. EPIC Healthcare Group proved that point in less than a year after the Dallas-based, employee-owned company was formed.

EPIC Healthcare Group emerged in September 1988 from an estimated $860-million leveraged buyout of 36 hospitals previously owned by American Medical International (AMI) of Beverly Hills, California. The transaction was led by Kenn S. George, EPIC Healthcare Group's chairman and chief executive officer and former senior vice president of AMI's Southwest region.

The buyout made EPIC Healthcare Group the nation's third-largest employee-owned company. And it also placed EPIC among the country's top 10 proprietary healthcare providers. EPIC Healthcare Group now owns and operates 38 hospitals in 10 states — California, Texas, Oklahoma, Louisiana, Florida, Georgia, South Carolina, Mississippi, Arkansas and Missouri. Employee-owners number 10,000; there are 6,000 medical staff

Kenn S. George, chairman and CEO of EPIC Healthcare Group.

members and 4,300 acute-care licensed beds.

In their first six months of operation, EPIC hospitals surpassed their performance as AMI hospitals only one year earlier. "This performance is especially rewarding because it underscores the positive results of employee ownership," Chairman and CEO Kenn S. George reports. "Where outsiders may have doubted our people's ability to positively impact quality and operations, we are proving them wrong and improving our company."

Improving the company means saving nearly $500,000 in pharmaceutical supply costs during 1989 thanks to guidelines formulated by an employee-owner cost-management task force. Improving the company also means saving, in just five months, nearly $300,000 in temporary help costs at Katy Medical Center in Katy, Texas. The employee-owners of this hospital developed and implemented a child care program for night-duty nurses that enabled more of them to return to full-time employment.

Making EPIC Healthcare group a better company is possible through the commitment of its employee-owners. Typical of that commitment is Wayne Provin, director of engineering at Westside Hospital in Los Angeles. When an unusual cold snap sank Southern California temperatures into the low 20s over a weekend in January 1989, Westside's heater boilers malfunctioned. The 69-bed hospital had only two empty beds; the contractor was unable to make repairs for two days. Provin spent his weekend hunting spare parts 25 miles away and repairing the boilers less than 24 hours after they first failed.

Although EPIC Healthcare Group's hospitals are autonomous and make decisions locally, they benefit from the company's Dallas Support Center, which provides resources in operations, finance, human

EPIC Healthcare Group manages 38 hospitals in 10 states from its Dallas Support Center in Oak Lawn.

resources, communications and marketing.

"I chose Dallas as our base because of the long-term economic opportunity I see here," George explains. Two excellent airports — Dallas/Fort Worth International and Love Field — make it easy for the EPIC support staff of 150 to visit any of our 38 hospitals.

"Dallas provides the right kind of environment for our company, for our vision is to become the nation's health care provider of choice and employer of choice," George adds. "Dallas business has a way of supporting the expectation of excellence, and we feel very at home here."

More than 100 years of leadership in the graphic arts industry in Dallas has positioned Williamson to pursue the future with anticipation and vigor. It is an optimism reinforced by the confidence that the best years lie ahead for Williamson Printing Corporation, its employees, customers, suppliers and friends.

— *Williamson Printing Corporation*

"There's a collective Dallas support for business that's helpful to me and other executives of my company. And I've found that being in the chemical business doesn't exclude me from good relationships with executives in other businesses in Dallas."

Ray R. Irani, Chairman
— Occidental Chemical Corporation

"Ventahood has experienced steady and consistent growth throughout its history and continues to have excellent growth potential. The company looks forward to a bright future along with the Dallas area."

— *Ventahood Company*

"Multi-Amp recognizes a commitment to support its customers, its employees and the community by providing quality products and services, a challenging work environment and the contribution of its talents and resources to the area's growth and prosperity."

— *Multi-Amp Corporation*

"The move to Dallas was very positive for Pro-Line. Our banking relationships were enhanced. The business community here was more receptive than some of the cities we studied. We were courted."

Comer J. Cottrell Jr., Chairman,
— *Pro-Line Corporation*

"Innovation has always been the hallmark governing Haggar Apparel Company, the Dallas-based men's and women's clothing manufacturer. Begun in 1926, Haggar moved quickly to the forefront of the men's apparel industry."

— *Haggar Apparel Company*

"Lennox International Inc. represents nearly a century of progress that has been marked by a continued willingness to expand, innovate and improve."

— *Lennox International*

CHAPTER 19

Manufacturing

Producing goods for individuals and industry world-wide, Dallas' manufacturing firms also provide employment for its residents and balance to its economic base.

WILLIAMSON PRINTING CORPORATION

Williamson Printing Corporation is one of the nation's premier printers, with more than a century of experience as a leader in Dallas business, and with a deep faith in the future of the city as a vibrant and dynamic center for communications and the graphic arts.

Drawing of the original Dorsey Company building circa 1884 located on Elm Street in Dallas.

Williamson was founded in 1884 as The Dorsey Company, a family-owned, family-operated office supply and printing firm. During the first two decades of the 20th century, The Dorsey Company established itself as "The Business Man's Department Store," one of the nation's premiere printing and office supply operations. Branch offices opened in Houston and Muskogee, Oklahoma, while salesmen traveled the entire country, including the Territory of Arizona and the Indian Territory of Oklahoma, selling everything from ledgers to bank vaults. Henry Dorsey led the company's print shop in pioneering the lithography process and in introducing new engraving techniques. Under his direction, The Dorsey Company was among the first in the Southwest to engrave using steel and copper plates.

A Dorsey catalog from November 1912 explained to its customers why the firm had become larger than all its Dallas competitors combined. "The central location of The Dorsey Company, with its mammoth stores, warehouses and factories at Dallas, Houston, and Muskogee; the exceptional railroad facilities of these cities with direct water-route connections with eastern markets, where raw materials are produced, enable the company to serve its patrons quicker and better than other concerns.

"Equipped with the latest improved machinery, the greatest time- and labor-saving methods and systems, and the highest class of workmanship known to the art of printing and kindred craft, the company is turning out a class of work that is equaled by the product of but few and surpassed for quality by that of none."

When James Dorsey died in 1913, Henry Dorsey bought his brothers' one-half interest and became the sole proprietor. As a charter member of the Dallas Chamber of Commerce, Henry Dorsey was active in the "150,000 Club." This group was dedicated to building the city's population to that magic number before the 1920 federal census. Dallas went over the top with 8,000 to spare.

The Great Depression years were difficult times, as businesses were forced to do without office supplies and commercial printing — practically everything The Dorsey Company brought to market. However, by

The original site of The Dorsey Company after the fire on May 27, 1898.

The Dorsey Company home on Elm and Poydras from 1902 to 1969.

1940, business had picked back up, and so had the company's business. That same year, a young executive named Bowen Williamson joined the firm. It was a good match, for Williamson thrived at the Dorsey Company, and through hard work he advanced to become sales manager, vice-president, and eventually, a member of the board of directors.

In 1964, Bowen Williamson assumed sole proprietorship of the printing side of The Dorsey Company. By 1970, he had purchased it outright and changed its name to Williamson Printing Corporation. Under his direction, the company experienced a tremendous growth in size and sales, establishing itself as an industry leader, with a reputation for its technical skills and the quality of its service. Since Bowen Williamson's death in 1983, Williamson Printing Corporation has continued to assert itself as one of the nation's premier printers.

In celebration of the firm's 100 years of operation, the Williamson family, including Mrs. Bowen Williamson, a member of the board; Jerry

Williamson, Chairman of the Board; Jesse Williamson, president; Becky Williamson Parker, sales person; and sisters Speight Anderson and Elaine Antone; along with the employees of the corporation, decided to make a contribution to the City of Dallas, Old City Park, and its print shop.

"Instead of having a big party in celebration, we decided to show our thanks for the good things that have happened to us over the past century," Jerry Williamson explains. "We commissioned an artist to do two posters depicting Old City Park. We printed and donated them to the park, and they are being sold to help raise money for the park. We are also establishing a trust fund that will finance a person to run the print shop at Old City Park. The print shop had been one of the park's most popular attractions, especially with young schoolchildren, but lack of funds forced the park to close the operation. This fund will allow the park to hire a printer and make it become operational again."

From 1969 to 1983 Williamson Printing Corporation called 2263 Valdina home.

Under the guidance of Bowen's sons, Williamson Printing has continued to expand, meeting the needs of a sophisticated and even more demanding national market. Today, as Williamson Printing Companies Group, Williamson is organized in six operating companies, each serving a specific segment of the graphic arts industry with its own separate management.

Since 1983 Williamson Printing Corporation has been located in this 200,000 square foot facility adjacent to Love Field Airport.

Williamson Printing Corporation offers high quality, multi-color, full service printing for advertising agencies, design studios and local and national companies.

Williamson Legal & Financial serves the highly specialized needs of the legal and financial communities by utilizing state of the art computer typesetting, media conversion, desk top publishing interface and related electronic technologies.

Classic Color Corporation offers high quality, full service color separations with the latest in electronic scanners and computer electronic imaging.

Printing Resources Management (PRM) provides complete business forms management, including design, printing, storage and computerized inventory control of forms and documents.

Image Express Printing (IEP) offers one, two and three color printing to serve the intensive budget and response requirements of commercial businesses.

The Fulfillment Center (TFC) provides turn-key processing for literature and product distribution, from order receipt and product or kit assembly to packing and shipping, with computerized storage, inventory controls and customer database management.

The Williamson Printing Companies remain completely up-to-date

with prevailing technologies and techniques; indeed, Williamson's Dallas facilities are often used as a primary test site for major equipment manufacturers. But however innovative technologically, a leading commercial printer depends upon the expert skills and abilities of its people to succeed in the marketplace. At Williamson, such excellence has resulted in the company being consistently ranked among the nation's top three award-winners in printing industry and graphic design competitions across the United States and Europe.

Williamson can attribute much of its success to Dallas. For more than a century, the city has been a center of commerce and trade, attracting new business and enabling the company to deliver its products quickly and easily. Dallas has provided a well-educated and industrious work force, and Dallas is home to an aggressive, entrepreneurial base of clients who demand and appreciate exceptional printing and innovative business solutions.

More than 100 years of leadership in the graphic arts industry in Dallas has positioned Williamson to pursue the future with anticipation and vigor. It is an optimism reinforced by the confidence that the best years lie ahead for Williamson Printing Corporation, its employees, customers, suppliers and friends.

OCCIDENTAL CHEMICAL CORPORATION

As a newcomer to Dallas in 1987, Occidental Chemical Corporation (OxyChem) found a warm welcome from the city and an attitude toward business that helped the company on its way to posting record profits in 1988.

OxyChem's business may not sound glamorous, but it is vitally important. A unit of Los Angeles-based Occidental Petroleum Corporation, OxyChem is a recognized leader in the chemical industry. The company manufactures and markets industrial and specialty chemicals, plastics and agricultural products.

In 1983, OxyChem was in a "condition of disaster," says Dr. Ray R. Irani, the company's chairman. Many observers thought it would be sold by its parent. Instead, Occidental Petroleum's chairman and chief executive, Dr. Armand Hammer, recruited Irani from his post as president of Olin Corporation and gave him the task of turning OxyChem around.

Irani's strategy was to take Oxy-Chem back to the basics. The goal was to become the lowest-cost producer of commodity chemicals such as chlorine and polyvinyl chloride (PVC). At the time, many chemical producers were abandoning commodities for higher-priced specialty chemicals. But Irani reasoned that even specialty producers would always need to buy the basic chemical feedstocks.

He recruited new key executives led by J. Roger Hirl, OxyChem's president and chief operating officer. Together, they then set about cutting OxyChem's costs through modernizing plants and production processes, and selling unrelated businesses. They also began to search for suitable acquisitions to help boost Oxy-Chem's market share of those basic chemicals.

In 1986, Occidental bought Diamond Shamrock Chemicals Co.,

based in Las Colinas just outside Dallas. At that point, OxyChem was headquartered in Darien, Conn., but the company decided to examine possible relocation sites. After considering several options, OxyChem chose Dallas, opening its offices opposite the Galleria on July 1, 1987.

"We found the business community to be a highly respected part of

OxyChem's worldwide headquarters are located at the intersection of the LBJ Freeway and the Dallas Tollway.

the whole community in Dallas," Hirl says. "There's a collective Dallas support for business that's helpful to me and other executives of my company."

Hirl points to "an advantageous

interaction within the Dallas business community" through organizations such as the Dallas Citizens Council. He also says the city's central location means less travel time when headquarters employees visit OxyChem's nearly 60 production facilities spread throughout the United States and abroad.

With the relocation to Dallas complete and the turnaround strategy well under way, OxyChem posted record earnings of $878 million on sales of $4.62 billion in 1988. Helping in this impressive achievement was Occidental's purchase of Houston-based Cain Chemical Inc., now called Oxy Petrochemicals Inc. Oxy paid $1.25 billion in cash for Cain and assumed roughly $1 billion of its debt.

The acquisition instantly made the company a significant producer of petrochemicals, one major industry segment expected to continue to grow even as demand in other areas is expected to lessen in 1990. Bryan Jacoboski, an industry analyst with Paine Webber in New York, has called Oxy Petrochemicals "a gold mine" for Occidental, adding that the purchase was "the best deal in the company's history."

Two of OxyChem's many commodity chemicals find their way into swimming pools: polyvinyl chloride (PVC) for pool liners and chlorine for water purification.

OxyChem employees are active through Adopt-a-School programs, helping children perform better in local public schools.

From its beginnings, through tough times to its current strong position, OxyChem has grown to become the nation's third-largest producer of ethylene and high-density polyethylene, the world's largest maker of phenolic molding materials, the country's largest merchant marketer of PVC resin, chlorine and caustic soda, the leading manufacturer of chrome chemicals, the second largest producer of silicates and the top producer of potassium hydroxide. The names may sound strange and bewildering, but the end products are found in our everyday life, in plastic bottles, wall coverings, detergents and a myriad of other household items.

With its domestic business thriving and carefully structured to minimize the impact of cyclical downturns, OxyChem now has an eye overseas. Asia and the Pacific Rim appear to hold the best expansion opportunities. Europe also is a possibility, provided OxyChem finds the right situation. But even as it seeks growth further and further away from Dallas, OxyChem will not forget its adopted hometown.

"Our focus is on educational support through a broad range of activities," Hirl says. Besides being one of the area's largest contributors to United Way, OxyChem's community involvement includes employee volunteer efforts in Junior Achievement and the Adopt-a-School program. As a company, OxyChem provides financial support for such endeavors as the Reading is Fundamental literacy program while combining education and the arts by supporting student performance programs.

"We probably generate as much sweat equity on behalf of the community as anyone in business," Hirl says.

VENTAHOOD COMPANY

There are many testaments to the entrepreneurial spirit so prevalent in Dallas. One of the most shining examples can be found in the story of Ventahood Company. Founded in 1933 as an outgrowth of Dallas Engineering Company, today's Ventahood was the first manufacturer of home cooking ventilation.

The first Ventahoods were manufactured in a house with a dirt floor in Dallas, then sold door-to-door. The primary ingredient in the success of Ventahood is its uniquely designed, fire safe "Magic Lung" blower system. Throughout the years the product has been improved, but the original concept is central to the design and remains unequalled.

Ventahood has developed an

A Ventahood employee smooths out corners on a custom unit. Ventahood offers a complete line of stock hoods, as well as custom units.

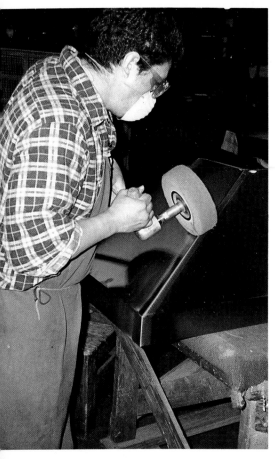

Two Ventahood employees put the finishing touches on an assembled unit before installing the fire safe "Magic Lung" ventilation motor.

excellent reputation throughout the industry by offering top quality in the "stock" line as well as handmade craftsmanship in the "custom" series. Each product manufactured by Ventahood is individually engineered for performance in addition to style. Company longevity and product quality have given the name Ventahood instant product recognition.

Today's family-owned company was originally financed by Carr P. Collins Sr., a Dallas financier and founder of Fidelity Union Life Insurance Company. Miles Woodall Jr.,

nephew of Collins, was recruited in 1937 to manage the company and continues in that capacity along with his son, Miles Woodall III.

Currently housed in a modern 100,000-square-foot manufacturing facility, Ventahood employs a highly skilled workforce to achieve quality craftsmanship. A national as well as international marketing program includes an impressive roster of distributors, many of which are second generation.

Ventahood has experienced steady and consistent growth throughout its history and continues to have excellent growth potential. The company looks forward to a bright future along with the Dallas area.

MULTI-AMP CORPORATION

Multi-Amp Corporation is an internationally recognized leader in the design and manufacture of high quality, specialized electrical test equipment and measuring instruments and also offers complete support in the areas of technical services and training. The company serves electric utilities and industrial operations around the world.

Founded in 1951, Multi-Amp pioneered the electrical power test industry with the design and manufacture of a portable protective relay test set. At the time, few organizations recognized the importance of testing electrical protective devices. But a massive power failure in 1965 left 30 million people without electricity in parts of the Northeastern United States and Canada and gave impetus to the need to test electrical systems and ensure their reliability. Under the leadership of Eduardo R. Redlhammer, who retired as company president in 1985, Multi-Amp was at the forefront of the electrical test industry's subsequent expansion.

Multi-Amp chose to locate its headquarters in Dallas in 1973 because of the city's proximity to Dallas/Fort Worth International Airport; the skills, talents and work ethics of

Multi-Amp Corporation located its headquarters in the Red Bird Industrial Park in Dallas in 1973 because of the city's positive business environment and the skills, talents and work ethics of the local residents. The company's facilities have doubled in size and continue to contribute to the community's growth and prosperity.

the local residents; and the city's positive business environment.

Since 1973, Multi-Amp has provided jobs for an increasing number of area residents and has more than doubled the space of its research and development and manufacturing facilities in Dallas. The company also operates a plant in Toronto and has sales offices throughout the United States and sales agents in more than 50 countries.

Today, Multi-Amp designs, manufactures and markets a wide variety of equipment, accessories and instruments used to test circuit breakers, transformers, watthour meters, cables, oil circuit reclosers and protective relays. Multi-Amp products have evolved from the early days of basic electromechanical design to the era of solid-state and now to state-of-the-art, microprocessor-controlled instruments and the development of advanced software for computerized protective relay testing.

Multi-Amp Services Corporation, a subsidiary of Multi-Amp Corporation, provides training courses and materials, and a broad range of technical services to support the start-up, commissioning or maintenance of generating plants, substations and industrial facilities. Multi-Amp Services has played an important role in start-up operations for numerous power plants across the country, including the Comanche Peak Steam Electric Station operated by Texas Utilities near Glen Rose, Texas.

Ruben E. Esquivel, president and chief executive officer of Multi-Amp Corporation, presents the latest technology in microprocessor-controlled relay test equipment. Multi-Amp is the leading producer of state-of-the-art electrical test instruments and a major supplier of technical services and training for the power industry.

The company's training operation, Multi-Amp Institute, has provided performance-based instruction to more than 50,000 technicians and engineers. Each year, the Institute hosts more than 1,000 students from throughout the world who come to Dallas to learn the latest techniques in electrical power system safety and maintenance.

Multi-Amp prides itself in its longstanding, customer-oriented philosophy that continues today with the guidance of President and Chief Executive Officer Ruben E. Esquivel, who joined the company in 1961. Multi-Amp's goal is to build on its strong reputation of meeting customer needs and direct its resources toward internal expansion of products and markets, and the acquisition of complementary products and services.

Multi-Amp recognizes a commitment to support its customers, its employees and the community by providing quality products and services, a challenging work environment and the contribution of its talents and resources to the area's growth and prosperity.

PRO-LINE CORPORATION

Few companies survive in the volatile and competitive personal-care-products industry. Yet Dallas-based Pro-Line Corporation did not just succeed, although that alone would have been remarkable. Pro-Line also was a pioneer, helping create an entire industry devoted to ethnic haircare products.

Pro-Line was founded in 1970 with $600 and a second-hand typewriter by Comer J. Cottrell Jr., company chairman. The Alabama native, 39 at the time, had a vision of supplying haircare products for African-Americans serving in the military. From his experience as a post exchange (PX) manager in the U.S. Air Force between 1949 and 1953, Cottrell knew there was nothing available suited to African-Americans' needs.

Comer J. Cottrell founded Pro-Line Corporation in 1970 and by doing so helped create a whole new industry.

Astonishingly, that void still had not been filled by the late 1960s when consumer demand changed as a result of a widespread trend toward Afro hairstyles. Cottrell, living in Los Angeles and one of Sears, Roebuck & Co.'s first black division managers, contacted his congressman and obtained a contract to supply military commissaries worldwide. He then turned to developing a product.

Pro-Line's first offering was an oil-based, strawberry-scented hairspray. Six months later, it added Comb Out and Holding Spray to its product line. First-year sales were $86,000. Cottrell says he did not realize initially that there was a market beyond military PXs. African-American servicemen, however, were taking his products with them when they left the military and creating consumer demand that the fledgling company was eager to supply.

At the end of its second year, Pro-Line's sales had more than doubled to $186,000, and the company began to open accounts with nonmilitary distributors within California and outside the state. By 1972, sales had climbed to $365,000.

The next year, Pro-Line revenues hit $1 million and the company bought its first manufacturing plant, an 11,000-square-foot facility in Gardena, Calif. "Hair Food," a gel hair conditioner, helped keep sales doubling from 1973 through 1976, when Pro-Line relocated to a 35,000-square-foot plant in Carson, Calif.

The entry of other manufacturers prompted Cottrell and his younger brother, James, to reassess and revamp Pro-Line's marketing strategy. The younger Cottrell, who has since retired as Pro-Line's executive vice president, had a flair for marketing and steered the company into children's products. The result was Kiddie Kit, designed to make children's hair easier to work with in the morning. It was a huge success

Pro-Line continued its steady growth until 1980, carefully adding new products and expanding geographic distribution to the East Coast, then overseas to Africa.

Also in 1980, Pro-Line launched Curly Kit, the first home-use hair curling kit. Rock star Michael Jackson used the product and steady growth became explosive overnight. Droves of consumers lined up to buy Curly Kit, which in one day alone generated $1.4 million in revenues. Once again, Pro-Line had blazed a trail, literally transforming the ethnic haircare market with one product.

That also was the year that Cottrell made a strategic business decision to relocate his company. The 14 Western states constituted just 10 percent of Pro-Line's business, while the rest was in Texas and further east. Also, rising energy prices were making it much more costly to transport products long distances. It made good business sense to move closer to Pro-Line's major markets.

After studying half-a-dozen cities, Cottrell opted for Dallas. Its central location put Pro-Line within a couple

Pro-Line employs 250 people at its Dallas facility, making it the Southwest's largest African-American-owned business.

Cottrell again blazed a new trail by substituting audio cassette instructions for the normal written directions in Pro-Line's home permanent kits. He also targeted the salon market by developing a computerized imaging system acquired when Pro-Line bought the Kosmetikos salon chain in California in 1987.

In 1989, Pro-Line projects annual sales of more than $36 million, employs 250 people and markets more than 40 products in the United States, Africa and Asia. It is the largest African-American-owned business in the Southwest.

Growing despite increased competition in the ethnic health and beauty products industry, Pro-Line plays an active civic role in its adopted city. Cottrell and his wife, Isabell, vice chairperson, offer financial and advisory support to more than 50 organizations in Dallas,

including the Dallas Symphony Orchestra, the Sickle Cell Anemia Foundation, the Dallas Museum of African-American Life and Culture and the Dallas Black Dance Theatre. The company's special emphasis is education. Pro-Line adopted Albert Sidney Johnston School in 1985, has sponsored high-school choir trips to Europe and bought needed equipment and supplies for schools.

In Cottrell's opinion, Pro-Line's greatest contribution is serving as a role model for other corporations, encouraging them to become involved as well.

Proline markets more than 40 products in the United States, Africa and Asia.

of hours' flying time of any of its domestic markets. The Central time zone also helped make the best use of the sales force's time. And Dallas was close to Houston, a major international shipping port through which Pro-Line products were moving abroad.

"The move to Dallas was very positive for Pro-Line," Cottrell says. "I found the banks here were far more receptive to my business than even in California. Our banking relationships were enhanced. The business community here was more receptive than some of the cities we studied. We were courted."

After relocating to Dallas, Pro-Line continued to grow and to break new ground. In 1985, the company became the first ethnic haircare products marketer to advertise on four consecutive segments of a top-rated primetime TV show, "Dynasty."

HAGGAR APPAREL COMPANY

Innovation has always been the hallmark governing Haggar Apparel Company, the Dallas-based men's and women's clothing manufacturer. Begun in 1926 by J.M. Haggar Sr., a 34-year-old Lebanese immigrant, Haggar moved quickly to the forefront of the men's apparel industry.

Armed with a handful of second-hand sewing machines, Mr. Haggar began revolutionizing the way men dressed. First, he created a new apparel category: tailored trousers that did not match a suit jacket and that could be worn either at work or during "slack" time. Haggar later coined the term "slacks" to market these trousers.

Not satisfied to stop with his first innovation, Haggar rapidly introduced mass production of clothing, and he was the first clothing manufacturer to offer customers products at one cost. (Up until that time, salesmen and customers negotiated prices.)

From 1942 to 1946, Haggar devoted 80 percent of his production

J.M. Haggar Sr. founded the Haggar Apparel Company on the principles of quality and innovation.

line to the manufacture of more than 10 million military garments. With the remaining 20 percent of his business devoted to the civilian cause, Mr. Haggar began writing another chapter in clothing history. The company became the first to advertise slacks nationally in print in 1942, with ads appearing in *Collier's, Esquire, Life, Look* and *The Saturday Evening Post.* Then in 1951, the company debuted the memorable "Dancing Slacks" ad and became the first slacks manufacturer to advertise on television.

Haggar continued its innovative ways of design, production and manufacturing with the introduction of wash-and-wear slacks in 1954 and in the same year featuring well-known sports figures in its advertising campaigns.

Wash-and-wear slacks were followed in 1959 by pre-packaged, pre-cuffed, ready-to-wear slacks. "Permanent press" became a household word in 1968 as a result of Haggar, and by 1981 the company had introduced machine washable men's suits.

Haggar diversified its clothing lines in 1983 by introducing its first line of women's apparel, and Reed St. James,® a brand directed to discount stores.

Today as always, Haggar continues to look to the future. Mr. Haggar, Sr. passed away in December, 1987 at the age of 94 but his sons, E.R. Haggar Sr. and J.M. Haggar Jr., as well as his grandsons, J.M. Haggar III and E.R. Haggar Jr., are all members of Haggar's senior management team. They have overseen the introduction of specialized lines of men's and women's clothing aimed at both upscale and specialty stores, as well as focusing on the tastes and buying habits of young professionals.

Nationally and overseas, Haggar employs approximately 6,500 people in 14 U.S. and seven foreign manufacturing and distribution facilities.

A new generation of Haggars is turning the company's attention to young professionals and upscale customers.

For Haggar Apparel Company, much has changed and little has changed. From the first day of business, J.M. Haggar took pride in providing a quality product, value to his customers and a satisfying work environment for his employees, principles that Haggar Apparel Company adheres to today.

LENNOX INTERNATIONAL INC.

Lennox is one of the newer breed of Dallas-based corporations, having moved here 12 years ago. The privately owned company has seen nearly 100 years of growth and continues to be a leader in the heating, ventilating, air conditioning and refrigeration (HVACR) industry.

1986 was a landmark year for the company as Lennox International Inc. was established as the parent company of Lennox Industries Inc. and Heatcraft Inc. And, in early 1989, Lennox International acquired Magic Chef Air Conditioning Inc. and renamed it Armstrong Air Conditioning Inc.

HISTORY

Lennox traces its roots to Marshalltown, Iowa, where machinist Dave Lennox developed a sheet metal furnace in 1895. The Lennox design was unique because it was lighter and more durable than cast-iron furnaces, the standard of that time. It also was easier to install and maintain, and resisted cracking.

Dave Lennox eventually sold the rights to D.W. Norris, whose philosophy for Lennox' success still holds true today: Build the best product and market it through the best installing contractors. In fact, it is continued by John W. Norris, Jr., current president and chief executive officer — and grandson of D.W. Norris.

During the 1930s Lennox established a Research and Development Department to add blowers, oil burners and gas furnaces to the company's product lines. That Research and Development Department has since become a state-of-the-art facility and assured many Lennox firsts in the HVACR industry.

Another factor in Lennox' success has been a continued commitment to quality from its leadership. In fact, throughout the 95-year history of this company, there have been only four chief executive officers: D.W. Norris; John W. Norris, Sr.; Ray C. Robbins (now chairman of the board); and John W. Norris, Jr. They have guided Lennox to the enviable position it now holds in the HVACR industry.

TODAY

Lennox International has widened its scope in the industry with Heatcraft Inc. and Armstrong Air Conditioning Inc., as well as Lennox Industries Inc.

Lennox Industries Inc., a major manufacturer of residential and commercial heating and air conditioning systems, is based in Dallas at Lennox International's World Headquarters. Within seven North American sales divisions, Lennox Industries operates five factories, more than 45 branch offices and distribution centers, a national parts distribution center and a research and development lab.

Lennox also manufactures HVAC systems in Basingstoke, England, with distribution throughout Europe. And Lennox' Export Division handles sales of equipment all over the world.

Heatcraft Inc., headquartered in Grenada, Mississippi, is the world's largest manufacturer of heat transfer products. Its divisions include the Heat Transfer Division, Tool and Die Division and Copper Tube Mill, also in Grenada; Refrigeration Products Division in Wilmington, North Carolina; Electrical Products Division in Murfreesboro, Tennessee; and the Copper Products Division in Bossier City, Louisiana.

Armstrong Air Conditioning Inc., based in Bellevue, Ohio, manufactures a complete line of residential and commercial gas, oil and electric furnaces, as well as air conditioning systems.

Lennox International Inc. — nearly a century of progress that has been marked by a continued willingness to expand, innovate and improve.

This artist's rendering shows Lennox' new World Headquarters being built in Richardson, just north of Dallas. Lennox will move into its new home in early 1990.

"You cannot think about being the dominant bank in the South without a major presence in Texas and particularly in Dallas. It's hard to look for good investment opportunities throughout the world without including Dallas."

Kenneth D. Lewis, President
— NCNB Texas.

"In deciding where to relocate, after a careful evaluation of the most likely sites, we settled on Texas and the Dallas Metroplex area. Quite simply, for J.C. Penney, this was the right move at the right time to the right area."

William Howell, Chairman and Chief Operating Officer
— J.C. Penney Company

"More and more people are realizing that Dallas is a prime area either for expansion or relocation. We intend to become a major banking player, contributing to all those areas of growth."

John Bunten, President
— First City, Texas

"Dallas is the best place in the world to be an entrepreneur. The business climate here is both welcoming to new people and receptive to new ideas. This precipitated the diversity that helped us in our recent difficult economic times."

Milledge A. Hart III, Founder
— The Hart Group

"The advantages Dallas has to offer a business like ours are obvious. But more than this, it's a spirit, a spirit that our future is secure and also very exciting."

W. Humphrey Bogart, President and Chief Executive Officer
— Fidelity Investments Southwest

"Dallas is an excellent place to do business, as evidenced by its longstanding stature as a major insurance center. ICH management feels that it is only right that the company should give something back to the community."

Thomas J. Brophy, Senior Executive Vice President and Chief Operating Officer
— ICH Corporation

"We see an opportunity to be a part of a dynamic transition of the Texas banking environment and the Texas economy. There are people in growing numbers, great resources and energy, a tradition of winning and love of victory. Bank One, Texas is proud to be a part of that."

John B. McCoy, Chairman and Chief Executive Officer
— Banc One Corporation

CHAPTER 20

Business & Finance

Banking institutions, insurance, securities and diversified holding companies provide the financial foundation for a host of Dallas enterprises.

NCNB TEXAS

Settlers who flocked to the Texas frontier in the early 1800s looked on their destination as the promised land. Texas' great cities still hold that allure. Dallas and the rest of the state continue to attract the bold and far-sighted, those for whom risk and reward go hand-in-hand. People like those at NCNB Texas National Bank.

While others forecast continued gloom for Texas banking in mid-1988, NCNB Corporation saw great promise in the subsidiary banks of First RepublicBank Corporation. NCNB believed the ominous clouds that surrounded the ailing banking giant in reality held a silver lining. They represented an opportunity to spread beyond NCNB's Southeastern presence into one of the most attractive banking markets in the nation.

In July 1988, top NCNB execu-

tives struck a unique deal with regulators. The result was the formation of NCNB Texas, a single statewide bank serving customers through its branch network in 63 Texas communities. While earning praise from industry analysts, the emergence of NCNB Texas also promised increased opportunities for its employees and customers. Even more important, it was a solid vote of confidence in Texas.

NCNB initially made a 20 percent equity investment in NCNB Texas in November 1988, with a five-year option to purchase the remainder of Texas' largest banking organization. It dramatically accelerated that process by purchasing an additional 29 percent in April 1989 and the remaining 51 percent a little more than three months later.

"We are extremely pleased with what we've seen in Texas, especially in Dallas," says Kenneth D. Lewis, the bank's president. "That's the reason why we accelerated our timetable for purchase of NCNB Texas so dramatically."

Kenneth D. Lewis, president of NCNB Texas.

When it completed its purchase of the Texas bank in less than one year, NCNB had invested more than $1.3 billion in Texas. As a result, NCNB Texas has the strongest capital base in the state. And the bank's capital strength tells customers throughout Texas that this bank is willing and able to help make their plans real.

Lending money is the cornerstone of banking. It is the fuel that can power an economy — help it get started and keep it moving on course. NCNB Texas' commitment to lending in Texas resulted in more than $1.5 billion in new loans during the first six months of 1989.

Although the structure of the NCNB Texas transaction has been quite positive, it was not the primary reason for NCNB's interest in Dallas and Texas, Lewis says. Corporate expansion strategy formulated long ago included establishing a Southwest operation.

"You cannot think about being the dominant bank in the South without a major presence in Texas, particularly in Dallas," he adds. "So we saw a tremendous opportunity

NCNB Texas is the Lone Star State's largest bank. The largest concentration of customers are served in Dallas at a variety of locations, including Park Cities.

in acquiring the First Republic franchise."

NCNB's goal to be the biggest and best in banking in the South and Southwest is in keeping with its corporate history and reputation for aggressiveness and innovation. It was formed in 1960 and, through acquisitions and internal growth, has become the nation's ninth largest banking organization.

NCNB now serves customers from Baltimore to Miami to El Paso. The seven states in which the company has banks contain a combined population of 40 million people — one-sixth of the U.S. total.

Lewis says that NCNB Texas has found a warm welcome in Texas. That has been especially true in Dallas, its headquarters city. "Dallas has the largest concentration of our customers. We make no apologies about our partiality to Dallas," he adds.

In his opinion, the city on the prairie is "very livable," and that makes it easy for us to attract top professionals." Dallas' many positive attributes make it the single best relocation point for companies throughout the country, and it will remain a relocation magnet for some time, Lewis adds.

Thus, the city reinforces the initial opportunity it held out to NCNB. Those major corporate relocations — not to mention all the leading businesses already based in Dallas — are all potential NCNB Texas customers, Lewis says.

NCNB Texas also sees potential customers in the many smaller companies that spring up in Dallas' fertile soil. The bank has made a strategic commitment to pursue business startups and small businesses.

NCNB's success in Texas goes beyond the strength of its performance indicators, Lewis maintains. "It comes from a belief in ourselves and a belief in Texas. Our bank's strong position will enable us to help lead

the way to recovery."

Lewis says that as a naturalized Texan, he views the city's economic downturn from a different perspective. "Dallas is really just catching its breath. All the fundamentals are here. It's hard to look for good investment opportunities throughout the world without including Dallas. Our city has a great future."

Kenneth D. Lewis, president of NCNB Texas, addresses recent graduates and new NCNB Texas employees. This year, NCNB Texas will hire almost three hundred graduates from universities all over Texas.

J.C. PENNEY COMPANY

It's not your father's drygoods store. In fact, it isn't even the J.C. Penney it was six years ago.

A lot has changed in retailing since 1902 when James Cash Penney opened his first dry goods and clothing store in Kemmerer, Wyoming. And the Penney Company's latest changes have dramatically altered the look and direction of America's only national department store.

In 1983, the company undertook a $1-billion modernization program to upgrade the shopping environment in its 1,400 stores. The changes led to elimination of many departments including auto services, appliances, paint and hardware, lawn and garden, fabrics, home electronics, hard sporting goods, and photo equipment, representing a loss of $1.5 billion in annual sales.

"We have made a full commitment to serving the fashion needs of middle and middle/upper income customers," says William R. Howell, chairman of the board and chief executive officer. "I think it's fair to say that during the last six years of the '80s no major retailer in America has changed as much as J.C. Penney."

The newly positioned stores particularly target fashionable women's wear.

"Our store mix has changed as a percent of our total merchandise sales," says Howell. "In 1981, home lines — at 37 percent — were larger than women's, which was just 30 percent. By the end of 1988, women's apparel and accessories sales had increased to 42 percent of our volume and home lines had dropped back to 18 percent. That trend is continuing. By 1993, combined women's and men's will represent 72 percent of our total merchandise sales."

But the change really started in 1974 after the company was positioned with the vast majority of its square footage located in regional

William R. Howell, Chairman of the Board and Chief Executive Officer.

malls rather than in freestanding stores. As the company began evaluating how mall space differed from freestanding store space, researchers learned that consumers buy about 72 percent of all women's apparel and 68 percent of men's apparel in malls. But they buy only about 38 percent of home products and less than 20 percent of materials like paint and hardware in malls. The Penney merchandise mix was not in line with these figures.

In 1982, the company issued a positioning statement which incorporated its evaluations with a marketing strategy and literally revolutionized almost everything about the

huge business. Now Penney has focused on what the regional mall customer prefers: apparel, home furnishings, accessories and shoes for the career minded and family oriented.

"In carrying out our strategies, we recognize that we're adjusting to the changing consumer in a way that's different from anyone else," says Howell. "We see our stores positioned to attract our target consumer in the regional comparison mall. We're convinced that's the best direction for us by far."

J.C. Penney's approach to its catalog business has been to build volume primarily through sales centers in stores. In-store catalog service enables customers to purchase items not available in stores and also expands the merchandise assortment of smaller stores. In effect, catalog is viewed as a huge 12-million-square-foot back-up store. It supplements stores with an enormous selection of sizes, colors, and styles that no retail store, by itself, can compete with.

The centers are not only located at J.C. Penney stores but also in selected drug stores operated by the company's Thrift Drug division, consisting of more than 400 stores. Also, a number of freestanding catalog sales centers are located in markets not served by the company's stores.

J.C. Penney's 16 toll-free sales centers, which utilize the company's extensive voice and electronic communications network, facilitate order placement by catalog customers 24 hours a day and seven days a week through advanced technology and 7,000 trained order takers. This technology permits customers to reserve specific merchandise in a matter of seconds and to have alternate merchandise suggested to them on out-of-stock items. Merchandise can be picked up, usually within two to three days, at the store or delivered directly to a customer's home by United Parcel Service (UPS) from one of the company's distribution centers.

Another strategic move for the Penney Company was its relocation to Dallas in 1988 from New York City, where it had been headquartered since 1914. The company had located in New York when it was the merchandising and financial capital of America.

"But by the 1970s, nationwide electronic systems, communications

and distribution had altered the picture," says Howell. "A New York headquarters was no longer a necessity." The Northeast Coast location had actually become a drawback for the coast-to-coast J.C. Penney Company.

The company wanted to locate near outstanding local colleges which could fill entry-level positions and create a loyal work force. "We discovered in our evaluations that the Metroplex more than satisfied our needs for education," he says.

"In deciding where to relocate," Howell adds, "we examined such

areas as the attitude of local government toward business, the transportation characteristics, lifestyle environment of each community, quality of education and availability of skilled help. After a careful evaluation of the most likely sites, we settled on Texas and the Dallas Metroplex area. Quite simply, for J.C. Penney, this was the right move at the right time to the right area."

A modernization program started in 1983 and a move from New York City to Dallas in 1988 are part of J.C. Penney Company's repositioning strategy for the future.

FIRST CITY, TEXAS

The Dallas/Fort Worth Metroplex is experiencing a resurgence of business activity and growth, and First City, Texas is positioning itself as a primary catalyst for that growth.

First City Center in downtown Dallas is the heart of First City, Texas' operations in the North Texas district.

Central to its role in contributing to economic growth is First City's bullish attitude about the region as a whole.

"We hold firmly to the belief that Dallas will continue to play a crucial role in the Texas economic recovery," says Darryl Pounds, chairman and chief executive officer and director for First City's North Texas Region. "And, no one has a stronger

commitment to the recovery than we do. After all, Texas is our home. We don't do business in North Carolina or in Ohio or New York City. The business of Texas has our undivided attention."

However, Texas is a huge state compared to most, with different economic dynamics and financial needs in different regions. Therefore, First City has divided its attention, creating seven regional banking districts by which to serve the state better. In North Texas, one of the most dynamic of these districts, the target is growth. From the working class individual to the high dollar professional, from the entrepreneur to the middle market corporation, First City, Texas stands ready to serve. First City is the "Bank of the Dallas Cowboys," and it is the bank of the Cowboys fan as well.

"We look to serve the entire

LEFT: Joining Milledge A. Hart, III are corporate officers including, from left to right, Robert V. Thurmond, Jr., Vice President, Axon, Inc.; John R. Rossiter, Secretary/Treasurer, The Hart Group, Inc.; Jennifer R. Riner, Vice President of Finance, The Hart Group, Inc., Axon, Inc. and Rmax, Inc.; Richard W. Griner, President, Rmax, Inc., Axon, Inc. and The Hart Group, Inc. and Lynne A. Kessinger, Vice President, Sales and Marketing, Rmax, Inc.

BELOW: The "Superhandyman" Al Carrel endorses the Axon line of building services. Axon is fast becoming a leader in the building maintenance field, offering services in heating, air conditioning, plumbing and landscaping.

annual sales dramatically during an era of erratic and sometimes flat activity in the national construction industry.

Several years before the awakening of America's interest in expanding its export industry and passage of the U.S. Export Trading Company Act, The Hart Group established Trade Max Inc. in 1980. Now called H.C. Distributors, the company exports consumer goods to Europe and imports merchandise from the Far East and Europe.

Unlike many of its recently formed competitors, which for the most part are brokers, H.C. Distributors takes ownership of goods and operates in a true buy/sell mode. H.C. Distributors accelerated its move into services in July 1985 in response to growing global demand for more-specialized trading approaches. Some of these involve countertrade, barter and switch transactions. H.C. Distributors is consolidating its highly regarded position in its Far East and European markets as it expands into South America.

The latest member of The Hart Group is Axon Inc., a residential and commercial service company with a goal of becoming a national leader in the service industry. In 1985, Axon acquired United Plumbing and Air Conditioning of Dallas, one of the city's largest and most-respected providers of diversified plumbing, air conditioning, heating and mechanical contracting services. With the

upgrading of Axon's mainframe computer and other vital service-related capabilities, the firm will enhance its already enviable position by providing computer-assisted scheduling of homeowner and general building services. Future expansion of Axon's services will take place in a variety of other communities and already has begun in other industry-related fields.

The first step in that expansion took place in 1986 with Axon's addition of Automatic Rain of Dallas, already a leader in the landscape irrigation industry. Automatic Rain's track record of dedication to integrity, quality and productivity in the Dallas/Fort Worth area has been enhanced by its joining Axon. The merger will accelerate Axon's goal of becoming a national leader in providing diversified services for residential and commercial buildings.

These firms represent only half of the overall commitment by The Hart Group to the community it serves and wishes to make better. One major area of focus by The Hart Group is finding and developing leaders for today as well as tomorrow. The idea began to take shape when Mitch Hart found a similarly directed organization in Atlanta: the Society of International Business Fellows (SIBF). He persuaded that organization's founder, Jim Crupi, to relocate SIBF to Dallas so that it could serve as a nucleus for a group eventually named the International Leadership

Center (ILC).

SIBF gives executives and managers the opportunity to network through regional conferences, retreats and other gatherings. Many of the personal and professional relationships established through such functions have served these people and their companies in many ways that would not seem related.

But SIBF only served one portion of the leadership-development agenda of The Hart Group: today's leader. As the need for developing tomorrow's leader became apparent, Hart discovered there was no true program for determining who those leaders might be, and then developing them. With these goals as a starting point, and with Hart's commitment to investing personal seed money for the concept, he established Leadership America in 1987.

Leadership America encourages leadership development by challenging college undergraduates to pursue more demanding leadership roles. Leadership America is uniquely positioned to serve as the major stimulus for that development at the college level.

It does so by providing a unique opportunity in the form of a 10-week summer session. Each year, 50 college students are chosen for the program from approximately 1,000 applicants from more than 250 different campuses.

Leadership America's objectives are threefold: recognizing and rewarding effective student leadership, helping participants become better prepared for the leadership challenges of their generation, and developing a leadership model built around the concepts of group process, global awareness and community service.

The program begins with an orientation session at Duke University, followed by a week at the Center for Creative Leadership. At the Center, participants engage in group dynamic seminars, as well as one-on-one meetings with psychologists who specialize in leadership dynamics and help the students identify their personal leadership strengths and weaknesses.

The next step takes them to Colorado Outward Bound, a one-week outdoor challenge which teaches them self-confidence and how to trust in others. This experience gives them a greater appreciation of the teamwork necessary to accomplish specific goals.

The next leg of Leadership America is in Dallas at a classroom session at Southern Methodist University. Here they engage in additional leadership study and also divide into small groups to undertake a contemporary social problem solving project.

After the Dallas session, the stu-

Two members of the Leadership America Program take a break during a session at the Center for Creative Leadership.

dents spend four weeks in a self-selected internship across the country and/or around the globe. Internships involve government, business and community service. The program concludes with a closing session in Washington, D.C.

After completing the program, these 50 students return to their respective campuses with a renewed direction and commitment to developing their leadership skills. In the words of one 1987 Leadership America participant, his experience has resulted in his making a major difference for the betterment of his university, community, home state and also his peers.

Today, other companies are helping The Hart Group and Hart sponsor Leadership America. American Airlines, IBM, The Henry Luce Foundation, USAA and the Coca Cola Company are but a few of the many who recognize Leadership America to be the primer of the pump that will produce tomorrow's leaders.

From quality businesses to ethical entrepreneurial practices to developing tomorrow's leaders, The Hart Group plays a major role in the future of Dallas, Texas and the world.

FIDELITY INVESTMENTS SOUTHWEST

Fidelity Investments has become a leader in the financial services industry by combining outstanding performance with innovative customer service.

Fidelity Investments, one of America's oldest, largest and most successful financial institutions, has established itself on the cutting edge of financial services, primarily because of its commitment to both innovation and customer service.

Under the direction of Edward C. Johnson, 3d, son of the company's founder, Fidelity Investments has attained that position through the introduction of services not previously utilized within the industry. For example, Fidelity was the first company to offer check writing on money market mutual funds, a practice that now is an industry standard. Additionally, Fidelity designed the capacity to price sector-specific funds hourly, a first in the mutual fund industry.

Fidelity Investments, which began in Boston in 1946, has remained a privately held company. In 1983, after a particularly crippling snow storm hit Boston, company executives felt it imperative that they find a backup base of operation and turned their search for such a location to the Sunbelt.

Dallas, because of its central location, its airport, the presence of its bulk mailing center and state-of-the-art telecommunication capabil-ities, plus a large, well-educated labor pool, caught the company's eye, and Fidelity's new telemarketing center was placed in Las Colinas.

When Fidelity began its operations in the Metroplex, it had only 100 employees. Within a year, however, Fidelity's mail operation in Irving began sending out 100 percent of the prospectuses for the entire company and, at times, as many as 50,000 pieces of mail each day.

The number of employees doubled each year from 1983 through 1987. During that time, Fidelity expanded its operations in the Metroplex beyond its initial telemarketing group. Today, a variety of divisions, including the company's in-house Transfer Agent, Software Development and Institutional Marketing Divisions, are based here.

In 1986, Fidelity built a 46,000-square-foot direct mail and warehouse facility to house its expanding operations, and a state-of-the-art Data Center, which serves as a backup to the company's computers in Boston. Now, nearly a dozen Fidelity businesses operate in Dallas.

"The past year has seen several Fidelity business units set up operations in Dallas," says W. Humphrey Bogart, president and CEO of Fidelity Investments Southwest. "As these diverse segments of our company move to Dallas, we magnify our ability to establish more business relationships in the area. In addition, we create more career opportunities for employees in Dallas. These moves illustrate the direction in which we would like to continue."

To continue in its leadership position, and to ensure its future as one of the most successful financial institutions in the country, Fidelity has continued to enhance investment performance and increase the level of service expected by investors.

"We know that our service organization performs better than any other in the industry," says Bogart. "But we need to do better. Our customers are demanding faster processing, fewer errors and more responsible service."

Despite the general downturn in the financial services industry precipitated by the October 1987 stock market crash, Fidelity has gone against the tide of poor performance experienced by similar institutions. For example, in 1988 the company posted a significant net operating profit, a fact that did not go unnoticed in the industry. While that figure was down from 1987, it reflected two things: Despite difficult market conditions and investor sentiment, Fidelity still showed an overall gain; and, perhaps more importantly, the company adapted to those difficult times by doing what was most sensible — cutting costs.

Fidelity Investments Southwest has nearly a dozen divisions operating in the Metroplex, including the company's in-house Transfer Agent, Software Development, Institutional Marketing and a state-of-the-art Data Center.

ICH CORPORATION

ICH Corporation and the pioneer insurance companies which it operates in Dallas are a primary reason the city has long been recognized as one of the nation's foremost insurance centers. Dallas-based ICH companies are among the largest and strongest in the Southwest and can trace their local and regional history back more than 85 years.

As one of the largest life and health insurance providers in the entire world, ICH Corporation has grown by acquiring subsidiary insur-

Lincoln Plaza is the home of Dallas ICH Companies, including Great Southern Life, Philadelphia Life and Southwestern Life Insurance Companies.

ance companies and implementing programs to reduce their operating costs and increase their production. Today, ICH's assets total more than $9.3 billion, with $80 billion worth of life insurance in force, and the strong new sales of the company's subsidiaries have been a key element in its competitive ability, internal growth and emergence as an industry leader.

ICH Corporation and its subsidiaries conduct business in all 50 states as well as in foreign countries utilizing the services of more than 3,000 home office employees, 4,000 full-time career agents and 39,000 independent insurance agents. Corporate offices are located in Louisville, Kentucky, and Denver, Colorado, and principal operating subsidiaries are managed in Chicago, Dallas and Denver.

In Dallas, ICH has acquired and consolidated three large insurance companies — Great Southern Life, Philadelphia Life and Southwestern Life. In addition, Union Bankers Life and Perich Systems/Citech also operate in the area. Each of the Dallas companies brings time-honored traditions and a rich heritage to ICH, the Metroplex and the state of Texas, as the following brief sketches reveal:

Great Southern Life Insurance Company traces its roots back to 1909, the year it was founded in Houston and began responding to the need for life insurance specially suited to the people of Texas. Since then, the company has scored numerous "firsts" in its outstanding record of commitment to the public. Great Southern was the first insurance firm in the state to write a policy for a death benefit of $100,000, the first to insure the lives of children, and the first to implement the "team concept" of improved service to policyholders. The company joined ICH in 1983 and moved its home office operations from Houston to Dallas in

1987. As it has for more than eight decades, Great Southern remains a true pioneer in its industry, and in the demanding marketplace of the 1990s, it will continue to lead the way with new products, technology and service.

Philadelphia Life Insurance Company is both rich in history and highly progressive in its thinking. Since 1906, it has maintained a tradition of service to policyholders, commitment to the development of quality life insurance products, and innovation in meeting the needs of the insurance consumer. The company survived the rigors of the Great Depression to experience phenomenal growth and become an industry giant. Upon joining ICH in 1986, Philadelphia Life relocated central operations to Dallas to coordinate with Great Southern and Southwestern Life. Since then, it has enhanced its heritage of excellence by achieving greater marketing momentum, broader distribution relationships and increased operating efficiency.

Southwestern Life Insurance Company is the oldest and largest of the legal reserve companies, and was a major force in making Dallas one of the four largest insurance centers in the United States. Since 1903, Southwestern Life has been helping Texas business grow and compiling a history of innovation. It was one of

Perich Systems provides streamlined data processing services for ICH and other companies in the insurance industry.

the first companies to issue "group" life insurance, to implement salary deduction and automatic bank draft methods of premium payment, and to lower premium rates for women. It also was first in the entire industry to install a complete in-house computer system. The company joined the ICH family in 1986, consolidating operations with Great Southern and Philadelphia Life at Lincoln Plaza in downtown Dallas, thereby adding greatly to its profitability and cost efficiency. In association with ICH, Southwestern Life remains a major force in its industry and one of the strongest institutions in Dallas.

Union Bankers Insurance Company, another Dallas institution, was founded in 1953 and has grown at a stunning pace. From modest beginnings, it has expanded into a substantial life and health insurance provider. Housed in a historic building, Union Bankers employs 340 home office personnel, uses the services of 25,000 insurance agents, and is licensed to do business in 45 states. The majority of its business is generated from sales of its outstanding health insurance programs.

Perich Systems is the newest member of the ICH family, created in 1989 to design and provide unique, streamlined data processing services for ICH and other companies in the insurance industry. The services are marketed through Citech, a partnership between ICH and Perot Systems. This relationship has allowed ICH to modernize and update its computer hardware and software, and to take advantage of state-of-the-art technology for a competitive edge in the insurance service field.

The ICH family of companies is strongly committed to its customers, its agents, its employees — and to the community. "Dallas is an excellent place to do business, as evidenced by its longstanding stature as a major insurance center," says Thomas J. Brophy, senior executive vice president and chief operating officer. "ICH management feels that it is only right that the company should give something back to the community."

With that in mind, civic pride and spirit are encouraged and promoted through an array of programs, including organized sports, arts and crafts shows, a company choir and participation in such community-wide programs as blood drives, disaster relief aid and the annual United Way campaign. Company-sponsored self-improvement classes help both employees and non-employees make better lives for themselves.

"For a corporation to be successful in the 1990s, it will need far more than mere financial strength," Brophy emphasizes. "It will require dedication to the people who make up the corporation and dedication to the community it serves. We believe the ICH companies in Dallas are a prime example of this kind of dedication and the success that can come from it."

Union Bankers Insurance Company occupies this historic structure in East Dallas.

BANK ONE, TEXAS

Momentum Place in Downtown Dallas

The newest force in the Dallas and Texas banking scene is truly excited about the positive economic future of its new markets.

In 1989, BANC ONE CORPORATION, based in the upper Midwest, successfully bid for the former MBank franchise. As a result, BANK ONE, TEXAS is assuming operating responsibilities for more than 20 former MBanks across Texas.

The reasons for the acquisition by one of the most widely-respected and stable financial institutions in the country is as much a story of opportunity as it is about the character of the people that make up BANK ONE, TEXAS.

John B. McCoy, Chairman and CEO for BANC ONE CORPORATION, has said about the Texas banking scene:

"There are many reasons for our move to Dallas. The growing diversity of business and industry here is one main factor. A healthy banking system already in existence is another. Expected population growth is important and the rebuilding economy signal great opportunities for our success."

The story of one of Dallas' oldest and widely respected financial institutions is a testament to the city it has been a proud partner to since the turn of the century.

"But the most important factor," adds McCoy, "is the people that make up BANK ONE, TEXAS. When we found out just how good the people at those banks are, that's when I really got interested." The people developed as a result of a very rich history.

The original Mercantile National Bank grew from a dream shared by three Dallas businessmen during World War I. In 1916 the bank opened in a one-room building under the name of Stiles, Thornton & Lund. The bank began with $20,000 in capital and took first-day deposits of more than $12,000, a very good beginning for the three bankers.

In 1917 the bank received its state charter and in 1920 joined the Federal Reserve system. Thirteen years later it was renamed Mercantile National Bank of Dallas.

Mercantile was on the cutting edge of the broad financial development in Dallas during the 1930s. This was a time of great growth in the banking business in the city with its close proximity to the booming East Texas oilfields.

That growth continued in the '40s with the purchase of land on which to construct a new home at Main and Ervay. The 33-story building, at the time the tallest building in Dallas, became a symbol of the great pride the bank had in the vigorous city of Dallas. For years, its unique silhouette, including the four-sided clock, was a signature for the city's growing skyline.

In 1948, founder R.L. Thornton, who had served as Mercantile's president since the beginning, became chairman of the board. Thornton presided over a period of phenomenal growth for the bank as assets rose from $219 million the year he assumed the position to $572 million the year of his death in 1964. Thornton, a prominent civic leader who helped found the Dallas Charter Association, was elected mayor of Dallas in 1952. His administration throughout most of the 1950s was a time of tremendous growth for Dallas as a whole, and Thornton is thought to be one of the most dynamic mayors Dallas has ever had.

1974 was a milestone year for Mercantile. At that time, assets broke the $1 billion barrier, and a holding company, Mercantile Texas, was established to assure future growth. At the time it was the biggest bank acquisition in Federal Reserve history, and it made Mercantile the fifth-largest bank holding company.

Mercantile continued to consolidate its position in Texas, adding banks in Abiline, Austin, Corpus Christi, El Paso, San Antonio, Sherman, Wichita Falls as well as Dallas and Houston.

But even more significant news was in the offing. For in 1984, Mercantile Texas merged with Houston-based Southwest Bancshares Inc. to form MCORP. The merger created an organization of 69 member banks across the state and allowed the larger organization to better-serve the middle market and business services in Texas.

In the 1980s the operation helped to pioneer the now-familiar MPACT card. A new theme centered around "Momentum" also took root, and even found its name in the bank's new building, Momentum Place, located across Main Street in Downtown Dallas from the building it took 40 years for the bank to outgrow.

BANK ONE, TEXAS plans to apply its personalized retail and middle-market banking style to the high-energy corporate lending foundation established by MCorp. The idea of operating a bank like a store is, in a manner of speaking, much like the storefront beginnings of "The Big Friendly Mercantile" more than 70 years ago.

According to McCoy, the new Banc One acquisition in Texas gives both his operation, as well as Dallas and Texas a new lease on life.

"We see, as do others, an opportunity to be a part of a dynamic transition of the Texas banking environment and the Texas economy. There are people in growing numbers, great resources and energy, a tradition of winning and love of victory. BANK ONE, TEXAS is proud to be a part of that."

"Dallas has changed in the last 20 years from a very nice, prosperous regional center to an international presence, which has allowed us to grow from 10 people to more than 500."

John Johnson, Chairman
— Johnson & Gibbs

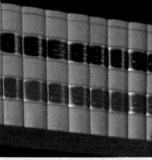

"We take great pride in the fact that our firm has been an integral part of the development of Dallas for so many years. As a firm policy, members of this firm have engaged in many kinds of community work, and the dividends have been enormous and highly gratifying."

Bill Keller, Senior Partner
— Clark, West, Keller, Butler & Ellis

"Dallas is still one of the few places left in this country where a person can start a business and build it into a successful company. There really are no limits to what a person can do here in Dallas as long as he or she is willing to work hard and do a good job."

Donald E. Godwin, Managing Director
— Godwin, Carlton & Maxwell

"We have a special, personal interest in the affairs of Dallas because we live here. We make a contribution to the city by helping to improve the quality of life."

Alberto Gutierrez, President
— Gutierrez, Smouse, Wilmut & Assoc. Inc.

"Dallas encourages innovation and rewards innovators. And I don't think that's always true of many older cities. We believe that the firm has to be a part of the community. We can't prosper unless the community prospers."

Mike Riddle, Managing Partner
— Riddle & Brown

"For 70 years the law firm of Carrington, Coleman, Sloman & Blumenthal has shared with Dallas its proud heritage. We look forward to another 70 years with those who would make Dallas their new home and part of their shining future."

James E. Coleman Jr., Managing Partner
— Carrington, Coleman, Sloman & Blumenthal

"For more than 20 years the accounting firm of Cheshier & Fuller has been providing expert professional service, with clients large and small benefitting from a full range of accounting services."

— Cheshier & Fuller Inc.

"Having recognized the opportunity of a Dallas location two decades ago, HOK has grown and prospered along with the city's accomplishments. The opportunity has allowed HOK to practice our art in significant ways."

Larry D. Self, AIA, Chief Administrative Officer
— Hellmuth, Obata & Kassabaum Inc.

"The leaders in Dallas by and large are dedicated to making this the finest place in the country to work and live."

Jerome H. Lane, Managing Partner
— Lane, Gorman, Trubitt & Co.

"We believe that housing is the most important basis of architectural design products. We give housing a special emphasis. Everything else spreads from a base of housing — industrial parks, strip shopping centers, commercial buildings."

Charles Womack, President
— Womack-Humphreys Architects

"Being headquartered in Dallas has benefitted the firm. The city's diverse economy provides many opportunities for a varied legal practice. Dallas is also a national headquarters for many national companies."

Brent Cooper, Founding Partner
— Cowles & Thompson

"KPMG Peat Marwick has helped establish Dallas as a highly respected international gateway for inbound and outbound investments with its unique blend of domestic and international reach and market specialization."

— KPMG Peat Marwick

"There is a unique quality about the culture here. There is an attitude here to take a young person who is willing and eager and open doors for them, to help them along."

Steve Garrison, President
— Ward Howell International

"Black & Veatch will celebrate its 75th anniversary as a firm, and its 20th anniversary in Dallas during 1990. We are proud to have been a part of Dallas' growth these 20 years."

C.W. Duncan, P.E., Resident Partner
— Black & Veatch

"We have a team concept: It's fairness, it's respect, it's camaraderie. I have always encouraged our lawyers to refer to ourselves as 'we' rather than 'I.' It's subtle, but I think the client understands that this is a team effort."

Richard D. Haynes, Founding Partner
— Haynes & Boone

"Dallas is a vibrant, exciting, alive city. It's not tightly controlled by a few big businesses or law firms. The quality of the Dallas legal community overall is quite high. More than in some other cities, Dallas lawyers exhibit a spirit of cooperation."

Robert M. Cohan, Partner
— Cohan, Simpson, Cowlishaw, Aranza & Wulff

"In addition to our tax, accounting, management and employee benefits consulting services geared for more mature companies, we've become highly successful in serving the needs of owner-managed businesses."

Jerry Walker, Managing Partner
— Coopers & Lybrand

"The thing that sets Dallas apart from other cities in the Southwest is that we have such a wide base of economic resources. It is our goal at Gardere & Wynne to help strengthen and broaden that base even further."

Barry Drees, Managing Partner
— Gardere & Wynne

"The attitude of the people of Dallas has always been positive toward growth, even during the last few tough years. The quality of the people of this city is very high, and that's definitely another one of the advantages of doing business in Dallas."

Cecil B. Phillips, Chairman and Chief Executive Officer
— M/A/R/C Inc.

"We will sacrifice short-term gains for long-term investments. That's why RTKL's expertise in mixed-use, hotel, resort and retail projects is in demand internationally as well as domestically."

Joseph Scalabrin, FAIA, Vice Chairman and Managing Principal
— RTKL Associates Inc.

"Dallas is a great city in which to do business. The business community is open to anyone with good ideas who's willing to work hard. Dallas has been very receptive to us."

James L. Baumoel, Regional Managing Partner
— Jones, Day, Reavis & Pogue

"Economic opportunity is the product of accessibility. A superior work force is the product of quality of life. Dallas is the only U.S. city which combines local and international accessibility with unparalleled quality of life."

Michael C. French, Managing Partner
— Jackson & Walker

Professions

Attorneys, accountants, architects, engineers and advertising professionals all provide essential services to the Dallas community.

JOHNSON & GIBBS, P.C.

Twenty years ago when five young lawyers started the firm known today as Johnson & Gibbs, they had a vision that was almost unheard of for a fledgling legal group: "We started with the idea of becoming an institution, not just a group of individuals," explains John R. Johnson, chairman and one of the founding attorneys.

In those days, he notes, no Dallas law firm had even 50 lawyers. Johnson & Gibbs was the first to reach 100 lawyers and today is the largest Dallas-based law firm, with more than 275 attorneys and a support staff of comparable size. While the greatest number of lawyers are based in Dallas, the firm has important offices in Austin, Houston and Washington, D.C. The firm's management believes in the "one-firm" concept, meaning that offices in cities other than Dallas are not viewed as "branches" but as integral parts of the overall firm. Johnson & Gibbs' professional resources are available to clients on a firm-wide basis regardless of location.

From the beginning, the firm's lawyers invoked an entrepreneurial spirit and a desire to develop a new and significant presence in the Southwest. They knew that a key to future success would rest with the quality of legal talent they could attract. "We assumed a lead role in aggressively recruiting lawyers from fine law schools throughout the country," Johnson says.

Today, Johnson & Gibbs has an exceptional recruiting and training program, one that attracts top law students from more than 46 law schools nationwide. In addition to in-depth technical training in their particular specialties, Johnson & Gibbs' lawyers are trained to be problem solvers, implementors and facilitators in the atmosphere of a cost-sensitive, full-service business organization.

Johnson & Gibbs is well known

In many ways, Johnson & Gibbs' growth is directly linked to that of Dallas, but the firm has expanded far beyond its original scope.

for its expertise in many areas, including corporate/securities, real estate, tax, litigation and financial services. In the past few years, the firm's tax practice has received national attention, with five members of the firm having served on the Council of the Section of Taxation of the American Bar Association. Most recently, Larry Gibbs served as Commissioner of the Internal Revenue Service from 1986-1989. He has now returned to join the firm's efforts in building one of the largest tax departments in the country, with capabilities in the areas of tax planning, tax controversy and civil and criminal tax litigation.

To meet the increasing demands of its client base, Johnson & Gibbs has formed smaller, interdisciplinary practice groups that function within the larger departments, including bankruptcy, energy, employee benefits, healthcare, intellectual property, international, labor and employment, legislative/administrative and public finance.

The firm has had an extremely high Dallas real estate profile in recent years, serving as council on recognizable projects such as Reunion Tower/Hyatt Regency Hotel, First City Center, Momentum Place, Dallas Galleria, Computer Associates International in Las Colinas and Cityplace Center. Additionally, Johnson & Gibbs represents large corporations in their relocation to or growth within the Metroplex, including Exxon Corporation, GTE Corporation, MCI Communications Corporation and Oryx Energy Company, as well as American Airlines on their new maintenance facility and expansion at Dallas/Fort Worth International and Alliance Airports.

Johnson & Gibbs has a history of successful involvement in public/private partnerships which are established to increase awareness and support of major community projects, such as the Dallas Arts District,

Reunion Arena and the Freeport Trade Center at D/FW Airport.

Founders Square, Johnson & Gibbs' Dallas headquarters, is a stunning historical landmark in Dallas' popular West End. The firm, in partnership with a major Dallas developer, restored the 75-year-old Higginbotham-Bailey-Logan Building, which was originally used for dry goods and wholesale distribution. Johnson & Gibbs moved into the award-winning building in 1984.

In many ways, the firm's growth is directly linked to that of Dallas, but the organization has expanded far beyond its original scope. The senior lawyers realized that the firm could make a significant contribution that would not only benefit the economic development of North Texas, but the state, and that would focus national and international attention on Texas. To that end, for example, Johnson & Gibbs' lawyers donated considerable legal time to the Texas National Research Laboratory Commission during their efforts to bring the Superconducting Super Collider to North Texas.

Johnson & Gibbs' commitment to its community and state does not stop there. The firm won the North Texas Legal Services' "Firm of the Year" award in 1988 for its *pro bono* work. In 1989, the organization devoted nearly 2,000 hours and more than 30 lawyers — ranging from first-

year associates to senior shareholders — to assist low-income and underprivileged families in Dallas County. Johnson & Gibbs' lawyers and staff also donate their time and expertise to the Multicultural Community Center, which assists some 50,000 refugees in Dallas County.

The firm has always been a strong supporter of the arts, as well as civic, charitable, religious and professional associations. Johnson & Gibbs' employees have consistently given their time, energy and creativity to such entities as the Chambers of Commerce of Dallas (of which John Johnson was chairman from 1984 through 1986), North Dallas

---

The commitment to the communities in which it operates underscores Johnson & Gibbs' presence as an exciting, forward-thinking, truly international corporation which still maintains its hometown roots.

Founders Square, Johnson & Gibbs' Dallas headquarters, is a stunning historical landmark in the popular West End.

---

and Oak Cliff, the Central Dallas Association, the Dallas Assembly, the Dallas Citizen's Council, the Dallas Symphony, the Dallas Museum of Art, the Dallas Opera, the Dallas Theater Center and the Greater Dallas Planning Council.

Johnson & Gibbs also supports Leadership Dallas, the Lyric Opera, the Shakespeare Festival and the United Way, plus several private and parochial schools, law schools, universities and religious organizations. The firm's community spirit extends beyond the Metroplex, with the pursuit of civic, artistic, educational and religious interests by Austin, Houston and Washington, D.C. employees.

The deep commitment to the communities in which it operates underscores Johnson & Gibbs' presence as an exciting, forward-thinking, truly international corporation which still maintains its hometown roots. John Johnson sums it up best: "We will continue our entrepreneurial endeavors even though we've become an institutional law firm. Dallas has been very good to us. Our commitment to this city and to Texas makes sense — as lawyers, and as citizens looking toward a brighter future."

CLARK, WEST, KELLER, BUTLER & ELLIS

For more than 100 years, the ideals of community involvement and providing highly personalized legal service to business clients of all sizes have guided the firm of Clark, West, Keller, Butler & Ellis.

Founded in 1886, the firm has a long and distinguished history. From its ranks have come the only Texan to serve as a justice on the U.S. Supreme Court and two U.S. attorney generals. Firm attorneys also have served as U.S. deputy attorney general, assistant attorney general in charge of the Justice Department's antitrust, civil, lands and criminal divisions, federal district judge, federal district attorney and in other federal and state legal positions.

With deep historical roots, Clark, West, Keller, Butler and Ellis looks to its future in Dallas. Today, the firm practices in virtually all areas of civil law, rendering a broad range of services to clients in real estate, litigation, banking, retail, oil and gas, utilities, manufacturing, tax, bankruptcy, corporate, antitrust, product liability, labor and employment law, occupational safety and health, and other matters. The firm, which places emphasis on its litigation capabilities, has participated in several major U.S. Supreme Court decisions. Its labor and employment law practice has been national in scope for many years.

"We take great pride in the fact that our firm has been an integral part of the development of Dallas for so many years," says Senior Partner Bill Keller. "As a firm policy, members of this firm have engaged in many kinds of community work, and the dividends have been enormous and highly gratifying. It is a great thrill to see a new building being erected — whether it be a church, school, library, sports arena, legal center or a place for the performing arts — when you know that somehow,

as a firm, you have made a contribution to that effort."

In recent years, a number of projects have kept the firm's lawyers in the mainstream of community work. They have supported the Dallas Independent School District, the Dallas County Community College District, private schools, Southern Methodist University and its Law School and moot court teams, other colleges and universities, the Greater Dallas Chamber and its committees, the Dallas Museum of Art, the Dallas Symphony, area theaters and sporting events.

The firm believes in and practices good citizenship. Its lawyers are encouraged to do *pro bono* work of various kinds. They work with battered spouses, neglected and abused children, the homeless, students and other needy groups. The firm awards a college scholarship to the outstanding graduating senior at its adopted North Dallas High School. One of its senior lawyers works regularly, as part of the Christian ministry, in state penal institutions. The firm's attorneys also accept court appointments in criminal cases. Members of the firm helped organize the first legal aid service organization in Dallas. Currently, through partner Mike Tabor, the firm is involved in the Leadership Dallas program.

"We are convinced that community service has made us much better citizens and a more effective law firm," says Senior Partner Allen Butler. "It has provided us with work opportunities, experience and acquaintances that result in our being better lawyers. We want our lawyers to have this valuable training in community work because we know that it gives them additional experience and strengths. We have no hesitancy in putting our lawyers in difficult situations or in any courtroom, from city courts to the Supreme Court."

Members of the firm have remained highly active in professional and bar association work. They have served as president of the National Federal Bar Association and the State Bar of Texas, as chairman of the Judicial Administration and the Labor and Employment Law sections of the American Bar Association, as a founder of the National Institute for Trial Advocacy, and as trustee and chairman of the Labor and Employment Law Division of the Southwest-

ern Legal Foundation. Partner Mark Shank has served as chairman of the Texas Young Lawyers' Association.

Over the years, members of the firm have lectured and participated in many legal programs from coast to coast about developments in different legal fields, including lectures to groups of visiting foreign lawyers about our systems of constitutional and criminal law. One senior partner has participated for 12 years in annual meetings in different foreign nations to study their systems of "the law of the workplace."

"We have worked in and been a part of this community for many years," says Senior Partner Melvyn Douglas. "We believe in close personal service to our clients. We are grateful for the opportunity to be of service to our clients and friends in Dallas. Dallas has a 'quality of life' — in the combined family, social, professional and commercial sense — of which we are fortunate to be a part.

With deep historical roots, Clark, West, Keller, Butler and Ellis looks to its future in Dallas, practicing in virtually all areas of civil law.

Great growth is sure to continue here. We fully intend to grow with this community for the next 100 years, and continue to enjoy life and make our contribution to the city and all its people."

GODWIN, CARLTON & MAXWELL

Members of the law firm Godwin, Carlton & Maxwell discuss a case in the firm's library.

In 1980 Donald E. Godwin, George R. Carlton and James S. Maxwell were partners with a prestigious law firm in Dallas. But the men had a dream. They saw the need in Dallas for a firm with a strong foundation in business litigation and insurance defense as opposed to transactional law. They decided to form such a firm and established their office in 2001 Bryan Tower. Theirs was one of the first law firms in Dallas to be a true "litigation boutique."

As of early 1990, the firm of Godwin, Carlton & Maxwell numbered more than 85 attorneys and 210 total employees occupying almost two-and-a-half floors in NCNB Plaza. The firm is the "fastest growing law

firm in Texas," according to the publication *Texas Lawyer*.

The growth of the firm can be traced directly to a certain amount of planned service expansion. However, according to Donald E. Godwin, managing director of the firm, "the idea initially was for the practice to evolve into one which would deal primarily with litigation. But it became apparent rather quickly that our clients needed a wider range of services. Those clients essentially told us that if we could handle some of their other legal matters, they would be

able to do more business with us. It was very simple: We had to either meet the needs of our clients or eventually risk losing their business."

Godwin, Carlton & Maxwell has evolved into a multifaceted firm that services corporate, institutional and individual clients in most areas of civil law, both in litigation and transactions. Several dynamics unique to the legal profession also are responsible for the firm's rapid yet well-planned growth.

"First of all, with the exception of our start-up costs in 1980, we have not incurred any significant debt in order to expand," says Godwin. "And secondly, we have always secured the business to warrant expansion rather than the other way around. When we established this firm, we envisioned our ultimate growth to conclude at around 20 or so attorneys. However, the concept of the firm has broadened, which makes our initial projections very outdated."

At this time, the firm has developed strong expertise in corporate, securities, employee benefits (ERISA), labor (management), banking, oil and gas, real estate, taxation, probate, estate planning, health care and bankruptcy as well as other types of litigation. The firm has attorneys that are certified by the Texas Board of Legal Specialization in the areas of civil trial law, bankruptcy law (both consumer and business), personal injury trial law, oil and gas and mineral law, tax law, estate planning and probate law.

The firm's Dallas location has had a profound impact on its development. "Dallas is still one of the few places left in this country where a person can start a business and build it into a successful company," says Godwin. "There really are no limits to what a person can do here in Dallas as long as he or she is willing to work hard and do a good job at a competitive price."

The future of Godwin, Carlton & Maxwell is as exciting as the growth already experienced by the firm. Within the next couple of years, Godwin projects, the firm will employ well over 100 lawyers. Primary additions will be in the banking, business, corporate and tax law and environmental areas.

"We also expect a shift in the type of representation we provide in the next few years," he says. "Recently, we have been in a high-litigation/low-transactional cycle. But as the 'golden age of litigation' runs its course and things settle down, there should be more transactional work and a proportional decrease in litigation. We are already preparing for that day."

One characteristic of Godwin, Carlton & Maxwell that all employees are proud of is the firm's commitment to giving back to the community. Public service efforts of individuals and the firm as a whole are indeed noteworthy. The firm does a greater-than-normal amount of *pro bono* work for those who require legal expertise but are unable to pay for such services.

Godwin, Carlton & Maxwell maintains a high visibility in the arts in Dallas, having purchased a corporate box at the new Morton H. Meyerson Symphony Center, as well as providing ongoing financial support to the Dallas Museum of Art, Dallas Theater Center and Dallas Summer Musicals. The firm also is a substantial contributor to the annual Crystal Charity Ball, a gala function that benefits a wide range of local charitable foundations.

Thomas Rosen, a senior partner with the firm, is a former director of the Greater Dallas Chamber and currently sits on the board of directors for the Sammons Center for the Arts. The firm has always believed in community involvement and the incumbency of individuals and companies who have been successful to give of themselves back to the community.

Godwin, Carlton & Maxwell also has a strong relationship with the Dallas Independent School District's Business Magnet School. This arrangement each year affords several students the opportunity to work for the firm as a part of their secondary educational curriculum.

Though the history of Godwin, Carlton & Maxwell is relatively short, it is bright with accomplishments — for the firm but also for Dallas.

"We are proud to be here," says Godwin. "And we are proud to be a part of the growth that our city is again experiencing."

From left, founding partners James S. Maxwell, Donald E. Godwin and George R. Carlton on the staircase of their downtown Dallas law firm.

GUTIERREZ, SMOUSE, WILMUT & ASSOC. Inc.

Gutierrez, Smouse, Wilmut & Assoc. Inc. is the third-largest Dallas-based general civil engineering firm. Founded in 1975 by Alberto F. Gutierrez, John Smouse and Charles Wilmut, the firm is nationally recognized and employs 50 people. It also operates branch offices in Houston and Big Spring, Texas.

The work that Gutierrez, Smouse, Wilmut performs has or will have a significant impact on Dallas. For example, the firm provided drainage and utility design for one of the state's most congested expressways — North Central Expressway.

The firm designed the effluent channel for the city's South Side wastewater treatment plant. Gutierrez, Smouse, Wilmut also provided water utility planning and design for Southland Corporation's Cityplace office, retail and residential development just outside downtown Dallas. Such work is absolutely essential to keep the city going and make it a healthy and safe place to live.

"We have a special, personal interest in the affairs of Dallas because we live here," says co-founder and president Alberto Gutierrez. "We make a contribution to the city by helping to improve the quality of life. At Gutierrez, Smouse, Wilmut, we go beyond the actual performance

Gutierrez, Smouse, Wilmut & Assoc. Inc. designed the effluent channel for Dallas' South Side wastewater treatment plant.

normally required. We want to leave a mark on the projects we undertake by providing long-term, permanent solutions to traffic or environmental problems rather than a quick fix."

Gutierrez and his family fled communist Cuba in 1960 for Miami, where he got a job as a draftsman for $60 a week. After a year in Miami, Gutierrez found a federal job as a sanitary engineer with the U.S. Public Health Service in Dallas and for nine years administered a multimillion-dollar construction grant program in Texas.

In 1972 he was transferred to the newly created Environmental Protection Agency. Eventually he was promoted to chief engineer, engineering and design section, Office of Grants Coordination for the Environmental Protection Agency's Region VI.

After 11 years in the public sector, Gutierrez opened an engineering division for a large corporation in Dallas in 1973. A year earlier, public law 92-500 was passed, providing federal grants to construct wastewater treatment facilities. Sensing an

Gutierrez, Smouse, Wilmut & Assoc. Inc. provided water utility planning and design for the 140-acre Southland Corporation Cityplace office, retail and residential development just outside downtown Dallas.

opportunity, Gutierrez teamed with Smouse and Wilmut to purchase the division with the help of a $100,000 Small Business Administration guaranteed loan. Their newly formed and renamed engineering firm offered specialized services for the federal wastewater program that included infiltration/inflow analysis, sewer system evaluation surveys and rehabilitation plans and specifications.

The firm diversified in 1980 when funding for the federal wastewater treatment grants was threatened. Today, Gutierrez, Smouse, Wilmut designs and plans paving and drainage, utility systems, water distribution and wastewater collection systems and provides solid/hazardous waste management and environmental studies, all with state-of-the-art computer-aided design capabilities.

Smouse, who moved to Dallas in 1956, has since retired from the firm, while Dallas native Wilmut is senior vice president. Under Gutierrez's leadership, the firm has become one of the 400 top Hispanic-owned businesses in the nation, according to *Hispanic Business.*

RIDDLE & BROWN, ATTORNEYS AND COUNSELORS

The three Hewlett-Packard 3000 computers that dominate the fourth floor offices of Riddle & Brown, Attorneys and Counselors, captures the essence of the firm: sleek and up-to-date.

There are no dusty law books lining waiting room walls; the chairs are not leather; the paneling is light.

"We're not hidebound by old world wood and leather," says Mike Riddle, founder and managing director of the firm. "We started this firm with the concept that you could offer very specialized legal services to financial institutions on a high volume, low-cost basis, nationwide."

It was a concept ahead of its time. But then, that is exactly where Riddle tries to steer the firm.

"The simple thing is to do what's obvious today," he says. "The much more challenging thing is to do the thing that's going to be obvious five years from now."

Today, Riddle & Brown services insurance companies, financial insti-

Riddle & Brown was founded on the concept of offering very special services to financial institutions on a high volume, low-cost basis. Today they service insurance and real estate companies, financial institutions and mortgage bankers, nationwide. Photo by Art Beaulieu.

tutions, real estate firms and the mortgage banking industry.

About 50 percent of Riddle & Brown's business is associated with real estate closings. From Maryland to Newport Beach, lending institutions contract with the firm to prepare closing documents on thousands of transactions each month. Riddle & Brown's use of the computer places the firm on the cutting edge of technology, enabling it to guarantee 24-hour turnaround — at substantial savings to clients.

Riddle explains that in the past such documentation was created one piece at a time, "as you would tailor-make suits." Such labor-intensive preparation is much more expensive, and the computer is usually more accurate.

When the firm began in 1980, no one had any idea it would swell to include 50 attorneys with offices in Dallas, Houston and New Orleans. In fact, the original lawyers broke away from large firms because they were too big.

Mike Riddle credits his Texas background, which encourages experimentation and achievement, for his willingness to start his own business. "I guess it's because Texans were all gamblers to start with. We had nothing to start with, and nothing to lose," he says.

Riddle came to Dallas from Lubbock because "this was where there was opportunity. I love Dallas because it's so open. I have never felt restrained in this city. If I could envision an opportunity and put together the people and resources to do it, nothing would stand in the way.

"Dallas encourages innovation and rewards innovators. I don't think that's always true of many older cities," he adds.

The firm recently donated $250,000 to Children's Medical Center. "We believe that the firm has to be a part of the community," Riddle says. "We can't prosper unless the community prospers."

Three Hewlett-Packard 3000 computers help Riddle & Brown process thousands of real estate closing documents each month. Photo by Art Beaulieu.

CARRINGTON, COLEMAN, SLOMAN & BLUMENTHAL

On my way to Cambridge, Massachusetts to enter law school, I visited a few days at my brother's home and was subjected at that time to a bombardment of criticism by my brother who urged me to abandon my ideas of life as a spokesman for others, a 'mouthpiece.' To that I had replied, I dreamed of a law firm made up of young, attractive, extremely able and promising partners, each of whom would enjoy the successes of the others and whose future together would not fail to develop each as citizens in every sense of the word and as lawyers of the highest professional attainments.

I arrived in Dallas about 7 a.m., January 8, 1919, intending to make my home and practice law in Dallas for the balance of my life.

From Paul Carrington's *A Dallas Lawyer for Sixty Years.*

Paul Carrington (1894-1988).

A brother's advice is rebuked with the high-minded eloquence that today sounds like something said in a Charlton Heston movie. Yes, Paul Carrington actually *talked* this way. For that was his style. And his decision in 1919 to make a new home in Dallas was the beginning of the law firm of Carrington, Coleman, Sloman & Blumenthal.

When Paul Carrington arrived in Dallas in 1919, the city had a population of 150,000. Today Dallas boasts a metropolitan population in excess of 3 million. When Mr. Carrington began his practice, the Dallas legal community had only about 300 members. Today almost 10,000 lawyers practice in the Dallas area. The city of 1919 has little similarity to the Dallas of the 1990s as ruins from some cultures have to their counterparts. One similarity, however, is that the lawyers of Carrington, Coleman strive to exemplify that which Paul Carrington wanted in his professional life: ability and promise, success, citizenship and high professional attainment.

As the 1990s arrive, Dallas/Fort Worth is one of America's most prominent metropolitan centers. Carrington, Coleman, Sloman & Blumenthal has grown as well and now has nearly 100 of those 10,000 attorneys.

Carrington, Coleman's practice involves virtually all areas of business law. The firm advises businesses in the areas of securities, mergers and acquisitions, antitrust and trade regulation, commercial finance, bankruptcy, environmental issues, employee relations and benefits, state and federal taxation, banking and financial institutions, oil and gas, real property and real estate development, utilities, health care, and trusts and estates.

Regrettably, advice about business transactions frequently is not enough, for this era has been called

James E. Coleman Jr. has been the managing partner of Carrington, Coleman since 1970.

the "golden age of litigation." The firm hopes that will change some day. But in the meantime, Carrington, Coleman has one of the largest trial and appellate practices in Dallas/Fort Worth, including the areas of securities, corporate, banking, product liability, antitrust, creditor/debtor rights, so-called business crimes, as well as other types of commercial litigation and arbitration.

Fortunately, very few clients need 100 attorneys. In popular parlance, Carrington, Coleman is a "full-service" firm. But that term does not convey much that is meaningful to a serious client. Experience shows that the typical Dallas client wants one or, when necessary, a few highly skilled, intelligent attorneys who are available when the client calls, understand the client's business, are loyal to the client's interests and will per-

Carrington, Coleman's principal offices are located at The Crescent.

form the required services (and only occasionally — a miracle). Additionally, the client's attorneys should be able to handle the client's needs in an acceptable time frame and at a reasonable cost.

Carrington, Coleman represents a broad range of publicly and privately held business entities, from local companies and entrepreneurial enterprises to large national and international companies which Dallas so successfully attracts. The firm serves as general and regional counsel to many major national and international businesses.

The firm also is proud to serve numerous charitable and civic organizations and to render individual and firm-sponsored pro bono services for those unable to pay.

Carrington, Coleman has its principal offices in The Crescent, an

architecturally acclaimed complex of offices and a hotel. The location on the north side of downtown Dallas' central business district is convenient to clients that want to avoid center city congestion or have quick access to airports. In order to better serve clients that are locating their businesses in the northern part of the

Dallas area, Carrington, Coleman has an office in Collin County.

Carrington, Coleman is pleased to have been asked to contribute to *Dallas: Proud Heritage, Shining Future.* It offers us the rare chance to re-affirm some traditional values about the practice of law in these commercially complex, law entangled times.

We feel that the law is still a profession and not just a business. We think that the term "legal ethics" is not self-contradicting. We also feel it is not our place to "name drop" our clients. We instead like to think that our clients are proud to tell others that we represent them. Finally, we feel that Dallas is a great city and that Texas is a great state . . . and lawyers should try to return to the community at least as much as they receive from it.

In short, Paul Carrington's vision for his life and law firm still lives at Carrington, Coleman, Sloman & Blumenthal.

To meet the needs of Dallas' growth to the north, Carrington, Coleman has offices in an historic Colonial Revival building in Collin County.

CHESHIER AND FULLER INC. P.C. — Certified Public Accountants

The choice of an accounting firm ranks as one of the most important financial decisions that both corporate officials and private individuals can make. Trust, expertise and experience are paramount in choosing the right firm to handle crucial and sensitive financial matters.

The Dallas accounting firm of Cheshier & Fuller has been providing such service for more than 20 years, with clients large and small benefitting from a full range of accounting services, from the very simple to the highly complex.

The firm's highly skilled professionals perform audits, reviews, compilations of financial statements, business valuations, assistance in obtaining financing, tax related planning, tax preparations, management advisory services and more.

Cheshier and Fuller's more than 20 certified public accountants and support staff work closely with management to analyze their needs, review their accounting systems and procedures, review internal controls and analyze financial results, highlighting potential strengths and weaknesses.

In accounting, as in any business, personalized service makes the difference. Because of its size, Cheshier

and Fuller is able to give its clientele close personal attention, which ultimately results in better service. The firm also is able to provide services similar to those of a large national firm because it is a member of Accounting Firms Associated Inc., a group of 50 independent accounting firms nationwide that networks their services.

With roots planted firmly in North Texas, Cheshier and Fuller understands the dynamics of conducting business in the North Texas area. Lee Cheshier, whose family settled in the area in 1850, graduated from the University of Texas in 1952 and began his practice in 1956. Harold Fuller's family settled in the Mid-Cities area in 1870. He is a 1953 graduate of North Texas State University, who started his accounting practice in 1960. In 1969 the accounting firms were merged and in 1970 incorporated as a professional corporation.

As the young firm gained new clients, it added more CPAs through

Accountants at Cheshier & Fuller have access to an extensive resource library to keep themselves abreast of changing tax laws and accounting practices.

a very selective recruiting process at colleges and universities primarily located in the Southwest. Cheshier and Fuller also has benefited from the hiring of experienced CPAs, adding immeasurably to the firm's scope and expertise. Today Cheshier & Fuller is ranked among the Dallas area's top 20 accounting firms overall and among the top five locally based firms.

Ever mindful of changing tax laws and accounting practices, accountants at Cheshier and Fuller do many things to keep abreast of this changing profession. They participate in continuing education courses and management development programs, and they voluntarily submit themselves to a review in which a firm is closely evaluated by its peers.

The CPAs of Cheshier and Fuller Inc. are members of the American Institute of Certified Public Accountants, Texas Society of Certified Public Accountants, Dallas Chapter of Texas Society of Certified Public Accountants and the Dallas Estate Planning Council.

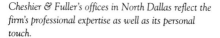

Cheshier & Fuller's offices in North Dallas reflect the firm's professional expertise as well as its personal touch.

HELLMUTH, OBATA & KASSABAUM

The Dallas Galleria, designed by HOK, combines retail, office, hotel and entertainment.

Recognizing that design influences the quality of life, Hellmuth, Obata & Kassabaum's goal has always been to create the best possible environment for the Dallas business community while at the same time addressing the city's broad-based needs.

Hellmuth, Obata & Kassabaum (HOK) is an international, multidisciplinary design organization of architects, engineers, planners, facility programmers, interior and lighting designers, landscape architects and graphic designers. One of the city's largest employers of design professionals, the firm also ranks as the nation's second-largest architectural/engineering and interior design firm.

During the past two decades, HOK's design vision has profoundly reshaped the profile of Dallas with such landmarks as Dallas/Fort Worth International Airport, which has contributed significantly to the overall economic growth of North Texas. In 1976, HOK designed the First International Building (now known as Renaissance Tower) which, at the time, was Texas' tallest skyscraper. HOK further influenced Dallas' architectural character in the early 1980s by designing the Dallas Galleria, an office/retail/hotel development in North Dallas. HOK's practice also includes a host of international business clients in Japan, the Middle East, Europe and Mexico.

HOK has provided services to help successfully relocate a number of major corporations to the Metroplex, including Exxon, GTE, MCI and Caltex. To accommodate the needs of developers, the real estate community and corporations, HOK provides an array of services including building analyses, build-to-suit, site selection, facility programming and interior design services.

HOK has addressed the rapidly changing nature of the high tech and telecommunications industries, but still maintains a very diverse client base. Recent clients include IBM, Mobil, ARCO, Convex Computers, First Boston, Oryx, and Baker and McKenzie.

HOK is active in public sector projects, including the Dallas Area Rapid Transit (DART) Starter Line. Other public work includes the Spring Creek Campus of Collin County Community College, and the Plano Civic Center, which is projected to increase business and tourism throughout North Texas.

HOK's visionary approach to design includes the use of its state-of-the-art CADD system which generates three-dimensional computer animation. This technique was used by HOK's Planning Group in the urban design of North Central Expressway.

"HOK is proud to have practiced in Dallas for more than 20 years," says Larry D. Self, HOK/DALLAS Managing Principal. "And we're committed to providing Dallas with environments that will reflect the culture and aspirations of its people and enhance the quality of their lives."

Hellmuth, Obata & Kassabaum was the design architect for the Dallas/Fort Worth International Airport, the 2nd busiest airport in the world.

LANE, GORMAN, TRUBITT & CO. CERTIFIED PUBLIC ACCOUNTANTS

When Jerome H. Lane visited Dallas in 1948, he found a working person's city.

While there were not any mountains or oceans to attract a growing population, he noted an overall feeling of civic pride. "The people were hard-working and caring, just as they are today," recalls Lane.

That same year he returned to Dallas to stay, and in 1950 established what is now Lane, Gorman, Trubitt & Co., one of the largest independent certified public accounting/management consulting firms in Dallas and the Southwest.

The partners and a dedicated professional staff have built the firm's reputation for quality and service. This is what attracts many of its cli-

ents which include some of Dallas' most successful and quality-conscious businesses.

Lane, Gorman, Trubitt & Co. is dedicated to offering its clients a broad range of services, close personal attention, timely service and forward-thinking advice. As a growth-oriented firm, the staff is trained in specific industries such as construction, health care, real estate, financial institutions, professions, manufacturing, wholesale, retail and technology.

Lane, Gorman, Trubitt & Co. is dedicated to offering its clients a broad range of services, close personal attention, timely service and forward-thinking advice.

Clients recognize that the firm has a unique ability to identify special needs and provide the resources to help achieve success. Emerging businesses will find Lane, Gorman, Trubitt & Co. in step with changing times as the firm adds new services based on tomorrow's demands.

"We take a businessperson's approach to accounting," notes Lane. "Our people initiate ideas and keep abreast of business developments."

Lane, Gorman, Trubitt & Co. is a firm of diverse services including traditional tax, audit and accounting and consulting services. The firm also provides many of the same non-traditional services as a national accounting firm such as management advisory services, personal financial planning, computer and software consulting, marketing and employee benefits.

The firm has enjoyed a steady growth since 1950, even during some

Keeping in touch with the present and future demands a full service firm that can effectively service multiple industries.

of Dallas' unpredictable economic times, because of hard work and dedication to its clients' best interests.

The firm has participated on a voluntary basis in the peer review monitored by the American Institute of Certified Public Accountants (AICPA) since the program was established in 1978.

"Our peers meticulously evaluate our compliance with professional standards and requirements," explains Wanda Lorenz, managing partner-elect. Lane, Gorman, Trubitt & Co. is a member of both the AICPA's Private Practice Section and the SEC Section. "Our participation in peer review allows our clients to be the benefactors of a performance that adheres to the strictest quality control standards," says Lorenz.

In addition, the firm belongs to three peer networks that allow the firm access to expertise and information from CPA firms across the country and internationally. While independent of each other, the groups keep abreast of what is new in the accounting profession while exchanging valuable ideas. The Southwest Practice Management Group includes firms from some of the largest independent CPA firms in Texas, Louisiana and Arkansas. CPA Management Systems is a group of independent CPA firms from coast to coast. For international support, Lane, Gorman, Trubitt & Co. is a member of GMN North America.

Lane finds that Dallas continues to be a working person's city, and the feeling of civic pride has never changed — not in his firm or among the firm's clients. Lane, Gorman, Trubitt & Co. believes that their goal is to provide clients with quality services that will help them become increasingly successful. They also believe in the continued strength and growth of Dallas.

WOMACK-HUMPHREYS ARCHITECTS

Perhaps as much a tribute to the diversity of its projects as to its youthful enthusiasm and style, Womack-Humphreys has risen to become one of the 10 largest architectural firms in the Metroplex and has firmly secured its place as one of the most respected and sought-after firms in the nation.

Womack-Humphreys was founded in 1976 by Charles Womack, a Dallas native, president of the firm. Three years later, he was joined by Mark Humphreys, who is executive vice president.

The organization, which has multiple offices nationwide and its staff of architects, planners, landscape architects and interior designers, has won an impressive array of awards. Included are many McSam Awards issued by the Home and Apartment Builders Association for design excellence, as well as numerous awards from other national associations and the AIA.

Unlike most large architectural firms, Womack-Humphreys uses the studio system which allows the client to work with the same talented individuals throughout the duration of the project. This system also lets the studios specialize in different architectural types calling on the diverse talents and experience of the staff. The reward of the system is to help the studios provide the personalized service characteristic of a smaller firm.

Womack-Humphreys has ongoing projects in 30 states and Canada. And, the company is seriously eyeing the international market. "In 1984, when the slow-down happened in Dallas, we didn't just jump into a widely diversified national market overnight," says Humphreys. "We were already there. We not only remained strong, but in fact continued to grow, primarily because of two critical factors: One, our design work and its quality, and two, our diversity."

Charles Womack (left) and Mark Humphreys

Bryan Place

The V.I.P. Residence at Stonebridge Ranch.

Womack-Humphreys designs everything from large residential communities to retail centers, commercial buildings, municipal structures, hotel/resort complexes and multifamily developments. One of the most outstanding projects, and a recipient of many awards, is the condominium complex located at Bryan Place just east of downtown Dallas.

"We believe housing is the architectural design foundation from which all other uses spring — whether it be retail or retirement facilities," says Womack. "The diversity of our firm causes us to be more aware of the communal matrix of the various building types creating our living environment. Our clients expect us to help them envision how the different elements fit together for our total living/working environment."

As leaders in a growing Dallas economy, Womack-Humphreys has become symbolic of the opportunities Dallas presents to the entrepreneur.

Decker Court

Bowie Market

COWLES & THOMPSON

With its headquarters in Dallas, Cowles & Thompson provides full-service legal counsel throughout Texas with a network of four additional offices in Austin, Sherman, Temple and Tyler.

Founded in 1978 by six attorneys from one of the oldest firms in Dallas, Cowles & Thompson is recognized as one of the premier litigation firms in Texas with a progressive and expanding business practice. Currently, the firm has 18 partners and 64 associates and is committed to excellence through timely and efficient delivery of legal services.

Cowles & Thompson is most widely known for its litigation and appellate expertise, especially in the areas of medical malpractice, aviation, products liability, insurance and commercial law. Other areas of practice include corporate and real estate law, eminent domain, tax, trust and probate, banking, oil and gas, construction, bankruptcy and professional liability.

Cowles & Thompson has one of the most comprehensive and sophisticated insurance practices in Texas, offering not only litigation services but coverage analysis, insurance regulatory and corporate representation. Cowles & Thompson is one of a small number of firms in the state that can represent its insurance clients before the State Board of Insurance and the Legislature. The Austin office offers all areas of representation, from legislation to insurance board filings and approvals to the sale or merger of insurance companies. Cowles & Thompson also can provide cost-effective worker's compensation representation through its statewide office network.

Cowles & Thompson is one of the first law firms in Texas to create a section devoted to appellate practice. The firm has one of the largest and most experienced appellate sections in the state and has been involved in numerous landmark legal decisions that have changed Texas common law.

Cowles & Thompson also is among the few Dallas firms that specialize in aviation law. With more than 25 years of aviation litigation experience, Cowles & Thompson is well known for representing aircraft manufacturers, fixed-base operators and aviation insurers.

Being headquartered in Dallas has benefitted the firm, says Brent Cooper, a founding partner. The city's diverse economy provides many opportunities for a varied legal practice. "Dallas is also a national headquarters for many national companies," he says. "This provides another tremendous opportunity for a law firm.

"Reasonable housing costs and cultural opportunities such as the opera and the symphony give our firm a lot to offer prospective lawyers to help them make the decision between Dallas and other cities," Cooper adds.

Cowles & Thompson is divided into areas of practice. Each attorney typically concentrates his or her practice within a particular industry, activity or area of law, such as real estate or banking. Each client matter is assigned to a supervising attorney who is responsible to the client throughout Cowles & Thompson's representation. If the matter requires resources and talent from several disciplines, a team will be selected to work with the responsible attorney.

Cowles & Thompson has in place the people, tools, resources and systems for full modern legal representation in any part of the state of Texas.

Cowles & Thompson's Dallas office combines the best of old and new.

KPMG PEAT MARWICK

MARWICK, MITCHELL, PEAT & CO.
CERTIFIED PUBLIC ACCOUNTANTS

DALLAS, 1908: Photo courtesy of the Dallas Public Library

When KPMG Peat Marwick first opened its Dallas office for business 75 years ago, the accounting firm already had a strong legacy fostered by its mother company, which was founded — and became quite successful — before the turn of the century.

In 1915, it was known as Marwick, Mitchell, Peat & Co., and grew to be among the largest full-service public accounting firms in the world, with annual revenues today of approximately $4 billion. KPMG Peat Marwick in Dallas is highly respected for the professionalism and international expertise of its 600 people and is one of 12 offices in Texas. Indeed, KPMG Peat Marwick over the years has served as business advisors to many of the Dallas entrepreneurs, visionaries and community leaders who have become a part of the city's rich fabric.

KPMG Peat Marwick has helped establish Dallas as a highly respected international gateway for inbound and outbound investments. The firm's unique blend of domestic and international reach and market specialization, combined with its service to growth-oriented companies comprising the middle-market sector, helped place KPMG at the top of its profession. The organization's accounting, tax and consulting expertise is provided to clients of all sizes at consistently superior quality regardless of location. Keenly attuned to ever-changing economic needs in Dallas, KPMG Peat Marwick's scope of services reflects the needs of the area.

In 1987, Peat Marwick International merged with Klynveld Main Goerdeler (KMG), greatly expanding the firm's global reach. Peat Marwick had a strong presence in the United States and England, and KMG was a powerhouse in continental Europe. The marriage put KPMG in an excellent position to remain an industry leader when Europe becomes a unified common market in 1992.

"This was a wonderful fit between our strengths and the strengths of the KMG firm in terms of global representation," says William L. Schilling, who served as Managing Partner of the Dallas office of the firm from 1971 through 1989. He fully understands the need for international scope, having also served as managing partner of Peat Marwick's continental European practice before coming to Dallas.

Peat, Marwick, Mitchell & Co.

In 1990, Schilling turned over the reins to C.H. Moore, a 27-year veteran who had served as partner-in-charge of the audit department since 1978.

Both men have watched KPMG Peat Marwick grow into a team of business advisors who are able to give Dallas companies new insights into future growth and to provide them with the strategies necessary to shape the vision of international commerce. They both are extremely active with their clients and in the community and are high-profile contributors of their time and resources.

Through the leadership of Schilling and Moore, the Dallas office has involved itself in many local projects that have benefitted the city. Peat Marwick, for example, plays an integral role in the arts, through its work with the Dallas Symphony Association, the Dallas Opera and the Dallas Museum of Art; in education, through the Edwin L. Cox School of Business at Southern Methodist University; and in the community, through the Dallas Economic Development Advisory Board and the Dallas Business Commission.

These two executives encourage KPMG Peat Marwick partners and staff to stay closely involved with the community and to give of their time and talents in productive and creative ways, thus helping nurture the city that has been home to their firm for three-quarters of a century.

DALLAS, 1968: Squire-Haskins Photography

DALLAS, 1989: J. Brousseau, The Image Bank

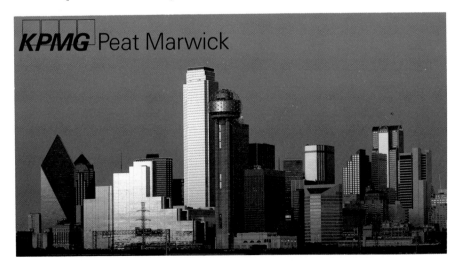

KPMG Peat Marwick

WARD HOWELL INTERNATIONAL

Stephen A. Garrison, Chairman and Chief Executive Officer of Ward Howell International.

Spanning five continents and 21 countries, Ward Howell International is one of the oldest and largest executive search firms in the world. Founded in 1951 by W. Wardwell Howell, a pioneer in the industry, it is the only major executive search firm owned equally by its principals.

Stephen A. Garrison founded the Dallas office in 1982, subsequently expanding Ward Howell's operations across the Southwest. He was named chairman and chief executive officer of Ward Howell International in 1988. Although the firm is headquartered in New York, Garrison has chosen to maintain his residence and office in Dallas with weekly commutes to the home office.

"My business has taken me all across this nation and to most of the major cities of the world, but there's no place I'd rather live or do business than in Dallas," Garrison observes. "There is a unique entrepreneurial spirit in Dallas. I think it has its roots in the indomitable attitudes of those early businessmen who built great fortunes and industries here. That heritage continues to influence the business climate in Dallas."

Garrison reflects on his own early experiences saying, "When I came to Dallas in 1976, I had to create a demand for our services. I was asking firms to rethink their corporate culture and trust me to place the right person for the right job — and they did," he recalls. "That 'open to new ideas' attitude prevails today."

Garrison gives credit to several Dallas businessmen who served as role models or mentors early in his career. Among those who have been important influences are Edmund Hoffman, Ed Cox, Ray Hunt and Trammell Crow. "They believed in the value of our services and invested personal time and effort to opening doors for us," he says. Garrison pauses to observe: "The strength of Dallas is its human resources. It's that intangible quality that makes this city great and capable of surviving any adversity."

Another quality of the Dallas business culture is its commitment to community affairs. Garrison believes that "contributing money isn't enough. We're results-oriented here and that takes a commitment of your personal resources of time and talents."

Garrison applies this measuring standard to his own company, donating about 25 percent of the Dallas office's work to worthy community causes. "There is no community effort that we have not touched in one form or another," he says. "We give back to the community in a significant way because as business leaders, it is important to know the needs of the city if you're going to be an architect of the future."

As it expands its European and Asian markets, Ward Howell International anticipates continued growth well past European unification in 1992. This will surely result in more travel demands, but Mr. Garrison will always return home to Dallas. He sums up his thoughts with, "There's no place I'd rather be."

BLACK & VEATCH

Black & Veatch, one of the largest engineering-architectural firms in the United States, recognized the vibrant spirit of Dallas and selected the city to be the firm's southern regional headquarters almost 20 years ago. From this base, Black & Veatch serves a variety of clients not only in the Dallas area but in Texas and surrounding states. Throughout the years, Black & Veatch has grown with Dallas, playing a key role in helping the city meet its diverse needs. The current staff of approximately 60 provides the full range of services available from Black & Veatch.

Founded in 1915, Black & Veatch will celebrate its 75th anniversary in 1990. The firm attributes its longevity and success to the principles established by founders E.B. Black and N.T. Veatch: honesty, integrity and consistently providing professional services of the highest possible quality.

Black & Veatch is an internationally recognized firm, providing services in every major field of engineering and architecture throughout the United States and in 40 foreign countries. The staff of more than 3,600 employees is comprised of civil, electrical, mechanical, nuclear, chemical, sanitary, architectural and structural engineers. Other skilled professionals include architects, planners, economic and financial specialists, hydrologists, chemists, biologists, meteorologists, lawyers, physicists, technicians and administrative personnel.

One of the firm's strengths is its ability to provide an unusually wide range of professional services. Black & Veatch is actively involved in civil and environmental projects, energy and resource recovery, industrial systems and processes, architecture, computer resources and financial planning and management for government and industry.

The firm has been responsible for more than 15,500 projects of varying size and scope for approximately 3,500 clients. Black & Veatch has served some of these clients since the inception of the firm. All aspects of each project can be handled within the organization because of the firm's wide range of capabilities and successful management approach.

To improve efficiency, accommodate growth and match capabilities to client's needs, Black & Veatch is organized into four major operating groups: Energy, Environmental, Facilities and Resources.

The Permian Basin Station near Monohans, Texas, demonstrates Black & Veatch's combustion turbine capability. TU Electric selected Black & Veatch to design 975 megawatts of additional capacity; these projects included three plants and 15 combustion turbines. The advantages of combustion turbines include efficiency and cost competitiveness.

The Energy Group provides complete engineering services to the electric utility industry for the generation, transmission and distribution of electric power. Additionally, the group provides design, engineering, procurement and construction for the petrochemical industries.

The Environmental Group provides study, design and construction-related services in water, wastewater, solid waste and transportation fields. Engineering services also include the cleanup of abandoned waste sites and treatment and disposal studies for control of hazardous materials.

A comprehensive range of planning and engineering services to federal agencies is provided by the Facilities Group. Architectural services for commercial, retail, educational, health care, industrial, retirement and public buildings also are a feature of this group.

The Resources Group maintains overseas offices to expeditiously accomplish international projects. The group also provides utilities with special services in valuation, rate, financial and feasibility matters.

As Black & Veatch continues to expand its capabilities to serve clients throughout the world, the firm looks forward to growing with Dallas and being a vital part of this city's bright future.

As part of a multiphase project involving Dallas' Southside Waste Water Treatment Plant, Black & Veatch prepared a master plan for the treatment plant service area and designed the Phase III plant expansion. Black & Veatch also provided study, design and construction administration services for Phases I and II of the plant. Screw pumps are used to discharge the effluent to the Trinity River, following treatment.

HAYNES AND BOONE

In 1964, Richard D. Haynes opened his solo office in Dallas for the practice of law after having been with another Dallas firm for a number of years. He was joined in June, 1967 by Michael M. Boone upon his graduation from law school. In 1970, the partnership of Haynes and Boone was formed.

Since then, Haynes and Boone has grown to be a full-service business law firm with a major regional presence as well as a growing national and international practice. The firm has offices in Austin, Dallas, Fort Worth and San Antonio, and a Houston office will open in 1990. The firm does not designate a home office; all offices and all clients enjoy equal importance and equal access to the firm's wide range of professional expertise and resources.

Through hard work and careful planning, Haynes and Boone has earned a reputation for excellence. As a result, during the past 10 years the firm consistently has been one of the fastest growing law firms headquartered in the Southwest.

As a growing full-service law firm, Haynes and Boone encourages its lawyers to become recognized experts in their areas of practice. This is done through teaching, legal writing, public speaking and participation in bar association activities. Also, Haynes and Boone has developed its own nationally recognized training and continuing legal education programs to assure the highest quality legal services for its clients.

That quality can be seen in the comprehensive range of legal services the firm provides for its business clients, including: appellate law, asset securitization, bank lending and regulation, corporate-securities, labor and employment law, tax, antitrust, intellectual property, environment, health care, real estate, oil, gas and natural resources, bankruptcy, specialized criminal defense, business litigation and international transactions.

These areas are serviced through 12 practice groups, many led by lawyers who are nationally recognized as being among the best in the United States. These practice groups have been added and developed over the years as the firm has acquired clients requiring representation in these areas.

Richard D. Haynes

Early in its history, Haynes and Boone recognized the need to establish a philosophy for managing itself and its relationships with its clients. That philosophy embraces delivering the highest quality legal services, responsiveness to client needs, understanding a client's business, strong communication, a caring attitude, excellent management of the delivery of legal services, citizenship, and respect for clients, lawyers and support staff.

Also present is a firm culture of teamwork and fairness. "There is an inherent fairness with each individual, whether he or she be a partner or an associate or a runner in the mail room," says Richard D. Haynes. "We have a team concept: It's fairness, it's respect, it's camaraderie. I have always encouraged our lawyers to refer to ourselves as 'we' rather than 'I.' It's subtle, but I think the client understands that this is a team effort rather than a one-man deal."

This culture has remained a guiding force as the firm has grown from two lawyers in 1970 to more than 200 today. And while the firm has grown steadily, the firm has been able to maintain a balance of large-firm expertise and small-firm personal service.

This is in large part because Haynes and Boone has applied the most up-to-date business procedures to firm management. "We were able to grow up in the era of the development of law office management," says Boone. "As a result, Haynes and Boone was responsive to meeting the changes in the marketplace, in law office management."

As a relatively young firm, much of Haynes and Boone's professional expertise has been developed from within. Each year Haynes and Boone conducts a detailed and exhaustive recruiting program at major law schools throughout the country and a comprehensive summer associate pro-

gram at its various offices.

In more recent years, Haynes and Boone has added to the depth and breadth of its practice by a selective process of lateral hiring from other firms as well as by merging or combining with other firms.

"Our decisions were always made to grow to meet the needs of our client business base," says Mike Boone. "We never made decisions to grow just for growth's sake." In all cases, Haynes and Boone has added associates and partners based on their legal talent, professionalism, personal character and commitment to their

practice and clients.

One of the major influences on the practice of law and firm management in the past 15 years has been the advent of the computer. Early on Haynes and Boone recognized the benefits of technology and has been a leader in the use of computers to help manage client documentation, office administration, billings and legal library resources.

The end result has been that Haynes and Boone lawyers are able to devote a maximum amount of time, as Mike Boone says, "to hard work doing first-class, quality legal work."

COHAN, SIMPSON, COWLISHAW, ARANZA & WULFF

Founded in July 1986, Cohan, Simpson, Cowlishaw, Aranza & Wulff brought together 10 attorneys who desired the best of both worlds: They wanted to practice law without the bureaucratic constraints inherent in large firms, but they wanted to bring big-firm sophistication to their practice as well.

Today, Cohan, Simpson, Cowlishaw, Aranza & Wulff has nine partners and nine associates and is one of Dallas' outstanding law firms. The firm's practice covers a broad spectrum of substantive areas: antitrust, banking, commercial transactions, real estate, lending (including loan workouts), insurance, corporations, securities, tax, environmental law, public utility regulation, bankruptcy, product liability, trade regulation, and commercial litigation.

The firm's clients range from individual entrepreneurs and small businesses to national corporations. The firm represents several clients in the financial services industry, including Bankers Trust Company

and Texas Commerce Bank; Alexander & Alexander Inc., a national insurance broker; S&A Restaurant Corporation, which operates the Steak and Ale and Bennigan's restaurant chains; Burger King Corporation; and Gulf States Utilities Company.

Other clients are in industries that range from telecommunications and computer software to brewing and horse breeding. The firm represents a number of major Dallas-based corporations as well as handling regional affairs for major corporations based outside the city.

The firm has a substantial trial practice in state and federal court, and is on the cutting edge of alternative dispute resolution. In 1988, the firm's attorneys resolved a major complex antitrust dispute in just three months through a unique arbitration process. By comparison, two to three years would have been required for litigation. For the effort, the firm received the Significant Achievement Award from the Center for Public Resources in New York.

The firm's attorneys attended top-flight colleges and law schools and earned considerable scholastic

The Transactions Group

honors. In 1988, a Dallas executive search and recruiting company gave Cohan, Simpson, Cowlishaw, Aranza & Wulff the highest rating of any Dallas law firm for its lawyers' distinguished academic backgrounds and achievements. The firm's founders also have Texas and Dallas roots: three of them grew up in the city.

Dallas has made a big contribution to the growth of the firm; and in turn, Cohan, Simpson, Cowlishaw, Aranza & Wulff encourages its attorneys to become involved in pro bono matters and be active in other professional, community and charitable organizations. For example, partner Lee Simpson served two terms on the Dallas City Council, several years on the board of the Dallas Area Rapid Transit Authority, and as a member of the Dallas Citizens Charter Review Committee. Partner Patrick Cowlishaw served as President of the Board of Legal Services of North Texas, and a number of attorneys have won awards for their pro bono work.

The Litigation Group

COOPERS & LYBRAND

A history of overcoming adversity has earned Dallas the reputation of a "can do" city. Whether through charitable contributions or civic leadership, Dallas' citizens get involved. Since 1930, Coopers & Lybrand professionals have been involved in Dallas giving of their time, their money and their expertise.

The Coopers & Lybrand Supporting Youth Education program holds special meaning to Dallas office personnel in that youth education has been identified as a critical area of need by city leaders. Both locally and nationally, Coopers & Lybrand places community involvement as a high priority. Specifically, Supporting Youth Education has been identified as the Firm's number one community involvement priority. This innovative program has received national recognition and is already making a difference for Dallas.

Responsive to Dallas' needs, Coopers & Lybrand has grown with the city. In fact, Coopers & Lybrand has been Dallas' fastest growing accounting and consulting firm over the past five years. As Dallas has diversified and expanded its economic base, Coopers & Lybrand has responded to the needs of the city's business community by training its professionals in the services and industries critical to Dallas' growth.

Just like Dallas, Coopers & Lybrand values and nurtures entrepreneurial spirit. Exemplifying this commitment, the Firm established a separate office in North Dallas in the Galleria to serve high growth, owner-managed businesses such as those in the high technology industry. Staff in this office focus on specific opportunities and solutions for emerging businesses.

With a work force of more than 500 partners and staff in its downtown and North Dallas offices, Coopers & Lybrand serves companies of all sizes. Some of the Firm's local

clients include ARCO Oil and Gas Company; BANK ONE, TEXAS, NA; Hall-Mark Electronics Corporation; I.C.H. Corp.; Lennox International Inc.; Parkland Memorial Hospital; Oryx Energy Company; Rexene Products Corporation; and Valhi, Inc.

As diverse as the city, Coopers & Lybrand Dallas has service focuses in banking, business reorganization services, energy, health care, information systems, insurance, international, litigation services, manufacturing, mergers & acquisitions, real estate, resource productivity, and retail/distribution.

Going forward, Coopers & Lybrand remains committed to applying creativity and innovation to meet the changing needs of the Dallas community. Combining all disciplines of the Firm — including audit, tax, management consulting and

Above are Coopers & Lybrand's Dallas Partners-in-Charge. From Left to Right: Murray H. Schofel — Management Consulting Services; Harry D. Spring — Actuarial, Benefits and Compensation; John S. Furst — Tax Services; Seated: Jerry W. Walker — Dallas Office Managing Partner

actuarial, benefits and compensation consulting — Coopers & Lybrand employs a team approach in achieving solutions for business.

Tracing its roots back nearly a century, Coopers & Lybrand was started in Philadelphia in 1898 and has grown to a worldwide organization with 50,000 partners and staff in 580 offices located in 102 countries. Headquartered in New York, Coopers & Lybrand is among the largest accounting and consulting firms in the world.

GARDERE & WYNNE

Businesses, from the largest Fortune 500 corporation to the smallest start-up enterprise, face an increasingly complex maze of legal issues. Gardere & Wynne recognizes that a law firm must anticipate and respond to business needs and emerging trends to fully serve its clients. To that end, the firm offers a full range of legal services for individuals and businesses, encompassing all levels of trial and appellate practice and all forms of business and financial transactions.

With more than 240 attorneys and paralegals, the firm has nine formal sections and numerous practice groups. In addition to the scope and depth of legal experience in traditional and specialized areas of law, the firm structures certain sections and practice groups along industry lines. Examples are in the fields of emerging technologies, energy, health care, communications, insurance and aviation. Other practice groups have been developed to provide legal guidance and services in areas — for example, bankruptcy, labor, environmental and intellectual property — that cut across industry lines and impact virtually every business. This organizational structure serves one objective: to provide clients with legal services that achieve their goals.

To take advantage of geographic diversity, Gardere & Wynne became a founding member of two national legal organizations — The Network and the TechLaw Group. The Network responds to clients' regional and international needs through a nexus of stellar firms in key states and countries. Gardere & Wynne clients benefit by having preferred access to "local" counsel wherever their business occurs. The TechLaw Group enhances Gardere & Wynne's resources and range of experience in technology law and related areas.

Gardere & Wynne's pride in excellence has been melded from the quality, hard work and professional devotion of its staff and members. Its imagination, drive and insight have resulted in enhanced legal services to clients. The firm has been, and continues to be, well-recognized as a leader in innovative bankruptcy, corporate, banking, finance and loan workout transactions. It has handled sophisticated work for some of the largest business transactions in modern Dallas history.

Gardere & Wynne's practice of controlled growth mirrors the growth and development of the Dallas business community as a whole. Continually expanding its depth of practice in the traditional areas, the firm also has aggressively expanded the breadth of its practice into several emerging areas. From less than 75 lawyers in 1980, the firm enters the 1990s more than 200 strong, ready to respond to the challenges of the coming decade.

Gardere & Wynne balances modern innovations with its many established traditions. They include timely and courteous responses from firm members, the nurturing of legal excellence and ethics, and an atmosphere of personability and conviviality.

Another long-standing tradition is the firm's commitment to its involvement in the community. Along with its active participation in traditional bar and chamber

---

GARDERE & WYNNE

Formal Sections

Banking and Creditors' Rights	Private Business
Corporate and Securities	Real Estate
Energy/Environmental	Tax
Intellectual Property	Trial
Labor	

Practice Groups

Antitrust	Health Care
Appellate	Immigration
Aviation	Insurance
Bankruptcy	International
Communications	Liquor Control
Construction/Surety	Legislative/Governmental Relations
Domestic Relations	
Emerging Technologies	Products Liability
Employee Benefits/ERISA	Toxic Torts
Estate Planning	White Collar Crime
Government Contracts	

Managing Partner Barry Drees oversees the entire range of Gardere & Wynne's practices and services.

activities, and in legal and business seminars, Gardere & Wynne personnel make significant donations of time and resources to a broad range of educational and charitable institutions. Many are board members or officers of cultural and arts organizations. Attorneys teach at local universities and tutor underprivileged students. For many years, Gardere & Wynne has actively participated in the funding and staffing of the city's law magnet high school.

In 1991, the firm will have one of its own serve as president of the Dallas Bar Association. Recently, the firm was recognized as "Firm of the Year" by Legal Services of North Texas for its unsurpassed contribution in the performance of pro bono legal work. The firm is a consistent supporter of the United Way campaign, and in 1989, the firm recorded the highest contribution among participating law firms. The firm and its lawyers have been founding and sustaining members of numerous business, arts and civic organizations, including the U.S./ Mexico Chamber of Commerce, The

Gardere & Wynne is one of the largest full-service law firms in the Southwest and a major player in Dallas' growth as a leading world center of business development and activity.

500 Inc. and the city of Dallas Environmental Health Commission.

Thus, Gardere & Wynne lives up to its responsibility as a full-service firm with its contributions to the profession and to the community. The history of Dallas business is reflected directly in the history of the firm: impelled by the one characteristic which sets Dallas apart from the rest of the nation — its indomitable and indefatigable spirit, drive, compassion and vision, which is often reduced to the single, symbolic rubric, "the entrepreneurial spirit."

"The characteristics that set Dallas apart from other cities in the Southwest are the diversity of its economic and human resources and the resilience of its business community," says Barry D. Drees, the firm's managing partner. "It is our goal at Gardere & Wynne to be an integral element in strengthening and broadening these attributes."

M/A/R/C INC.

Marketing research — the discipline of taking a representative sample of consumers and asking them what they bought and what they thought of their purchase — was virtually nonexistent back in 1950 when Cecil B. "Bud" Phillips began building a research division for Dallas advertising agency Tracy-Locke.

Today, marketing research is a $2.3 billion industry, of which M/A/R/C Inc. is a recognized leader.

In the 1950s manufacturers rarely tested concepts, products and advertising before spending vast sums of money. Few analyzed data collected from consumers to solve marketing problems. And tracking consumer behavior to determine the effectiveness of an ad campaign or to uncover trends in consumer habits was the exception, not the rule. A few packaged goods giants, such as Procter & Gamble or General Foods America, had embryonic organized research facilities, but the Southwest had none.

In this atmosphere, the region's first marketing research department, Marketing And Research Counselors (now M/A/R/C), started pounding the pavement for business. One major Tracy-Locke client, when presented with a report on how consumers were using his company's product, unceremoniously dumped the work in the trash. "You're wasting your time," he said.

Other clients, however, reacted enthusiastically to the department's efforts. In just a few years, almost every Tracy-Locke client became a research believer, including the client who had first responded negatively.

M/A/R/C also began to receive requests for studies from marketers that were not Tracy-Locke clients. At first these were turned down, but as their volume increased it became clear that there was a tremendous demand for M/A/R/C's services and a genuine need for research on a much

*Bud Phillips
Chairman & CEO*

wider scale. As a result, in 1965 Tracy-Locke spun off M/A/R/C into a subsidiary, still headed by Phillips. In 1985, M/A/R/C was first publicly traded.

Today M/A/R/C is engaged in two main businesses: custom marketing research and highly sophisticated database marketing. M/A/R/C, in fact, is the nation's second-largest custom marketing researcher. This discipline gathers information on consumer attitudes and buying behaviors. M/A/R/C maintains the nation's largest electronic data collection network through eight full-service offices in addition to its headquarters in Las Colinas. M/A/R/C's blue-chip clients market everything from snack foods to financial services.

M/A/R/C also offers database marketing, a new and sophisticated form of direct marketing that uses computer technology and advanced analysis. As the hottest area of consumer marketing, database marketing can enhance actual sales or boost coupon redemption, and M/A/R/C is setting trends in perfecting its applications.

Because its clients are spread throughout the country, M/A/R/C has always benefitted from Dallas' central location and its modern airport. "Dallas/Fort Worth International Airport is a vital asset to us and to the city," says Phillips, company chairman and chief executive officer. Dallas also offers an intangible asset: "It's the attitude of the people of Dallas — it's always been positive toward growth, even during the last few tough years. The quality of the people of this city is very high, and that's definitely another one of the advantages of doing business in Dallas."

Headquartered in a six-story, 146,000-square-foot facility, M/A/R/C has 437 full-time employees. Apart from Phillips, top management includes Sharon M. Munger, president; Elmer L. Taylor, vice chairman; and Peter B. Bogda, executive vice president.

RTKL ASSOCIATES INC.

Celebrating a decade of design excellence, the Dallas office of RTKL Associates Inc. opened with a staff of seven in 1979. Now, nearing the 120 mark in personnel, it is the second largest RTKL office, offering full architectural design services, planning and urban design, interiors and graphic design.

Since its founding in 1946, the architectural firm's growth has spiraled from an Annapolis, Maryland basement to contemporary headquarters in Baltimore. Its gross billings topped $52 million in 1988, covering retail, mixed-use, hotel, institutional and medical projects worldwide.

With more than 600 employees in five offices (Baltimore, Dallas, Fort Lauderdale, Washington, D.C. and Los Angeles), RTKL's scope of services encompasses programming, planning and urban design, graphics, interiors and structural, mechanical and electrical engineering. Ranked as the sixth-largest architectural firm nationwide by *Building Design & Construction* magazine, the firm has been the recipient of more than 100 regional and national awards.

Although the firm's projects dot the globe, RTKL of Dallas remains an integral part of the community, both individually and collectively. In its commitment to urban revitalization, RTKL provided the master plan for the State-Thomas and Bryan Place projects, both adjacent to downtown Dallas. The office has offered its planning expertise to the neighboring cities of Richardson and Arlington. Further, staff members have been involved in planning committees affecting Dallas' growth.

Additionally, the firm has contributed significantly to the Dallas Museum of Art, the Dallas Symphony Association, McKinney Avenue Transit Authority, the Dallas Opera, Junior League, Texas Society of Architects, Dallas Zoological Society and North Texas Public Broadcasting, among others. Employees have actively participated in the United Way and March of Dimes Walkathon.

RTKL also sponsors scholarships to outstanding architectural students and participates in the Dallas Independent School District's executive classroom program every year. Upon graduation, some interns are offered permanent positions with RTKL.

"We only get better by working with talented people," says Joseph Scalabrin, FAIA, vice chairman and RTKL managing principal in Dallas. "That's why we have such a strong national recruiting program."

Whether they are recent graduates or 10-year veterans, RTKL's professionals function as a group of teams. "Teamwork is at the heart of our philosophy," a brochure states. "Our work and projects are too complex for an individual."

RTKL believes that its design teams should use technology to its fullest while focusing on one purpose: to serve human needs. The company recognizes that people want to be comfortable and feel good about the buildings around them. Thus, appropriateness underlies RTKL's attitude toward design. Structures are created with respect for natural and man-made surroundings.

Tysons Corner Center, McLean Virginia. Photo by Hedrick-Blessing.

For those reasons, RTKL has gathered recognition and "a reputation so good it's our best form of marketing," says Scalabrin. In fact, 80 percent of RTKL's business is repeat clientele.

While the Dallas office is noted for its national and regional architecture (i.e. The Quadrangle and Berkshire Court in Dallas), the international market has opened up in the past two years. Projects are under way in England, Japan and Australia, among others, which comprise 20 percent of the office's business.

"We look beyond the boundaries," says Scalabrin, adding that the process is made easier by the access to national and international markets via Dallas/Fort Worth International Airport.

"We very much believe in the long view — not necessarily the next year, but the next 10," Scalabrin continues. "We will sacrifice short-term gains for long-term investments. That's why RTKL's expertise in mixed-use, hotel, resort and retail projects is in demand internationally as well as domestically."

The Quadrangle, Dallas, Texas. Photo by Joe C. Aker.

JONES, DAY, REAVIS & POGUE

By the time Jones, Day, Reavis & Pogue formed its Dallas office on January 1, 1981, the law firm was well on its way to becoming a major national presence with international reach.

"Our firm's philosophy is to service our clients wherever they might be," says James L. Baumoel, regional managing partner. "It was clear when we opened our Dallas office that Dallas was and would continue to be a very important business and financial center, and we needed to be here."

Jones Day Dallas began with approximately 35 lawyers through a merger with the Dallas law firm of Meyers, Miller, Middleton, Weiner & Warren.

Today, Jones Day Dallas has matured to an office of about 140 attorneys engaged in broad-based corporate, real estate, tax and litigation practice. Jones Day is unique in the city's legal community. As a separate entity, the Dallas office of Jones Day would be among the city's largest law firms. However, Jones Day Dallas is also part of one of the world's largest law firms, with more than 1,156 lawyers and 17 offices worldwide. In July 1989, with the opening of the Tokyo office, Jones Day became the first law firm in Texas to establish an office in the Pacific Rim. And in October 1989, it opened the doors of an office in Brussels, the capital of the European Community.

As an integral part of the world's second-largest law firm, Jones Day Dallas brings unique resources, expertise and capabilities to practicing law in Dallas. "Dallas is a great city in which to do business," Baumoel says. "The business community is open to anyone with good ideas who is willing to work hard. Dallas has been very receptive to us."

Robert L. Meyers III, head of the firm's Construction Section, James L. Baumoel, Regional Managing Partner, and Francis P. Hubach Jr., head of the firm's Real Estate Group.

In Dallas, as in the firm's other offices, lawyers are organized by major practice groups to facilitate practice development, training and quality control. The groupings stress the global focus of the firm rather than an individual office orientation. Yet the divisions are not rigid; there is regular interaction and coordination among five practice groups, which are:

The Corporate Group — The Corporate Group handles mergers, acquisitions, reorganizations and joint ventures. This group is involved in equity and debt offerings and initial public offerings and has particular expertise in "securitized" financings. Jones Day Dallas also has a rapidly expanding creditors' rights and bankruptcy practice.

The Litigation and Government Regulations Groups — The practice of the Litigation and Government Regulations Group include product liability, white-collar crime, corporate and securities, trademark disputes, unfair competition, copyright, labor, taxation and all types of commercial litigation. The Dallas office has special capabilities in grand jury representation and takeover and director liability litigation and is well known for its antitrust expertise. These groups also are involved extensively in environmental, occupational and health laws and other government regulatory matters.

The Real Estate/Construction Group — The Real Estate/Construction Group has been at the forefront in the securitization of the real estate industry through creating real estate investment trusts, so-called vulture funds, pooled disposition and acquisitions funds and other transactions. The Dallas Construction Section represents all aspects of the construction industry. Jones Day lawyers have participated in all types of major real estate and construction projects, including hotels, office complexes,

Robert A. Profusek, head of the firm's Mergers and Acquisitions Section, and Richard K. Kneipper, head of the firm's Financial Institutions Section.

ger of two Cleveland law firms. The firm opened an office in Washington, D.C. in 1946, and by 1973, the concept of a national law firm began to take shape with the opening of an office in Los Angeles. Other offices followed: Columbus, Ohio in 1980, Dallas in 1981, and Austin, Texas in 1984. In 1986, the firm merged with Surrey & Morse. With offices in London, New York, Paris, Riyadh as well as Washington, D.C., Surrey & Morse brought acknowledged expertise in international law to Jones Day.

Subsequent to the merger, Jones Day continued its pattern of geographic expansion, opening offices in Hong Kong in 1986, Chicago and Geneva in 1987, and Atlanta, Pittsburgh, Tokyo and Brussels in 1989. The Atlanta office resulted from a merger with Hansell & Post, one of

the Southeast's most distinguished law firms.

Throughout its growth and expansion, Jones Day has always recognized its obligation to contribute to the community. Because of its commitment, its lawyers participate actively in a broad range of community service and civic organizations in each of the cities in which Jones Day has offices.

In Dallas, the firm supports, and Jones Day lawyers are active participants in the "Adopt-A-Monument" program, the Dallas Symphony Orchestra, the Dallas Museum of Art, the Dallas Opera, the Dallas Theater Center, The 500 Inc., the Dallas Summer Musicals, the Dallas Repertory Theater, the Dallas County Historical Society, the Historic Preservation League, the Dallas Easter Seal Society, the American Diabetes Association, the Arthritis Foundation, the Kent Waldrep National Paralysis Foundation, the Wadley Guild, the Dallas Arboretum and Botanical Society, the Science Place, the Central Dallas Association and the United Way.

Litigation partners Terence M. Murphy, Chester J. Hinshaw and Sydney B. McDole stand in the firm's mock courtroom located in its new Litigation Center.

multifamily residential buildings, pollution control facilities, sports arenas and shopping centers.

The Tax Group — The Tax Group specializes in real estate, international, corporate transactions, oil and gas, financial, public finance and ERISA/benefit-related matters. Dallas tax lawyers participate in the most sophisticated and creative tax structuring projects throughout the firm's domestic and international offices, and are involved regularly in creating new securitized products and tax strategies in the compensation area.

The roots of Jones Day reach back nearly 100 years to 1893, when the firm first was formed by the mer-

JACKSON & WALKER

Photo by Jim Sims.

Jackson & Walker is one of the 10 largest Texas-based law firms with more than 200 attorneys located in Dallas, Fort Worth, Houston and New Orleans.

With one of the region's longest and most distinguished legal traditions, Jackson & Walker has its origins in Dallas because the firm has found substantial advantages to practicing law in this distinctive city.

As Managing Partner Michael C. French explains it: "One of Dallas' primary advantages is its diverse economic base, which has resulted in nearly 100 companies relocating their headquarters to the area since 1980. Since Dallas combines local and international accessibility with unparalleled quality of life it offers opportunities to all types of industries either located or doing business in the area."

Since its inception Dallas has been a major trade and distribution center. Established in the late 1800's, the firm's founding partners played key roles in the development of Dallas and the formation of a number of its major corporations. Although the firm has expanded throughout Texas and into Louisiana, Jackson & Walker continues to take an active role in the Dallas/Fort Worth economy.

Jackson & Walker has a diverse local and international client base that includes private and public corporations, individuals, partnerships, trusts, estates and other enterprises ranging in size from start-up operations to Fortune 500 companies.

The stability and loyalty of clients, as well as the members of the firm, have been major building blocks for growth. The firm's growth and success have coincided with the progress of its clients as the firm has strived to anticipate and meet clients' rapidly changing needs and provide high-quality, cost-effective service. In doing so, the firm has expanded through hiring superior attorneys, providing thorough supervision and training, and adding or expanding practice areas of particular importance to the client base. The firm expects future growth to be governed and driven by this same philosophy.

As a full-service firm, Jackson & Walker has the capabilities to advise clients in the full range of opportunities and problems they may face in such areas as:

- corporate
- securities
- mergers and acquisitions
- litigation
- banking and financial institutions
- bankruptcy, creditors' rights and corporate reorganization
- taxation (including international tax issues)
- estate planning and administration (including trust and fiduciary matters)
- employee benefits and executive compensation (including ERISA)
- real estate
- energy
- environmental

- labor & employment
- patent, trademark & copyright
- media and first amendment matters
- international (including letters of credit and debt swaps)
- aviation
- appellate
- computer
- construction
- entertainment
- health care
- insurance
- venture capital
- professional liability
- product liability
- white collar criminal defense

To further its commitment to the highest level of professional services, Jackson & Walker maintains state-of-the-art research and support facilities. This includes a number of separate libraries serving all aspects of its prac-

Photo by Martin Vandiver

Photo by Gerry Kano.

tice and access to the most advanced on-line research and information services from individual personal computers. The entire firm operates on a Novell wide-area network utilizing the most current personal computer technology, which allows for rapid and efficient document generation. This includes the linking of all offices by data and phone systems. The firm-wide system is constantly upgraded as new technological developments occur.

Jackson & Walker makes an effort to return something to the community which has witnessed and helped sustain its continued success. Many of the firm's attorneys are involved in pro bono work including efforts for the South Dallas legal clinic. Jackson & Walker has received the "Outstanding Service" award for its work with the clinic.

The firm's attorneys take an active role in lecturing for seminars, writing articles and initiating various programs to either contribute to con-

tinuing legal education or to present current legislative issues to community groups, industry trade groups and clients. The firm also takes an active role in a community literacy program to help address one of the nation's leading concerns.

Many of the firm's attorneys also are active in public affairs. Glenn E. Box, an associate in the firm, devotes 30-40 hours each week as a member of the Dallas City Council — a demanding and time-consuming post that pays a modest weekly stipend.

Jackson & Walker has been and continues to be involved in the formation and development of the West End Historic District in downtown Dallas. Jackson & Walker also contributes financially to more than 100 civic and cultural organizations.

Jackson & Walker is proud to have been a part of Dallas for more than 100 years.

CHAPTER 22

Building Greater Dallas

"We take great pride in calling Dallas home. We are proud of what we have accomplished in this city that is an important part of our successful reputation."

Denny Alberts, Chairman and Chief Executive Officer
— Rosewood Property Company

"A major reason for our move was that Dallas is a good environment for business. Not only does local local government reflect a 'pro-business' attitude, but the workforce of Dallas is exceptionally well-educated."

M. Thomas Lardner, President and Chief Executive Officer
— The Lehndorff (USA) Group of Companies

"Our standards are simple, but that doesn't mean they're easy. When someone in the industry calls my style 'innovative' or 'aggressive,' I have to smile. It's simply a willingness to go the extra mile."

Ellen Terry, Founder
— Ellen Terry Realtors

"Founded in Dallas in 1918, Austin Industries Inc. has grown to become the largest and most diversified construction contractor in the Metroplex, and one of the five largest contractors based in the southern half of the United States."

— Austin Industries

"There's still a great sense of human spirit here. It's been knocked around a bit the last few years, but you can still see the excitement."

Raymond Nasher, Founder The Nasher Company

"Since the company's founding 40 years ago, Centex and Dallas have each played an important role in the development of the other. Centex is proud to have helped build Dallas and we look forward to many more years of progress and prosperity."

Laurence E. Hirsch, President and Chief Executive Officer
— Centex Corporation

Dallas' real estate and construction industry shapes tomorrow's skyline, providing working and living space for its people and attracting new businesses and residents to the area.

ROSEWOOD PROPERTY COMPANY

The Shops and Galleries at The Crescent

The Mansion on Turtle Creek

Long acknowledged as a leader in the development of and investment in high-quality real estate, Rosewood Property Company's success is founded on a "tradition of excellence."

All of Rosewood's properties — from its hotel and office developments to its retail and residential ventures — share a common heritage. As part of the Caroline Hunt Trust Estate, whose extensive holdings include land, oil and gas and other investments, the Dallas-based company is rooted in a commitment to creating unique, high-quality environments enhanced by unparalleled service.

Although Rosewood's outstanding reputation is known worldwide,

Dallas is and always will be a focal point for the company's activities. "We take great pride in calling Dallas home," says Denny Alberts, chairman and chief executive officer of Rosewood Property Company. "We are proud of what we have accomplished in this city which is an important part of our successful reputation."

Perhaps the most visible sign of Rosewood's success is showcased in the company's landmark mixed-use project — The Crescent. The project has been heralded as one of the most extraordinary hotel, retail and office projects in Dallas.

But Rosewood's expertise in high-quality developments extends beyond The Crescent. Its hotel and resort properties as well as restaurants and private clubs epitomize a level of service that is all too rare today. This excellence is exemplified by The Mansion on Turtle Creek and the Hotel Crescent Court. Like the highly esteemed Hotel Bel-Air and other hotels located worldwide, these Rosewood hotels have been consistently honored for their unique design and superlative service.

Rosewood's "tradition of excellence" is also evident in the company's Commercial Group, which has become a symbol of achievement for its high-quality design and expert leasing and management. The group's philosophy is to develop and invest intelligently in projects that embody the Rosewood spirit. In each market area — from The Crescent Office Towers in downtown Dallas to Parkwood Square Shopping Center in suburban Plano — Rosewood's projects offer the prestigious image and quality amenities successful business people demand.

Through the years Rosewood has built an impressive portfolio of land holdings in strategic locations. Many of those acquisitions have been targeted for retail development, a niche which has been an important part of the company's growth and history, with more than a million square feet

Premier Place

in Dallas alone. Rosewood is augmenting its retail portfolio by diversifying its expertise into an expanding array of retail projects.

Completing the Rosewood real estate circle is the company's Residential Group, which specializes in the development of high-quality multi-family properties. The group's vision of the future extends beyond Dallas with additional offices located in key markets throughout the United States.

THE LEHNDORFF (USA) GROUP OF COMPANIES

The Lehndorff Group was founded in Hamburg, West Germany in 1965 by Dr. Hans Abromeit and Jan von Haeften. Their goal was to create a vehicle for direct and pooled investment in North American income-producing property.

In 1971, M. Thomas Lardner opened the first United States office for Lehndorff, managing a $12-million real estate portfolio and staff of four. Today, Lehndorff is one of America's most prominent real estate investment, management and development firms, employing more than 800 people. On behalf of itself and its clients, The Lehndorff Group owns and manages a portfolio of U.S. commercial real estate valued in excess of $4 billion.

Originally based in Chicago, Lehndorff USA moved its headquarters to Dallas in 1978. The city's location in the center of the country, combined with the presence of Dallas/Fort Worth International Airport and Love Field, were major factors in Lehndorff's decision to move here. The move to Dallas put all of Lehndorff's properties within one day's trip, and D/FW Airport also gives Lehndorff executives easy access to Europe and the Far East, where the firm also conducts business.

According to Lardner, now president and chief executive officer, the decision to relocate to Dallas was based on more than the city's strategic location.

"A major reason for our move was that Dallas is a good environment for business," he says. "Not only does local local government reflect a 'pro-business' attitude, but the workforce of Dallas is exceptionally well-educated and performs as if nothing is impossible. The quality of life here is superior. Dallas has a thriving arts community, and the cost of living is relatively low, as evidenced by our taxes and housing costs. All of these factors combine to

make Dallas a world-class city."

Lehndorff is co-developer of the State-Thomas Master Plan, a mixed-use project which will revitalize the city's historic State-Thomas district near downtown. When completed, State-Thomas will be a "new" urban neighborhood, reminiscent of the neighborhoods that have always existed in major metropolitan centers such as New York, Chicago and Toronto.

At 100 acres, the State-Thomas district is the largest tract of undeveloped land situated immediately adjacent to the central business district of a major city in North America. Lehndorff's plans for the area include upscale residential, retail and office development designed to create an urban neighborhood where people can live and work within a short walk of entertainment, restaurants and specialty retail shops.

Ground will be broken in early 1990 on the first residential State-Thomas project, a community of mid-rise luxury flats which will be targeted to young professionals who prefer to live near their downtown offices. Research sponsored by the Central Dallas Association Housing Committee shows there is an affluent market awaiting development of the State-Thomas area.

"We know the market is ready for uptown living," Lardner says. "It's going to be the best of both worlds — an old-fashioned neighborhood with character and a sense of community, sitting literally in the shadow of the Central Business District, in one of the most modern cities in the world."

The State-Thomas Master Plan is evidence of Lehndorff's development capability, which is but one facet of the company's reputation as a leader in the U.S. real estate market, the foundation of which is expertise in the acquisition and management of quality office, retail and industrial

M. Thomas Lardner, President and CEO, The Lehndorff Group.

properties in major urban markets across the country. Lehndorff's portfolio includes some of the most preeminent office buildings and shopping centers in the United States.

These properties include:

• Tysons Corner Center in McLean, Virginia. This enclosed mall has 1.95 million square feet, 220 tenants and is anchored by Bloomingdale's, Hecht's, Woodward & Lothrop and the first Nordstrom on the East Coast. Lord & Taylor will open in the spring of 1990.

• 1001 Pennsylvania Avenue in Washington, D.C., an office building with 755,986 square feet of net rentable space.

• Four Oaks Place in Houston's Galleria area, a 1.7-million-square-foot office complex consisting of four office towers.

Lehndorff also maintains an experienced professional staff to provide asset management and advisory services. In addition, the firm directly manages more than 20 million square feet of commercial and retail properties.

ELLEN TERRY, REALTORS

Ask Ellen Terry, the petite mother of two who is the founder and driving force behind hugely successful Ellen Terry, Realtors, her formula for success, and she is likely to offer this axiom: "If you think you can, or if you think you can't — you're right."

And few have lived this philosophy with more verve and courage than Terry, who in 1976 found herself in a shattered marriage and in the midst of financial adversity. She channeled her emotional energy into finding a way to support her children and found she had an inherent talent for selling real estate. She joined Coldwell Banker and before long became the top residential salesperson in Texas and number two in the nation with that firm.

Buoyed by this success, Terry decided in 1981 to open her own business, specializing in higher-end properties. She never has had to look back. Because Terry's personal commitment to excellence has filtered down through her highly professional work force of more than 40 sales

Finding a way to support her children led Ellen Terry to discover an inherent talent for selling quality homes. Ellen is shown here with her children, Amy, 20, and Todd, 22. They have seen their mother accept many challenges and turn them into opportunities for growth. She tells them, "Life is 10 percent what you make it, and 90 percent how you take it."

associates and 13 support staff, her firm in 1988 sold more million dollar plus homes than anyone in Dallas County.

But the accolades do not stop there. ABC Television has called Ellen Terry, Realtors one of the most successful real estate firms in America. Indeed, the sales associates are believed to have among the highest annual dollar volume sales of any single office company in the business; in the company's first eight years it had sales of more than $900 million.

Ellen Terry's story has been featured in a number of magazine and newspaper articles, including *USA Today*. She received the Distinguished Alumni Award from Southern Methodist University, where she graduated in 1961, and she was named Realtor of the Year by the Greater Dallas Board of Realtors. Terry is also a sought-after motivational speaker who has parlayed her life experiences into common-sense advice and inspiration.

Perhaps the most prestigious honor for Terry's corporation, however, has been its affiliation with Sotheby's International Realty and the very exclusive Estates Club of world-class real estate firms. Ellen Terry, Realtors, as of 1989, is one of only seven firms in the United States invited to belong to both.

Ellen Terry's company has a very high presence in Dallas' most exclusive neighborhoods, and its reputation of integrity, professionalism, productivity and client satisfaction is stellar.

"Our standards are simple" says Terry. "But that doesn't mean they're easy. When someone in the industry calls my style 'innovative,' I have to smile. It's simply a willingness to go the extra mile." She adds, "Of course, I'm flattered when others in the industry emulate our methods and techniques."

Ellen Terry's desire to stay on

Ellen Terry's own life underscores her company's philosophy that high standards and strong desire produce excellence. Ellen Terry, Realtors is Dallas' premier residential real estate firm, specializing in the city's most prestigious homes.

that cutting edge was her motivation behind the addition of a Leasing and Property Management Division in 1987. Her goal was to enhance the company's ability to offer this complete service to fulfill all residential real estate needs. Ability to provide this type of superior service caught the attention of executives relocating to Dallas who suggested that Terry create a division dedicated to fulfilling the needs unique to the relocating executive. In March of 1989 the Relocation Division was created for just this purpose.

Amazing as it may seem, in less than a decade Ellen Terry has come from what one might call "the bottom of the minus-minus-minus column" to creating a company that has been referred to as the Cadillac of residential real estate brokerage firms in the Dallas area. And neither Ellen Terry nor her company show any signs of slowing down.

AUSTIN INDUSTRIES, INC.

Founded in Dallas in 1918, Austin Industries, Inc. has grown to become the largest and most diversified construction contractor in the Metroplex, and one of the five largest contractors based in the southern half of the United States.

Austin Industries is employee owned, with 6,000 employee-owners. The company's four subsidiaries — Austin Bridge, Austin Commercial, Austin Industrial and Austin Paving — perform heavy, commercial and industrial construction.

From the beginning, Austin Industries was instrumental in building Dallas, from the now-famous Triple Underpass to NCNB Plaza, the

Austin Industries built office, computer and garage facilities for American Airlines at CentrePort IV.

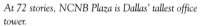

At 72 stories, NCNB Plaza is Dallas' tallest office tower.

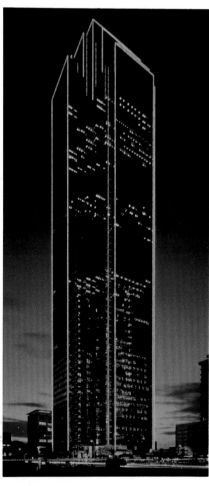

largest and tallest building in the city. The company also has constructed many of the electrical power stations that furnish power for the Metroplex and a variety of manufacturing and commercial facilities.

Throughout the years, Austin constructed large portions of the city's major transportation arteries: Central Expressway, Stemmons Freeway, LBJ Freeway and the Dallas North Tollway. Currently, the company is building the largest highway project in North Texas: the five-level Interstate 20/35W interchange in Tarrant County.

Many well-known Dallas commercial building landmarks were constructed by Austin, including NCNB Plaza, Texas Commerce Tower, the Loews Anatole Hotel and the Towers at Williams Square.

Austin Industries also has worked closely with most of Dallas' leading corporations, including constructing facilities for:

- American Airlines
- *The Dallas Morning News*
- Electronic Data Systems (EDS)
- GTE
- Methodist Hospitals of Dallas
- Neiman-Marcus
- Presbyterian Hospital of Dallas
- Southwest Airlines
- Texas Instruments

Dallas and Austin Industries have grown together for more than 70 years. Today, Austin Industries continues earning its reputation — achieving superior performance through people who are the best at what they do.

THE NASHER COMPANY

NorthPark is a fully integrated development that includes shops and restaurants, office buildings and residential sites.

Driven by a passion for excellence and guided by an uncompromising commitment to quality, NorthPark founder and owner Raymond D. Nasher has created a testament to the vision and spirit of Dallas pioneers.

For more than 30 years, The Nasher Company has imaginatively fostered and carefully crafted the growth and development of more than 200 acres at the crossroads of North Central Expressway and Park Lane.

The master-planned community, from fields of cotton, includes NorthPark Center, NorthPark National Bank, NorthPark Office Center and the luxurious Lane Park residential subdivision.

Widely recognized as one of North Texas' most distinctive and popular retail complexes, NorthPark Center reflects the style and ambiance created through uniformity of design and bold cultural expression. Anchored by Neiman Marcus, Lord & Taylor, Dillards, and JC Penney, more than 150 specialty shops, boutiques, restaurants and theaters feature year-round family entertainment, trendsetting styles and contemporary accessories for home and office.

In 1966, NorthPark National Bank was founded in response to a need for a more personalized style of banking. In 1970, assets were $18.5 million; by 1989, assets had shown dramatic growth to $730 million, making it the largest independent bank in Texas.

On the east side of Central Expressway, the first building in NorthPark Office Center, One NorthPark, was completed in 1973.

The second building was added in 1976, the third in 1978 and Four NorthPark in 1982. The four now provide over one million square feet of quality office space.

In 1985, The Nasher Company developed Lane Park, an upscale residential community near NorthPark where residents take pride in one of the city's most prestigious neighborhoods.

It is unusual for an individual developer to remain in one place for 30 years, maintaining and expanding his original concept. Despite expansive involvement in numerous other governmental, cultural, educational and development projects, Nasher has fulfilled his vision and commitment to providing NorthPark-area residents with an enhanced, aesthetically pleasing community — from housing, banking, business and shopping to entertainment and culture.

Nasher says he came to Dallas in the 1950s because he recognized it as one of the key growth areas in the United States. "Texas had great opportunity, and I thought it would be exciting to be a part of the enthusiasm and pioneering of the area," he says.

"There's still a great sense of spirit here," he adds. "You can feel the excitement."

Currently, NorthPark is only half completed. A 55-acre tract to the southwest to be known as NorthPark Plaza is in the planning stages, and much of the remaining area awaits development. Plans include orderly growth and expansion of the shopping center, the addition of a hotel and improved transit within the NorthPark area.

NorthPark Center was the first fully enclosed shopping mall in the Metroplex and remains one of the area's most elegant and distinctive retail centers.

CENTEX CORPORATION

While the Dallas real estate development and construction industries were struggling through some of the worst times in their history in the late 1980s, Centex Corporation — a company whose name is synonymous with residential and commercial building in Dallas — was enjoying record business volume and reaping record profits.

In fiscal 1989, for example, despite the depressed Texas economy, Centex's revenues soared to an all-time high of nearly $1.85 billion. It

Through the years, Centex, through its Dallas-based general construction subsidiary J.W. Bateson, has completed some of the area's most renowned structures, including Texas Stadium in 1970, top, and the Morton H. Meyerson Symphony center in the fall of 1989, lower.

was the second straight record-breaking year for company revenues and the 20th consecutive fiscal year of profitability since the company became publicly held in 1969.

These remarkable achievements came as no surprise, however, to those who have watched Centex grow from a small regional company in 1950 into one of the largest nationwide builders in America.

Over the past four decades, Centex management has demonstrated a rare talent for turning adversity into opportunity, and at no time in its history has that talent been more amply demonstrated than during the recent real estate development crisis.

In the fields of homebuilding, general construction and construction products, Centex was among the most successful companies during the dramatic ups and downs of the 1980s. The decade saw Centex emerge as one of only a handful of truly national homebuilders, while also firmly establishing itself as the leading homebuilder in Texas. In the 1990s, the company will be building and selling quality homes in 34 markets across the country.

As a multi-market homebuilder, Centex has few peers. The company's reputation for building quality homes was enhanced by its merger in the early 1970s with Fox & Jacobs, the largest single-family homebuilder in the Southwest at that time. By 1980, Centex subsidiaries had built and sold 100,000 homes.

Since then, the pace has quickened even more as Centex increased its homebuilding markets from eight to 34. By the end of 1989, more than 150,000 homes had been built by the company, and Centex had established its own title and insurance businesses and savings bank as important adjuncts to its new home sales operation.

"In the 1990s, we anticipate substantial growth in our homebuilding operation as Centex moves into higher-priced markets where margins are usually higher," says Laurence E. Hirsch, president and CEO. "We plan to direct our focus toward the move-up market, while continuing to strengthen our first-time buyer market through quality and innovation."

Meanwhile, Centex also has become one of the nation's busiest companies in general construction, an area in which it has excelled since purchasing Dallas-based J.W. Bateson Construction Company in the mid 1960s. Included among the major Dallas projects built by Centex are such landmarks as Southland Life Building, One Dallas Centre, Arco Tower, the former Republic Bank complex (now NCNB), Texas Stadium, the Dallas Museum of Art and the Morton H. Meyerson Symphony Center.

In the 1980s, Centex expanded geographically and undertook general construction projects from one end of the country to the other. In 1989, while winning contracts for more than $1 billion in major projects scattered from California to Florida to Maine, Centex also boosted its gen-

© 1989 Nathaniel Lieberman

eral construction revenues and its backlog of projects to all-time highs. At the same time, the company was working to complete its largest single project ever — the $172-million Veterans Administration Medical Center in Houston.

"One key to the success of our general construction operation is the solid financial base provided by Centex," says Paul R. Seegers, board chairman. "This enables us to obtain bonding for larger projects and results in less competition in the bidding process."

Innovation has always been an integral part of the Centex approach to building. In the 1950s, when it was still a small company largely unknown outside Texas, Centex began developing Elk Grove Village in Illinois, one of the nation's first master-planned communities and now a large Chicago suburb. In addition to thousands of homes, the company built shopping centers, commercial buildings and industrial parks at Elk Grove Village.

In the mid-1960s, Centex pioneered another innovation in the construction industry when it entered the cement manufacturing and readymix concrete businesses, producing construction products on an ever-increasing scale. Today the company has cement plants and terminals in Texas, Nevada, California, Wyoming and Illinois, and has leased a major aggregate reserve in northern California. In 1986, the company acquired its own gypsum wallboard manufacturing plant and is currently more than doubling the plant's capacity, further enhancing its building materials business.

The 1980s were largely a period of transition, rapid growth and diversification for Centex, setting the stage for the next step in the company's evolution and expansion during the 1990s. As amazing as its growth has been during its first 40 years,

The 2300-square-foot "Charleston," named "Best Product Design" by the Home and Apartment Builders of Metropolitan Dallas in 1988, is one of more than 65,000 homes built in the area by Centex subsidiary Fox & Jacobs.

Hirsch has no doubt that even greater challenges lie ahead.

"As we move into the future, our natural aggressiveness will be tempered by our knowledge of each operation's unique position in its cycle, as well as by our recognition of the fragile economic environment. But as past experience has proved so often, what looks like adversity at first glance may actually be opportunity in disguise."

Because of its financial strength and reputation for quality, Seegers points out, Centex was able to boost its market share in Texas substantially during the slump of the mid-to-late-1980s and is now in excellent position to take advantage of that fact.

"We know that Texas and Dallas are rapidly rebounding from the economic reverses of the past few years," he says. "And while we aren't nearly as dependent on these nearby markets for our overall success as we once were, we are positioned to take full advantage of that rebound."

Centex subsidiary Fox & Jacobs is the largest home builder both in Dallas and in Texas. Originally a builder of first-time homes, F&J now addresses the move-up market with products like the 2600-square-foot "Potomac," priced at less than $135,000.

"The Friday's concept as we know it today was refined at the Greenville Avenue location. New menu items were cultivated and refined, the service style was augmented and the design of future restaurants was developed."

Richard E. Rivera, President and Chief Executive Officer
— TGI Fridays

"Dallas' unique can-do spirit of enthusiasm and entrepreneurship has made Dallas a world-famous city. It has been the perfect climate for helping Mary Kay Cosmetics become one of the largest and most successful cosmetics companies in the world. Thank you Dallas!"

Mary Kay Ash, Chairman Emeritus
— Mary Kay Cosmetics Inc.

"Dallas has always had a strong entrepreneurial spirit. The city has been and continues to be one of BeautiControl's strongest markets. I wouldn't live or work anywhere else."

Richard W. Heath, President and Chief Executive Officer
— BeautiControl Cosmetics Inc.

"The Grand Kempinski Dallas has brought a heretofore unknown brand of European luxury to the city's hotel industry. The tradition of continental excellence traces its roots to the turn of the century."

— Grand Kempinski Dallas

"Dallas is critical to Doubletree because it is a city that is experiencing an economic resurgence and therefore the community is very supportive of business growth."

William Stanton, Regional Vice President/General Manager
— Doubletree Hotels

"I've seen 49 years of growth far beyond the vision of the eye. But most of all, I have been privileged to see the people of Dallas grow with success — for without growth-minded people, there would be no Big D."

Donald J. Carter, President
— Home Interiors & Gifts Inc.

"Our middle and upper management group has 'We try harder' as their own personal work ethic. These are people who like to work harder to give good service, and it's made us an excellent company to do business with."

John West, President
— Hayes Leasing Company

"Guests will be delighted to discover this quiet hotel, resting in the shadow of Dallas' impressive skyline and within minutes of the bustling city. To stay at the Ambassador Plaza Hotel is to step back in time."

— Ambassador Plaza Hotel

"I have a gathering of very loyal and dedicated people who treat our company as though it were their own. In this business where there's not a lot of difference in the products, our customers really seem to appreciate the personal touch of service."

Michael Tidburt, Vice President
— Accent Auto Leasing

"The Southland Corporation, the world's leading convenience retailer and the developer of Cityplace, has forged a proud heritage and looks forward to a bright future in Dallas, the city in which convenience retailing was born."

— *The Southland Corporation*

"Dallas is a city of opportunities. It offers the type of attractions, entertainment and business climate that is attractive to meeting planners and individual travelers alike."

Charlotte St. Martin, President and Chief Executive Officer
— *Loews Anatole Hotel*

"Stouffer believes in Dallas and is betting on Dallas. We are strongly committed to this city and to supporting its economic growth."

William N. Hulett, President
— *Stouffer Hotel Company*

CHAPTER 23

The Marketplace

Dallas' retail establishments, service industries and leisure/ convention facilities offer an impressive variety of choices for Dallas residents and visitors alike.

T.G.I. FRIDAY'S

It was a phrase coined by hard-working young professionals and put to use in a New York City bistro. The phrase — "Thank goodness it's Friday!" — became the highly successful casual theme for T.G.I. Friday's. It also became an American legend.

When the first T.G.I. Friday's opened in 1965 at First Avenue and 63rd Street in Manhattan, it called attention to the dawning of a new era — the singles scene. Arbiters of taste such as *Newsweek* magazine and *Saturday Evening Post* proclaimed Friday's success at capturing the fancy of this booming generation.

It was more than just a new restaurant or bar. It was a new environment — comfortable and relaxing, where customers could enjoy their food and drink.

As the decade progressed, more Friday's opened around the country, including a Dallas location on Greenville Avenue. That location, in

The first T.G.I. Friday's, which opened at First Avenue and 63rd Street in Manhattan, called attention to the dawning of a new era — the singles scene.

Old Town Shopping Center, became the bell cow for the chain and proved that the concept could have nationwide appeal.

By its 25th anniversary in 1990, T.G.I. Friday's operated more than 160 units in the United States and Great Britain, and had signed agreements which would take the chain even further throughout the world.

Dallas is the corporate home for T.G.I. Friday's. The chain was acquired in 1975 by Carlson Companies, Inc., which was the sole shareholder from 1981 to 1983, when the company made its initial public offering. Friday's was taken private again by its chairman, Curtis L. Carlson, in early 1990.

In a highly volatile industry, Friday's boasts impressive statistics such as the highest per-unit sales volume of any nationwide chain. Even though the chain is seeing an entire second generation of customers — in addition to its original customers — Friday's has managed to remain contemporary, doing 50 percent more volume than its closest competitor.

"We stay fresh because we've maintained a broad appeal," says Richard E. Rivera, president and CEO. "We modify the menu without

eliminating old favorites." The timeless appeal of Friday's also has much to do with some of the innovations put in place when Dan Scoggin opened his Greenville Avenue franchise in 1972.

America owes the popularization of frozen and ice cream drinks to Friday's. Friday's created an assortment of smooth frozen alcoholic beverages as well as an array of frozen non-alcoholic ice cream and fruit drinks to satisfy the desires of its customers.

Friday's led the industry in creativity with the invention of finger foods such as potato skins and the popularization of fried zucchini.

The eclectic decor was deliberate and carefully thought out. Memorabilia was and still remains an integral and legendary part of the Friday's look.

"The Friday's concept as we know it today was refined at the Greenville Avenue location," says Rivera. New menu items were culti-

Friday's four-sided bar is surrounded by tiered seating. This creates increased visibility and contributes to the character and atmosphere of the restaurant.

vated and refined, the service style was augmented and the design of future restaurants, down to the exact placement of memorabilia, was developed.

Most Friday's restaurants are designed with large four-sided bars surrounded by tiered seating. Customers have increased visibility, and company officials believe this contributes to the character and atmosphere of its restaurants. Every detail, down to the number of steps to the bar, the lighting and plants is carefully planned.

Also carefully planned is the level of service that customers have come to expect from Friday's employees. To assure quality service, Friday's conducts a strong four-month manager training program which includes a week of "cultural" training in Dallas. Hourly employees are tested, and upon passing, they are certified. The company's performance incentives and extensive recognition programs make the training and certification process fun and rewarding.

As the company reached its quarter-century mark, plans were under way to pursue a more aggressive development program, according to Rivera. The plans include joint ventures, management contracts and franchising as well as company-owned or leased locations.

Franchise development agreements already in place will result in five additional Friday's restaurants in the New York City area, more than 50 Friday's in 15 western European countries and numerous other franchise agreements in the United States.

One of Friday's most successful units has been the one in London,

Memorabilia remains an integral and legendary part of the Friday's look. The eclectic decor is deliberate and thought out.

where British customers flock to the all-American bistro known for its trend-setting menus and eclectic decor.

In keeping with the company's tenet to stay abreast of trends, an experimental concept called Dalts was founded in 1980. More of a grill with lighter entrees and less bar emphasis, Dalts is said to complement Friday's.

Rivera told *Restaurant Hospitality* magazine: "One of the most significant changes in casual dining is that people who started using casual theme restaurants as so-called dating bars have gotten older, so restaurants have had to evolve with the guests." The way Friday's customers use the restaurant has changed, and as its customers grow older, Friday's has evolved to assure that customer needs are being met.

To keep abreast of generational changes, Friday's looks carefully at emerging trends ranging from liquor consumption to noise levels and eating habits.

T.G.I. Friday's is keenly aware of its place in American popular culture, and as the restaurant forges ahead into new world-wide markets, it will bring with it concepts that were first developed in Dallas.

The way Friday's customers use the restaurant has changed, and as its customers grow older, Friday's has evolved to assure that customer needs are being met.

MARY KAY COSMETICS

Mary Kay Ash founded Mary Kay Cosmetics in 1963 to fulfill her dream of an unlimited career opportunity for women everywhere. Currently, nearly 200,000 women in the U.S., Canada and 10 other countries have discovered their potential through Mary Kay careers.

In 1963, Mary Kay Ash filled two important gaps in the marketplace when she founded Mary Kay Cosmetics. She offered women an unprecedented career opportunity and personal instruction in skin care and makeup. Since then, the company that began in a tiny storefront with just Mary Kay and her young son, Richard Rogers, now employs more than 1,500 people, and has nearly 200,000 independent Mary Kay beauty consultants worldwide.

At the age of 25, Rogers received the Marketing Man of the Year award from the American Marketing Association and became one of the youngest presidents of a multimillion-dollar company in the United States.

Today, almost half of all women in the United States have experienced a Mary Kay skin care class or facial. In a national study among consumers who use two or more skin care products a week, those who believe there is a best brand of skin care products named Mary Kay more often than any other single brand.

It all goes back to the proud heritage and shining future of Dallas that Mary Kay echoes. She is the epitome of entrepreneurship, as reflected in the approximately $1 billion in retail sales generated by the sales force each year. As the "first lady of cosmetics," she single-handedly created a company that has enhanced Dallas' fame and wealth. Herself a living legend, Mary Kay has shared the spotlight of success and recognition with the city of Dallas. Her tremendous national recognition, including appearances on "60 Minutes," "Good Morning America" and other network television programs, helps create almost universal brand awareness and focuses attention on Dallas as a quality place to live and do business.

Based on compensation paid to Dallas employees, seminar expenditures and gross income, commissions and incentives earned by more than 14,000 Texas beauty consultants, Mary Kay's total economic effect on Texas is $345 million annually. A large part of that affects Dallas. From cancer research and breast cancer awareness campaigns to the arts and the environment, Mary Kay makes an impact.

Every summer, Dallas' "beauty quotient" goes into triple digits when attractive, intelligent, energetic women entrepreneurs from all over the world gather in the city for the annual Mary Kay Cosmetics Seminar.

When the first seminar was held in 1964, Mary Kay herself hosted a mere 200 people, cooking for all and cleaning up afterward. The event is now Dallas' largest continuously held convention, welcoming 25,000 beauty consultants to four back-to-back three-day extravaganzas. Ten Dallas hotels are booked 10 years in advance to accommodate participants from the United States, Canada, Mexico and other countries including Australia, New Zealand,

West Germany, Argentina, Singapore, Malaysia, Chile, Thailand, Panama and Uruguay. In fact, Dallasites visiting any restaurant, hotel or shop near downtown can be assured of running into at least one famous pink car.

The fact that the annual seminar is held in the middle of the summer gives the local convention business a boost at a time of year when it needs it. Hundreds of workers are needed to construct the stage and run the show, and millions of dollars are spent in local businesses by the company and its beauty consultants.

During the past 25 years, it is estimated that more than a quarter of a million people have come to Dallas for these seminars, many for the first time. Dallas' friendly warmth and hospitality always makes the trip memorable and enjoyable for people who may never have visited Dallas if it were not for the Mary Kay event. Mary Kay's annual seminar and scores of other meetings held in Dallas year-round show a community consciousness reflected throughout the entire corporate culture.

Mary Kay Ash, with more than 25 years of experience in direct selling in 1963, saw a huge lack of economic opportunity for women. She was convinced that women, if only given the chance, could and would achieve greatness. And she was right.

Every beauty consultant begins at the same level, purchasing a beauty showcase. From there, it is up to her to decide how much time and energy she wants to expend on her career. Some women are happy to have a part-time career that earns spending money for clothes, vacations or a college education. Other women go for the top — and get there by advancing at their own pace and promoting themselves through successful selling and recruiting. Top achievers earn as much as $400,000 a year and enjoy rewards like pink cars, luxury vacations and jewelry. And then there is the incredible feeling of new-found self-esteem, confidence and accomplishment that goes with it.

Mary Kay beauty consultants sell by appointment directly to women who appreciate the convenience of personal attention in their homes and offices. Knowledgeable about skin care, glamour and fashion trends, beauty consultants are trained to help women create personalized skin care routines and glamour looks that will fit their lifestyles.

Of Mary Kay's employee base of approximately 1,500, more than 1,000 live in the Dallas/Fort Worth area. The contribution in salaries,

Mary Kay President Richard Bartlett encourages everyone to focus on providing quality products and services. His interest in conservation and other environmental concerns has sparked a successful employee recycling program and other socially conscious projects.

wages, sales and taxes is enormous, but beyond that, Mary Kay shows the direction that a major corporation can take in being a good neighbor and responsible citizen, caring for more than company balance sheets.

The responsible role Mary Kay Cosmetics has taken in making the Dallas area a better place to live and work can be seen particularly in the special relationships between the arts and educational communities and the company.

Mary Kay Cosmetics has supported the Dallas-area Adopt-a-School program, supplying employee volunteers to help enrich the educational experiences of children. Company executives serve as advisors to several area universities, including Baylor University, University of Texas at Dallas and the University of Dallas.

It is the belief of Mary Kay Cosmetics that a community without arts is a dead society. Of particular importance are the performing arts such as the Dallas Opera and the Dal-

Mary Kay's manufacturing facility, located just a block from corporate headquarters, is the largest manufacturer of cosmetics in the Southwest and one of the most efficient cosmetics producers in the world.

Mary Kay's legendary pink cars are awarded to top performers. More than 5,000 Mary Kay cars are on the road from coast to coast.

BELOW: Mary Kay Manufacturing employs more than 450 people who develop, process, assemble, package and ship more than 100 million product units in a typical year.

las Symphony. To show its support, the company donates dollars as well as manpower to the arts.

Mary Kay's unique marketing abilities make it possible to provide a substantial amount of pro bono contributions. The Dallas Opera has received show production assistance from Mary Kay's graphic production and visual communications departments, and design and production assistance on opera programs and other literature from the creative services and reprographics staff.

The company also has underwritten production costs on several arts-related television specials broadcast locally and in other Texas cities. "Birth of an Opera: The Aspern Papers" exposed a wide new audience to the joys of opera, while "Images of Woman: Selections from the Permanent Collection at the Dallas Museum of Art" enabled Dallasites to appreciate the masterpieces of important artists. "Prelude to Greatness" chronicled the development of one of Dallas' most recent and most highly anticipated assets: the Morton H. Meyerson Symphony Center. Many of these programs are now available for schools and universities to use for instruction in the humanities.

But no matter how much more attractive a community is with an active arts program, it cannot be truly beautiful if the landscape is blighted, the water polluted and the air unbreathable. So in early 1989, Mary Kay Cosmetics became one of the first cosmetics companies in the nation to include on its product containers the recycling code from the Society of Plastics Industry. This code identifies the various plastic resins in the containers so those same containers may be recycled efficiently and used again to make stuffing for pillows or plastic lumber, for example.

Additionally, Mary Kay products are packaged in containers free of chloroflourocarbons (CFC) suspected of depleting the earth's ozone. Ozone is that layer of multiatomed oxygen molecules that gives the earth a protective sun screen. None of Mary Kay's aerosol products use CFCs as a propellant either.

On a larger scale, Mary Kay Cosmetics is a leader in encouraging states to adopt the Society of Plastics Industry's uniform coding system to identify all plastics that can be recycled. It is estimated that this would reduce by 30 to 50 percent the volume of domestic garbage that goes into landfills.

The sense of responsibility at Mary Kay toward the quality of the environment is shared by employees with the backing and encouragement of management.

An employee-led recycling program, strongly supported by President Richard Bartlett, an active conservationist and vice chairman of the Texas Nature Conservancy, has been a major success. Such things as non-biodegradable and non-recyclable styrofoam cups are being phased out. Collection bins outdoors and in office and manufacturing areas allow employees to bring recyclable items like glass, aluminum, plastics and newspapers from home. The collected material is sold to recycling centers and a portion of the money is sent to the Texas Nature Conservancy. It is a help to the beauty of mother nature from those who have made the beauty of women a consuming passion.

Cancer research is another project Mary Kay personally feels strongly about. Her compassion has spread company-wide, as shown by support from the Mary Kay Foundation and the sales force of two major cancer research organizations: The Susan G. Komen Foundation and the Wadley Cancer Research Center.

A four-year grant to the Komen Foundation has been established to help in the advancement of breast cancer research. Strong corporate lobbying efforts for insurance coverage of mammogram examinations for women 35 and over are also aimed at increasing awareness and early detection of breast cancer.

And each year at seminar, Mary Kay makes a personal appeal to attendees to support cancer research on behalf of sales force members who have been stricken with the disease and for their own future well-being.

Mary Kay Cosmetics has brought the Texas spirit of entrepreneurship to women all over the world. Through Mary Kay's own brand of motivation, inspiration and enthusiasm, women the world over have achieved greatness.

In Texas alone, approximately 300 women were awarded the use of automobiles from Mary Kay for meeting and exceeding their goals. That brings to more than 5,000 the number of Mary Kay cars on the road nationwide. And while there may be those who make fun of the distinctive pink Mary Kay cars, the question asked over and over by those who drive them is: "What color was the car your company gave you?"

At the top of the Mary Kay sales structure are the esteemed National Sales Directors. Numbering more than 60, they are a strong band of leaders that the sales force looks up to as examples of how far one can advance in Mary Kay. Each of them started at the bottom and set out to change their lives. They sold, they recruited, they overcame obstacles. They rose through their own hard

work, dedication and belief in themselves to become successful entrepreneurs. They soared on wings of an unbeatable spirit they never knew they had.

That spirit is represented in the lobby of Mary Kay's corporate headquarters by a large bronze cast sculpture titled, "On Silver Wings." For those with the dedication and serious ambitions of greatness, it is a symbol of the Mary Kay spirit. Beneath the sculpture are four lines of poetry. There is no author's name, for no one is sure who the author is. But the lines are pure inspiration for anyone who seeks the "American dream" of free enterprise:

I have a premonition that soars on silver wings.
It's a dream of your accomplishment of many wondrous things.
I do not know beneath which sky, or where you'll challenge fate.
I only know it will be high! I only know it will be great!

This bronze sculpture, displayed in the corporate lobby, was especially commissioned by Mary Kay Cosmetics to commemorate the company's 25th anniversary. Mary Kay's favorite poem, "On Silver Wings," served as the inspiration for New Mexico sculptor Norman Boyles.

Seminar, held at the Dallas Convention Center, is the annual event celebrating and recognizing success for thousands of Mary Kay beauty consultants.

BEAUTICONTROL® COSMETICS, INC. SUCCEEDING IN STYLE

In less than a decade, BeautiControl Cosmetics has become a recognized leader in the direct sales cosmetics industry. Headquartered in the Dallas suburb of Carrollton, Texas, BeautiControl has created a unique niche in the marketplace by offering clients a complete image consulting service. The company had over 19,500 Image Consultants in the United States and Canada and sales in excess of $44 million at the end of 1989. Today, it remains the fastest growing cosmetics concern in North America.

Total Image Resource

BeautiControl functions as a Total Image Resource, offering clients more than just innovative products.

The company starts with scientifically advanced skin care systems and conveniently organized, color-coded cosmetics — all of which are fragrance-free, dermatologist, sensitivity and allergy tested. What sets the company apart, however, are its professional, fully-trained Image Consultants and the services they provide.

BeautiControl was the first in the industry to offer free color analysis to determine a client's most flattering makeup and clothing colors. Computer-assisted Personal Image Profiles© — developed and offered exclusively by BeautiControl — help clients make the right fashion choices by determining body type, facial shape and desired makeup and fashion personality. Color-coded fashions and accessories that complement the company's cosmetics and image services are offered exclusively by mail.

Since more women are working than ever before, BeautiControl brings these products and services to them in the workplace through Image Update Workshops™ sponsored by businesses, organizations and clubs. Of course, Consultants continue to provide Image Improvement Clinics at their clients' home or

BeautiControl's unique program of scientifically advanced skin care systems, free color analysis, color-coded cosmetics and Personal Image Profiling helps women project a more coordinated, confident image. . . and can actually save them time and money in the process.

BeautiControl offers women flexible, independent career opportunities that let them control the delicate balance between work and family plus offer exceptional earning potential

pany of entrepreneurs," explains Jinger Heath. "We pride ourselves on offering women the means to enter business for themselves, at a time when increasing numbers are looking for just such an opportunity."

BeautiControl Image Consultants enjoy freedom of self-employment and the ability to control their own lives, coupled with the security of being associated with "The World's Premier Image Company." Training and achievement recognition programs provide continuous support and encouragement. As a woman's career proceeds, BeautiControl's Leadership Development Program guides her as she works her way from individual Consultant to Unit Director with her own sales organization. The appeal of these opportunities is evident: BeautiControl's Consultant turnover rate is half the industry average.

Only in Dallas

Dallas' supportive atmosphere has been instrumental in fostering BeautiControl's growth. The city's commercial orientation, superior

office, and direct mail catalogs make reordering as simple as picking up the phone to call their Consultant or BeautiControl's 800 Reorder Line.

Entrepreneurial Enterprise

Entrepreneurship, as much as image, is in many ways what Beauti-Control is all about. In 1981, Dick and Jinger Heath pooled their life savings to acquire a struggling cosmetics company. Their efforts transformed BeautiControl into one of the decade's greatest success stories.

Today, the Heaths head an established, publicly-traded corporation that has gathered a multitude of honors from the investment community, including recognition by *Forbes* Magazine (November 13, 1989 issue) as the 20th best small company in America. The company provides direct employment for 300 people at its Dallas-area facility, where 77% of all its product offerings are manufactured or assembled.

BeautiControl's entrepreneurial success was recognized in 1989 when Dick, who serves as President and Chief Executive Officer, and Jinger, Chairman of the Board, were named Entrepreneurs of the Year by *Inc.* magazine, Arthur Young and Co. and *The Dallas Morning News.*

"BeautiControl is, in fact, a com-

Innovative, easy-to-use skin care and cosmetics provide the visible results consumers demand.

Jinger and Dick Heath turned a struggling cosmetics company into a recognized industry leader.

The international headquarters and manufacturing facilities for BeautiControl Cosmetics are located in Carrollton, Texas.

quality of life and moderate cost of living combine to provide an incomparable business environment.

BeautiControl, in turn, has generously supported the community through contributions to various charities including the United Way, Children's Hospital and the National Diabetes Association. In addition, the Heaths serve as board or executive committee members with the Susan G. Komen Foundation for breast cancer research, MD Anderson Hospital, the Swiss Avenue Counseling Center, the Salvation Army, the Kidney Foundation and the Dallas Easter Seals Society for Children.

Throughout its history, Dallas has proved to be an exemplary business address, and BeautiControl is pleased to call it home. The future promises only to reinforce the spirit that has contributed to both the city's and company's success.

"Dallas always has had a strong entrepreneurial spirit," says Dick Heath. "It has been and continues to be one of BeautiControl's strongest markets. I wouldn't live or work anywhere else."

BeautiControl's color-coded and clinically pure makeup is fragrance-free, dermatologist, sensitivity and allergy tested.

BeautiControl Image Consultants offer Image Update Workshops to businesses and organizations to help employees and members develop a more polished image. These presentations are an excellent source of new clients for the Consultants.

GRAND KEMPINSKI DALLAS

Though the Grand Kempinski Dallas has only been in existence since 1987, it has brought a heretofore unknown brand of European luxury to the city's hotel industry.

The tradition of continental excellence traces its roots to the turn of the century when the corporation was formed with its first operation near the internationally famous "Unter den Linden" section of Berlin.

The hotel's cafes, suites and salons were a rendezvous location not only for the German rich and powerful but also for European gentry. The one hotel eventually evolved into three highly visible and luxurious properties during the first two decades of the 20th century, eventually becoming a meeting place for Berlin society during the 1920s.

The hotel chain was all but destroyed during World War II, losing its property first to Allied bombs,

then to demarkation as all three sites were in East Berlin.

Undaunted, though its properties and assets were reduced to rubble and ashes, the company shifted its emphasis to West Germany, eventually establishing properties in Munich, Frankfurt, Berlin and Hamburg.

The acquisition of its Dallas property in 1987 followed the merger of Kempinski and German Lufthansa Airlines to become Kempinski International.

Almost simultaneous to the Dallas acquisition, the corporation acquired properties in Hong Kong, Istanbul, Santiago de Chile, Chicago, Toronto and Buenos Aires. Projected

The atrium of the Grand Kempinski Dallas is a favorite rendezvous point.

The Grand Kempinski Dallas offers elegant European-style accommodations in the heart of vibrant North Dallas.

expansion includes the establishment of a hotel in Beijing and Bangkok.

The Grand Kempinski Dallas, located on the vibrant corridor of the Dallas North Tollway, offers more than 530 superbly appointed rooms and suites. All that anyone could expect is available at the Grand Kempinski: on-site health club and tennis courts, limousine service, the finest shops in the city, convenient location and other amenities the discriminating guest has come to expect from the finest European-style accommodations in the world.

The Grand Kempinski Dallas is widely-known to area residents for its superb Malachite Showroom Sunday Brunch as well as its Mediterranean restaurant, Monte Carlo; the cozy Le Cafe; the high-energy night club, Kempi's; the Crystal Ballroom, cornerstone of the hotel's thriving convention trade; and the atrium area, a breathtaking rendezvous point for Dallas' gentry.

So the tradition begun by the company a century ago is alive and well at the Grand Kempinski Dallas, a new face in the long-proud Dallas Heritage.

DOUBLETREE HOTELS

Doubletree Hotels, characterized by a successful management triangle — focusing on costs, revenues and service — has become something of a turnaround expert in the upscale hotel market.

Begun in 1969 by J. Peter Bidstrup, who remains Doubletree's chairman, the Phoenix-based chain has experienced a 300 percent growth in recent years. In the past two years alone the chain has grown from 10 to 33 properties representing more than 10,000 rooms in 15 states and 16 cities. Annual revenues are approximately $230 million nationwide, and the chain expects to double in size within the next five years.

Doubletree Hotel at Lincoln Center is one of two Doubletree properties in Dallas and 33 in 15 states.

As a result of its highly successful and aggressive expansion campaign, Doubletree attracted the attention of Metropolitan Life Insurance Company of New York, which in 1987 purchased 20 percent ownership in the company.

Unlike many hotel chains, however, Doubletree's primary mode of expansion has been through acquisition, not construction. Doubletree has carved out a substantial niche by purchasing the management contracts of upscale hotels that have failed to live up to their potential.

"Our mission in life is the same now as it was at its inception," explains Claudia Potter, Director of Marketing at the Doubletree Hotel at Lincoln Center. "Our CARE program, which stands for Caring and Responsive Employees, has been our key for successfully turning around a great many upscale hotel properties that simply haven't been doing well. That CARE program is ingrained in us from the day we begin our jobs."

Doubletree maintains 50 CARE standards which all employees must adhere to. These include answering telephones by the third ring, instant check-in and check-out services, room service breakfasts delivered within 15 minutes and five-minute table service at hotel restaurants.

Doubletree also has initiated a "white glove" test for room cleanliness. Guests are challenged to "white glove" their room, and if there is a problem, Doubletree promises to immediately correct it or place the guest in a new room. And there is a touch of tender loving care, something that has become a Doubletree tradition: a welcome gift of freshly baked chocolate chip cookies on the guest's first night stay. In 1988 alone, more than 3 million cookies were distributed.

While the CARE standards remain the same for all Doubletree properties, the modus operandi used

From bedside to poolside, Doubletree employees offer the best in first-class hotel service, making the chain one of the most successful in the business.

in the turnaround of specific properties is highly individualized.

A "conversion team" is sent to a hotel whose management contract has been acquired by Doubletree. They analyze the operation to find the reasons why that particular hotel has not done well. Often, potential customer groups have been ignored due to lack of advertising or lack of sensitivity to their particular needs. Doubletree management teams target those problems and immediately begin steps to rectify them, all the while keeping the hotel running smoothly.

Additionally, in 1987 Doubletree Hotels at Allen Center and Intercontinental Airport in Houston introduced a community service program called "Room at the Inn." The purpose of the program, conducted during the Christmas holidays, is to provide short-term lodging to those in need.

Each of those hotels reserves 10 rooms per night between December 1 and December 31 for use specifically by individuals who are referred by Houston area hospitals and the Ronald McDonald House. William Stanton, Regional Manager, says the program "gives each hotel and its employees an opportunity to thank the community during a season when blessings are customarily counted." The program has been expanded to include all Doubletree Hotels across the country.

Doubletree's CARE program is a set of 50 operating principles that assure guests will get the best service possible.

As a result, nearly all of Doubletree's acquired properties have shown substantial gains within the first year under Doubletree management. With such an outstanding turnaround record, Doubletree's management teams have become increasingly sought-after, not only because they are good, but because of the competitive nature of the hotel business.

Because Doubletree has been expanding so rapidly, it has developed an on-site training program attended by all management to assure each property has a full complement of competent personnel. And to make sure the CARE principles continue to be applied on a daily basis, CARE committees are established at each hotel. Evaluations in all major areas of service are posted daily so that individual employees have incentive to improve in broad areas, as well as in individual service.

The overall CARE attitude is not limited to guest needs, however, says Potter. "Mr. Bidstrup stresses three broader concepts. Those are: Care about each other, Care about family, and Care about those in need."

As a result of this corporate philosophy, Doubletree employees at each hotel donate an estimated 1,000 hours monthly to a variety of charitable organizations. The Make A Wish Foundation has been one of the primary benefactors in Texas of both corporate money and employee volunteer activities.

HOME INTERIORS AND GIFTS INC.

The vast merchandising organization known as Home Interiors and Gifts Inc. stands today as a monument to one woman's love of beauty and her determination to "be somebody."

When Mary C. Crowley founded the company in the garage of her home in 1957, her only assets were her enthusiasm, determination and solid contacts with a number of suppliers. By the end of the 1980s, Home Interiors and Gifts Inc. had grown into a national giant in its field, with annual sales of more than $430 million and a family of affiliated companies engaged in activities ranging from manufacturing to oil and gas production to professional sports.

Although Crowley died in 1986 and her son and longtime partner, Don Carter, succeeded her as company president, she gave thousands of women the opportunity to "be somebody" during her colorful career, and she brought joy and beauty into millions of American homes.

Crowley was raised by her grandparents after her mother died of pneumonia when she was 18 months old. It was her grandparents who taught her self-determination and nurtured her unwavering belief in Jesus — beliefs that had profound affects on her life and career.

Her first job was as a 21-year-old sales clerk in Sherman, Tex., earning $7 a week during the Great Depression. Later, she moved to Dallas, where a $100 scholarship from the Rotary Club enabled her to enroll in Dallas Business College. Later, she found a job with an insurance company and attended Southern Methodist University's evening business courses. In 1948, she married David M. Crowley Jr. whom she met while working for the insurance company.

While her children were in high school, Crowley was an accountant for a large furniture company where she also gave advice on decorating to

Home Interior's innovative sales techniques and inspirational business approach reflect the nature of Mary C. Crowley, the company's founder.

young couples. In 1949 she quit her secure job and began working full time with Stanley Home Products where she became a top salesperson. After a few months, she became manager of her own Stanley unit.

In 1954, Crowley joined a new direct sales company that sold gifts and decorative accessories from many countries and became sales manager. However, a difference of opinion with the owner led her to resign and eventually start her own company.

From the time she conducted her first merchandise show in December 1957 at the home of a close friend, orders began pouring in and business boomed. With the help of a timely loan from a friendly banker, the active assistance of her husband, Dave Crowley, and her son's management of the 2,500-square-foot warehouse when the family garage got too small, the company grew phenomenally over the next few years.

Crowley considered this growth a genuine miracle and never failed to express her thanks to God for allowing it to happen. But she also subscribed to the belief that "God helps them who help themselves," and she used all her physical and mental energy to propel the company to new heights.

Home Interiors and Gifts utilizes a sales system in which hostesses sponsor decorating and gift shows conducted in their homes by members of a nationwide team of some 35,000 sales representatives or "displayers." These techniques have been copied by numerous companies since they were originated by Crowley, who also was a pioneer in offering exotic trips, mink coats and expensive jewelry as rewards and incentives for high sales.

"Mrs. Crowley's original selling plan is still the cornerstone of the company," says William Hendrix, vice president of finance, who has seen the company's annual sales increase almost 15-fold since he joined the team in 1973. "And another major reason for our success is the network of suppliers developed by Don Carter. We have plants in Mexico and the Far East which were built specifically to manufacture products for us, and this is unique among companies in our field."

In addition to her tremendous business success, Mary Crowley also achieved great personal recognition

during her lifetime. She received the Horatio Alger Award in 1978, was among 25 top business leaders invited to a White House conference in 1977, and was the first woman to serve as a director of the Billy Graham Evangelistic Association, The Direct Sales Association and the Greater Dallas Chamber of Commerce. In addition, she became a best-selling author of inspirational books for women.

Today, under the direction of Don Carter, who is best known in Dallas as president of the Dallas Mavericks of the National Basketball Association, Home Interiors and Gifts carries on the tradition of excellence established by Crowley.

From the company's rambling headquarters in North Dallas, more than 1,300 employees distribute more

As president of Home Interiors and Gifts, Don Carter operates the company under the same time-proven principles that have made it one of the largest organizations of its kind in the world and enabled countless women to "be somebody."

than 500 products to customers throughout the United States. And despite its past growth, the company continues to build its sales and broaden its product lines while pursuing a program of controlled expansion.

"We foresee continued steady growth in the 1990s," says Hendrix, "but we aren't looking simply for growth for growth's sake. We want to grow only fast enough to keep providing the same excellent service that our customers are accustomed to. Even now, we've really only scratched the surface of our potential market, so we see a very promising future for the company."

As one of the largest interstate shippers in the Southwest, Hendrix points out, the central location of the Dallas area and its outstanding interstate transportation system are major assets to the company, enabling it to ship goods efficiently and economically to all parts of the nation. But in addition to these practical considerations, the company also feels a strong emotional attachment to the city where it was born.

"Mary Crowley loved Dallas, just as she loved helping women by bringing beauty into their lives and helping them achieve," Hendrix says. "And although we do business in 49 states, the heart of our company is here."

As the company focuses on the future, it continues to operate under the same time-proven principles that have made it one of the largest organizations of its kind in the world and enabled countless women to "be somebody." And the guiding, determined spirit of its founder remains very much a part of today's Home Interiors and Gifts.

"I don't foresee any changes in our basic business plan," Hendrix concludes. "Mrs. Crowley had a unique gift for keeping things fresh, and Don Carter has that same gift."

HAYES LEASING COMPANY INC.

Earl Hayes knew a good deal when he saw it, though some may have challenged his decision back in 1954 when he paid $150 for the exclusive Avis franchise for Dallas County. The well-known Chevrolet dealer, community leader, and philanthropist has since proved that his business foresight was on target.

Today, nearly 40 years later and a decade since Earl Hayes died, Hayes Leasing Company Inc. remains the exclusive Avis licensee in Dallas, Fort Worth, San Antonio and Austin — and yet it is an "invisible company," in the words of Hayes President John West, since the Avis name is the one with which the public identifies. While most Avis licensee operations are fairly small, Hayes Leasing is the second-largest in the United States.

In addition to automobile rentals, Hayes Leasing operates the Shelter Park business at Love Field, and is the only Dallas County dealer in Nissan's UD medium-duty diesel trucks, in combination with its

JoAnn and Robert T. Hayes, chairman of Hayes Leasing Company Inc.

extensive Avis truck rental and sales operation which dates to 1961. West believes theirs is the widest variety rental fleet in the United States.

West explains that Warren Avis, a Detroit Ford dealer, predicted after World War II that commercial aviation in the United States would grow and that airports would need car rental facilities to provide air travelers — especially business people — convenient ground transportation.

"In those days," says West, "this was considered heresy, since most car rentals were either at train stations or at downtown hotels. Certainly few people believed that air travel would become as popular as it did."

But Avis began his Avis Airlines Rent-a-Car System in 1946, and it became one of the great American success stories, typified by a classic motto created in 1962: "We're only No. 2. We try harder," has been universally acknowledged as one of the 10 best ad slogans of all time.

It is the spirit of the slogan that has been ingrained in the Hayes operation going back to 1952 when the founder organized Earl Hayes Rents Cars & Trucks with five vehicles, a $2,000 bankroll and the exclusive car rental concession at Love Field.

Today the profile of Hayes Leasing is much different: The total work force numbers around 400 at some 10 locations. The company's top 25 managers have an average of 15 years' service with Hayes, and of these managers, half are women. Locally, Avis rentals run neck-and-neck with the firm's top competitor, Hertz, although Avis edged out Hertz at both Love Field and Dallas/Fort Worth International Airport in 1987 and 1988, according to West.

Linda Childs, a 20 year veteran and vice president of Hayes Leasing, presents an illustration of Avis' phenomenal growth in the years since D/FW Airport was built: "In 1974 when the airport opened, Hayes

Earl F. Hayes, founder of Hayes Leasing Company Inc.

Leasing was doing about 4,000 transactions a month at D/FW Airport and 1,000 at Love Field. Today, in peak months, we complete about 25,000 rentals a month, 75 percent of which are at D/FW Airport. I can hardly believe it."

Chairman Robert T. Hayes links the growth of Hayes Leasing to "the legacy left to us by city leaders who were very pro-business," such as former Dallas Mayor Erik Jonsson who was so instrumental in the development of D/FW Airport.

As to the company's future, Hayes is confident that it "directly relates to the future of D/FW Airport.

Hayes Leasing's Avis locations employ the most up-to-date means to get customers from airport terminals to their rental cars quickly and comfortably.

As the airport grows larger with more daily flights, the Metroplex will in turn grow and continue to be attractive for corporate relocations. And, of course, our business is directly impacted by that."

Earl Hayes was deeply involved in the area's growth, having worked with "Goals for Dallas" in the late 1960s, among his many other civic activities. He and his wife, Alline, who was extremely active in Dallas cultural, civic and charitable affairs, worked tirelessly within their own community of Oak Cliff. As a result, Hayes was named Oak Cliff Man of the Year in 1968 and received accolades from such luminaries as then-Congressman George Bush, Governor Preston Smith and Mayor Jonsson.

Robert T. (Bob) Hayes carries on his father's commitment to Dallas and to Texas. He was president and chairman of the board of the United Cerebral Palsy Association of Dallas County in 1965-67, president of the Oak Cliff Chamber of Commerce in 1979-80, served five years as a member of the Dallas County Hospital District Board (Parkland) and one year as its vice chairman, and chairman of the Texas Automobile Dealers

Hayes Leasing is the only Dallas County dealer in Nissan's UD medium-duty diesel trucks, in combination with its extensive Avis truck rental and sales operation which dates to 1961.

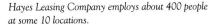

Hayes Leasing Company employs about 400 people at some 10 locations.

Association in 1983. In the past 29 years he has served as director, trustee or committeeman of various charitable and civic organizations such as the Greater Dallas Chamber, the Dallas Citizens Council, the Dallas Chapter of the American Red Cross, the Dallas Museum of Art, the United Way and the Dallas Opera.

Evidencing the early intentions of the family to give back to the community, they founded the Earl Hayes Foundation in 1949 to funnel some of the company's profits to a variety of local charities such as the arts, medical facilities and education.

Likewise, Hayes Leasing Company Inc. involves itself in a number of important civic projects, perhaps the most visible being its work with KERA, the local public broadcasting television station. Each year, Hayes donates autos to the Channel 13 auction and Avis trucks to help carry donated items to their destinations. Avis employees volunteer their time to work at the TV station on pledge nights.

John West observes that such involvement illustrates that "we are an invisible company with a good

corporate personality which has prospered and in turn given back to the community."

What is the company's formula for excellence? "Our middle and upper management group has 'We try harder' as their own personal work ethic," responds John West. "These are people who like to work harder to give good service, and it's made us an excellent company to do business with.

"We are a group of people with a common work ethic; it's the glue that joined us together and keeps us together."

Hayes Leasing Company operates the Shelter Park business at Love Field.

AMBASSADOR PLAZA HOTEL

The history of the Ambassador Plaza Hotel is as rich and colorful as that of Dallas itself. Indeed, the hotel, which opened as the Majestic in 1905, is Dallas' oldest hotel. It has earned its status as both a Texas and a Dallas Historic Landmark, and it is being considered for a National Register Landmark designation.

Gracious Old World charm, beautifully furnished rooms, outstanding dining facilities and proximity to downtown Dallas have made the Ambassador Plaza a favorite hotel of visitors to Dallas for more than eight decades.

When the property was in its turn-of-the-century heyday, it boasted the first hotel elevator west of the Mississippi and played host to such luminaries as President Theodore Roosevelt and Sarah Bernhardt, who resided there during her Texas tour. Later, Presidents William Taft and Woodrow Wilson patronized the hotel, which was renamed the Park in 1907. Composer John Philip Sousa stayed there when he performed at Old City Park, adjacent to the hotel and itself a picturesque Dallas landmark.

In 1931, the hotel changed owners to become the Ambassador, and major architectural alterations were made to enhance the facility's "lux-

Suites at the Ambassador Plaza include comfortable living areas for relaxing and visiting.

ury" image. Some 22 years later, the property was sold to a consultant to the White House Conference on Aging and became a residential and retirement hotel. By 1966, it was evident that the Ambassador's glory days were gone, but the deteriorating building nonetheless was designated an Historic Landmark of the State of Texas.

Sensing an opportunity to revitalize a portion of Dallas' past, TAP Historic Properties purchased the hotel in 1983 and undertook a major restoration to return it to its original charm and elegant ambience. Renamed the Ambassador Park, it became the Ambassador Plaza in 1985 when it was purchased by its present owner, Evangeline Federal Savings and Loan.

Today, the Ambassador Plaza Hotel boasts 114 elegantly furnished guest rooms, including eight suites; featured are wet bars, entry lounges, radios and televisions. Guests may enjoy full concierge and room service, a complimentary shuttle to downtown Dallas and Love Field, free valet parking and limousine service on request. Hotel staff also will be pleased to arrange a horse-drawn surrey to transport guests to the exciting

West End Historic District, only minutes from the hotel.

Dining is a pleasure in the warm, handsome surroundings of the Embassy Room. The Embassy Lounge serves cocktails from 11 a.m. to 2 a.m. daily, and guests may enjoy complimentary hors d'oeuvres weekdays between 5 and 7 p.m. In addition, a number of delightful room-plus-dining weekend packages are available, as well as special seasonal, corporate, government, military and group tour rates for lodging.

Guests will be delighted to discover this quiet hotel, resting in the shadow of Dallas' impressive skyline and within minutes of the bustling city. To stay at the Ambassador Plaza Hotel is to step back in time.

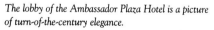

The lobby of the Ambassador Plaza Hotel is a picture of turn-of-the-century elegance.

Elegant dining and impeccable service are the hallmarks of the Ambassador Plaza's Embassy Room.

ACCENT AUTO LEASING INC.

When measured against the long history of Dallas business activity, Accent Auto Leasing is in its infancy. Yet that has not stopped the rental firm from establishing itself as a leader in both product quality and outstanding customer service.

Accent opened its first office in October 1986, according to Michael Tulburt, vice president. Tulburt brought some 15 years of experience in the auto leasing business when he teamed up with Arlington physician Dr. David Rasmussen, Accent's founder and president.

Says Tulburt, "I had the experience and he had the financing," so they formed a specialized leasing company aimed at price-conscious customers who believe that personalized service is important, too.

By April 1987, Accent had opened its second location, in Plano, and four months later established its newest rental center in Dallas convenient to the Dallas Convention Center, the Dallas Market Center and some of the city's largest and most popular hotels.

Tulburt believes Accent's excellent rapport with the area's hotels is

one of the keys to the company's success. "We are unique in that we will bring a customer's car directly to the hotel," whereas most car rental firms require a trip via shuttle bus to a central location. In fact, Accent is prepared to deliver a car to a customer at any time of day or night. At least one of Tulburt's 13 employees is on call every hour of the day to assist a customer in need. "I have a gathering of very loyal and dedicated people who treat our company as though it were

their own," he notes proudly.

The 24-hour on-call amenity ties closely to Accent's role as an insurance replacement renter. Whereas many auto rental firms are not always available after hours or on weekends to replace stolen or damaged vehicles, Accent always is.

Today the company has a fleet of 250 Chrysler vehicles ranging from economy to luxury size. "We also have mini-vans and convertibles," Tulburt points out, adding that Accent is planning to diversify its fleet soon to include other car makes. There is also an expansion planned in 1990 that will place an Accent leasing office near Dallas/Fort Worth International Airport.

Tulburt says that because Accent's overhead is so low, the company is able to keep its rates at about 75 percent of the rates charged by larger car rental firms. Unlimited free local mileage is included in the daily rate.

Tulburt says Accent gets a great deal of repeat business, with customers bypassing the hotel connection and calling his office direct: "In this business where there's not a lot of difference in the products, our customers really seem to appreciate the personal touch of service."

THE SOUTHLAND CORPORATION

John P. Thompson (left) and Jere W. Thompson have built the small ice company started in 1927 by their father into the world's largest convenience store chain and one of the United States' largest independent gasoline retailers.

The Southland Corporation, based in Dallas, is the world's largest convenience store chain and one of the United States' largest independent gasoline retailers. Its stores operate predominantly as 7-Eleven, one of the most recognized names in America.

Southland was founded by Joe C. Thompson Sr. in 1927 as an ice company in the Oak Cliff section of Dallas. Today, more than 12,000 7-Eleven stores are operated by Southland, its franchisees, licensees and affiliates in the United States and 21 foreign countries. As a result, 12 million customers shop at their neighborhood 7-Eleven stores every day.

Southland's convenience stores are supported by five Southland Distribution Centers and the Southland Foods Division's six fast food production facilities. The company also owns a 50-percent interest in Citgo Petroleum Corporation, a petroleum refining, marketing and transportation operation.

Despite its size, Southland's cornerstone philosophy has always revolved around anticipating and meeting the needs of the local neighborhoods where each of its stores operates. "We've built our 7-Eleven business over the last 62 years by providing our customers what they want, where they want it, and when they want it," says Jere W. Thompson, Southland's president and chief executive officer. "The people who run our stores usually live fairly close to where they work. So they know their customers. They're part of the neighborhood, and they get involved in issues and events that are important to that community. That makes a big difference in how a business is perceived by its customers."

Southland originated the convenience retailing concept in 1927, when a Southland Ice Company employee named John "Uncle Johnny" Green began selling milk, eggs and bread at his ice dock as a service to his customers. People responded enthusiastically to the convenient service and friendly employees, and the convenience store industry was born.

"We're in the business of selling convenience, and today, convenience has to be a lot more than just a good location," Thompson continues. "People want high-quality products and services for a fair price, and they really appreciate good, friendly customer service. At 7-Eleven, we do our best to measure up to those standards every day, and judging by how we've grown, we think we've done a pretty good job."

The early Southland convenience stores were known as Tote'm stores, and genuine Alaskan totem poles were installed at the front of each location. In 1946, the name 7-Eleven was coined for the growing chain of stores, which were open from 7 a.m. until 11 p.m.

The first 7-Eleven stores outside Texas were opened in Miami and Jacksonville, Fla., in 1954. Within a few years, the company had more than 300 stores and had expanded the convenience store concept to other parts of the United States.

Founder Joe C. Thompson Sr. died in 1961 at the age of 60. At that time, his oldest son John was named president of the company, and his second son Jere was elected to the company's board of directors.

Southland opened its first 24-hour 7-Eleven store in Las Vegas in 1963 and began franchising its convenience stores in California the following year. Today, 95 percent of all 7-Eleven stores are open around the clock, and almost 12 percent of all 7-Eleven shoppers visit the stores between 11 p.m. and 7 a.m. In addition, Southland celebrated its 25th anniversary in franchising in 1989, with more than 40 percent of its 7-Eleven stores in the United States now operating under franchise agreements. The company is regularly included among listings of the top franchisors in the country by several well-known business publications.

Southland grew rapidly throughout the 1970s, opening stores in Canada, Mexico and Japan. The company also announced its support of the Jerry Lewis Labor Day Telethon and the fight against crippling neuromuscular disease. Since that time, the combined efforts of Southland employees, franchisees and customers have generated more than $60 million in donations to the Muscular Dystrophy Association (MDA).

In addition to MDA, Southland management and 7-Eleven have been deeply committed to community activities in all neighborhoods where the company does business, from Little League and local hospital work to children's shelters and educational endeavors. Also, the company contributes to the arts and cultural events and was a major sponsor of the 1984 Olympic Games in Los Angeles.

By 1987, Southland had more than 10,000 stores worldwide. In addition to its half-interest in Citgo Petroleum Corporation, the company also included a manufacturing and distribution division, a chain of regional dairies, a chemical division, a movie rental operation and a chain of auto parts stores.

From time to time during the mid-1980s, Southland was the subject of rumors that it was a takeover candidate, and its common stock experienced unusual trading activity. In June of 1987, John, Jere and Jodie Thompson, sons of the company's founder, concluded that it would be in the best interest of Southland and its shareholders to take the company private through a leveraged buyout.

The buyout was announced on July 5, 1987, and was finalized on December 15 of the same year. Southland subsequently announced that it would focus on its convenience retailing business for the long term, and the company was reorganized. All non-convenience store oper-

ations, excluding the distribution centers, food center and Southland's interest in Citgo, were divested over the next year.

Today, as the largest privately held company in Dallas, Southland is stronger than ever and remains the undisputed leader in the convenience retailing industry. The company has more than 50,000 employees, including more than 4,000 in the Dallas/ Fort Worth Metroplex, and operates approximately 2,000 more convenience stores in the United States and Canada than its next largest competitor.

Southland's rapid expansion during the 1970s and 1980s created a growing need for a new headquarters facility. With its roots in the Dallas area, the company's management team saw the opportunity to renew its commitment to the city by building a new headquarters facility within an exciting mixed-use community that would be located near its existing building, just north of Dallas' central business district.

Under the auspices of Southland's wholly-owned subsidiary, Cityplace Development Corporation, 160 acres of land were assembled for the new development. At the same time, Southland engaged a team of internationally known architects, planners and traffic consultants to create Cityplace, which soon became known as one of the most unique inner city developments in the world.

Recently, Southland moved to its new corporate headquarters in the 42-story Cityplace Center East, the first Cityplace project to be completed, located across the street from the company's former headquarters building. Planning is well under way for developing the remainder of Cityplace over a 15-to-20-year period, including a second 42-story tower which, with the recently opened building, will form the core of the development, Cityplace Center.

The core of Southland's business is its more than 12,000 7-Eleven stores worldwide. Southland also owns half interest in Citgo Petroleum Corporation.

The rest of the project will encompass retail and entertainment centers, hotels, residential and other office development. The entire area is being enhanced by attractive landscaping, wide boulevards and parks throughout the community. Cityplace will become the new gateway to downtown Dallas.

From its small beginnings on an ice dock in Oak Cliff to its undisputed leadership in the rapidly growing convenience store industry, Southland has forged a proud heritage of its own as part of Dallas.

"The Thompson family has never been interested in preserving the status quo," says John P. Thompson, Southland's chairman. "We like to grow, to expand, and watch people develop, and Dallas, as our home, has been very conducive to that process over the years."

"Certainly we intend to remain the leaders in the convenience retailing industry," Thompson continues. "And with the development of Cityplace now well under way, we've underscored our commitment to Dallas with a project that will meet many needs of the community at the same time that it will celebrate the people who are that community. Without a doubt, we're looking forward to sharing in the growth and dynamism of Dallas for many more years to come."

Cityplace Center East, at 42 stories, is Southland's new headquarters and the first phase of a multi-use development that eventually will encompass retail and entertainment centers, hotels, residential and other office development.

LOEWS ANATOLE HOTEL

Dallas' Loews Anatole Hotel is virtually a village within the city of Dallas. Its unparalleled meeting space makes it one of the most complete convention hotels in America. On its premises, there are more than 240,000 square feet of flexible, versatile meeting space (58 meeting rooms including five ballrooms, six theaters and a 73,000 square-foot exhibit hall) as well as 1,620 guest rooms counting 145 suites, a complete health and fitness facility, 18 restaurants and lounges, three swimming pools and boulevards strewn with impressive works of art and boutiques.

Developer Trammell Crow first conceived the idea of this multipurpose hotel in the early '70s to service the Dallas Market Center which sits across from its site on Interstate 35. But soon after the Anatole was built with 900 guestrooms in 1979, it began attracting lucrative convention business.

Sumptuous decor and a variety of amenities have made the Loews Anatole Hotel a major draw for conventions and meetings coming to Dallas.

Charlotte St. Martin, president and chief executive officer of the Anatole, states that this convention side of the hotel has had a significant impact on Dallas. "In 1979, the advent of the Anatole gave the city another desperately needed large hotel to assist the convention bureau in filling the Dallas Convention Center," she says. "With the hotel's expansion in 1984, the Anatole became the largest hotel in guest rooms and meeting facilities in Texas."

Last year, the Loews Anatole entertained more than 20,000 conventions, meetings, banquets and receptions. The hotel services more than 500,000 guests each year and employs more than 1,500 people. And good business for the Anatole translates into good tourism dollars for Dallas. Proof of the Anatole's contribution to the city's convention business lies in a recent survey that lists Dallas as the third-largest convention city in the United States, just behind New York and Chicago.

St. Martin explains, "The Anatole has opened up new markets for Dallas and has attracted business which Dallas wouldn't be able to handle if the Anatole weren't here. And with the Anatole's new 73,000-square-foot exhibit hall, it will bring more new business to Dallas." The hotel, which celebrated its 10th anniversary in 1989, aims to be the top convention hotel in the world.

In addition to being a magnet for group meetings, the hotel's personalized service and array of amenities also attract business and pleasure travelers to Dallas. Its generous and varied number of quality restaurants, lounges and shops; rare art collection; state-of-the-art health and fitness complex rated in the world's top 10; seven-acre park offering a lagoon of Japanese Coi, croquet court, horseshoe pit, exotic aviary and gardens; 24-hour room service; private con-

With 1,620 guest rooms, 145 suites, 58 meeting rooms, five ball rooms and 8 restaurants, the Loews Anatole Hotel is the largest hotel in Texas.

cierge floors; video game room; business center; and three transportation services desks in addition to two lobby concierge desks add up to outstanding privileges.

"Whereas the Anatole is a village of opportunities, Dallas is a city of opportunities," St. Martin adds. "It offers the type of attractions, entertainment and a business climate that is attractive to meeting planners and individual travelers alike. Its central location as well as the wonderful support of the international airport combine for an extremely appealing and convenient visit. The Anatole and Dallas sell off of each other in a complementing way."

Other than helping bring the world to Dallas, the hotel plays host to a wide array of charity functions and has become recognized as a great hotel within the community. Celebrities like the Princely Family of Monaco, Prince Charles of Wales, U.S. Presidents and superstars like Michael Jackson have all graced Anatole suites.

One might wonder if catering to conventions, business travelers, tourists and social functions would wear the Anatole staff thin or narrow its focus. "Absolutely not — we're selling 'Anatole-Dallas' to all of our clients, in everything we do, all of the time," St. Martin says. "We've become a marketing partner to the city itself."

STOUFFER DALLAS HOTEL

With its clean, contoured, contemporary lines, the 30-story pink granite monolith rises above the 175-acre Dallas Market Center. The Stouffer Dallas Hotel stands not only as an architectural landmark in Dallas, but serves as a hallmark for excellence in service and personalized attention world-wide.

With 41 hotels and resorts in the United States, the Virgin Islands and Mexico, Stouffer Hotels & Resorts has enjoyed unprecedented growth as well as enthusiastic response from business travelers and casual vaca-tioners. Most recently, Stouffer added to its collection of luxurious properties by purchasing the Standford Court, a landmark hotel in San Francisco's exclusive Nob Hill area, and by opening the $117 million Stouffer Esmeralda Resort at Indian Wells, California.

Much of Stouffer Hotels' success can be attributed to the company's dedication to twin goals: offering old-

The physical elegance of the Stouffer Dallas Hotel is matched by its world-class accommodations and service.

world charm and elegance (evident at the Stouffer Dallas with its long spiraling crystal chandelier and numerous objets d'art), and dealing with guests' needs and desires quickly and efficiently.

"Stouffer is committed to providing first-class, memorable service at the Stouffer Dallas Hotel and all other Stouffer properties," says William N. Hulett, president of the Stouffer Hotel Company. "Service is the foundation of the hotel industry and our top priority."

To illustrate Hulett's point, under his leadership Stouffer has instituted a number of company-wide, precedent-setting programs that have garnered considerable praise, particularly from business guests. For example, guests staying at any Stouffer Hotel or Resort receive complimentary coffee and newspaper with their wake-up calls. Other exclusive Stouffer features include the elimination of many categories of telephone surcharges (long a sore spot with frequent business travellers) and convenient FAX machine service that is complimentary for faxes received and charged at nominal rates for faxes sent.

And, Hulett, who has not necessarily been sold on all the merits of computers, has limited the number of computer stations in the front desk area in an attempt to maintain the

personal touch he feels is so vital in the hotel business.

"These are just a few of the many services we offer at all of our Stouffer Hotels and Resorts," says Hulett. "And, to guarantee that our guests receive nothing but the best in service and attention, we have instituted a direct, 24-hour 'hot-line' to our general managers that will ensure problems are resolved as quickly as possible."

Stouffer Dallas Hotel, as with most Stouffer Hotels, is in a geographically strategic location. Surrounded by the world's largest wholesale market, Stouffer Dallas is only seconds away from the Dallas Apparel Mart, Market Hall, Menswear Mart, the World Trade Center and INFOMART. The hotel also is only minutes from downtown, the Dallas Arts District, the Dallas Convention Center, the West End Historic District, the Cotton Bowl, Texas Stadium, and Reunion Arena.

Stouffer Dallas Hotel is particularly convenient for business travelers, since it is only 20 freeway minutes from Dallas/Fort Worth International Airport, and only 10 minutes from Dallas Love Field.

The 540 newly refurbished guest rooms and suites at the Stouffer Dallas Hotel are representative of the luxury and distinction found in Stouffer Hotels & Resorts everywhere. Suites offer separate guest room and parlor facilities and some have bars. The Club Floors offer exclusive deluxe accommodations with private butler service, and the ultimate in luxury — the $1,500-per-night Presidential Suite, constructed at a cost of $250,000 with fireplace, whirlpool and a spectacular view of the city of Dallas.

Responding to the desires of its guests, Stouffer offers dining ranging from casual all-day fare to gourmet dining. In Dallas, the new Charisma offers all-day fare, and an outstanding Mediterranean dinner menu is the focus of an elegant evening setting. For those who prefer the ultimate in private dining, 24-hour room service is available. Cocktails, live music and a relaxed atmosphere in the Lobby Bar provide the perfect setting for winding down after a busy day of sightseeing or business.

Stouffer Hotels' meeting facilities are versatile for banquets, receptions, meetings and workshops. The Dallas hotel offers 15,000 square feet of function space. The 4,664-square-foot Grand Ballroom has been completely refurbished. The Ellipse Ballroom and eight additional meeting rooms — including the newly constructed, luxurious Stanford and Waverly rooms — accommodate groups of 15 to 500. A professional catering and convention services staff handles all the details from room setups to custom-designed menus.

If you want a vigorous workout or just a quiet time to lounge, both can be enjoyed in the hotel's rooftop health club and pool. Included are a Nautilus weight room, heated outdoor lap pool, jacuzzi, steam room and sauna. Men's and women's locker rooms and towels are provided. Open daily, the health club and pool are available free of charge to registered guests.

World-wide, Stouffer has more than 12,000 employees, including 320 in Dallas. "As Stouffer expands its portfolio of luxury properties, superior service will continue to be the primary goal of every employee," says Hulett.

History, elegance, innovation, commitment to service and trendsetting leadership make Stouffer Hotels and Resorts one of the premier, pacesetting hotel companies of the present and the future.

Charm and elegance are hallmarks of all Stouffer properties, and especially Stouffer Dallas Hotel with its unique crystal chandelier.

CHAPTER 24

Technology

"The Dallas and North Texas area has become one of the world's leading high tech centers due largely to a quality of life that not only attracts new companies but fosters growth and expansion of existing businesses."

Kent M. Black, Executive Vice President and Chief Operating Officer
— Rockwell International

"Quality is the only thing that keeps us in business. One thing we do is heavily train in quality improvement methods. Something that takes another company six weeks to build will take us a week."

Jeff Ryno, Founder
— Cuplex

"Texas is a great state to do business in. Dallas has always been progressive and very supportive of its entrepreneurs and of industry moving in, all of which is a good omen for those of us who are here."

Paul Dickenson, President and CEO
— H R. Industries

"Hitachi Semiconductor (America) Inc. needed lots of reasonably priced land, a pro-business climate, a high-quality labor force and proximity to a good airport. In 1978, those requirements prompted the company to locate its U.S. headquarters in the Dallas area."

— Hitachi Semiconductor (America) Inc.

"The positive business attitude, solid high tech environment and growth-oriented philosophy of Dallas have been important factors in our success. The area is already firmly established as one of the country's top five telecommunications manufacturing centers."

James L. Donald, Pesident and Chief Executive Officer
— DSC Communications Corporation

A large and diverse group of businesses have gathered to make Dallas one of the world's leading centers of technology innovation, development, manufacturing and employment.

377

ROCKWELL INTERNATIONAL CORPORATION

Rockwell International Corporation, with $12 billion in annual sales, is a diversified, high technology company serving markets throughout the world. It holds leadership positions in its four major businesses — electronics, aerospace, automotive and graphics.

Rockwell has approximately 110,000 employees worldwide and operates more than 150 plants and research and development facilities in Australia, Brazil, Canada, Europe, the Far East, Mexico and the United States. Rockwell is the largest employer in the Dallas suburb of Richardson and the fifth-largest manufacturing employer in the Dallas Metroplex, employing approximately 6,000 people.

As a high technology corporation, Rockwell employs nearly 27,000 engineers, scientists and technical support people.

The company has compiled an impressive growth record in the past decade and a half. Earnings have gained sharply, too. From 1975 to 1988, net income and earnings per share increased almost sixfold.

People worldwide know Rockwell for a variety of products: trucks use Rockwell heavy-duty axles and breaks; cars use Rockwell components; pilots use Rockwell-Collins avionics; newspapers are printed on Rockwell Goss printing presses; telephone calls are transmitted by Rockwell telecommunications products;

and satellites are launched from the Rockwell-built NASA space shuttle.

Rockwell's corporate headquarters are in El Segundo, California. The company is headed by Donald R. Beall, chairman and CEO.

Two of the company's major businesses are located in Richardson, where Rockwell is involved in the design and manufacture of communications products and systems for both commercial and defense applications.

To trace Rockwell's history in the Dallas area, it is necessary to go back to Collins Radio Company, which Rockwell acquired in 1973. Collins Radio moved part of its operations to Dallas in 1951. In 1957, Collins built a 123,000 square-foot building on a 200-acre site in Richardson. Today, Rockwell occupies nearly 1.8 million square feet of office and manufacturing facilities in that city.

As a major North American telecommunications supplier, Rockwell manufactures a wide range of products and systems for telephone company, business and government customers.

A pioneer in microwave transmission systems, the company is

Collins Defense Communications is a leading supplier of command and control communications systems for the U.S. strategic Minimum Essential Emergency Communications Network (MEECN), including the Airborne Command Post fleet.

expanding the application of this technology for use in remote rural areas and cellular telephone networks. Rockwell has provided high-performance, high-capacity microwave products to major industries, including telephone, transportation, oil and gas and manufacturing for more than 30 years.

The company is now one of the largest suppliers of lightwave, or fiber optic, transmission systems in North America. Its newest lightwave system can carry more than 16,000 telephone conversations simultaneously over a strand of fiber about the size of a human hair. All seven regional Bell operating companies, as well as MCI, Sprint and Telecom Canada, have purchased Rockwell lightwave systems.

In specialized switching equipment, Rockwell call management systems serve telephone company and business customers. The Rockwell Automatic Call Distributor (ACD) is used by businesses handling large volumes of incoming or outgoing telephone calls such as major airlines, car rental companies and hotel, motel and retail chains. More than 50 percent of the "800" toll free calls in the United States are managed by Rockwell ACD systems. Telephone company applications include E911 routing, equal access and directory assistance. The company also produces management and control systems for public and private communications networks.

Rockwell's defense communications business in Richardson produces a variety of command, control, communications and intelligence (C^3I) systems which are used extensively by the U.S. Government, NATO allies and more than 60 other countries to improve the reliability and security of communications among their military forces.

The company participates in virtually every U.S. strategic communi-

cation system. Its equipment provides, for example, a survivable communications link between command authorities and strategic submarines.

Rockwell's development of advanced, jam-resistent terminals for the military strategic tactical relay (Milstar) satellite network continues to be a high priority Air Force strategic communications program.

Rockwell is proud of its aviation and space heritage. The company has built more military aircraft than any other American company. In April 1988, the company delivered the 100th B-1B advanced bomber to the Air Force.

Rockwell is also a recognized world leader in design and production of spacecraft, space systems and rocket propulsion systems. More recently, it has served as the prime contractor for the NASA space shuttle.

Rockwell provides a variety of electronics products and systems developed and manufactured outside Richardson. For example, the company provides guidance and navigation for many U.S. strategic systems such as submarines and intercontinental ballistic missiles (ICBMs). For naval forces, Rockwell produces command and control systems, antisubmarine warfare electronics and integrated combat systems for submarines and ships.

The company delivers avionics for most commercial jetliners in the free world, and is a leading supplier of avionics for business aircraft and commuter airliners.

It also is the world's largest supplier of high- and medium-speed modems that are integrated into products such as facsimile machines and personal computers.

A subsidiary of Rockwell, Allen-Bradley, is a leading manufacturer of industrial automation controls. The company has earned a reputation for high quality, excellent customer service and a broad product line, including electro-mechanical and electronic devices, and systems that control manufacturing machinery and processes, and collect and communicate quality and production data. Allen-Bradley also is recognized as an innovative producer of equipment for computer-integrated manufacturing.

Serving vehicle manufacturers for 80 years, Rockwell is among the world's leading producers of components for heavy- and medium-duty trucks, trailers, buses and heavy-duty off-highway vehicles. In keeping up with the automotive industry, Rockwell, long known for the manufacture of individual automotive components, is now placing more emphasis on complete component systems.

Rockwell leads the world in the manufacture of newspaper production systems and is emerging as a leader in selected segments of the commercial printing market.

Two of every three daily newspapers in the United States as well as large-circulation newspapers in 95 other countries are printed on Rockwell's Goss presses. With its vast line of presses, Rockwell provides the color capability and print quality that newspapers require, colors with water-based inks that do not rub off, full-color inserts and flyers for retail advertisers and serves the catalog, book, periodical, financial and general commercial printing markets.

Rockwell is committed to maintaining and enhancing its position as a responsible corporate citizen. In doing so, the company is involved in, and contributes financially to, a broad range of educational, non-profit service and civic organizations. In fiscal 1989, the company and its trust fund contributed nearly $12 million to these types of organizations. Rockwell's employees supplemented the company's contributions with

Microwave and lightwave transmission systems produced at Rockwell International's facility in Richardson, Texas, help customers around the world communicate with each other easily and conduct their business more efficiently.

donations of their own totaling more than $4 million.

Education is one of Rockwell's primary concerns as the company acknowledges the nation's growing need for qualified engineers and scientists. Nearly 40 percent of Rockwell's charitable contributions are made to educational institutions. Rockwell has worked closely with University of Texas at Dallas officials to bring into existence the Erik Jonsson School of Engineering and Computer Science.

United Way continues to receive a large portion of the company's contributions — in addition to the substantial amounts pledged by Rockwell employees.

The balance of contributions are made to other health and human service organizations, civic and community development agencies, national research and public policy groups, and cultural and performing arts organizations.

CUPLEX

Cuplex was started in 1973 by Ron and Jeff Ryno with a $20,000 loan and three employees. They sold $93 worth of printed circuit boards their first month.

Today, Cuplex produces more than $28 million worth of circuit boards each year for more than 200 companies around the world, often working on more than 300 jobs at once. Of the more than 1,000 independent printed circuit board manufacturers in the United States, only 25 are larger, and Cuplex is the largest in Texas.

Although their major markets are on the East and West Coasts and in the Far East, the Rynos began their business in the Dallas area because they both love Texas. "Texas is the place to be," they say. "The area is blessed with a history and an attitude that is exceptional."

Cuplex makes boards for commercial manufacturers of computers, telecommunications equipment and industrial controls. Clients include IBM, Tandem Computers, Rockwell International, Northern Telecom, & General Datacom.

Cuplex's Garland plant runs 24 hours a day, seven days a week to keep up with customer demand for quick turnaround and very high quality.

"Quality is the thing that keeps us in business," says Jeff Ryno, adding that they compete with quality and not just price. "One thing we do is heavily train in quality improvement methods." Of the 300 people currently employed by Cuplex, many have been through the statistical process control course offered at Cuplex through Southern Methodist University.

Cuplex is devoted to the concept that all members of the team need training in quality control, and to ensure that, the company pays 100 percent of its employees' higher education cost at local institutions.

The plant is housed in an 86,000-square-foot facility in Gar-land. It operates 24 hours a day, seven days a week using a high tech conglomeration of machines from Germany, Italy, Japan, Israel, England and the United States. The primary goal is to produce a very high-quality product and meet the demand for quick turn-around prototypes.

"Something that takes another company six weeks to build will take us a week," they report.

The boards, thin layers of epoxy and fiberglass with fine copper connections throughout, are used in everything electronic, from computers to telephone switching equipment. Cuplex makes no product of its own but builds boards to customers' specifications.

Both Rynos are highly involved in their company, often walking the plant floor, checking quality, working with employees and frequently sitting in on Quality Improvement Teams. Both are former employees of Texas Instruments where they learned not only about the manufacture of printed circuit boards but also a great deal about sound management practices.

Cuplex builds circuit boards designed for almost any kind of electronic equipment, from computers to telephones.

HR. INDUSTRIES

Like many entrepreneurial firms, HR. Industries has felt the full force of the wringer of financial setbacks coupled with growth and change.

But the company came through the wringer and emerged as a leading circuit board manufacturer and the fifth-largest Hispanic-owned firm in the Dallas/Fort Worth Metroplex.

The firm was founded in 1976 by New Yorkers Horst Reetz and Ron Howard. "They were some of the first entrepreneurs in the circuit board industry in the state of Texas," says Paul Dickinson, current president and CEO. "They brought what was then state-of-the-art technology to Dallas from New York."

In 1982, TMG, a Dallas-based Hispanic conglomerate, bought HR. Industries Inc. and appointed Dickinson to head the operation. The company, however, was on the decline, its troubles culminating in a fire in 1984.

That disaster "almost put us out of business," Dickinson says, but the company fought back, and volume has tripled since July 1987 when Dickinson acquired control of the firm.

The company has turned itself around by evolving from a manufacturer of fairly low-tech products — boards as simple as though used in video games — to a builder of very complex boards with up to 16 layers for use in computers, telecommunications and oil field instrumentation systems.

The company now utilizes state-of-the-art technology to produce surface-mount circuit boards which do not require extensive drilling but which according to Dickinson "can compress an enormous amount of information into a very small space."

But with each new wrinkle in the manufacturing process, the plant must retool — a very expensive proposition since many new processes demand equipment costing $1 million or more. Dickinson, who has an MBA from the Wharton School of Finance, has relied on his academic background and experience in accounting to creatively finance the new equipment needed.

"This is not a business for the meek," he says. "You have to be ready to take quite a few risks."

For his risks and the success which has stemmed from them, Dickinson was named Minority Entrepreneur of the year in 1989 by Arthur Young & Co. That makes him especially happy, because he is proud to represent Dallas.

"I like Dallas very much," he says. "I'm a sports freak, and Dallas is a major league town in every possible way. We have tremendous cultural opportunity, tremendous educational opportunity.

'Texas is a great state to do business in. Dallas has always been progressive and very supportive of its entrepreneurs and of industry moving in, all of which is a good omen for those of us who are here."

Paul Dickinson, President and CEO

HITACHI SEMICONDUCTOR (AMERICA) INC.

A pro-business climate, a high-quality labor force, proximity to an international airport and reasonably priced land prompted Hitachi Semiconductor (America) Inc., an electronic circuitry manufacturer, to locate its U.S. headquarters in the Dallas area.

Today, 11 years after its establishment, Hitachi Semiconductor (America)'s Las Colinas facilities span 114,000 square feet, including a 42,000-square-foot wafer fabrication plant. The company employs approximately 400 highly educated, dedicated and skilled workers who make some of the tiny electronic devices that have become an integral part of our everyday lives. Although usually hidden, semiconductors are all around us; they are in the cars and planes we ride in, the equipment we use to manufacture many products, the televisions we watch, the elevators we use to get to the office, even the toys that amuse our children.

The watchword at Hitachi Semiconductor (America) is meticulous.

That word applies to every stage of production. Rigorously trained and supervised employees operate one of the finest manufacturing facilities of its kind, producing a line of 256K and 1 megabit, dynamic random access memories, (DRAM), and 16K, 64K and 256K static random access memories, (SRAMs). Hitachi Semiconductor (America) engineers are prepared as well to meet the challenge of custom applications and to work closely with customers to assure maximum reliability and performance.

Hitachi Semiconductor (America) employees are serious about reliability and performance. They know that a failed circuit can mean a failed system, and such failures simply are not acceptable. That is why the company redefined the word "precision" with its quality assurance program. This program includes extensive reliability testing of each product. Silicon chips are examined microscopically before being bonded to the leadframes. Two extreme temperature

Hitachi Semiconductor (America)'s Las Colinas facilities span 114,000 square feet, including a 42,000-square-foot wafer fabrication plant. The company produces some of the tiny electronic devices that have become an integral part of our everyday lives.

tests eliminate marginal devices. Three separate electrical tests verify product integrity, and each device receives no fewer than five visual inspections.

Products also are pulled off the line randomly for further exhaustive testing. Ion chromatography, scanning electronic microscopy, dynamic life tests, liquid or air thermal shock tests, pressure cooker tests and temperature and humidity tests are conducted in the company's reliability laboratory.

Hitachi Semiconductor (America) is a wholly owned subsidiary of Hitachi America Limited, which itself is a unit of the more than $48-billion-dollar international giant, Hitachi Ltd. Hitachi is one of the world's top 10 electrical and electronic equipment manufacturers. It has been said that Hitachi makes "everything that has electricity in it," with a lineup of more than 20,000 products that range from tiny semiconductors to nuclear power plants.

Hitachi has five product divisions, each representing a major market focus and research and development thrust; power systems and equipment; consumer products; information and communications systems and electronic devices; industrial machinery and plants; and wire, cable, metals, chemicals and other products.

Hitachi has one of the largest organizations in the world, with 24 research laboratories and more than 16,000 R&D personnel. Hitachi has

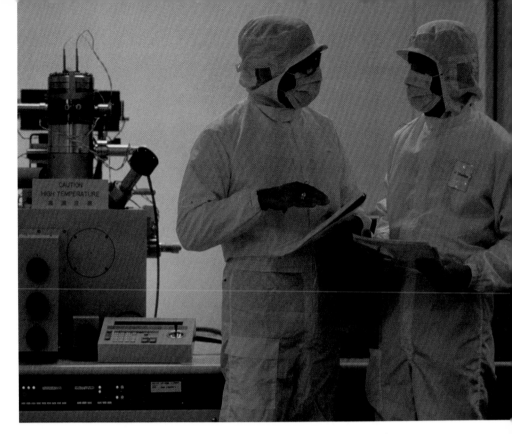

Hitachi has one of the largest research organizations in the world, with 24 research laboratories and more than 16,000 R&D personnel.

an annual research budget of nearly $2 billion. In recent years, more than 50 percent of that budget has been focused on electronic products of the kind made by Hitachi Semiconductor (America).

Founded by Namihei Odaira in Japan in 1910, Hitachi began as a small electrical machinery shop. Its first products were three 5-horsepower electrical motors. The technology was entirely original, as was Odaira's vision for Hitachi's future.

Today, Hitachi Limited truly is a global enterprise, with 104 manufacturing subsidiaries and sales and service facility outside Japan, Hitachi has major operations in North and South America, Europe, Australia, Asia, Africa and the Middle East. Its total employment is more than 279,000 people. Hitachi's goal is to continue to expand its international operations and to employ primarily local workers.

In the United States, Hitachi America, Ltd. was formed in 1959, principally as a sales organization for Japanese products. But today Hitachi America is a truly American company, with sales of $1.66 billion. It employs more than 3,700 people in 65 offices and manufacturing facilities throughout the United States. Through units such as Hitachi Semi-

conductor (America), Hitachi America combines the best of East and West, blending Japanese and U.S. technological, engineering and production capabilities.

It is of fundamental importance to each Hitachi company to be a "good neighbor" to its American sponsor community by providing human and material resources to help achieve community goals. On a larger scale, Hitachi is working to enhance East-West relations through increasing purchases of U.S. goods, expansion of Hitachi America, and creation of the $20-million Hitachi Foundation to promote cultural, educational and scientific exchange between the two nations.

Hitachi has been and always will be an organization that plans for the future. Hitachi's current R&D efforts include highly advanced fields such as ultra-large-scale integrated circuits, artificial intelligence, nuclear fusion, new ceramics, bioengineering and other emerging fields.

President, Hitachi Semiconductor (America) Inc., Mr. Masao Uchihashi.

DSC COMMUNICATIONS CORPORATION

As one of the first companies to deliver digital tandem switches to U.S. long distance telephone carriers, DSC Communications Corporation has played a key role in the emergence of the Dallas area as a major high technology center.

Today, the Metroplex boasts one of the nation's largest concentrations of high tech development, and DSC has become a leader in the field of telephony. The company is internationally recognized as a technology leader in the production of tandem/cellular switches, signal transfer points, digital cross-connects and other sophisticated telecommunications equipment.

"We are proud of the leadership position that DSC has established in a wide range of technologies and the contribution that it has made to our community," says chairman and CEO James L. "Jim" Donald. "For example, we have shipped more digital tandem switches to the non-AT&T long distance carrier market than anyone, and our cellular switch, a derivation of the tandem, is recognized worldwide as one of the best available.

Each of these products has been designed, developed and manufactured locally.

"DSC delivered the first Common Channel Signaling No. 7 (CCS7) configured signal transfer point for use in the United States and now has one of the largest Signal Transfer Point (STP) bases within the long distance and local exchange carrier markets," Donald points out. "In the cross-connect technology arena, the company's leadership position was established with the introduction of one of the first software programmable machines in the mid-1980s. Today, the company offers one of the most complete product lines and largest capacity cross-connects in the industry."

Nearly half of DSC's employees hold technical degrees. Engineering specialists in hardware and software design, many with backgrounds in electrical engineering and computer science, have been key contributors to the success of the company as a leading designer, developer and manufacturer of telecommunications equipment.

DSC has seen its revenue grow from zero in 1981 to an all time high of more than $400 million in 1989. The company has achieved this phenomenal level of success against a host of significant worldwide competitors, including many large foreign-owned equipment suppliers.

"Our success is due to a variety of factors," Donald says. "But the key is that we listen to our customers; then we design, develop and manufacture products that meet their requirements."

And yet, none of it might ever have happened if it had not been for a "window of opportunity" which began to open in the latter half of the 1970s and early 1980s. It was at this time that competition was introduced into the telecommunications long distance business and alternative suppliers of equipment entered the marketplace.

In 1976, Digital Switch Corporation, the forerunner of today's DSC, set up operations in Virginia. The company foresaw tremendous demand for a telephone switching system utilizing state-of-the-art digital technology to process and bill telephone calls, and soon began work on such a system.

But five years passed and it was not until the arrival in 1981 of Jim Donald, who had extensive experience in telecommunications, a strong perception of the market and a solid management background — did the struggling venture become a success. By June of that year, Donald had become the company's chief executive officer, and had moved DSC to the Dallas area.

Donald was a former president of Danray, Inc., where he had been brought in to manage the new telecommunications equipment manufacturer. In addition, he brought with him 18 years of experience with Texas Instruments, one of the early leaders in the high tech field. After Danray

was acquired by Northern Telecom in 1978, Donald became aware of Digital Switch Corporation and the potential of the company, seeing it as a vehicle that could take advantage of a vast opportunity — one that might not remain open for very long. The telecommunications industry was experiencing its most rapid growth in history, and Donald sensed that the company's technological expertise could lead to sharing in this tremendous growth.

Obviously, DSC and Donald have done precisely that. From the tiny nucleus of just six employees who made the move from Virginia to Dallas in 1981, DSC has grown into a large-scale operation with more than 3300 employees and worldwide operations conducted from locations in Japan, England, Puerto Rico, Canada and throughout the United States. Headquartered in Plano, it ranks as a leading designer, developer, manufacturer and marketer of digital switching, transmission and network system products for the public and private telecommunications industry.

After operating as Digital Switch Corporation for nearly a decade, the company's name was changed in April 1985 to DSC Communications Corporation to better reflect its position as a leading worldwide supplier of both switching and transmission telecommunications systems. Later that same year, it became the first U.S. switch manufacturer to gain entry into the Japanese market.

DSC's strategies in the rapidly changing telecommunications marketplace are to continue to broaden its product offerings and customer base, to combine new and existing technology and to form corporate partnerships that address specific market segments. The company's principal strength as it addresses the needs of the marketplace in the 1990s is its ability to offer innovative, cost-effective, reliable technological

DSC Communications Corporation Plano, Texas

business solutions for its customers.

Under the continuing leadership of Donald and other members of its management team, DSC is poised today for new rounds of growth. It is building toward the future on the same foundation of highly skilled people, quality products and financial strength that has served it so well in the past.

"The positive business attitude and solid high tech environment of the Dallas area location in combination with the growth-oriented philosophy of DSC have been important factors in the company's success," says Donald. "The North Dallas/Richardson/Plano/Garland area is already firmly established as one of the country's top telecommunications manufacturing centers and we feel the future is very bright both for DSC and the area in general."

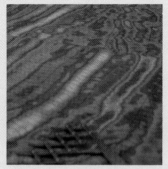

"Energy plays a key role in the viability of any city or region. We're proud of our long and successful operating history and our role in the future development of Dallas."

David W. Biegler, Chairman and Chief Operating Officer
— Lone Star Gas Company

"Dallas is a dynamic city that provides high-caliber employees, and Dallas provides an effective interface with other key players in the oil and chemicals industries."

Ron W. Haddock, President and Chief Executive Officer American Petrofina Inc.

"In its second half-century, DeGolyer and MacNaughton continues its founders' criteria for performance which have set the standard for the industry it began: knowledge, integrity and service."

— DeGolyer and MacNaughton

"Integrity and excellence are the principles that guide Netherland, Sewell & Associates. They are basic, unchanging and uniquely distinguish the petroleum consulting services offered by the firm."

— Netherland, Sewell & Associates

Photo by Martin Vandiver

"The Dallas area is the best location in the Southwest for a corporate headquarters. It's the major crossroads of the 'oil patch,' the major transportation crossroads of the entire region, and a great place to do business."

Allan J. Tomlinson, President
— Champlin Refining Company

"Dallas enjoys an enviable reputation as a great place to live and work — and for good reason. That's why ARCO has been here so long."

James A. Middleton, President
— ARCO Oil and Gas Company

"Dallas is a can-do, dynamic city that has endured some less-than-favorable economic times and yet maintained a positive outlook. Dallas has a lot of the same attributes we see in Oryx Energy Company."

Robert P. Hauptfuhrer, Chairman and Chief Executive Officer
— Oryx Energy Company

"We felt strongly that it was in our best long-term interest to locate in a business and transportation center such as Dallas. Our experience here has met or exceeded our expectations in every sense."

Charles K. Vaughan, President and Chief Executive Officer
— Atmos Energy Corporation

CHAPTER 25

Energy

Energy companies headquartered in Dallas are a vital sector of the local economy as they bring energy and power to businesses and residents throughout the world.

LONE STAR GAS COMPANY

In 1909 the state of Texas chartered Lone Star Gas Company, thus beginning the story of large-scale natural gas development in Texas. The discovery of natural gas in Clay County a year earlier led directly to the creation of this new company and the first long-distance pipeline in Texas.

The first delivery of natural gas to the Lone Star system was through a pipeline from the Petrolia Field, running 100 miles south to Fort Worth and 35 miles east to Dallas. Gas was turned on in both cities in 1910. A single gas well furnished the demands of all 15,000 customers in the two cities.

The arrival of natural gas ushered in an era of more comfortable, gracious living. The gas age brought improved home heating, water heating, cooking and clothes drying.

The advantages of natural gas also were apparent to business and industry. As long-range gas supplies became stable, more and more commercial enterprises were attracted to Dallas because of the availability of this incomparable fuel.

New industrial and commercial applications are still being "born" every day, based on the economy, efficiency and environmentally benign qualities of natural gas.

Natural gas has helped keep the skies of Texas blue, and will continue to be part of the solution to many environmental concerns of the future.

Lone Star today ranks among the six largest integrated transmission/distribution companies in the United States, and owns and operates a giant interconnected network of gas transmission lines, gathering lines, underground storage reservoirs, distribution systems and associated measurement and treatment facilities.

Through more than 30,000 miles of pipeline, the company transports and distributes natural gas to approximately 1.25 million residential, commercial, industrial and electric generation customers.

Through the years Lone Star's engineers and technical specialists have gained industry-wide respect and earned a leadership role based on successful innovation and refinements of many techniques and processes.

New knowledge and techniques will continue to ensure the widest and most cost-effective uses of natural gas in both present and future energy environments.

Lone Star's transmission network includes more than 10,000 miles of intrastate pipelines that tap into eight major natural gas basins in the Southwest and provide connections to numerous other major pipelines and markets.

Lone Star is both an "open access" and an intrastate transporter. This flexibility, coupled with Lone Star's ability to provide storage, compression, gathering and treating services, allows the company to meet a shipper's special needs on a very competitive basis.

Lone Star is primarily a service operation — serving the energy needs of nearly 600 communities in Texas and Oklahoma. But that is not all it does.

Whether it is working with local chambers of commerce to attract new business and industry to the area, or helping children to improve their reading skills, or the elderly to repair their homes, Lone Star's people are continually working to improve the

Convenience, comfort and economy are reasons natural gas remains the energy of choice for homes, businesses and industry.

quality of life in their communities. No job is more important.

Natural gas is increasingly seen as a long-term solution to the nation's energy needs. It is plentiful, economical and does not harm the atmosphere. Increased use of this highly efficient fuel is good for consumers, Dallas and the environment.

The use of compressed natural gas (CNG) as a vehicle fuel has gained popularity in recent years. The primary benefits of using CNG as a motor fuel are cost savings (fuel costs, and maintenance costs) and improved air quality. While the formerly higher prices and supply shortage problems of gasoline led initially to the CNG conversion drive, compliance with new air quality standards makes natural gas an even more compelling choice as a motor vehicle fuel.

The Environmental Protection Agency (EPA) recently released a new set of guidelines to help major U.S. metropolitan areas attain minimum air quality standards. These guidelines indicate that substitution of CNG for gasoline can reduce hydrocarbon exhaust emissions by 40 percent, carbon monoxide emissions by 50 percent, and completely eliminate evaporative hydrocarbon emissions.

Clean air is a precious asset, and regaining control over this important factor in our lives has become a top priority. Natural gas is the cleanest-burning hydrocarbon found in nature, and simply switching to this fuel whenever possible will go a long way toward meeting our aspirations for cleaner air and blue skies.

At a time when oil imports are at record levels, it is important to note that the nation has an abundant supply of natural gas, 26 percent of it in Texas. The conversion of fleet vehicles to CNG holds the promise of furthering the efforts in many locales as

they seek to comply with clean air standards.

Dallas has a proud past, and there is no doubt the city and region are poised for continued growth and prosperity. And, for the last 80-plus years, Lone Star Gas has been proud to play its part in serving the energy needs of this great city. The best is yet to come.

Lone Star's extensive pipeline system gives customers strong access to all major natural gas basins in the United States, thus ensuring long-term availability of supplies.

AMERICAN PETROFINA, INC.

Ron W. Haddock, Fina's president and chief executive officer.

American Petrofina, Inc. is the only fully integrated petroleum company headquartered in Dallas. Through its main operating subsidiary, Fina Oil and Chemical Co., American Petrofina is active in exploration and production of oil and gas, refining, marketing and transportation of crude oil and natural gas, and chemical manufacturing and marketing.

Dallas has always been home to Fina. The company was organized in 1956 as a publicly held affiliate of Petrofina S.A. Based in Brussels, Belgium, Petrofina S.A. is an international organization of approximately 200 companies operating in 33 countries.

Dallas' central location was a key factor in choosing a place to start an oil company. The city has contributed to Fina's success, says Ron W. Haddock, Fina's president and chief executive officer.

"Dallas is a dynamic city that provides high-caliber employees," Haddock says. "The city has strong financial resources and an efficient transportation system. Just as important, Dallas provides an effective interface with other key players in the oil and chemicals industries."

Today, Fina has roughly 3,400 distributor-served or company-owned retail outlets located in 22 southwest, midwest and southeast states. It operates refineries in Big Spring and Port Arthur, Texas, with total capacity of more than 160,000 barrels a day, and chemical manufacturing plants in Carville, Louisiana, and LaPorte, Texas. In addition, Fina has a 1,600-mile network of crude-gathering pipelines and two finished-product pipelines.

Fina products are available in more than 220 terminals, providing easy access to Fina jobbers. In 1988, the company posted record net earnings of $132.9 million — a 60 percent increase over 1987 — on sales of $2.6 billion.

Fina started out on a smaller scale with the acquisition of several oil companies. These included Panhandle Oil Company of Wichita Falls, Texas, American Liberty Oil Co. in Mt. Pleasant, Texas, and Petro-Atlas with its refinery in El Dorado, Kansas. Fina introduced the Fina brand name and the first Fina products in 1958, and began to distribute Fina credit cards.

In 1963, with the purchase of Cosden Oil and Chemical Company, Fina doubled its number of retail outlets. Ten years later Fina took another big step when it bought assets of British Petroleum Company, including 1,000 service stations and BP's 84,000-barrel-per-day Port Arthur refinery.

Fina strengthened its presence in the Midwest and Southwest in 1984 with the purchase of Champlin Petroleum and its 172 service stations. In

1987, Fina bought 31 retail outlets from Texaco Inc. in the Minneapolis-St. Paul metropolitan area, becoming a major industry influence in that midwest community.

In 1988, Fina launched a $150-million fuels modernization project at Port Arthur to give the plant a new 45,000-barrel-per-day catalytic cracker, a 110,000-barrel-per-day atmospheric crude unit and a 16,000-barrel-per-day saturate liquids recovery unit. When these improvements are completed in 1991, the refinery will be among the best in the industry.

In 1988, Fina more than doubled its oil and natural gas reserves when it paid about $600 million for all the exploration and production assets of Tenneco Inc.'s Gulf Coast and Southwestern divisions. This acquisition included Tenneco's operations in parts of Arkansas and New Mexico, most of Texas with the exception of some of the Texas Panhandle, and all of Alabama, Florida, Louisiana and

Mississippi. In addition to producing properties, the purchase included undeveloped leasehold, mineral and royalty acreage with good exploration potential. The largest concentration of fee minerals and property is in south Louisiana, including the 180,000 net acre LaTerre property in Terrebonne Parish.

A major accomplishment has been the smooth transition of the Tenneco assets into Fina's ongoing operations. The Tenneco division office in San Antonio was closed and its activities relocated to Fina's office in Midland, Texas. The Fina office in Corpus Christi, Texas, was also closed. Two new divisions were created: South Texas and South Louisi-

Fina has roughly 3,400 distributor-served or company-owned retail outlets located in 22 southwest, midwest and southeast states. Photograph by Stewart Cohen.

ana, both headquartered in the former Tenneco office in Houston.

Fina also stepped up its own exploration activities in 1988. At the end of the year, the company had a working interest in 185 total gross wells, resulting in about 32 net exploratory wells and 20 development wells. Fina achieved a success rate of 62 percent for exploratory and 100 percent for development wells.

Fina operates refineries in Big Springs and Port Arthur, Texas, and chemical manufacturing plants in Carville, Louisiana and Laforte, Texas. Photograph by Stuart Cohen.

Fina is the nation's No. 3 producer of polypropylene, used primarily in flexible packaging, fibers, housewares and the automotive industry. Photograph by Stewart Cohen.

As a result of both acquisitions and increased efforts, Fina's year-end proved reserves rose dramatically in 1988. Crude oil and condensate reserves increased 80 percent, from 31.2 to 56.3 million barrels. Natural gas reserves soared 136 percent, from 291.7 to 687.8 billion cubic feet. Sales volumes of natural gas, crude oil, condensate and gas liquids also increased in 1988. Total natural gas sales were 37.3 billion cubic feet compared to 27.5 billion cubic feet in 1987. Total crude oil, condensate and gas liquid sales increased from 5.9 million to 6.4 million barrels.

Average crude prices fell from $16.91 in 1987 to $14.26 in 1988. Fina, however, has been able to hold total operating costs (excluding the Tenneco acquisitions) essentially flat since the 1986 reduction of 25 percent. Although low crude prices yielded disappointing financial results in this segment of Fina's business, the company now has record reserves and production capacity and is well positioned to benefit from an expected increase in natural gas prices.

The natural gas market is changing rapidly, but with reserves more than doubled, Fina remains committed to it. In 1988, the company suc-cessfully implemented programs that improved its competitive position and ability to market natural gas profitably. Among the results were a 12 percent increase in sales volumes (excluding the acquired Tenneco properties) and an average 6 percent rise in prices. Fina also expanded its natural gas marketing organization to tap new, more attractive markets, to settle existing pipeline contract disputes on favorable terms, and to cut gas transportation costs.

In 1988, Fina profited handsomely from the highest margins in the refining industry since 1979. The company succeeded in meeting its key goals of lowering costs and improving yields. Output at Big Spring and Port Arthur reached 167,000 barrels per day, 2 percent higher than in 1987.

At Port Arthur, a new cogeneration plant opened on August 1, 1988, two months ahead of schedule. This unit generates roughly 75 percent of the electricity and most of the steam needed at the refinery; based on ini-tial operating experience, it should reduce total operating costs by about 10 percent. Along with the fuels modernization program begun in 1988, Port Arthur developed an improved catalyst to produce benzene and xylene from toluene. This catalyst, which was devised by Fina's research and development group, contributed to a record 8,700 barrels per day of aromatics produced at the refinery in 1988.

Volatile crude price swings in 1988 presented a challenge. Fina responded, resulting in a trading profit of more than $15 million. The company began using an improved computerized approach to risk and inventory management. Fina also started using a new system to improve the effectiveness of crude acquisitions, allowing for quicker and more accurate economic analysis of potential purchases.

Fina has made major strides in becoming more efficient in other areas as well. One of these is marketing: awareness and acceptance of the Fina brand name grows every year. In 1988, Fina withdrew from some unattractive markets and discontinued business with a number of poor quality distributors. Despite increased competition, sales of gasoline, distillates, jet fuel, asphalt and other Fina products rose 15 percent from 1987 levels and were at their highest since 1978.

Since the middle of 1987, Fina has been involved in a major project to strengthen its brand name image.

Fina traders buy and sell crude oil and products to supply the company's raw materials. Fina utilized an improved computerized approach to risk and inventory management.

The company has rebuilt or modernized more than 1,000 existing company-operated or distributor-served retail gasoline outlets. In addition, Fina opened 43 new stations in 1988. All display the new Fina logo. The goal is to offer quality products at clean, attractive outlets. During the year, Fina also installed advanced retail automation systems at 162 company-operated stores.

To enhance marketing efforts even further, Fina introduced its Distributor Awards Retirement Program in 1988. This plan, a first for the industry, offers retirement benefits to distributors who meet the high standards established by the company. Fina distributors have responded to the program enthusiastically.

Fina's chemical business posted record profits and revenues in 1988. It continues to be a strong contributor, although margins are down due to softer export markets, increased cost of raw materials and increased supplies. In 1988, Fina became the nation's number three producer of polypropylene. Completion of a major expansion at the LaPorte plant boosted capacity from 600 million to 840 million pounds annually. Polypropylene is used primarily in flexible packaging, fibers, housewares and the automotive industry.

Fina is consolidating all polystyrene production at its Carville, Louisiana plant. By early 1990, a new production line at Carville should be finished, completing the consolidation. Polystyrene is used in appliance and electrical components, housewares, toys and rigid packaging. Fina also is expanding its styrene monomer production capacity at Carville. Styrene is used in synthetic rubber for tires, for unsaturated polyester for fiberglass boats and to produce polystyrene.

Although Fina is fully involved in business activities, the company also has time for community service.

At the end of 1988, Fina had a working interest in 185 total gross wells, resulting in about 32 net exploratory wells and 20 development wells. Fina achieved a success rate of 62 percent for exploratory and 100 percent for development wells. Photograph by Stewart Cohen.

Ron Haddock, since becoming chief executive officer in early 1989, encourages employees to participate in events such as the March of Dimes Walk-A-Thon. Fina employee participation directly benefits the charity. Haddock says the company also gets a return.

"It builds morale and esprit de corps — it builds a team," Haddock says. "We have a lot to contribute to the community in the way of talent and resources."

DEGOLYER AND MACNAUGHTON

When DeGolyer and Mac-Naughton was founded in 1936 to serve as a consultant to the growing oil and gas industry, it was the first organization of its type in the world. Today the firm is considered by many to be the leading authority in assessing the extent and worth of petroleum reserves around the globe.

The Dallas firm was begun as a partnership between the late Everette Lee DeGolyer and Lewis W. Mac-Naughton in direct response to the needs of an industry that was suffering from the effects of "boom and bust" cycles, accelerated depletion, inaccurate and incomplete assessments of reservoir conditions and inefficient and primitive production practices. DeGolyer, regarded by oilmen as a pioneer in geophysics and other phases of oil exploration, and MacNaughton, an extraordinarily talented geologist, recognized the demand for reliable, realistic consultation and created the first organization to perform such services for financial institutions and oil companies worldwide.

One concept developed by the firm was the use of oil and gas reserves as collateral in securing financing for exploration and development. Today this is a common practice embraced not only by financial institutions but also by those involved in the purchase and sale of oil and gas properties.

Its expertise in serving these needs further enhanced DeGolyer and MacNaughton's reputation as an experienced and impartial assessor of the worth of petroleum and mineral properties and reserves. Today the firm is relied upon by the U.S. Securities and Exchange Commission and its Canadian counterpart, as well as by other government agencies around the world, for its dependable evaluations of hydrocarbon and mineral reserves.

In addition to working with domestic and foreign government entities, financial institutions and major oil companies, DeGolyer and MacNaughton provides its services to many individuals, smaller oil companies and firms outside the energy industry. Many of DeGolyer and MacNaughton's clients are of long standing and rely on recurring service.

Some of the firm's services have resulted in major milestones in the industry. A prominent example can be found in DeGolyer and Mac-Naughton's initial appraisal of the Prudhoe Bay oil field on the Alaskan North Slope. The firm's 1969 estimate of recoverable oil (5 to 10 billion barrels) was instrumental in the determination that the field was indeed a major discovery. And in the late 1970s during the merger of the

The DeGolyer and MacNaughton board room houses some of the more than 11,000 reports the firm has prepared since its inception. The bronze bust is a likeness of founder Everette Lee DeGolyer. Photo by Ron Clark.

Getty and Skelly oil companies, DeGolyer and MacNaughton's assessment of their reserves and worth formed a basis not only for the merger but also for its successful subsequent legal defense.

The firm's only office and its sole base of operations is in Dallas. The privately held, employee-owned corporation has a staff of 150, including more than 60 professionals. Each member of the professional staff has previously worked in the industry an average of 12 years before joining the firm, and average total experience exceeds 25 years. DeGolyer and Mac-Naughton has prepared more than 8,600 domestic and 3,000 international reports over the years.

In its second half-century, DeGolyer and MacNaughton continues its founders' criteria for performance, which have set the standard for the industry: knowledge, integrity and service. Its pioneering spirit and fearless innovation ensure that the firm will evolve with the industry and the city of Dallas into the 1990s and the 21st century.

NETHERLAND, SEWELL & ASSOCIATES, INC.

Netherland, Sewell & Associates, Inc. is a petroleum consulting firm that provides independent engineering, geologic, geophysical and economic analyses on behalf of petroleum companies, financial institutions, investment bankers, law firms and government agencies, domestically and throughout the world.

The company was formed in 1961 when Clarence M. Netherland opened his own consulting firm in Dallas. Eight years later he was joined by Frederic D. Sewell. Currently employing more than 50 petroleum professionals and support staff, Netherland, Sewell has evolved into one of the industry's leading petroleum consulting firms due to the excellence of its work and the skills and character of its people.

From the outset, Netherland, Sewell has been committed to providing superior service to its clients. The firm employs people of high academic achievement and proven professional performance. The company's engineers, geologists and geophysicists have between five and 10 years of proven performance with major petroleum companies and average more than 15 years overall experience in their respective fields. A high experience level is also found in the firm's computer experts, systems analysts, engineering technicians and support staff.

Clients depend on Netherland, Sewell for analyses of the highest caliber, from complex technical studies to the most detailed economic evaluations. The company provides reserve estimates combined with economic forecasts; property evaluations for sales, acquisitions and trades; comprehensive field studies; workover and performance evaluations; pipeline and gas gathering studies; determinations of gas deliverability; reservoir simulations and unitization studies. Netherland, Sewell also provides technical counsel to investors and management and expert witness testimony before government regula-

Clarence M. Netherland (left) and Frederic D. Sewell have built Netherland, Sewell & Associates, Inc. into one of the industry's leading petroleum consulting firms.

tory bodies and courts of law. In addition, the firm evaluates prospects and exploration potential as well as helping clients identify potential petroleum reserves.

Netherland, Sewell has had the opportunity to evaluate onshore and offshore oil and gas properties throughout the world. The company has performed geologic, engineering and economic analyses of petroleum reserves in North and South America, Africa, Indonesia, the West Indies and the North Sea. As a result of its skills and reputation, the firm has been involved in some of the most substantial and qualitative consulting work in the oil and gas industry.

Netherland, Sewell is a petroleum consulting firm of integrity and excellence. The firm's commitment to excellence is evident throughout its work, from attention to detail in its analyses to the presentation of results. Such excellence has its foundation in the integrity of the people. The firm's technical evaluations are based on independent investigation, interpretation and presentation.

Integrity and excellence are the principles that guide Netherland, Sewell & Associates, Inc. They are basic and unchanging and distinguish the petroleum consulting services offered by the firm.

Netherland, Sewell & Associates, Inc. has had the opportunity to evaluate onshore and offshore oil and gas properties throughout the world. As a result of its skills and reputation, the firm has been involved in some of the most substantial and qualitative consulting work in the oil and gas industry.

CHAMPLIN REFINING AND CHEMICALS INC.

Highly skilled technicians constantly check and analyze crude to assure a consistent high grade of gasoline and other products.

Champlin Refining and Chemicals provides consistent high-quality gasoline and diesel fuels and petrochemical products to a wide range of customers throughout the United States.

The $1.5-billion enterprise operates the largest refinery in the Port of Corpus Christi, Texas, and maintains petrochemical offices in Humble, Texas and corporate headquarters in Dallas.

Champlin's continuing success in a volatile industry is attributed to the standard of excellence evident in each product, a team of dedicated employees, and a management philosophy that encourages and rewards quality, creativity, innovation and productivity.

While the oil industry slumped over the past decade, Champlin's responsiveness to the constantly changing market conditions enabled the company to build a reputation as a dependable manufacturer of quality products in two major categories.

First, gasoline and diesel products are sold to 10,000 private brand retailers (gasoline stations, convenience stores and truck stops) through a marketing and distribution network across 10 Southeast and Southwest states.

Champlin has established a cost-effective distribution system which allows these independents to have maximum flexibility and control of product movement. For instance, motor fuels are transported by pipeline, truck, tanker and barge from the Corpus Christi refinery to destinations in any of the 10 states. Leased and company-owned terminals are strategically located throughout the region and are equipped with computerized loading systems for convenient, 24-hour-a-day access to Champlin products.

In addition, Champlin's marketing representatives serve as primary contacts with the fuels customers. Each representative has the authority to respond immediately to any concerns that may arise within that geographic area. As a result, Champlin has developed a strong rapport with customers who look to the company for quality, dependable products.

Champlin's second major area of emphasis is the marketing of consistent, high-quality petrochemicals such as cumene, cyclohexane and methyl butyl ether (MTBE) to chemical, plastic and synthetic fiber customers. MTBE and similar aromatic fractions are used as octane enhancers for today's high-performance, lead-free gasolines.

Traditionally a supplier of gasoline and diesel fuels, Champlin has been upgrading its products to higher

value petrochemicals. The Company is adding continuously to petrochemical capacity and is planning for new products based on increasing market demand.

The centerpiece for Champlin's petrochemical and gasoline products is its state-of-the-art refinery in Corpus Christi. With a capacity of 160,000 barrels per day, the huge complex converts low-gravity, high-sulphur Venezuelan crude into the vast array of Champlin products.

These refining facilities utilize advanced processing technology and energy recovery systems, as well as statistical process controls to maximize yields and ensure product quality. In addition, a sophisticated laboratory provides testing, analysis and

monitoring capabilities. This push for quality and efficiency has netted Champlin several prestigious awards for its products.

"People often ask us why we at Champlin put so much emphasis on quality," says CEO Allan Tomlinson. "I tell them because our customers are setting ever higher performance standards and that I feel being a leader will keep us well ahead of competition. We believe that consistency and dependability in meeting customer requirements are very much part of quality."

Plant operations are monitored from modern control rooms.

ATLANTIC RICHFIELD COMPANY (ARCO)

Dallas has been an important location for Atlantic Richfield Company (ARCO) since the early 1900s. While there are many who recognized the North Texas area as a favorable location for finance, insurance and other industries, ARCO was among the first to recognize it as a hub for future oil and gas production activities.

The company, then known as

ARCO Oil and Gas Company is based in ARCO Tower, a 49-story granite structure designed by I.M. Pei, located in the heart of Dallas' downtown business district.

Atlantic Refining of Philadelphia, sent E.H. Blum to set up a Dallas office in 1920. His mission was to locate and secure valuable oil reserves which were developing in Oklahoma, South and East Texas, and the Permian Basin in West Texas. Blum began by leasing office space in the landmark Magnolia Building in downtown Dallas. The success which followed is a tribute to the synergy that results when a growing industry and city come together.

The subsequent growth of the company led Atlantic to establish a laboratory for research activities in 1942 at Mockingbird Lane and Lemmon Avenue. Atlantic's research and development facilities remained at this location until 1967, when its new Production Research Center opened in Plano.

While the ensuing years have brought many changes, challenges and exciting achievements for ARCO throughout the world, the contributions and influence of its operations in Dallas and the surrounding area have been vital to its progress and are significant to its strength today.

A merger with California-based Richfield Oil Corporation in 1966 created Atlantic Richfield Company. Its Dallas-based operations, known as the North American Producing Division, were responsible for domestic oil and gas exploration and production efforts throughout the United States, including Alaska. The discovery in 1968 of Alaska's Prudhoe Bay Field, the largest oil field discovery in U.S. history, and the construction of the trans-Alaskan pipeline which began pumping oil from the field in 1977, were managed from ARCO's Dallas offices. Development of that field has meant a 25 percent increase in U.S. oil reserves.

Other ARCO acquisitions, such as Sinclair Oil Corporation in 1969, have helped bring ARCO to its cur-

rent position as an industry leader. Despite low crude oil and natural gas prices in recent years, today's ARCO ranks as one of the nation's largest energy companies and is among the 20 largest industrial concerns in the United States. It is a large, integrated hydrocarbons company engaged in all aspects of the oil and gas business from the exploration and production of crude oil, natural gas liquids and natural gas to the refining and marketing of petroleum products. The company also mines and markets coal and has interests in two companies that produce and market petrochemical products.

Also, just as it did in 1920, ARCO recognizes the importance of its operational base in the Dallas area, which is now the home of two major operating divisions created during a 1979 restructuring: ARCO Oil and Gas Company and ARCO International Oil and Gas Company.

ARCO Oil and Gas Company is a far cry from E.H. Blum's one-man operation, yet the territory remains very similar. This division is responsible for exploration and production in the lower 48 states. Current production of some 200,000 barrels of crude oil and natural gas liquids and more than 1.4 billion cubic feet of natural gas per day makes ARCO one of the nation's largest domestic energy producers.

ARCO Oil and Gas Company employs some 4,000 individuals in offices and facilities throughout Texas, including about 2,200 in the Dallas/Plano area. Other ARCO Oil and Gas Company employees report to the Dallas headquarters from locations in California, Oklahoma, New Mexico, Louisiana and elsewhere.

No longer housed in leased office space as was necessary in the early years, ARCO Oil and Gas Company now occupies 49-story ARCO Tower featuring the triangular geometry favored by its designer, I.M. Pei.

Completed in 1983, the building sits on property acquired by the company for its original 10-story building constructed in 1950.

While the 1920 office was noted for being the first air conditioned office space in Dallas, and the Atlantic Building of 1950 was known for having the first high-speed automatic elevators, ARCO Tower was built with the comfort, safety and efficiency of its employees in mind. It includes a number of space-age innovations, including video conferencing that can take the board room to the oil patch on command.

The research facilities in Plano have been expanded in recent years and now form the core of ARCO's worldwide research program, helping the company achieve its goals of being the best, expanding when it makes economic sense and remaining profitable. Effective use of advanced exploration technology has resulted in ARCO's position as one of the most successful, low-cost producers in the United States.

ARCO International Oil and Gas Company relocated to enlarged facilities in Plano in early 1989. This division is responsible for exploration and production activities outside the United States.

The Plano location brought ARCO International closer to the technology available at the research operation and meant convenient access to transport needs associated with activities in Indonesia, Dubai, Turkey, the North Sea and New Zealand. It continues to increase its operational scope through acquisition and exploration, such as its 1988 acquisition of Tricentrol PLC, a London-based company with significant oil and gas reserves in the United Kingdom.

ARCO is widely recognized for its corporate citizenship, and nowhere is this more evident than in Dallas. Its limited consumer orienta-

ARCO's complex in Plano near North Dallas is the site of the company's research and development operations as well as home of ARCO International Oil and Gas Company.

tion here has enabled ARCO to focus its philanthropy away from high-visibility projects and toward those that afford long-term impact and high potential for success. The company has been honored as the Corporate Philanthropist of the Year by the Dallas Chapter of the National Society of Fundraising Executives.

ARCO is proud of its collaborative efforts with educational institutions and cultural and community organizations. The relationship has created opportunities for thousands of disadvantaged youngsters and others. ARCO and the Dallas County Community College District created a summer introductory engineering program for minority high school students. The Girls Clubs of Dallas participate in an arts introduction program designed for them by ARCO and the Dallas Opera. Hundreds of youngsters have participated in Project Discovery, an audience development project sponsored with the Dallas Theater Center.

ARCO employees contribute substantially to the Dallas community through their civic leadership and personal volunteer time. Additionally, the company sponsors a number of release-time activities for volunteers. This was the first major employer in Dallas to release employees to deliver Meals on Wheels for the Visiting Nurses Association. ARCO continues to maintain a contingent of 200 volunteers who deliver meals daily to the homebound in an inner-city neighborhood. Also, teams of ARCO volunteers work throughout the year at public schools, festivals and community events.

The company actively promotes community involvement within and outside the workplace. It has been a longtime sponsor of community volunteer recognition and promotion efforts, including those of the Volunteer Centers of Dallas and Plano and the Retired Senior Volunteer Program of the Senior Citizens of Dallas.

"ARCO's roots go deep in the Dallas area," said James A. Middleton, president of ARCO Oil and Gas Company. "We are committed to it. Our company and its employees are involved in the community, our schools and our government. We have enjoyed considerable success here and look forward to playing an active role in the bright future of our city,"

ORYX ENERGY COMPANY

Oryx Energy Company is something of a pleasant paradox. It has a new name, but it is one of Dallas' oldest and most respected companies. For more than 70 years, Oryx had been part of the mammoth Sun Oil Company as its exploration and production arm in Dallas. Then in November 1988, history was made when Sun Exploration and Production became a stand-alone company and the largest independent oil and gas producer in North America — possibly in the world — with assets of $4 billion and reserves of nearly 1 billion barrels.

But it was not enough to simply spin off; it was time for a completely new persona, one that conveyed excitement, pride, resourcefulness — all of the qualities for which Philadelphia-based Sun and its sub-

With 2 million net developed acres and 3 million net undeveloped acres, Oryx Energy can be found in every major domestic basin.

sidiaries have been known for so many years.

"We took on the task of forging an entirely new identity for our company," says James E. McCormick, president and chief operating officer for Oryx. He explains that Oryx commissioned the Dallas-based Richards Group to analyze and develop corporate names that would be appropriate. "We were not looking for one of those computer-generated names."

What emerged was beautifully symbolic and immediately embraced by the company's officers and shareholders. The oryx antelope, which, according to Chairman and Chief Executive Officer Robert P. Hauptfuhrer, "has qualities we see in Oryx Energy Company: strength, spirit, aggressiveness and the ability to prosper in any environment. A new name helps establish our independence as a stand-alone company."

And so on May 3, 1989, one day after Sun Exploration and Production shareholders voted to change the name, Oryx Energy was born. Old logos came down and the graceful new red, white and black antelope-in-motion logo came up. (So tied is the new company to the Oryx image that it immediately "adopted" a live

African Oryx, which resides at Fossil Rim Wildlife Ranch in Glen Rose, southwest of Fort Worth.)

Like its namesake, Oryx Energy is lean and strong. About 1,200 of its 3,200 employees work in several locations in Dallas, including those at corporate headquarters and some 225 geoscientists at Synergy Park adjacent to the University of Texas-Dallas.

Construction will begin in early 1990 on a new corporate headquarters building at the Galleria, with occupancy expected by Christmas 1991.

Oryx is divided into four major regions — Houston, Midland, Tex., Oklahoma City and Valencia, Calif. — and has 50 small field offices throughout the United States. Oryx Energy employees also work at a cogeneration plant near Taft, Calif., at a marketing storage terminal in West Memphis, Ark., on production platforms off the coast of California and in the Gulf of Mexico; and at more than 35 natural gas-producing facilities.

Oryx Energy's daily production in 1989 averages 115,000 barrels of liquids and 735 million cubic feet of natural gas.

The company, with 2 million net developed acres and 3 million net undeveloped acres, can be found in every major domestic basin. Daily production in 1989 averages 115,000 barrels of liquids and 735 million cubic feet of natural gas. In 1988, Oryx drilled 107 net exploratory and 240 net development wells, making it the No. 1 wildcatter in terms of wells drilled and new field discoveries.

Finding and producing oil and gas is what Oryx is about — but that is not all it is about.

Oryx and its predecessor have been very active in Dallas community affairs, says Hauptfuhrer, noting that participation has been low key but extremely strong. In fact, President George Bush in 1989 presented Oryx with the coveted Presidential "C" Flag for its outstanding community involvement in the Metroplex.

Not only does Oryx provide generous financial support — for example, employees consistently rally to the local United Way cause, and the company matches contributions dollar for dollar — it also stresses volunteerism among its employees, from "our top executives to our most junior workers," says Hauptfuhrer.

Oryx volunteers participate in the Channel 13 Public Television pledge and auction nights, the March of Dimes Walkathon, the Walt Garrison Rodeo benefitting muscular dystrophy, the Shakespeare Festival and the Adopt-A-School Program.

Senior executives serve on the boards of the Dallas Symphony Orchestra, the Dallas Museum of Natural History, the Metropolitan Dallas United Way, the Volunteer Center of Dallas County, the YMCA, the Dallas Arboretum and Botanical Society and the Circle 10 Council of the Boy Scouts of America.

The company also provides in-kind contributions of office furniture, equipment and other needs to hospi-

tals, police storefronts and non-profit organizations.

But by far the biggest corporate emphasis has been in the area of elementary and secondary education. Oryx is proud of its commitment to the I Have a Dream Foundation, which encourages 6th and 7th graders in inner-city schools to pledge they will graduate from high school; upon graduation, a college scholarship awaits. For this program, Oryx provides both dollars and about 25 volunteers, who meet with students at least once a month to offer encouragement and support.

Through the Reading is Fundamental (RIF) Program, Oryx buys books for three Dallas schools: Amelia Earhart, Stonewall Jackson and Obediah Knight. The company also works with Dallas CAN Academy, a non-profit organization that assists high school dropouts in returning to their studies and obtaining their GED certificates.

And as if that were not enough, Oryx has its own in-house volunteer

program called the Responsible Citizen Program (RCP). It is operated by a council of employees and regularly features speakers from outside the company who explain to RCP participants how they may become more involved in the community. The program, says McCormick, has been a huge success and continues to foster excellent morale among employees.

Indeed, Oryx Energy is an exemplary corporate citizen with a solid history — and an even stronger future.

Seismic data and core samples are compiled and analyzed at geophysical workstations.

ATMOS ENERGY CORPORATION

Atmos Energy Corporation, taking its name from the Greek root word *atmos* for "vapor or gases in the air," is both an old and a new company poised on the cutting edge of an increasingly used energy source: natural gas.

Tracing its roots back to 1906 and the Amarillo Gas Company of Amarillo, Texas, Atmos originally provided natural gas to its customers through a coal gasification process. Following the discovery, early in the 20th century, of the expansive Texas Panhandle gas fields, coal gasification became outdated, and the company, which later became known as Pioneer Natural Gas, began building pipelines to connect its customers with this newfound energy source.

In the early 1980s, Pioneer Corporation created a separate natural gas distribution arm called Energas, which subsequently was spun-off to shareholders as a wholly independent company in 1983.

Charles K. Vaughan, Atmos chairman, president and chief executive officer, has led the company through a period of impressive growth fueled by acquisitions and a much greater public awareness of natural gas.

After the spin-off, Energas found itself with both the heritage of an experienced business and many of the problems of an infant company. Energas immediately embarked on an aggressive expansion campaign fueled primarily through the acquisition of other gas distribution companies. Then, as now, the company is involved only in natural gas distribution, not exploration or production.

By 1986, the company made its first purchase: Trans Louisiana Gas Company. For a variety of reasons, primarily accessibility to the Louisiana market and positioning for future growth, Energas moved its corporate headquarters from Amarillo to Dallas following the purchase.

According to Charles K. Vaughan, Atmos chairman, president and chief executive officer, "We felt strongly that it was in the best long-term interest of our company, its shareholders and employees that we locate in a business and transportation center such as Dallas. We anticipated additional growth, and that has, in fact, materialized. Our experience in the Dallas area has met or exceeded our expectations in every sense."

One year later, the company continued to appraise the natural gas distribution market in search of another acquisition. This time, Energas purchased Western Kentucky Gas Company.

Following the acquisition, the company began to detect some confusion within the business and investment communities between the Energas that supplied West Texas and the Energas corporate entity that had embarked on an aggressive growth campaign through acquisitions as well as operating other gas utilities such as Western Kentucky and Trans Louisiana.

The company determined that it was in their best interest to separate the corporate entity from the operat-

Company-wide, including three individual utilities, Atmos has more than 1,400 employees with approximately 200 in the Dallas-based corporate headquarters.

ing companies. In 1988, the corporate name was changed to Atmos. While Atmos controls the operation of Energas Company, headquartered in Lubbock, Texas, Trans Louisiana Gas Company, based in Lafayette, and Western Kentucky Gas Company, headquartered in Owensboro, the separate names give customers and employees a sense of local identity with their own individual utility, and at the same time provide them with participation in a much larger picture.

"We have found the name change to be highly successful on all levels," states Vaughan.

Today, Atmos Energy is one of the largest independent natural gas distribution companies in the country, serving more than 520,000 customers over a three-state service area. Company-wide, including the three individual utilities, Atmos has more than 1,400 employees with approximately 200 in the Dallas-based corporate headquarters.

Atmos, which continues to assess the marketplace for other

potential acquisitions, is bullish on the future of natural gas. Currently, Energas in West Texas claims at least an 80 percent market penetration with its primary customers being residential, small commercial and agricultural users. Market penetration in Kentucky and Louisiana presently stands in the 50 to 65 percent range with more than half of the company's deliveries in Kentucky going to industrial customers.

"Atmos continues to entertain growth by acquisition while working aggressively to increase its market share in its respective marketplaces," says Vaughan. "We think that natural gas has a very bright future."

Natural gas could well benefit from the very real concerns that exist about the environment. Natural gas is one of the cleanest burning fuels known to man. In many boiler applications, either alone or in combination with another fuel source such as coal, natural gas can reduce emissions which contribute to the acid rain problem. The industry is also receiving positive signals from the Bush administration. There are abundant domestic supplies of natural gas, and there is increasing interest in the use of compressed natural gas as a vehicle fuel in some fleet operations.

"In Texas, for instance," says Vaughan, "legislation was passed this year mandating the use of alternative fuels in certain public authority fleet vehicles by the mid-1990s. We believe that compressed natural gas will be the fuel of choice for many of these vehicles."

By operating companies in three different geographic regions, Atmos is in a much better position to withstand fluctuations in local economies and weather conditions. For example, the Kentucky economy is growing and a large number of new jobs have been created in that state through expansion of existing facilities and the opening of new ones. The West

Texas and Louisiana economies have experienced some hard times in recent years but have begun to show signs of rebounding.

"We are proud of the fact that even when those two economies were not doing well, our company continued to grow and prosper," says Vaughan. "Our acquisitions and internal growth, combined with a much greater public awareness of natural gas, are helping us to sustain our very impressive growth pattern."

For Atmos, whose top management has more than 100 years combined experience in the gas distribution business — Vaughan alone has been with the company 32 years — the future is bright indeed.

Energas, one of Atmos' three natural gas distribution utilities, has an 80 percent market penetration in West Texas with its primary customers being residential, small commercial and agricultural users.

INDEX

Corporate Profile Index

General Index

Italicized numbers indicate illustrations.